Robert Louis Stevenson

The Letters of Robert Louis Stevenson to His Family and Friends

Volume I

Robert Louis Stevenson

The Letters of Robert Louis Stevenson to His Family and Friends
Volume I

ISBN/EAN: 9783337016586

Printed in Europe, USA, Canada, Australia, Japan

Cover: Foto ©ninafisch / pixelio.de

More available books at **www.hansebooks.com**

THE LETTERS OF
ROBERT LOUIS STEVENSON

TO HIS FAMILY AND FRIENDS

SELECTED AND EDITED WITH
NOTES AND INTRODUCTIONS BY

SIDNEY COLVIN

VOLUME I

LONDON
METHUEN AND CO.
36 ESSEX STREET
1899

Edinburgh: T. and A. CONSTABLE, Printers to Her Majesty

CONTENTS

INTRODUCTION, ... xv-xliv

I
STUDENT DAYS AT EDINBURGH
TRAVELS AND EXCURSIONS

INTRODUCTORY, ... 3
LETTERS :—
    To Mrs. Thomas Stevenson, ... 15
    To the Same, ... 17
    To the Same, ... 19
    To the Same, . . 20
    To Mrs. Churchill Babington, . . 24
    To Alison Cunningham, . . . 26
    To Charles Baxter, . . . 27
    To the Same, ... 29
    To Mrs. Thomas Stevenson, ... 30
    To the Same, ... 32
    To the Same, ... 33
    To Thomas Stevenson, . . . 36
    To Mrs. Thomas Stevenson, ... 38
    To Charles Baxter, ... 40

CONTENTS

II

STUDENT DAYS—*continued*

ORDERED SOUTH

	PAGE
INTRODUCTORY, ...	45

LETTERS:—

To Mrs. Thomas Stevenson, ...	48
To Mrs. Sitwell, ...	49
To the Same, ...	51
To the Same, ...	53
To the Same, ...	57
To the Same, ...	61
To Mrs. Thomas Stevenson, . .	62
To Mrs. Sitwell, ...	65
To Mrs. Thomas Stevenson, ...	67
To the Same, ...	69
To Mrs. Sitwell, ...	71
To the Same, ...	73
To Mrs. Thomas Stevenson, ...	74
To Mrs. Sitwell, ...	75
To the Same, ...	77
To the Same, . . .	79
To the Same, . .	81
To the Same, . .	83
To Sidney Colvin, ...	84
To Mrs. Sitwell, ...	85
To Sidney Colvin, ...	87
To Mrs. Sitwell, ...	88
To the Same, ...	88
To the Same, ...	91
To the Same, ...	92

CONTENTS vii

	PAGE
To the Same,	95
To the Same,	95

III
ADVOCATE AND AUTHOR
EDINBURGH—PARIS—FONTAINEBLEAU

INTRODUCTORY,	99
LETTERS:—	
To Mrs. Thomas Stevenson,	104
To Mrs. Sitwell,	104
To Sidney Colvin,	106
To Charles Baxter,	109
To Sidney Colvin,	110
To Mrs. Sitwell,	111
To Mrs. de Mattos,	112
To Mrs. Sitwell,	114
To Sidney Colvin,	115
To the Same,	115
To Mrs. Sitwell,	116
To W. E. Henley,	117
To Mrs. Sitwell,	118
To Sidney Colvin,	119
To Mrs. Sitwell,	120
To A. Patchett Martin,	121
To the Same,	122
To Sidney Colvin,	124
To the Same,	125
To Mr. and Mrs. Thomas Stevenson,	126
To Mrs. Thomas Stevenson,	126
To the Same,	127

CONTENTS

	PAGE
To W. E. Henley, . .	128
To Charles Baxter, ...	128
To Mrs. Thomas Stevenson, . .	129
To W. E. Henley, . . .	129
To Edmund Gosse, .	130
To W. E. Henley, . .	132
To Edmund Gosse, .	134
To Sidney Colvin, . .	136
To Edmund Gosse,	136

IV

THE AMATEUR EMIGRANT
MONTEREY AND SAN FRANCISCO

INTRODUCTORY, . .	141
LETTERS:—	
To Sidney Colvin, .	144
To the Same, .	144
To W. E. Henley, . .	146
To Sidney Colvin, . .	147
To the Same, . .	148
To the Same, . . .	149
To Edmund Gosse,	150
To W. E. Henley, . .	151
To the Same, .	152
To P. G. Hamerton, .	155
To Edmund Gosse, .	156
To Sidney Colvin, . .	157
To Edmund Gosse, . .	158
To Sidney Colvin, . . .	160
To the Same, . .	162

CONTENTS

	PAGE
To Charles Baxter,	164
To Sidney Colvin,	165
To W. E. Henley,	167
To Sidney Colvin,	169
To Edmund Gosse,	169
To Dr. W. Bamford,	170
To Sidney Colvin,	171
To the Same,	171
To the Same,	172
To C. W. Stoddard,	173
To Sidney Colvin,	174

V
ALPINE WINTERS
AND HIGHLAND SUMMERS

INTRODUCTORY,	179
LETTERS:—	
To A. G. Dew-Smith,	185
To Thomas Stevenson,	187
To Edmund Gosse,	188
To the Same,	189
To C. W. Stoddard,	191
To Mr. and Mrs. Thomas Stevenson,	192
To Sidney Colvin,	194
To Mrs. Thomas Stevenson,	195
To Sidney Colvin,	197
To Horatio F. Brown,	199
To the Same,	200
To the Same,	200

CONTENTS

	PAGE
To Mr. and Mrs. Thomas Stevenson,	201
To Edmund Gosse,	202
To Sidney Colvin,	204
To Professor Æneas Mackay,	205
To the Same,	205
To Edmund Gosse,	206
To the Same,	207
To P. G. Hamerton,	208
To Sidney Colvin,	209
To W. E. Henley,	211
To the Same,	212
To Sidney Colvin,	213
To Dr. Alexander Japp,	215
To Mrs. Sitwell,	216
To Edmund Gosse,	217
To the Same,	218
To the Same,	219
To W. E. Henley,	219
To Dr. Alexander Japp,	221
To W. E. Henley,	222
To Thomas Stevenson,	223
To P. G. Hamerton,	224
To Charles Baxter,	226
To Mrs. Thomas Stevenson,	227
To Alison Cunningham,	228
To Charles Baxter,	228
To W. E. Henley,	229
To the Same,	230
To Alexander Ireland,	233
To Edmund Gosse,	235
To Dr. Alexander Japp,	236

CONTENTS

	PAGE
To the Same,	236
To W. E. Henley,	238
To Mrs. T. Stevenson,	240
To Edmund Gosse,	241
To the Same,	242
To W. E. Henley,	242

VI

MARSEILLES AND HYÈRES

INTRODUCTORY,	247
LETTERS:—	
To the Editor of the *New York Tribune*,	251
To R. A. M. Stevenson,	252
To Thomas Stevenson,	253
To Mrs. Thomas Stevenson,	254
To Charles Baxter,	254
To Alison Cunningham,	256
To W. E. Henley,	257
To Mrs. Thomas Stevenson,	261
To Thomas Stevenson,	262
To Mrs. Sitwell,	263
To Edmund Gosse,	265
To Mr. and Mrs. Thomas Stevenson,	266
To the Same,	267
To Edmund Gosse,	268
To the Same,	269
To W. E. Henley,	270
To the Same,	271
To the Same,	272

CONTENTS

	PAGE
To the Same,	273
To the Same,	274
To Alison Cunningham,	275
To W. E. Henley,	277
To Edmund Gosse,	278
To W. E. Henley,	279
To Edmund Gosse,	283
To Sidney Colvin,	284
To W. H. Low,	286
To R. A. M. Stevenson,	288
To Thomas Stevenson,	291
To W. H. Low,	292
To W. E. Henley,	294
To Mrs. Thomas Stevenson,	295
To Sidney Colvin,	296
To Mrs. Milne,	297
To Miss Ferrier,	299
To W. H. Low,	300
To Thomas Stevenson,	301
To Mr. and Mrs. Thomas Stevenson,	302
To Mrs. Thomas Stevenson,	303
To Mr. and Mrs. Thomas Stevenson,	304
To Sidney Colvin,	305
To Mr. Dick,	308
To Cosmo Monkhouse,	310
To Edmund Gosse,	312
To Miss Ferrier,	313
To W. H. Low,	314
To Thomas Stevenson,	315
To Cosmo Monkhouse,	316
To W. E. Henley,	318

CONTENTS

	PAGE
To Edmund Gosse,	319
To Mr. and Mrs. Thomas Stevenson,	320
To Sidney Colvin,	321

VII
LIFE AT BOURNEMOUTH

INTRODUCTORY,	325
LETTERS :—	
To Mr. and Mrs. Thomas Stevenson,	328
To W. E. Henley,	328
To the Rev. Professor Lewis Campbell,	330
To Andrew Chatto,	331
To W. H. Low,	332
To Thomas Stevenson,	334
To W. E. Henley,	335
To Thomas Stevenson,	335
To Charles Baxter,	337
To the Same,	337
To Miss Ferrier,	338
To Edmund Gosse,	339
To Miss Ferrier,	340
To Henry James,	341
To Mr. and Mrs. Thomas Stevenson,	343
To W. E. Henley,	344
To the Same,	345
To H. A. Jones,	346
To Sidney Colvin,	346
To Thomas Stevenson,	347
To Sidney Colvin,	348
To the Same,	349

CONTENTS

	PAGE
To J. A. Symonds,	350
To Edmund Gosse,	352
To W. H. Low,	354
To P. G. Hamerton,	356
To William Archer,	358
To Mrs. Fleeming Jenkin,	359
To the Same,	360
To W. H. Low,	361
To W. E. Henley,	363
To William Archer,	364
To Thomas Stevenson,	367
To Henry James,	368
To William Archer,	369
To the Same,	371
To W. H. Low,	374

Frontispiece—PORTRAIT OF R. L. STEVENSON, *æt.* 35
From a photograph by Mr. LLOYD OSBOURNE

INTRODUCTION

ONE day in the autumn of 1888, in the island of Tahiti, during an illness which he supposed might be his last, Stevenson put into the hands of his stepson, Mr. Lloyd Osbourne, a sealed paper with the request that it should be opened after his death. He recovered, as every one knows, and had strength enough to enjoy six years more of active life and work in the Pacific Islands. When the end came, and the paper was opened, it was found to contain, among other things, the expression of his wish that I should be asked to prepare for publication 'a selection of his letters and a sketch of his life.' The journal letters written to myself from his Samoan home, subsequently to the date of the request, offered the readiest material towards fulfilling promptly a part at least of the duty thus laid upon me; and a selection from these was accordingly published in the autumn following his death.[1]

The scanty leisure of an official life (chiefly employed as it was for several years in seeing my friend's collected and posthumous works through the press) did not allow me to complete the remainder of my task without considerable delay. For one thing, the body of corre-

[1] *Vailima Letters:* Methuen and Co., 1895.

spondence which came in from various quarters turned out much larger than had been anticipated, and the labour of sifting and arranging it much greater. The author of *Treasure Island* and *Across the Plains* and *Weir of Hermiston* did not love writing letters, and will be found somewhere in the following pages referring to himself as one 'essentially and originally incapable of the art epistolary.' That he was a bad correspondent had even come to be an accepted view among his friends; but in truth it was only during one particular period of his life (see below, vol. i. p. 103) that he at all deserved such a reproach. At other times, as is now apparent, he had shown a degree of industry and spirit in letter-writing extraordinary considering his health and occupations, and especially considering his declared aversion for the task. His letters, it is true, were often the most informal in the world, and he generally neglected to date them, a habit which is the despair of editors; but after his own whim and fashion he wrote a vast number; so that for every one here included some half-a-dozen at least have had to be rejected.

In considering the scale and plan on which my friend's instruction should be carried out, it seemed necessary to take into account, not his own always modest opinion of himself, but the place which, as time went on, he seemed likely to take ultimately in the world's regard. The four or five years following the death of a writer much applauded in his lifetime are generally the years when the decline of his reputation begins, if it is going to suffer decline at all. At present, certainly, Stevenson's name

INTRODUCTION   xvii

seems in no danger of going down. On the stream of daily literary reference and allusion it floats more actively than ever. In another sense its vitality is confirmed by the material test of continued sales and of the market. Since we have lost him other writers, whose beginnings he watched with sympathetic interest, have come to fill a greater immediate place in public attention; one especially has struck notes which appeal to dominant fibres in our Anglo-Saxon stock with irresistible force; but none has exercised Stevenson's peculiar and personal power to charm, to attach, and to inspirit. By his study of perfection in form and style—qualities for which his countrymen in general have been apt to care little—he might seem destined to give pleasure chiefly to the fastidious and the artistically minded. But as to its matter, the main appeal of his work is not to any mental tastes and fashions of the few; it is rather to universal, hereditary instincts, to the primitive sources of imaginative excitement and entertainment in the race.

By virtue, then, of this double appeal of form and matter; by his especial hold upon the young, in whose spirit so much of his best work was done; by his undecaying influence on other writers; by the spell which he still exercises from the grave, and exercises most strongly on those who are most familiar with the best company whether of the living or the dead, Stevenson's name and memory, so far as can be judged at present, seem destined not to dwindle, but to grow. The voice of the *advocatus diaboli* has been heard against him, as it is right and proper that it should be heard

b

against any man before his reputation can be held fully established. One such advocate in this country has thought to dispose of him by the charge of 'externality.' But the reader who remembers things like the sea-frenzy of Gordon Darnaway, or the dialogue of Markheim with his other self in the house of murder, or the re-baptism of the spirit of Seraphina in the forest dews, or the failure of Herrick to find in the waters of the island lagoon a last release from dishonour, or the death of Goguelat, or the appeal of Kirstie Elliot in the midnight chamber—such a reader can only smile at a criticism like this and put it by. These and a score of other passages breathe the essential poetry and significance of things as they reveal themselves to true masters only—are instinct at once with the morality and the romance which lie deep together at the soul of nature and experience. Not in vain had Stevenson read the lesson of the Lantern-Bearers, and hearkened to the music of the pipes of Pan. He was feeling his way all his life towards a fuller mastery of his means, preferring always to leave unexpressed what he felt that he could not express perfectly; and in much of his work was content merely to amuse himself and others. But even when he is playing most fancifully with his art and his readers, as in the shudders, tempered with laughter, of the Suicide Club, or the airy sentimental comedy of Providence and the Guitar, or the schoolboy historical inventions of Dickon Crookback and the old sailor Arblaster, a writer of his quality cannot help striking notes from the heart of life and the inwardness

INTRODUCTION xix

of things deeper than will ever be struck, or even apprehended, by another who labours, with never a smile either of his own or of his reader's, upon the most solemn enterprises of realistic fiction, but is born without the magician's touch and insight.

Another advocate on the same side, in the United States, has made much of the supposed dependence of this author on his models, and classed him among writers whose inspiration is imitative and second-hand. But this, surely, is to be quite misled by the well-known passage of Stevenson's own, in which he speaks of himself as having in his prentice years played the 'sedulous ape' to many writers of different styles and periods. In doing this he was not seeking inspiration, but simply practising the use of the tools which were to help him to express his own inspirations. Truly he was always much of a reader; but it was life, not books, that always in the first degree allured and taught him.

> 'He loved of life the myriad sides,
> Pain, prayer, or pleasure, act or sleep,
> As wallowing narwhals love the deep'—

so with just self-knowledge he wrote of himself; and the books which he most cared for and lived with were those of which the writers seemed—to quote again a phrase of his own—to have been 'eavesdropping at the door of his heart'; those which told of moods, impressions, experiences or cravings after experience, pains, pleasures, opinions or conflicts of the spirit, which in the eagerness of youthful living and thinking had already been his own. No man, in fact, was ever less inclined to take anything at second-hand. The root of all originality was in him, in the shape of an extreme natural vividness of perception, imagination, and feeling. An instinctive and inbred unwillingness to accept the accepted and conform to the conventional was of the essence of his character, whether in life or art, and was a source to him both of strength and weakness. He would not follow a general rule—least of all if it was a prudential rule—of conduct unless he was clear that it was right according to his private conscience; nor would he join, in youth, in the ordinary social amusements of his class when he had once found out that they did not amuse *him*; nor wear their clothes if he could not feel at ease and be himself in them; nor use, whether in speech or writing, any trite or inanimate form of words that did not faithfully and livingly express his thought. A readier acceptance of current usages might have been better for him, but was simply not in his nature. 'Damp gingerbread puppets' were to him the persons who lived and thought and felt and acted only as was expected of them. 'To see people skipping all round us with their eyes sealed up with indifference, knowing nothing of the earth or man or woman, going automatically to offices and saying they are happy or unhappy, out of a sense of duty I suppose, surely at least from no sense of happiness or unhappiness, unless perhaps they have a tooth that twinges—is it not like a bad dream?' No reader of this book will close it, I am sure, without feeling that he has been throughout in the company of a spirit various

INTRODUCTION

indeed and many-sided, but profoundly sincere and real. Ways that in another might easily have been mere signs of affectation were in Stevenson only the signs of a nature ten times more spontaneously itself and individually alive than that of others. Self-consciousness, in many characters that possess it, deflects and falsifies conduct; and so does the dramatic instinct. Stevenson was self-conscious in a high degree, but only as a part of his general activity of mind; only in so far as he could not help being an extremely intelligent spectator of his own doings and feelings; these themselves came from springs of character and impulse much too deep and strong to be diverted. He loved also, with a child's or actor's gusto, to play a part and make a drama out of life:[1] but the part was always for the moment his very own: he had it not in him to pose for anything but what he truly was.

When a man so constituted had once mastered his craft of letters, he might take up whatever instrument he pleased with the instinctive and just confidence that he would play upon it to a tune and with a manner of his own. This is indeed the true mark and test of his originality. He has no need to be, or to seem, especially original in the form and mode of literature which he attempts. By his choice of these he may at any time give himself and his reader the pleasure of recalling, like a familiar air, some strain of literary association; but in so doing he only adds a secondary charm to his work; the vision, the temperament, the mode of conceiving and handling, are in every case

---

[1] Compare *Virginibus Puerisque*: the essay on 'The English Admirals.'

strongly personal to himself. He may try his hand in youth at a Sentimental Journey, but R. L. S. cannot choose but be at the opposite pole of human character and feeling from Laurence Sterne. In tales of mystery, allegorical or other, he may bear in mind the precedent of Edgar Poe, and yet there is nothing in style and temper much wider apart than *Markheim* and *Jekyll and Hyde* are from the *Murders in the Rue Morgue* or *William Wilson*. He may set out to tell a pirate story for boys 'exactly in the ancient way,' and it will come from him not in the ancient way at all, but re-minted; marked with a sharpness and saliency in the characters, a private stamp of buccaneering ferocity combined with smiling humour, an energy of vision and happy vividness of presentment, which are shiningly his own. Another time, he may desert the paths of Kingston and Ballantyne the brave for those of Sir Walter Scott; but literature presents few stronger contrasts than between any scene of *Waverley* or *Redgauntlet* and any scene of the *Master of Ballantrae* or *Catriona*, whether in their strength or weakness: and it is the most loyal lovers of the older master who take the greatest pleasure in reading the work of the younger, so much less opulently gifted as is probable—though we must remember that Stevenson died at the age when Scott wrote *Waverley*—so infinitely more careful of his gift. Stevenson may even blow upon the pipe of Burns, and yet his tune will be no echo, but one which utters the heart and mind of a Scots poet who has his own outlook on life, his own special and profitable vein of smiling or satirical contemplation.

INTRODUCTION xxiii

Not by reason, then, of 'externality,' for sure, nor yet of imitativeness, will this writer lose his hold on the attention and regard of his countrymen. The debate, before his place in literature is settled, must rather turn on other points: as whether the genial essayist and egoist or the romantic inventor and narrator was the stronger in him—whether the Montaigne and Pepys elements prevailed in his literary composition or the Scott and Dumas elements—a question indeed which among those who care for him most has always been at issue. Or again, what degree of true inspiring and illuminating power belongs to the gospel, or gospels, airily encouraging or gravely didactic, which are set forth in the essays with so captivating a grace? Or whether in romance and tale he had a power of happily inventing and soundly constructing a whole fable comparable to his unquestionable power of conceiving and presenting single scenes and situations in a manner which stamps them indelibly on the reader's mind. And whether his figures are sustained continuously by the true, large, spontaneous breath of creation, or are but transitorily animated at critical and happy moments by flashes of spiritual and dramatic insight, aided by the conscious devices of his singularly adroit and spirited art? This is a question which no criticism but that of time can solve; it takes the consenting instinct of generations to feel whether the creatures of fiction, however powerfully they may strike at first, are durably and equably, or ephemerally and fitfully, alive. To contend, as some do, that strong creative impulse, and so keen an artistic self-consciousness as Stevenson's was, cannot exist together, is quite idle. The truth, of course, is that the deep-seated energies of imaginative creation are found sometimes in combination, and sometimes not in combination, with an artistic intelligence thus keenly conscious of its own purpose and watchful of its own working.

Once more, it may be questioned whether, among the many varieties of work which Stevenson has left, all touched with genius, all charming and stimulating to the literary sense, all distinguished by a grace and precision of workmanship which are the rarest qualities in English art, there are any which can be pointed to as absolute masterpieces, such as the future cannot be expected to let die. Let the future decide. What is certain is that posterity must either be very well, or very ill, occupied if it can consent to give up so much sound entertainment, and better than entertainment, as this writer afforded his contemporaries. In the meantime, among judicious readers on both sides of the Atlantic, Stevenson stands, I think it may safely be said, as a true master of English prose; unsurpassed for the union of lenity and lucidity with suggestive pregnancy and poetic animation; for harmony of cadence and the well-knit structure of sentences; and for the art of imparting to words the vital quality of things, and making them convey the precise—sometimes, let it be granted, the too curiously precise—expression of the very shade and colour of the thought, feeling, or vision in his mind. He stands, moreover, as the writer who, in the last quarter of the nineteenth

INTRODUCTION xxv

century, has handled with the most of freshness and inspiriting power the widest range of established literary forms—the moral, critical, and personal essay, travels sentimental and other, romances and short tales both historical and modern, parables and tales of mystery, boys' stories of adventure, memoirs—nor let lyrical and meditative verse both English and Scottish, and especially nursery verse, a new vein for genius to work in, be forgotten. To some of these forms Stevenson gave quite new life; through all alike he expressed vividly an extremely personal way of seeing and being, a sense of nature and romance, of the aspects of human existence and problems of human conduct, which was essentially his own. And in so doing he contrived to make friends and even lovers of his readers. Those whom he attracts at all (and there is no writer who attracts every one) are drawn to him over and over again, finding familiarity not lessen but increase the charm of his work, and desiring ever closer intimacy with the spirit and personality which they divine behind it.

As to the fitting scale, then, on which to treat the memory of a man who fills five years after his death such a place as this in the public regard, the words 'selection' and 'sketch,' have evidently to be given a pretty liberal interpretation. Readers, it must be supposed, will scarce be content without both a fairly full biography, and the opportunity of a fairly ample intercourse with the man as he was accustomed to reveal himself in writing to his familiars. As to form—Stevenson's own words and the nature of the material alike seem to indicate that the *Life* and the *Letters* should be kept separate. There are some kinds of correspondence which can conveniently be woven into the body and texture of a biography, though indeed I think it is a plan to which biographers are much too partial. Nothing, surely, more checks the flow of a narrative than its interruption by stationary blocks of correspondence; nothing more disconcerts the reader than a too frequent or too abrupt alternation of voices between the subject of a biography speaking in his letters and the writer of it speaking in his narrative. At least it is only when letters are occupied, as Macaulay's for instance were, almost entirely with facts and events, that they can without difficulty be handled in this way. But events and facts, 'sordid facts,' as he called them, were not very often suffered to intrude into Stevenson's correspondence. 'I deny,' he writes, 'that letters should contain news (I mean mine; those of other people should). But mine should contain appropriate sentiments and humorous nonsense, or nonsense without the humour.' Business letters, letters of information, and letters of courtesy he had sometimes to write: but when he wrote best was under the influence of the affection or impression, or the mere whim or mood, of the moment; pouring himself out in all manner of rhapsodical confessions and speculations, grave or gay, notes of observation and criticism, snatches of remembrance and autobiography, moralisings on matters uppermost for the hour in his mind, comments on his own work or other people's, or mere idle fun and foolery.

INTRODUCTION xxvii

With a letter-writer of this character, as it seems to me, a judicious reader desires to be left as much alone as possible. What he wants is to relish the correspondence by itself, or with only just so much in the way of notes and introductions as may serve to make allusions and situations clear. Two volumes, then, of letters so edited, to be preceded by a separate introductory volume of narrative and critical memoir, or *étude*—such was to be the memorial to my friend which I had planned, and hoped by this time to have ready. Unfortunately, the needful leisure has hitherto failed me, and might fail me for some time yet, to complete the separate volume of biography. That is now, at the wish of the family, to be undertaken by Stevenson's cousin and my friend, Mr. Graham Balfour. Meanwhile the *Letters*, with introductions and notes somewhat extended from the original plan, are herewith presented as a substantive work by themselves.

The book will enable those who know and love their Stevenson already to know him more intimately, and, as I hope, to love him more. It contains, certainly, much that is most essentially characteristic of the man. To some, perhaps, that very lack of art as a correspondent of which we have found him above accusing himself may give the reading an added charm and flavour. What he could do as an artist we know—what a telling power and heightened thrill he could give to all his effects, in so many different modes of expression and composition, by calculated skill and the deliberate exercise of a perfectly trained faculty. This is the quality which nobody denies him, and which so deeply impressed his fellow-craftsmen of all kinds. I remember the late Sir John Millais, a shrewd and very independent judge of books, calling across to me at a dinner-table, 'You know Stevenson, don't you?' and then going on, 'Well, I wish you would tell him from me, if he cares to know, that to my mind he is the very first of living artists. I don't mean writers merely, but painters and all of us: nobody living can see with such an eye as that fellow, and nobody is such a master of his tools.' Now in his letters, excepting a few written in youth, and having more or less the character of exercises, and a few in after years which were intended for the public eye, Stevenson the deliberate artist is scarcely forthcoming at all. He does not care a fig for order or logical sequence or congruity, or for striking a key of expression and keeping it, but becomes simply the most spontaneous and unstudied of human beings. He will write with the most distinguished elegance on one day, with simple good sense and good feeling on a second, with flat triviality on another, and with the most slashing, often ultra-colloquial, vehemence on a fourth, or will vary through all these moods and more in one and the same letter. He has at his command the whole vocabularies of the English and Scottish languages, classical and slang, with good stores of the French, and tosses and tumbles them about irresponsibly to convey the impression or affection, the mood or freak of the moment. Passages or phrases of the craziest schoolboy or seafaring slang come tumbling after and capping others of classical cadence and purity, of poetical and heartfelt eloquence. By this medley of moods and manners, Stevenson's letters at their best—the pick, let us say, of those in the following volumes which were written from Hyères or Bournemouth—come nearer than anything else to the full-blooded charm and variety of his conversation.

Nearer, yet not quite near; for it was in company only that this genial spirit rose to his very best. Those whom his writings charm or impress, but who never knew him, can but imagine how doubly they would have been charmed and impressed by his presence. Few men probably, certainly none that I have ever seen or read of, have had about them such a richness and variety of human nature; and few can ever have been better gifted than he was to express the play of being that was in him by means of the apt, expressive word and the animated look and gesture. *Divers et ondoyant*, in the words of Montaigne, beyond other men, he seemed to contain within himself a whole troop of singularly assorted characters—the poet and artist, the moralist and preacher, the humourist and jester, the man of great heart and tender conscience, the man of eager appetite and curiosity, the Bohemian, impatient of restraints and shams, the adventurer and lover of travel and of action: characters, several of them, not rare separately, especially among his Scottish fellow-countrymen, but rare indeed to be found united, and each in such fulness and intensity, within the bounds of a single personality.

Before all things Stevenson was a born poet, to whom the world was full of enchantment and of latent romance, only waiting to take shape and substance in the forms of art. It was his birthright—

> 'to hear
> The great bell beating far and near—
> The odd, unknown, enchanted gong
> That on the road hales men along,
> That from the mountain calls afar,
> That lures the vessel from a star,
> And with a still, aerial sound
> Makes all the earth enchanted ground.'

At the same time, he was not less a born preacher and moralist after his fashion. A true son of the Covenanters, he had about him little spirit of social or other conformity; but an active and searching private conscience kept him for ever calling in question both the grounds of his own conduct and the validity of the accepted codes and compromises of society. He must try to work out a scheme of morality suitable to his own case and temperament, which found the prohibitory law of Moses chill and uninspiring, but in the Sermon on the Mount a strong incentive to all those impulses of pity and charity to which his heart was prone. In youth his sense of social injustice and the inequalities of human opportunity made him inwardly much of a rebel, who would have embraced and acted on theories of socialism or communism, could he have found any that did not seem to him at variance with ineradicable instincts of human nature.[1]

---

[1] The fragment called *Lay Morals*, at present only printed in the Edinburgh edition (*Miscellanies*, vol. iv.), contains the pith of his mental history on these subjects.

All his life the artist and the moralist in him alike were in rebellion against the bourgeois spirit,—against timid, negative, and shuffling substitutes for active and courageous well-doing, and declined to worship at the shrine of what he called the bestial goddesses Comfort and Respectability. The moralist in him helped the artist by backing with the force of a highly sensitive conscience his instinctive love of perfection in his work. The poet and artist qualified the moralist by discountenancing any preference for the harsh, the sour, or the self-mortifying forms of virtue, and encouraging the love for all tender or heroic, glowing, generous and cheerful forms.

In another aspect of his many-sided being Stevenson was not less a born adventurer and practical experimentalist in life. Many poets are content to dream, and many, perhaps most, moralists to preach; but Stevenson must ever be doing and undergoing. He was no sentimentalist, to pay himself with fine feelings whether for mean action or slack inaction. He had an insatiable zest for all experiences, not the pleasurable only, but including even the more harsh and biting— those that bring home to a man the pinch and sting of existence as it is realised by the disinherited of the world, and excluding only what he thought the prim, the conventional, the dead-alive, and the cut-and-dry. On occasion the experimentalist and man of adventure in him would enter into special partnership with the moralist and man of conscience; he loved to find himself in difficult social passes and ethical dilemmas for the sake of trying to behave in them to the utmost according to his own personal sense of the obligations of honour, duty, and kindness. In yet another part of his being, he cherished, as his great countryman Scott had done before him, an intense underlying longing for the life of action, danger, and command. 'Action, Colvin, action,' I remember his crying eagerly to me with his hand on my arm as we lay basking for his health's sake in a boat off the scented shores of the Cap St. Martin. Another time—this was on his way to a winter cure at Davos—some friend had given him General Hamley's *Operations of War*:—'in which,' he writes to his father, 'I am drowned a thousand fathoms deep, and O that I had been a soldier is still my cry.' In so frail a tabernacle was it that the aspirations of the artist, the unconventional moralist, the lover of all experience, and the lover of daring action had to learn to reconcile themselves as best they might. Frail as it was, it contained withal a strong animal nature, and he was as much exposed to the storms and solicitations of sense as to the cravings and questionings of the spirit. Fortunately, with all these ardent and divers instincts, there were present two invaluable gifts besides—that of humour, which for all his stress of being and vivid consciousness of self saved him from ever seeing himself for long together out of a just proportion, and kept wholesome laughter always ready at his lips; and that of a perfectly warm, loyal, and tender heart, which through all his experiments and agitations made the law of kindness the one ruling law of his life. In the end, lack of health determined his career, giving the chief part in his life to the artist and man of imagination, and keeping the man of action a prisoner in the sickroom until, by a singular turn of destiny, he was able to wring a real, prolonged, and romantically successful adventure out of that voyage to the Pacific which had been, in its origin, the last despairing resource of the invalid.

To take this multiple personality from another point of view, it was part of his genius that he never seemed to be cramped like the rest of us, at any given time of life, within the limits of his proper age, but to be child, boy, young man, and old man all at once. There was never a time in his life when Stevenson had to say with St. Augustine, 'Behold! my childhood is dead, but I am alive.' The child, as his *Garden of Verses* lives to testify, and as will be seen by abundant evidence in the course of the following pages, lived on always in him, not in memory only, but in real survival, with all its freshness of perception unimpaired, and none of its play instincts in the least degree extinguished or made ashamed. As for the perennial boy in Stevenson, that is too apparent to need remark. It was as a boy for boys that he wrote the best known of his books, *Treasure Island;* with all boys that he met, provided they were really boys and not prigs nor puppies, he was instantly at home; and the ideal of a career which he most inwardly and longingly cherished, the ideals of practical adventure and romance, of desirable predicaments and gratifying modes of escape from them, were from first to last those of a boy. At the same time, even when I first knew him, there were about him occasional traits and glimpses of old sagacity, of premature life-wisdom and experience, such as find expression, for instance, in the essay *Virginibus Puerisque*, among other matter more according with his then age of twenty-six.

Again, it is said that in every poet there must be something of the woman—the receptivity, the emotional nature. If to be impressionable in the extreme, quick in sympathy and feeling, ardent in attachment, and full of pity for the weak and suffering, is to be womanly, Stevenson was certainly all those; he was even like a woman in being ἀρτίδακρυς, easily moved to tears at the touch of pity or affection, or even at any specially poignant impression of art or beauty. But yet, if any one word were to be chosen for the predominant quality of his character and example, I suppose that word would be manly. In all his habits and instincts he was the least effeminate of men; and effeminacy, or aught approaching sexlessness, was perhaps the only quality in man with which he had no patience. In his gentle and complying nature there were strains of iron tenacity and will. He had both kinds of physical courage—the active, delighting in danger, and the passive, unshaken in endurance. In the moral courage of facing situations and consequences, of cheerful self-discipline and readiness to pay for faults committed, of outspokenness, admitting no ambiguous relations and clearing away the clouds from human intercourse, I have not known his equal. His great countryman Scott, as this book will prove, was not more manfully free from artistic jealousy or the least shade of irritability under criticism, or more modestly and unfeignedly inclined to exaggerate the qualities of other people's work and to underrate those of his own. His severest critic was always himself; the next most severe, those of his own household and intimacy, whose love made them jealous lest he should fall short of his best; for he lived in an atmosphere of love, indeed, but not of flattery. Of the humorous and engaging parts of vanity and egoism, which led him to make infinite talk and fun about himself, and use his own experiences as a key for unlocking the confidences of others, Stevenson had plenty; but of the morose and fretful parts never a shade. 'A little Irish girl,' he wrote once during a painful crisis of his life, 'is now reading my book aloud to her sister at my elbow; they chuckle, and I feel flattered.—Yours, R. L. S. *P.S.* Now they yawn, and I am indifferent. Such a wisely conceived thing is vanity.' If only vanity so conceived were commoner! And whatever might be the abstract and philosophical value of that somewhat grimly stoical conception of the universe, of conduct and duty, at which in mature years he had arrived, want of manliness is certainly not its fault. Nor is any such want to be found in the practice which he founded on or combined with it; in his invincible gaiety and sweetness under sufferings and deprivations the most galling to him; in the temper which made his presence in health or sickness a perpetual sunshine to those about him. Take the kind of maxims of life which he was accustomed to forge for himself and to act by:—'Acts may be forgiven; not even God can forgive the hanger-back.' 'Choose the best, if you can; or choose the worst; that which hangs in the wind dangles from a gibbet.' '"Shall I?" said Feeble-mind; and the echo said, "Fie!"' '"Do I love?" said Loveless; and the echo laughed.' 'A fault known is a fault cured to the strong; but to the weak it is a fetter riveted.' 'The mean man doubts, the great-hearted is deceived.' 'Great-heart was deceived. "Very well," said Great-heart.' '"I have not forgotten my umbrella," said the careful man; but the lightning struck him.' 'Nullity wanted nothing; so he supposed he wanted advice.' 'Evil was called Youth till he was old, and then he was called Habit.' 'Fear kept the house; and still he must pay taxes.' 'Shame had a fine bed, but where was slumber? Once he was in jail he slept.' With this moralist maxims meant actions; and where shall we easily find a much manlier spirit of wisdom than this?

There was yet another and very different side to Stevenson which struck others more than it struck myself, namely, that of the perfectly freakish, not perfectly human, irresponsible madcap or jester which sometimes appeared in him. It is true that his demoniac quickness of wit and intelligence suggested occasionally a 'spirit of air and fire' rather than one of earth; that he was abundantly given to all kinds of quirk and laughter; and that there was no jest (saving the unkind) he would not make and relish. In the streets of Edinburgh he had certainly been known for queer pranks and mystifications in youth; and up to middle life there seemed

INTRODUCTION xxxvii

to some of his friends to be much, if not of the Puck, at least of the Ariel, about him. The late Mr. J. A. Symonds always called him Sprite; qualifying the name, however, by the epithets 'most fantastic, but most human.' To me the essential humanity was always the thing most apparent. In a fire well nourished of seasoned ship-timber, the flames glance fantastically and of many colours, but the glow at heart is ever deep and strong; it was at such a glow that the friends of Stevenson were accustomed to warm their hands, while they admired and were entertained by the shifting lights.

It was only in talk, as I have said, that all the many lights and colours of this richly compounded spirit could be seen in full play. He would begin no matter how— in early days often with a jest at his own absurd garments, or with the recitation, in his vibrating voice and full Scotch accent, of some snatch of poetry that was haunting him, or with a rhapsody of analytic delight over some minute accident of beauty or expressiveness that had struck his observation, and would have escaped that of everybody else, in man, woman, child, or external nature. And forthwith the floodgates would be opened, and the talk would stream on in endless, never importunate, flood and variety. A hundred fictitious characters would be invented, differentiated, and launched on their imaginary careers; a hundred ingenious problems of conduct and cases of honour would be set and solved, in a manner often quite opposed to conventional precept; romantic voyages would be planned and followed out in vision, with a thousand incidents, to all the corners of our own planet and of others; the possibilities of life and art would be illuminated with glancing search-lights of bewildering range and penetration, the most sober argument alternating with the maddest freaks of fancy, high poetic eloquence with coruscations of insanely apposite slang—the earthiest jape anon shooting up into the empyrean and changing into the most ethereal fantasy—the stalest and most vulgarised forms of speech gaining brilliancy and illuminating power from some hitherto undreamt-of application—and all the while an atmosphere of goodwill diffusing itself from the speaker, a glow of eager benignity and affectionate laughter emanating from his presence, till every one about him seemed to catch something of his own gift and inspiration. This sympathetic power of inspiring others was the special and distinguishing note of Stevenson's conversation. He would keep a houseful or a single companion entertained all day, and day after day and half the nights, yet never seemed to dominate the talk or absorb it; rather he helped every one about him to discover and to exercise unexpected powers of their own. The point could hardly be better brought out than it is in a fragment which I borrow from Mr. Henley of an unpublished character-sketch of his friend: 'I leave his praise in this direction (the telling of Scottish vernacular stories) to others. It is more to my purpose to note that he will discourse with you of morals, music, marbles, men, manners, metaphysics, medicine, mangold-wurzel—*que scays-je?*—with equal insight into essentials and equal pregnancy and felicity of utterance; and that he will stop with you to make mud pies in the first gutter, range in your company whatever heights of thought and feeling you have found accessible, and end by guiding you to altitudes far nearer the stars than you have ever dreamed of footing it; and that at the last he makes you wonder which to admire the more—his easy familiarity with the Eternal Veracities or the brilliant flashes of imbecility with which his excursions into the Infinite are sometimes diversified. He radiates talk, as the sun does light and heat; and after an evening—or a week—with him, you come forth with a sense of satisfaction in your own capacity which somehow proves superior even to the inevitable conclusion that your brilliance was but the reflection of his own, and that all the while you were only playing the part of Rubinstein's piano or Sarasate's violin.'

All this the reader should imagine as helped by the most speaking of presences: a steady, penetrating fire in the wide-set eyes, a compelling power and sweetness in the smile; courteous, waving gestures of the arms and long, nervous hands, a lit cigarette generally held between the fingers; continual rapid shiftings and pacings to and fro as he conversed: rapid, but not flurried nor awkward, for there was a grace in his attenuated but well-carried figure, and his movements were light, deft, and full of spring. When I first knew him he was passing through a period of neatness between two of Bohemian carelessness as to dress; so that the effect of his charm was immediate. At other times of his youth there was something for strangers, and even for friends, to get over in the odd garments which it was his whim to wear—the badge, as they always seemed to me, partly of a genuine carelessness, certainly of a genuine lack of cash (the little he had was always absolutely at the disposal of his friends), partly of a deliberate detachment from any particular social class or caste, partly of his love of pickles and adventures, which he thought befel a man thus attired more readily than another. But this slender, slovenly, nondescript apparition, long-visaged and long-haired, had only to speak in order to be recognised in the first minute for a witty and charming gentleman, and within the first five for a master spirit and man of genius. There were, indeed, certain stolidly conventional and superciliously official kinds of persons, both at home and abroad, who were incapable of looking beyond the clothes, and eyed him always with frozen suspicion. This attitude used sometimes in youth to drive him into fits of flaming anger, which put him helplessly at a disadvantage unless, or until, he could call the sense of humour to his help. For the rest, his human charm was the same for all kinds of people, without the least distinction of class or caste; for worldly wise old great ladies, whom he reminded of famous poets in their youth; for his brother artists and men of letters, perhaps, above all; for the ordinary clubman; for his physicians, who could never do enough for him; for domestic servants, who adored him; for the English policeman even, on whom he often tried, quite in vain, to pass himself as one of the criminal classes; for the common seaman, the shepherd, the street arab, or the tramp. Even in the imposed silence and restraint of extreme sickness the magnetic power and attraction of the man made itself felt, and there seemed to be more vitality and fire of the spirit in him as he lay exhausted and speechless in bed than in an ordinary roomful of people in health.

But I have strayed from my purpose, which is only to indicate that in the best of these letters of Stevenson's you have some echo, far away indeed, but yet the nearest, of his talk—talk which could never be taken down, and has left only an ineffaceable impression in the memory of his friends. The letters, it should be added, do not represent him at all fully until about the thirtieth year of his age, the beginning of the settled and married period of his life. From then onwards, and especially from the beginning of Part VI. (the Hyères period), they present a pretty full and complete autobiography, if not of doings, at any rate of moods and feelings. In the earlier periods, his correspondence for the most part expresses his real self either too little or else one-sidedly. I have omitted very many letters of his boyish and student days as being too immature or uninteresting; and many of the confidences and confessions of his later youth, though they are those of a beautiful spirit, whether as too intimate, or as giving a disproportionate prominence to passing troubles. When he is found in these days writing in a melancholy or minor key, it must be remembered that at the same moment, in direct intercourse with any friend, his spirits would instantly rise, and he would be found the gayest of laughing companions. Very many letters or snatches

d

of letters of nearly all dates to his familiars have also been omitted as not intelligible without a knowledge of the current jests, codes, and catchwords of conversation between him and them. At one very interesting period of his life, from about his twenty-fifth to his twenty-ninth year, he disused the habit of letter-writing almost entirely.

In choosing from among what remained I have used the best discretion that I could. Stevenson's feelings and relations throughout life were in almost all directions so warm and kindly, that next to nothing had to be suppressed from fear of giving pain. On the other hand, he drew people towards him with so much confidence and affection, and met their openness with so much of his own, that an editor could not but feel the frequent risk of inviting readers to trespass too far on purely private affairs and feelings, including those of the living. This was a point upon which in his lifetime he felt strongly. That excellent critic, Mr. Walter Raleigh, has noticed, as one of the merits of Stevenson's personal essays and accounts of travel, that few men have written more or more attractively of themselves without ever taking the public unduly into familiarity or overstepping proper bounds of reticence. Public prying into private lives, the propagation of gossip by the press, and printing of private letters during the writer's lifetime, were things he hated. Once, indeed, he very superfluously gave himself a dangerous cold by dancing before a bonfire in his garden at the news of a 'society' editor having been committed to prison; and the only approach to a difference he ever had with one of his lifelong friends arose from the publication, without permission, of one of his letters written on his first Pacific voyage (see below, vol. ii. p. 121).

How far, then, must I regard his instructions about publication as authorising me to go after his death beyond the limits which he had been so careful in observing and desiring others to observe in life? How much may now fairly become public of that which had been held sacred and hitherto private among his friends? To cut out all that is strictly personal and intimate were to leave his story untold and half the charm of his character unrevealed; to put in too much were to break all bonds of that privacy which he so carefully regarded while he lived. I know not if I have at all been able to hit the mean, and to succeed in making these letters, as it has been my object to make them, present, without offence or intrusion, a just, a living, and a proportionate picture of the man, so far as they will yield it. There is one respect in which his own practice and principle has had to be in some degree violated, if the work was to be done at all. Except in the single case of the essay 'Ordered South,' he would never in writing for the public adopt the invalid point of view, or invite any attention to his infirmities. 'To me,' he says, 'the medicine bottles on my chimney and the blood on my handkerchief are accidents; they do not colour my view of life; and I should think myself a trifler and in bad taste if I introduced the world to these unimportant privacies.' But from his letters to his family and friends, these matters could not possibly be quite left out.

The tale of his life, in the years when he was most of a correspondent, was in truth a tale of daily and nightly battle against weakness and physical distress and danger. To those who loved him, the incidents of this battle were communicated, sometimes gravely, sometimes laughingly. I have very greatly cut down such bulletins, but could not manage to omit them altogether. Generally speaking, I have used the editorial privilege of omission without scruple where I thought it desirable. And in regard to the text, I have not held myself bound to reproduce all the author's minor eccentricities of spelling and the like. As all his friends are aware, to spell in a quite accurate and grown-up manner was a thing which this master of English letters was never able to learn; but to reproduce such trivial slips in print is, I think, to distract the reader's attention from the main matter. A normal orthography has therefore been adopted throughout.

Lastly, I have to express my thanks to my friend Mr. George Smith, proprietor of the *Dictionary of National Biography*, for permission to reprint in this and in following sectional introductions a few paragraphs from that work.

S. C.

August 1899.

I

STUDENT DAYS AT EDINBURGH

TRAVELS AND EXCURSIONS

1868—1873

ERRATA.

Vol. i. p. 364, l. 18, *for* 'gorgonically' *read* 'Gongorically.'

Vol. ii. p. 298, footnote 2, *for* 'Joseph-Marie' *read* 'José Maria.'

THE following section consists chiefly of extracts from the correspondence and journals addressed by Louis Stevenson, as a lad of eighteen to twenty-two, to his father and mother during summer excursions to the Scottish coast or to the continent. There exist enough of them to fill a volume; but it is not in letters of this kind to his family that a young man unbosoms himself most freely, and these are perhaps not quite devoid of the qualities of the guide-book and the descriptive exercise. Nevertheless, they seem to me to contain enough signs of the future master-writer, enough of character, observation, and skill in expression, to make a few worth giving by way of an opening chapter to the present book. Among them are interspersed one or two of a different character addressed to other correspondents.

But, first, it is desirable that readers not acquainted with the circumstances and conditions of Stevenson's parentage and early life should be here, as briefly as possible, informed of them. On both sides of the house he came of capable and cultivated stock. His grandfather was Robert Stevenson, civil engineer, highly distinguished as the builder of the Bell Rock lighthouse. By this Robert Stevenson, his three sons, and two of his grandsons now living, the business of civil engineers in general, and of official engineers to the Commissioners of Northern Lights in particular, has been carried on at Edinburgh with high credit and public utility for almost a century. Thomas Stevenson, the youngest of the three sons of the original Robert, was Robert Louis Stevenson's father. He was a man not only of mark, zeal, and inventiveness in his profession, but of a singularly interesting personality; a staunch friend and sagacious adviser, trenchant in judgment and demonstrative in emotion, outspoken, dogmatic,—despotic, even, in little things, but withal essentially chivalrous and soft-hearted; apt to pass with the swiftest transition from moods of gloom or sternness to those of tender or freakish gaiety, and commanding a gift of humorous and figurative speech second only to that of his more famous son.

Thomas Stevenson was married to Margaret Isabella, youngest daughter of the Rev. Lewis Balfour, for many years minister of the parish of Colinton in Midlothian. This Mr. Balfour (described by his grandson in the essay called 'The Manse') was of the stock of the Balfours of Pilrig, and grandson to that James Balfour, professor first of moral philosophy, and afterwards of the law of nature and of nations, who was held in particular esteem as a philosophical controversialist by David Hume. His wife, Henrietta Smith, a daughter of the Rev. George Smith of Galston, to whose gift as a preacher Burns refers scoffingly in the *Holy Fair*, is said to have been a woman of uncommon beauty and charm of manner. Their daughter, Mrs. Thomas Stevenson, suffered in early and middle life from chest and nerve troubles, and her son may have inherited from her some of his constitutional weakness as well as of his social and intellectual vivacity and his taste for letters. Robert Louis (baptized Robert Lewis Balfour) Stevenson was born on November 13, 1850, at 8 Howard Place, Edinburgh, and was the only child of his parents. His health was infirm from the first, and he was with difficulty kept alive by the combined care of a capable and watchful mother and a perfectly devoted nurse, Alison Cunningham; to whom his lifelong gratitude will be found touchingly expressed in the course of the following letters. In 1858 he was near dying of a gastric fever, and was at all times subject to acute catarrhal and bronchial affections and extreme nervous excitability. In January 1853 his parents moved to 1 Inverleith Terrace, and in May 1857 to 17 Heriot Row, which continued to be their Edinburgh home until the death of Thomas Stevenson in 1887. Much of his time was also spent in the manse of Colinton on the Water of Leith, the home of his maternal grandfather. Of this place his childish recollections were happy and idyllic, while those of city life were coloured rather by impressions of sickness, fever, and nocturnal terrors. If, however, he suffered much as a child from the distresses, he also enjoyed to the full the pleasures, of imagination. Illness confined him much within the house, but imagination kept him always content and busy. In the days of the Crimean war some one gave the child a cheap toy sword; and when his father depreciated it, he said, 'I tell you, the sword is of gold, and the sheath of silver, and the boy is very well off and quite contented.' As disabilities closed in on him in after

life, he would never grumble at any gift, however
niggardly, of fortune, and the anecdote is as characteristic of the man as of the child. He was eager and full
of invention in every kind of play, whether solitary or
sociable, and seems to have been treated as something
of a small, sickly prince among a whole cousinhood of
playmates of both the Balfour and the Stevenson con-
nections. He was also a greedy reader, or rather listener
to reading; for it was not until his eighth year that he
began to read easily or habitually to himself. He has
recorded how his first conscious impression of pleasure
from the sound and cadence of words was received from
certain passages in M'Cheyne's hymns as recited to him
by his nurse. Bible stories, the *Pilgrim's Progress*, and
Mayne Reid's tales were especially, and it would seem
equally, his delight. He began early to take pleasure in
attempts at composition of his own. A history of Moses,
dictated in his sixth year, and an account of travels in
Perth, in his ninth, are still extant. Ill health prevented
him getting much regular or continuous schooling. He
attended first (1858-61) a preparatory school kept by a
Mr. Henderson in India Street; and next (at intervals
for some time after the autumn of 1861) the Edinburgh
Academy. One of his tutors at the former school writes:
'He was the most delightful boy I ever knew; full of fun,
full of tender feeling, ready for his lessons, ready for a
story, ready for fun.' From very early days, both as
child and boy, he must have had something of that power
to charm which distinguished him above other men in
after life. '.I loike that bo-o-o-o-y,' a heavy Dutchman

was heard saying to himself over and over again, whom at the age of about thirteen he had held in amused conversation during a whole passage from Ostend. The same quality, with the signs which he always showed of quick natural intelligence when he chose to learn, must have helped to spare him many punishments from teachers which he earned by persistent and ingenious truantry. 'I think,' remarks his mother, 'they liked talking to him better than teaching him.'

For a few months in the autumn of 1863, when his parents had been ordered to winter at Mentone for the sake of his mother's health, he was sent to a boarding-school kept by a Mr. Wyatt at Spring Grove, near London. It is not my intention to treat the reader to the series of childish and boyish letters of these days which parental fondness has preserved. But here is one written from his English school when he was about thirteen, which is both amusing in itself and had a certain influence on his destiny, inasmuch as his appeal led to his being taken out to join his parents on the French Riviera; which from that day forward he never ceased to love, and for which the longing, amid the gloom of Edinburgh winters, often afterwards gripped him by the heart.

Spring Grove School, 12*th November* 1863.

MA CHERE MAMAN,—Jai recu votre lettre Aujourdhui et comme le jour prochaine est mon jour de naisance je vous écrit ce lettre. Ma grande gatteaux est arrivé il leve 12 livres et demi le prix etait 17 shillings. Sur la soirée de Monseigneur Faux il y etait quelques belles feux d'artifice. Mais les polissons entrent dans notre champ et nos feux d'artifice et handkerchiefs disappeared quickly, but we charged them out of the field. Je suis presque driven mad par une bruit terrible tous les garcons kik up comme grand un bruit qu'il est possible. I hope you will find your house at Mentone nice. I have been obliged to stop from writing by the want of a pen, but now I have one, so I will continue.

My dear papa, you told me to tell you whenever I was miserable. I do not feel well, and I wish to get home. Do take me with you.   R. STEVENSON.

This young French scholar has yet, it will be discerned, a good way to travel; in later days he acquired a complete reading and speaking, and pretty complete writing, mastery of the language, and was as much at home with French ways of thought and life as with English.

For one more specimen of his boyish style, it may be not amiss to give the text of another appeal which dates from two and a half years later, and is also typical of much in his life's conditions both then and later :—

2 Sulyarde Terrāce, Torquay, Thursday (April 1866).

RESPECTED PATERNAL RELATIVE,—I write to make a request of the most moderate nature. Every year I have cost you an enormous—nay, elephantine—sum of money for drugs and physician's fees, and the most expensive time of the twelve months was March.

But this year the biting Oriental blasts, the howling tempests, and the general ailments of the human race have been successfully braved by yours truly.

Does not this deserve remuneration?

I appeal to your charity, I appeal to your generosity, I

appeal to your justice, I appeal to your accounts, I appeal, in fine, to your purse.

My sense of generosity forbids the receipt of more—my sense of justice forbids the receipt of less—than half-a-crown.—Greeting from, Sir, your most affectionate and needy son, R. STEVENSON.

From 1864 to 1867 Stevenson's education was conducted chiefly at Mr. Thomson's private school in Frederick Street, Edinburgh, and by private tutors in various places to which he travelled for his own or his parents' health. These travels included frequent visits to such Scottish health resorts as Bridge of Allan, Dunoon, Rothesay, North Berwick, Lasswade, and Peebles, and occasional excursions with his father on his nearer professional rounds to the Scottish coasts and lighthouses, as well as several longer journeys to the south of England or the Continent. The love of wandering, which was a rooted passion in Stevenson's nature, thus began early to find satisfaction. From 1867 the family life became more settled between Edinburgh and Swanston Cottage, Lothianburn, a country home in the Pentlands which Mr. Stevenson first rented in that year, and the scenery and associations of which sank deeply into the young man's spirit, and vitally affected his after thoughts and his art.

By this time Louis Stevenson seemed to show signs of outgrowing his early infirmities of health. He was a lover, to a degree even beyond his strength, of outdoor life and exercise (though not of sports), and it began to be hoped that as he grew up he would be fit to enter the family profession of civil engineer. He was accordingly entered as a student at Edinburgh University, and for several winters attended classes there with such regularity as his health and inclinations permitted. This was in truth but small. The mind on fire with its own imaginations, and eager to acquire its own experiences in its own way, does not take kindly to the routine of classes and repetitions, nor could the desultory mode of schooling enforced upon him by ill-health answer much purpose by way of discipline. According to his own account he was at college, as he had been at school, an inveterate idler and truant. But outside the field of school and college routine he showed an eager curiosity and activity of mind. 'He was of a conversable temper,' so he says of himself, 'and insatiably curious in the aspects of life, and spent much of his time scraping acquaintance with all classes of men and womenkind.' Of one class indeed, and that was his own, he had soon had enough, at least in so far as it was to be studied at the dinners, dances, and other polite entertainments of ordinary Edinburgh society. Of these he early wearied. At home he made himself pleasant to all comers, but for his own resort chose out a very few houses, mostly those of intimate college companions, into which he could go without constraint, and where his inexhaustible flow of poetic, imaginative, and laughing talk seems generally to have rather puzzled his hearers than impressed them. On the other hand, during his endless private rambles and excursions, whether among the streets and slums, the gardens and graveyards of the city, or farther afield among the Pentland hills or on the shores of Forth, he was never tired of studying character and seeking acquaintance among the classes more nearly exposed to the pinch and stress of life.

In the eyes of anxious elders, such vagrant ways naturally take on the colours of idleness and a love of low company. Stevenson was, however, in his own fashion an eager student of books as well as of man and nature. He read precociously and omnivorously in the *belles-lettres*, including a very wide range of English poetry, fiction, and essays, and a fairly wide range of French; and was a thorough student of Scottish history, especially from the time of the persecutions down, and to some extent of history in general. The art of literature was already his private passion, and something within him even already told him that it was to be his life's work. On all his truantries he went pencil and copybook in hand, trying to fit his impression of the scene to words, to compose original rhymes, tales, dialogues, and dramas, or to imitate the style and cadences of the author he at the moment preferred. For three or four years, nevertheless, he tried dutifully, if half-heartedly, to prepare himself for the family profession. In 1868, the year when the following correspondence opens, he went to watch the works of the firm in progress first at Anstruther on the coast of Fife, and afterwards at Wick. In 1869 he made the tour of the Orkneys and Shetlands on board the steam yacht of the Commissioners of Northern Lights, and in 1870 the tour of the Western Islands, preceded by a stay on the Isle of Earraid (afterwards turned to account in the tale of *Kidnapped*), where the works of the Dhu Heartach Lighthouse were then in progress. He was a favourite, although a very irregular pupil, of the professor of engineering, Fleeming Jenkin, whose friendship and that of Mrs. Jenkin were of great value to him, and whose life he afterwards wrote; and must have shown some aptitude for the family calling, inasmuch as in 1871 he received the silver medal of the Edinburgh Society of Arts for a paper on a suggested improvement in lighthouse apparatus. The outdoor and seafaring parts of an engineer's life were in fact wholly to his taste. But he looked instinctively at the powers and phenomena of waves and tide, of storm and current, of reef, cliff, and rock, with the eye of the poet and artist, and not those of the practician and calculator; for desk work and office routine he had an unconquerable aversion; and his physical powers, had they remained at their best, must have proved quite unequal to the workshop training necessary to the practical engineer. Accordingly in 1871 it was agreed, not without natural reluctance on his father's part, that he should give up the hereditary vocation and read for the bar; literature, on which his heart was set, and in which his early attempts had been encouraged, being held to be by itself no profession, or at least one altogether too irregular and undefined. For the next several years, therefore, he attended law classes instead of engineering and science classes in the University, giving to the subject a certain amount of serious, although fitful, attention until he was called to the bar in 1875.

So much for the course of Stevenson's outward life during these days at Edinburgh. To tell the story of his inner life would be a far more complicated task, and cannot here be attempted even briefly. The ferment of youth was more acute and more prolonged in him than in most men even of genius; and for several years he was torn hither and thither by fifty conflicting currents of speculation, impulse, and desire. In the introduction I have tried to give some notion of the many various strains and elements which met in him, and which were in these days pulling one against another in his half-formed being, at a great expense of spirit and body. Add the storms, which from time to time attacked him, of shivering repulsion from the climate and conditions of life in the city which he yet deeply and imaginatively loved; the seasons of temptation, most strongly besetting the ardent and poetic temperament, to seek escape into freedom and the ideal through that grotesque back-door opened by the crude allurements of the city streets; the moods of spiritual revolt against the harsh doctrines of the creed in which he had been brought up, and to which his parents were deeply, his father even passionately, attached.

In the later and maturer correspondence which will appear in these volumes, the agitations of the writer's early days are often enough referred to in retrospect. In the boyish letters to his parents, which make up the chief part of this first section, they are naturally hardly allowed to find expression at all; nor will these letters be found to differ much in any way from those of any other lively and observant lad who is also something of a reader and has some natural gift of writing. At the end of the section I have indeed printed one cry of the heart, written not to his parents, but about them, and telling of the strain which matters of religious difference for a while brought into his home relations. These had until now been thoroughly happy. The attachment between the father and son from childhood was exceptionally strong; and as the latter grew up, their habits of sympathy, companionship, and affection had grown ever closer, remaining quite unshaken by the son's Bohemian ways, or even by disappointment about his choice of a profession. But the father was staunchly wedded to the hereditary creeds and dogmas of Scottish Calvinistic Christianity; while the course of the young man's reading, with the spirit of the generation in which he grew up, had loosed him from the bonds of that theology, and even of dogmatic Christianity in general, and had taught him to respect all creeds alike as expressions of the cravings and conjectures of the human spirit in face of the unsolved mystery of things, rather than to cling to any one of them as a revelation of ultimate truth. This, in the main, was his attitude throughout life towards religion, though as time went on he grew more ready, in daily life, to use the language and fall in with the observances of the faith in which he had been brought up. And even in youth, he was never, in my experience, the least blatant or offensive in the expression of his views. But the shock to the father was great when they came to his knowledge; and there ensued a time of extremely painful discussion and private tension between father and son. In due time this cloud upon a family life otherwise very harmonious and affectionate passed quite away. But the greater the love, the greater the pain; when I first knew Stevenson this trouble gave him no peace, and it has left a strong trace upon his mind and work. See particularly the bitter parable called 'The House of Eld,' in his collection of *Fables*, and the many studies of difficult paternal and filial relations which are to be found in *The Story of a Lie*, *The Misadventures of John Nicholson*, *The Wrecker*, and *Weir of Hermiston*.

TO MRS. THOMAS STEVENSON

1868.
AET. 18.

In July 1868 R. L. S. went to watch the harbour works at Anstruther, and afterwards, in the company of his father, those at Wick, where he was presently left by himself. The following is the second letter written home after his father had left. An early Portfolio paper *On the Enjoyment of Unpleasant Places*, as well as the second part of the *Random Memories* essay, written twenty years later, refer to the same experiences as the following letters:—

Wick, Friday, September 11, 1868.

MY DEAR MOTHER,— . . . Wick lies at the end or elbow of an open triangular bay, hemmed on either side by shores, either cliff or steep earth-bank, of no great height. The grey houses of Pulteney extend along the southerly shore almost to the cape; and it is about half-way down this shore—no, six-sevenths way down—that the new breakwater extends athwart the bay.

Certainly Wick in itself possesses no beauty: bare, grey shores, grim grey houses, grim grey sea; not even the gleam of red tiles; not even the greenness of a tree. The southerly heights, when I came here, were black with people, fishers waiting on wind and night. Now all the S.Y.S. (Stornoway boats) have beaten out of the bay, and the Wick men stay indoors or wrangle on the quays with dissatisfied fish-curers, knee-high in brine, mud, and herring refuse. The day when the boats put out to go home to the Hebrides, the girl here told me there was 'a black wind'; and on going out, I found the epithet as justifiable as it was picturesque. A cold, *black* southerly wind, with occasional rising showers of rain; it was a fine sight to see the boats beat out a-teeth of it.

In Wick I have never heard any one greet his neighbour with the usual 'Fine day' or 'Good morning.' Both come shaking their heads, and both say, 'Breezy, breezy!' And such is the atrocious quality of the climate, that the remark is almost invariably justified by the fact.

The streets are full of the Highland fishers, lubberly, stupid, inconceivably lazy and heavy to move. You bruise against them, tumble over them, elbow them against the wall—all to no purpose; they will not budge; and you are forced to leave the pavement every step.

To the south, however, is as fine a piece of coast scenery as I ever saw. Great black chasms, huge black cliffs, rugged and over-hung gullies, natural arches, and deep green pools below them, almost too deep to let you see the gleam of sand among the darker weed: there are deep caves too. In one of these lives a tribe of gipsies. The men are *always* drunk, simply and truthfully always. From morning to evening the great villainous-looking fellows are either sleeping off the last debauch, or hulking about the cove 'in the horrors.' The cave is deep, high, and airy, and might be made comfortable enough. But they just live among heaped boulders, damp with continual droppings from above, with no more furniture than two or three tin pans, a truss of rotten straw, and a few ragged cloaks. In winter the surf bursts into the mouth and often forces them to abandon it.

An *émeute* of disappointed fishers was feared, and two ships of war are in the bay to render assistance to the municipal authorities. This is the ides; and, to all intents and purposes, said ides are passed. Still there is a good deal of disturbance, many drunk men, and a double supply of police. I saw them sent for by some people and enter an inn, in a pretty good hurry: what it was for I do not know.

You would see by papa's letter about the carpenter who fell off the staging: I don't think I was ever so much excited in my life. The man was back at his work, and I asked him how he was; but he was a Highlander, and —need I add it?—dickens a word could I understand of his answer. What is still worse, I find the people hereabout—that is to say, the Highlanders, not the northmen —don't understand *me*.

I have lost a shilling's worth of postage stamps, which has damped my ardour for buying big lots of 'em: I'll buy them one at a time as I want 'em for the future.

The Free Church minister and I got quite thick. He left last night about two in the morning, when I went to turn in. He gave me the enclosed.—I remain your affectionate son, R. L. STEVENSON.

TO MRS. THOMAS STEVENSON

Wick, September 5, 1868. Monday.

MY DEAR MAMMA,—This morning I got a delightful haul: your letter of the fourth (surely mis-dated); Papa's of same day; Virgil's *Bucolics*, very thankfully received; and Aikman's *Annals*,[1] a precious and most acceptable donation, for which I tender my most ebullient thanksgivings. I almost forgot to drink my tea and eat mine egg.

It contains more detailed accounts than anything I ever saw, except Wodrow, without being so portentously tiresome and so desperately overborne with footnotes, proclamations, acts of Parliament, and citations as that last history.

[1] Aikman's *Annals of the Persecution in Scotland*.

1868.
AET. 18.

I have been reading a good deal of Herbert. He's a clever and a devout cove; but in places awfully twaddley (if I may use the word). Oughtn't this to rejoice Papa's heart—

> 'Carve or discourse; do not a famine fear.
> Who carves is kind to two, who talks to all.'

You understand? The 'fearing a famine' is applied to people gulping down solid vivers without a word, as if the ten lean kine began to-morrow.

Do you remember condemning something of mine for being too obtrusively didactic. Listen to Herbert—

> 'Is it not verse except enchanted groves
> And sudden arbours shadow coarse-spun lines?
> Must purling streams refresh a lover's loves?
> *Must all be veiled, while he that reads divines
> Catching the sense at two removes?*'

You see, 'except' was used for 'unless' before 1630.

Tuesday.—The riots were a hum. No more has been heard; and one of the war-steamers has deserted in disgust.

The *Moonstone* is frightfully interesting: isn't the detective prime? Don't say anything about the plot; for I have only read on to the end of Betteredge's narrative, so don't know anything about it yet.

I thought to have gone on to Thurso to-night, but the coach was full; so I go to-morrow instead.

To-day I had a grouse: great glorification.

There is a drunken brute in the house who disturbed my rest last night. He's a very respectable man in general, but when on the 'spree' a most consummate fool. When he came in he stood on the top of the stairs and preached in the dark with great solemnity and no audience from 12 P.M. to half-past one. At last I opened my door. 'Are we to have no sleep at all for that *drunken brute*?' I said. As I hoped, it had the desired effect.

Drunken brute!' he howled, in much indignation; then after a pause, in a voice of some contrition, 'Well, if I am a drunken brute, it's only once in the twelvemonth!' And that was the end of him; the insult rankled in his mind; and he retired to rest. He is a fish-curer, a man over fifty, and pretty rich too. He's as bad again to-day; but I'll be shot if he keeps me awake, I'll douse him with water if he makes a row.—Ever your affectionate son,

1868.
AET. 18.

R. L. STEVENSON.

TO MRS. THOMAS STEVENSON

Wick, September 1868. *Saturday*, 10 A.M.

MY DEAR MOTHER,—The last two days have been dreadfully hard, and I was so tired in the evenings that I could not write. In fact, last night I went to sleep immediately after dinner, or very nearly so. My hours have been 10—2 and 3—7 out in the lighter or the small boat, in a long, heavy roll from the nor'-east. When the dog was taken out, he got awfully ill; one of the men, Geordie Grant by name and surname, followed *shoot* with considerable *éclat*; but, wonderful to relate! I kept well. My hands are all skinned, blistered, discoloured, and engrained with tar, some of which latter has established itself under my nails in a position of such natural strength that it defies all my efforts to dislodge it. The worst work I had was when David (MacDonald's eldest) and I took the charge ourselves. He remained in the lighter to tighten or slacken the guys as we raised the pole towards the perpendicular, with two men. I was with four men in the boat. We dropped an anchor out a good bit, then tied a cord to the pole, took a turn round the sternmost thwart with it, and pulled on the anchor line. As the great, big, wet hawser came in it soaked you to the skin: I was the sternest (used, by way of variety, for sternmost) of the lot, and had to coil it—a work which involved, from *its* being so stiff and *your* being busy pulling with all your might, no little trouble and an extra ducking. We got it up; and, just as we were going to sing 'Victory!' one of the guys slipped in, the pole tottered—went over on its side again like a shot, and behold the end of our labour.

You see, I have been roughing it; and though some parts of the letter may be neither very comprehensible nor very interesting to *you*, I think that perhaps it might amuse Willie Traquair, who delights in all such dirty jobs.

The first day, I forgot to mention, was like mid-winter for cold, and rained incessantly so hard that the livid white of our cold-pinched faces wore a sort of inflamed rash on the windward side.

I am not a bit the worse of it, except fore-mentioned state of hands, a slight crick in my neck from the rain running down, and general stiffness from pulling, hauling, and tugging for dear life.

We have got double weights at the guys, and hope to get it up like a shot.

What fun you three must be having! I hope the cold don't disagree with you.—I remain, my dear mother, your affectionate son, R. L. STEVENSON.

TO MRS. THOMAS STEVENSON

The following will help the reader to understand the passage referring to this undertaking in Stevenson's biographical essay on his father; where he has told how in the end 'the sea proved too strong for men's arts, and after expedients hitherto unthought of, and on a scale hyper-Cyclopean, the work must be deserted, and now stands a ruin in that bleak, God-forsaken bay':—

Pulteney, Wick, Sunday, September 1868.

MY DEAR MOTHER,—Another storm: wind higher, rain thicker: the wind still rising as the night closes in and the sea slowly rising along with it; it looks like a three days' gale.

Last week has been a blank one: always too much sea. 1868.
I enjoyed myself very much last night at the R.'s. AET. 18.
There was a little dancing, much singing and supper.

Are you not well that you do not write? I haven't heard from you for more than a fortnight.

The wind fell yesterday and rose again to-day; it is a dreadful evening; but the wind is keeping the sea down as yet. Of course, nothing more has been done to the poles; and I can't tell when I shall be able to leave, not for a fortnight yet, I fear, at the earliest, for the winds are persistent. Where's Murra? Is Cummie struck dumb about the boots? I wish you would get somebody to write an interesting letter and say how you are, for you're on the broad of your back I see. There hath arrived an inroad of farmers to-night; and I go to avoid them to M—— if he's disengaged, to the R.'s if not.

Sunday (later).—Storm without: wind and rain: a confused mass of wind-driven rain-squalls, wind-ragged mist, foam, spray, and great, grey waves. Of this hereafter; in the meantime let us follow the due course of historic narrative.

Seven P.M. found me at Breadalbane Terrace, clad in spotless blacks, white tie, shirt, et cætera, and finished off below with a pair of navvies' boots. How true that the devil is betrayed by his feet! A message to Cummy at last. Why, O treacherous woman! were my dress boots withheld?

Dramatis personæ: père R., amusing, long-winded, in many points like papa; mère R., nice, delicate, likes hymns, knew Aunt Margaret ('t'ould man knew Uncle Alan); fille R., nommée Sara (no h), rather nice, lights up well, good voice, *interested* face; Miss L., nice also, washed out a little, and, I think, a trifle sentimental; fils R., in a Leith office, smart, full of happy epithet, amusing. They are very nice and very kind, asked me to come back—'any night you feel dull; and any night

1868.
AET. 18.

doesn't mean no night: we'll be so glad to see you.'
C'est la mère qui parle.

I was back there again to-night. There was hymn-singing, and general religious controversy till eight, after which talk was secular. Mrs. S. was deeply distressed about the boot business. She consoled me by saying that many would be glad to have such feet whatever shoes they had on. Unfortunately, fishers and seafaring men are too facile to be compared with! This looks like enjoyment: better speck than Anster.

I have done with frivolity. This morning I was awakened by Mrs. S. at the door. 'There's a ship ashore at Shaltigoe!' As my senses slowly flooded, I heard the whistling and the roaring of wind, and the lashing of gust-blown and uncertain flaws of rain. I got up, dressed, and went out. The mizzled sky and rain blinded you.

C D is the new pier.
A the schooner ashore. B the salmon house.

She was a Norwegian: coming in she saw our first gauge-pole, standing at point E. Norse skipper thought it was a sunk smack, and dropped his anchor in full drift of sea: chain broke: schooner came ashore. Insured: laden with wood: skipper owner of vessel and cargo: bottom out.

I was in a great fright at first lest we should be liable; but it seems that's all right.

Some of the waves were twenty feet high. The spray

rose eighty feet at the new pier. Some wood has come ashore, and the roadway seems carried away. There is something fishy at the far end where the cross wall is building; but till we are able to get along, all speculation is vain.

1868.
AET. 18.

I am so sleepy I am writing nonsense.

I stood a long while on the cope watching the sea below me; I hear its dull, monotonous roar at this moment below the shrieking of the wind; and there came ever recurring to my mind the verse I am so fond of:—

> 'But yet the Lord that is on high
> Is more of might by far
> Than noise of many waters is
> Or great sea-billows are.'

The thunder at the wall when it first struck—the rush along ever growing higher—the great jet of snow-white spray some forty feet above you—and the 'noise of many waters,' the roar, the hiss, the 'shrieking' among the shingle as it fell head over heels at your feet. I watched if it threw the big stones at the wall; but it never moved them.

Monday.—The end of the work displays gaps, cairns of ten ton blocks, stones torn from their places and turned right round. The damage above water is comparatively little: what there may be below, *on ne sait pas encore*. The roadway is torn away, cross heads, broken planks tossed here and there, planks gnawn and mumbled as if a starved bear had been trying to eat them, planks with spales lifted from them as if they had been dressed with a rugged plane, one pile swaying to and fro clear of the bottom, the rails in one place sunk a foot at least. This was not a great storm, the waves were light and short. Yet when we are standing at the office, I felt the ground beneath me *quail* as a huge roller thundered on the work at the last year's cross wall.

1871.
AET. 21.

How could *noster amicus Q. maximus* appreciate a storm at Wick? It requires a little of the artistic temperament, of which Mr. T. S.,[1] C.E., possesses some, whatever he may say. I can't look at it practically however: that will come, I suppose, like grey hair or coffin nails.

Our pole is snapped: a fortnight's work and the loss of the Norse schooner all for nothing!—except experience and dirty clothes.—Your affectionate son,

R. L. STEVENSON.

TO MRS. CHURCHILL BABINGTON

I omit the letters of 1869, which describe at great length, and not very interestingly, a summer trip on board the lighthouse steamer to the Orkneys, and Shetlands; as well as others, not very interesting either, of 1870. This, addressed to a favourite married cousin of the Balfour clan, belongs to the summer of 1871. 'Mrs. Hutchinson' is, of course, Lucy Hutchinson's famous Life of her husband the regicide.

[*Swanston Cottage, Lothianburn, Summer* 1871.]

MY DEAR MAUD,—If you have forgotten the handwriting—as is like enough—you will find the name of a former correspondent (don't know how to spell that word) at the end. I have begun to write to you before now, but always stuck somehow, and left it to drown in a drawerful of like fiascos. This time I am determined to carry through, though I have nothing specially to say.

We look fairly like summer this morning; the trees are blackening out of their spring greens; the warmer suns have melted the hoarfrost of daisies of the paddock; and the blackbird, I fear, already beginning to 'stint his pipe of mellower days'—which is very apposite (I can't spell anything to-day—*one* p or *two*?) and pretty. All the same, we have been having shocking weather—cold winds and grey skies.

I have been reading heaps of nice books; but I can't go

[1] Thomas Stevenson.

back so far. I am reading Clarendon's *Hist. Rebell.* at present, with which I am more pleased than I expected, which is saying a good deal. It is a pet idea of mine that one gets more real truth out of one avowed partisan than out of a dozen of your sham impartialists—wolves in sheep's clothing—simpering honesty as they suppress documents. After all, what one wants to know is not what people did, but why they did it—or rather, why they *thought* they did it; and to learn that, you should go to the men themselves. Their very falsehood is often more than another man's truth.

I have possessed myself of Mrs. Hutchinson, which, of course, I admire, etc. But is there not an irritating deliberation and correctness about her and everybody connected with her? If she would only write bad grammar, or forget to finish a sentence, or do something or other that looks fallible, it would be a relief. I sometimes wish the old Colonel had got drunk and beaten her, in the bitterness of my spirit. I know I felt a weight taken off my heart when I heard he was extravagant. It is quite possible to be too good for this evil world; and unquestionably, Mrs. Hutchinson was. The way in which she talks of herself makes one's blood run cold. There—I am glad to have got that out—but don't say it to anybody—seal of secrecy.

Please tell Mr. Babington that I have never forgotten one of his drawings—a Rubens, I think—a woman holding up a model ship. That woman had more life in her than ninety per cent. of the lame humans that you see crippling about this earth.

By the way, that is a feature in art which seems to have come in with the Italians. Your old Greek statues have scarce enough vitality in them to keep their monstrous bodies fresh withal. A shrewd country attorney, in a turned white neckcloth and rusty blacks, would just take one of these Agamemnons and Ajaxes quietly by his beautiful, strong arm, trot the unresisting statue down a little gallery of legal shams, and turn the poor fellow out at the other end, 'naked, as from the earth he came.' There is more latent life, more of the coiled spring in the sleeping dog, about a recumbent figure of Michael Angelo's than about the most excited of Greek statues. The very marble seems to wrinkle with a wild energy that we never feel except in dreams.

I think this letter has turned into a sermon, but I had nothing interesting to talk about.

I do wish you and Mr. Babington would think better of it and come north this summer. We should be so glad to see you both. *Do* reconsider it.—Believe me, my dear Maud, ever your most affectionate cousin,

LOUIS STEVENSON.

TO ALISON CUNNINGHAM

The following is the first of many letters to the admirable nurse whose care, during his ailing childhood, had done so much both to preserve Stevenson's life and awaken his love of tales and poetry, and of whom until his death he thought with the utmost constancy of affection. The letter bears no sign of date or place, but by the handwriting would seem to belong to this year:—

1871?

MY DEAR CUMMY,—I was greatly pleased by your letter in many ways. Of course, I was glad to hear from you; you know, you and I have so many old stories between us, that even if there was nothing else, even if there was not a very sincere respect and affection, we should always be glad to pass a nod. I say 'even if there was not.' But you know right well there is. Do not suppose that I shall ever forget those long, bitter nights, when I coughed and coughed and was so unhappy, and you were so patient and loving with a poor, sick child. Indeed, Cummy, I wish I might become a man worth talking of, if it were only that you should not have thrown away your pains.

Happily, it is not the result of our acts that makes them brave and noble, but the acts themselves and the unselfish love that moved us to do them. 'Inasmuch as you have done it unto one of the least of these.' My dear old nurse, and you know there is nothing a man can say nearer his heart except his mother or his wife—my dear old nurse, God will make good to you all the good that you have done, and mercifully forgive you all the evil. And next time when the spring comes round, and everything is beginning once again, if you should happen to think that you might have had a child of your own, and that it was hard you should have spent so many years taking care of some one else's prodigal, just you think this—you have been for a great deal in my life; you have made much that there is in me, just as surely as if you had conceived me; and there are sons who are more ungrateful to their own mothers than I am to you. For I am not ungrateful, my dear Cummy, and it is with a very sincere emotion that I write myself your little boy,   LOUIS.

TO CHARLES BAXTER

After a winter of troubled health, Stevenson had gone to Dunblane for a change in early spring; and thence writes to his college companion and life-long friend, Mr. Charles Baxter.

Dunblane, Friday, 5th March 1872.

MY DEAR BAXTER,—By the date you may perhaps understand the purport of my letter without any words wasted about the matter. I cannot walk with you to-morrow, and you must not expect me. I came yesterday afternoon to Bridge of Allan, and have been very happy ever since, as every place is sanctified by the eighth sense, Memory. I walked up here this morning (three miles, *tu-dieu!* a good stretch for me), and passed one of my favourite places in the world, and one that I very much affect in spirit when the body is tied down and brought immovably

1872.
AET. 22.

to anchor on a sickbed. It is a meadow and bank on a corner on the river, and is connected in my mind inseparably with Virgil's *Eclogues*. *Hic corulis mistos inter consedimus ulmos*, or something very like that, the passage begins (only I know my short-winded Latinity must have come to grief over even this much of quotation); and here, to a wish, is just such a cavern as Menalcas might shelter himself withal from the bright noon, and, with his lips curled backward, pipe himself blue in the face, while *Messieurs les Arcadiens* would roll out those cloying hexameters that sing themselves in one's mouth to such a curious lilting chant.

In such weather one has the bird's need to whistle; and I, who am specially incompetent in this art, must content myself by chattering away to you on this bit of paper. All the way along I was thanking God that he had made me and the birds and everything just as they are and not otherwise; for although there was no sun, the air was so thrilled with robins and blackbirds that it made the heart tremble with joy, and the leaves are far enough forward on the underwood to give a fine promise for the future. Even myself, as I say, I would not have had changed in one *iota* this forenoon, in spite of all my idleness and Guthrie's lost paper, which is ever present with me—a horrible phantom.

No one can be alone at home or in a quite new place. Memory and you must go hand in hand with (at least) decent weather if you wish to cook up a proper dish of solitude. It is in these little flights of mine that I get more pleasure than in anything else. Now, at present, I am supremely uneasy and restless—almost to the extent of pain; but O! how I enjoy it, and how I *shall* enjoy it afterwards (please God), if I get years enough allotted to me for the thing to ripen in. When I am a very old and very respectable citizen with white hair and bland manners and a gold watch, I shall hear three crows cawing in my heart, as I heard them this morning: I vote for old age and eighty years of retrospect. Yet, after all, I dare say, a short shrift and a nice green grave are about as desirable.

Poor devil! how I am wearying you! Cheer up. Two pages more, and my letter reaches its term, for I have no more paper. What delightful things inns and waiters and bagmen are! If we didn't travel now and then, we should forget what the feeling of life is. The very cushion of a railway carriage—'the things restorative to the touch.' I can't write, confound it! That's because I am so tired with my walk. . . . Believe me, ever your affectionate friend,
R. L. STEVENSON.

TO CHARLES BAXTER

The 'Spec.' is, of course, the famous and historical debating society (the Speculative Society) of Edinburgh University, to which Stevenson had been elected on the strength of his conversational powers, but where it is said that in set debate he did not shine.

Dunblane, Tuesday, 9th April 1872.

MY DEAR BAXTER,—I don't know what you mean. I know nothing about the Standing Committee of the Spec., did not know that such a body existed, and even if it doth exist, must sadly repudiate all association with such 'goodly fellowship.' I am a 'Rural Voluptuary' at present. *That* is what is the matter with me. The Spec. may go whistle. As for 'C. Baxter, Esq.,' who is he? 'One Baxter, or Bagster, a secretary,' I say to mine acquaintance, 'is at present disquieting my leisure with certain illegal, uncharitable, unchristian, and unconstitutional documents called *Business Letters: The affair is in the hands of the Police.*' Do you hear *that*, you evildoer? Sending business letters is surely a far more hateful and slimy degree of wickedness than sending threatening letters; the man who throws grenades and torpedoes is less malicious; the Devil in red-hot hell rubs his hands with glee as he reckons

1872.
AET. 22.

up the number that go forth spreading pain and anxiety with each delivery of the post.

I have been walking to-day by a colonnade of beeches along the brawling Allan. My character for sanity is quite gone, seeing that I cheered my lonely way with the following, in a triumphant chaunt: 'Thank God for the grass, and the fir-trees, and the crows, and the sheep, and the sunshine, and the shadows of the fir-trees.' I hold that he is a poor mean devil who can walk alone, in such a place and in such weather, and doesn't set up his lungs and cry back to the birds and the river. Follow, follow, follow me. Come hither, come hither, come hither—here shall you see—no enemy—except a very slight remnant of winter and its rough weather. My bedroom, when I awoke this morning, was full of bird-songs, which is the greatest pleasure in life. Come hither, come hither, come hither, and when you come bring the third part of the *Earthly Paradise*; you can get it for me in Elliot's for two and tenpence (2s. 10d.) (*business habits*). Also bring an ounce of honeydew from Wilson's.   R. L. S.

TO MRS. THOMAS STEVENSON

In the previous year, 1871, it had become apparent that Stevenson was neither fitted by bodily health nor by inclination for the family profession of civil engineer. To the great and natural regret of his father, who, however, wisely bowed to the inevitable, it was agreed that he should give it up, and should read instead for the Scottish Bar. Accordingly his summer excursions were no longer to the harbour works and lighthouses of Scotland, but to the ordinary scenes of holiday travel abroad.

Brussels, Thursday, 25th July 1872.

MY DEAR MOTHER,—I am here at last, sitting in my room, without coat or waistcoat, and with both window and door open, and yet perspiring like a terra-cotta jug or a Gruyère cheese.

We had a very good passage, which we certainly

deserved, in compensation for having to sleep on the cabin floor, and finding absolutely nothing fit for human food in the whole filthy embarkation. We made up for lost time by sleeping on deck a good part of the forenoon. When I woke, Simpson was still sleeping the sleep of the just, on a coil of ropes and (as appeared afterwards) his own hat; so I got a bottle of Bass and a pipe and laid hold of an old Frenchman of somewhat filthy aspect (*fiat experimentum in corpore vili*) to try my French upon. I made very heavy weather of it. The Frenchman had a very pretty young wife; but my French always deserted me entirely when I had to answer her, and so she soon drew away and left me to her lord, who talked of French politics, Africa, and domestic economy with great vivacity. From Ostend a smoking-hot journey to Brussels. At Brussels we went off after dinner to the Parc. If any person wants to be happy, I should advise the Parc. You sit drinking iced drinks and smoking penny cigars under great old trees. The band place, covered walks, etc., are all lit up. And you can't fancy how beautiful was the contrast of the great masses of lamplit foliage and the dark sapphire night sky with just one blue star set overhead in the middle of the largest patch. In the dark walks, too, there are crowds of people whose faces you cannot see, and here and there a colossal white statue at the corner of an alley that gives the place a nice, *artificial*, eighteenth century sentiment. There was a good deal of summer lightning blinking overhead, and the black avenues and white statues leapt out every minute into short-lived distinctness.

1872.
AET. 22.

I get up to add one thing more. There is in the hotel a boy in whom I take the deepest interest. I cannot tell you his age, but the very first time I saw him (when I was at dinner yesterday) I was very much struck with his appearance. There is something very leonine in his face, with a dash of the negro especially, if I remember aright, in the mouth. He has a great quantity of dark hair, curling in great rolls, not in little corkscrews, and a pair of large, dark, and very steady, bold, bright eyes. His manners are those of a prince. I felt like an overgrown ploughboy beside him. He speaks English perfectly, but with, I think, sufficient foreign accent to stamp him as a Russian, especially when his manners are taken into account. I don't think I ever saw any one who looked like a hero before. After breakfast this morning I was talking to him in the court, when he mentioned casually that he had caught a snake in the Riesengebirge. 'I have it here,' he said; 'would you like to see it?' I said yes; and putting his hand into his breast-pocket, he drew forth not a dried serpent skin, but the head and neck of the reptile writhing and shooting out its horrible tongue in my face. You may conceive what a fright I got. I send off this single sheet just now in order to let you know I am safe across; but you must not expect letters often.—R. L. STEVENSON.

P.S.—The snake was about a yard long, but harmless, and now, he says, quite tame.

TO MRS. THOMAS STEVENSON

Hotel Landsberg, Frankfurt, Monday, 29th July 1872.

... LAST night I met with rather an amusing adventurette. Seeing a church door open, I went in, and was led by most importunate finger-bills up a long stair to the top of the tower. The father smoking at the door, the mother and the three daughters received me as if I was a friend of the family and had come in for an evening visit. The youngest daughter (about thirteen, I suppose, and a pretty little girl) had been learning English at the school, and was anxious to play it off upon a real, veritable Englander; so we had a long talk, and I was shown photographs, etc., Marie and I talking, and the others looking on with evident delight at having such a linguist in the family.

As all my remarks were duly translated and communicated to the rest, it was quite a good German lesson. There was only one contretemps during the whole interview—the arrival of another visitor, in the shape (surely) the last of God's creatures, a wood-worm of the most unnatural and hideous appearance, with one great striped horn sticking out of his nose like a boltsprit. If there are many wood-worms in Germany, I shall come home. The most courageous men in the world must be entomologists. I had rather be a lion-tamer.

1872.
AET. 22.

To-day I got rather a curiosity—*Lieder und Balladen von Robert Burns*, translated by one Silbergleit, and not so ill done either. Armed with which, I had a swim in the Main, and then bread and cheese and Bavarian beer in a sort of café, or at least the German substitute for a café; but what a falling off after the heavenly forenoons in Brussels!

I have bought a meerschaum out of local sentiment, and am now very low and nervous about the bargain, having paid dearer than I should in England, and got a worse article, if I can form a judgment.

Do write some more, somebody. To-morrow I expect I shall go into lodgings, as this hotel work makes the money disappear like butter in a furnace.—Meanwhile believe me, ever your affectionate son,

R. L. STEVENSON.

TO MRS. THOMAS STEVENSON

Hotel Landsberg, Thursday, 1st August 1872.

... YESTERDAY I walked to Eckenheim, a village a little way out of Frankfurt, and turned into the alehouse. In the room, which was just such as it would have been in Scotland, were the landlady, two neighbours, and an old peasant eating raw sausage at the far end. I soon got into conversation; and was astonished when the landlady, having asked whether I were an Englishman,

VOL. I.—C

1872.
AET. 22.

and received an answer in the affirmative, proceeded to inquire further whether I were not also a Scotchman. It turned out that a Scotch doctor—a professor—a poet—who wrote books—*gross wie das*—had come nearly every day out of Frankfurt to the *Eckenheimer Wirthschaft*, and had left behind him a most savoury memory in the hearts of all its customers. One man ran out to find his name for me, and returned with the news that it was *Cobie* (Scobie, I suspect); and during his absence the rest were pouring into my ears the fame and acquirements of my countryman. He was, in some undecipherable manner, connected with the Queen of England and one of the Princesses. He had been in Turkey, and had there married a wife of immense wealth. They could find apparently no measure adequate to express the size of his books. In one way or another, he had amassed a princely fortune, and had apparently only one sorrow, his daughter to wit, who had absconded into a *kloster*, with a considerable slice of the mother's *geld*. I told them we had no klosters in Scotland, with a certain feeling of superiority. No more had they, I was told—'*Hier ist unser Kloster!*' and the speaker motioned with both arms round the taproom. Although the first torrent was exhausted, yet the Doctor came up again in all sorts of ways, and with or without occasion, throughout the whole interview; as, for example, when one man, taking his pipe out of his mouth and shaking his head, remarked *àpropos* of nothing and with almost defiant conviction, '*Er war ein feiner Mann, der Herr Doctor*,' and was answered by another with '*Yaw, yaw, und trank immer rothen Wein.*'

Setting aside the Doctor, who had evidently turned the brains of the entire village, they were intelligent people. One thing in particular struck me, their honesty in admitting that here they spoke bad German, and advising me to go to Coburg or Leipsic for German.—'*Sie sprechen da rein*' (clean), said one; and they all nodded their heads together like as many mandarins, and repeated *rein, so rein* in chorus.

1872.
AET. 22.

Of course we got upon Scotland. The hostess said, '*Die Schottländer trinken gern Schnapps*,' which may be freely translated, 'Scotchmen are horrid fond of whisky.' It was impossible, of course, to combat such a truism; and so I proceeded to explain the construction of toddy, interrupted by a cry of horror when I mentioned the *hot* water; and thence, as I find is always the case, to the most ghastly romancing about Scottish scenery and manners, the Highland dress, and everything national or local that I could lay my hands upon. Now that I have got my German Burns, I lean a good deal upon him for opening a conversation, and read a few translations to every yawning audience that I can gather. I am grown most insufferably national, you see. I fancy it is a punishment for my want of it at ordinary times. Now, what do you think, there was a waiter in this very hotel, but, alas! he is now gone, who sang (from morning to night, as my informant said with a shrug at the recollection) what but *'s ist lange her*, the German version of Auld Lang Syne; so you see, madame, the finest lyric ever written *will* make its way out of whatsoever corner of patois it found its birth in.

'*Mein Herz ist im Hochland, mein Herz ist nicht hier.
Mein Herz ist im Hochland im grünen Revier.
Im grünen Reviere zu jagen das Reh;
Mein Herz ist im Hochland, wo immer ich geh.*'

I don't think I need translate that for you.

There is one thing that burthens me a good deal in my patriotic garrulage, and that is the black ignorance in which I grope about everything, as, for example, when I gave yesterday a full and, I fancy, a startlingly incorrect account of Scotch education to a very stolid German on a garden bench: he sat and perspired under it, however, with much composure. I am generally glad enough to fall back again, after these political interludes, upon Burns, toddy, and the Highlands.

I go every night to the theatre, except when there is no opera. I cannot stand a play yet; but I am already very much improved, and can understand a good deal of what goes on.

Friday, August 2, 1872.—In the evening, at the theatre, I had a great laugh. Lord Allcash in *Fra Diavolo*, with his white hat, red guide-books, and bad German, was the *pièce-de-résistance* from a humorous point of view; and I had the satisfaction of knowing that in my own small way I could minister the same amusement whenever I chose to open my mouth.

I am just going off to do some German with Simpson. —Your affectionate son, R. L. STEVENSON.

TO THOMAS STEVENSON

Frankfurt, Rosengasse 13, *August* 4, 1872.

MY DEAR FATHER,—You will perceive by the head of this page that we have at last got into lodgings, and powerfully mean ones too. If I were to call the street anything but *shady*, I should be boasting. The people sit at their doors in shirt-sleeves, smoking as they do in Seven Dials of a Sunday.

Last night we went to bed about ten, for the first time *householders* in Germany—real Teutons, with no deception, spring, or false bottom. About half-past one there began such a trumpeting, shouting, pealing of bells, and scurrying hither and thither of feet as woke every person in Frankfurt out of their first sleep with a vague sort of apprehension that the last day was at hand. The whole street was alive, and we could hear people talking in their rooms, or crying to passers-by from their windows, all around us. At last I made out what a man was saying in the next room. It was a fire in Sachsenhausen, he said (Sachsenhausen is the suburb on the other side of the Main), and he wound up with one of the most tremendous falsehoods on record, '*Hier alles ruht*—here all is still.' If it can be said to be still in an engine factory, or in the stomach of a volcano when it is meditating an eruption, he might have been justified in what he said, but not otherwise. The tumult continued unabated for near an hour; but as one grew used to it, it gradually resolved itself into three bells, answering each other at short intervals across the town, a man shouting, at ever shorter intervals and with superhuman energy, '*Feuer— im Sachsenhausen*, and the almost continuous winding of all manner of bugles and trumpets, sometimes in stirring flourishes, and sometimes in mere tuneless wails. Occasionally there was another rush of feet past the window, and once there was a mighty drumming, down between us and the river, as though the soldiery were turning out to keep the peace. This was all we had of the fire, except a great cloud, all flushed red with the glare, above the roofs on the other side of the Gasse; but it was quite enough to put me entirely off my sleep and make me keenly alive to three or four gentlemen who were strolling leisurely about my person, and every here and there leaving me somewhat as a keepsake. . . . However, everything has its compensation, and when day came at last, and the sparrows awoke with trills and *carol-ets*, the dawn seemed to fall on me like a sleeping draught. I went to the window and saw the sparrows about the eaves, and a great troop of doves go strolling up the paven Gasse, seeking what they may devour. And so to sleep, despite fleas and fire-alarms and clocks chiming the hours out of neighbouring houses at all sorts of odd times and with the most charming want of unanimity.

We have got settled down in Frankfurt, and like the place very much. Simpson and I seem to get on very well together. We suit each other capitally; and it is an

1872.
AET. 22.

awful joke to be living (two would-be advocates, and one a baronet) in this supremely mean abode.

The abode is, however, a great improvement on the hotel, and I think we shall grow quite fond of it.—Ever your affectionate son, R. L. STEVENSON.

TO MRS. THOMAS STEVENSON

13 Rosengasse, Frankfurt, Tuesday Morning, August 1872.

. . . Last night I was at the theatre and heard *Die Judin* (*La Juive*), and was thereby terribly excited. At last, in the middle of the fifth act, which was perfectly beastly, I had to slope. I could stand even seeing the cauldron with the sham fire beneath, and the two hateful executioners in red; but when at last the girl's courage breaks down, and, grasping her father's arm, she cries out—O so shudderfully!—I thought it high time to be out of that *galère*, and so I do not know yet whether it ends well or ill; but if I ever afterwards find that they do carry things to the extremity, I shall think more meanly of my species. It was raining and cold outside, so I went into a *Bierhalle*, and sat and brooded over a *Schnitt* (half-glass) for nearly an hour. An opera is far more *real* than real life to me. It seems as if stage illusion, and particularly this hardest to swallow and most conventional illusion of them all—an opera—would never stale upon me. I wish that life was an opera. I should like to *live* in one; but I don't know in what quarter of the globe I shall find a society so constituted. Besides, it would soon pall: imagine asking for three-kreuzer cigars in recitative, or giving the washerwoman the inventory of your dirty clothes in a sustained and *flourishous* aria.

I am in a right good mood this morning to sit here and write to you; but not to give you news. There is a great stir of life, in a quiet, almost country fashion, all about us here. Some one is hammering a beef-steak in the *rez-de-chaussée*: there is a great clink of pitchers and noise of the pump-handle at the public well in the little square-kin round the corner. The children, all seemingly within a month, and certainly none above five, that always go halting and stumbling up and down the roadway, are ordinarily very quiet, and sit sedately puddling in the gutter, trying, I suppose, poor little devils! to understand their *Muttersprache*; but they, too, make themselves heard from time to time in little incomprehensible antiphonies, about the drift that comes down to them by their rivers from the strange lands higher up the Gasse. Above all, there is here such a twittering of canaries (I can see twelve out of our window), and such continual visitation of grey doves and big-nosed sparrows, as make our little bye-street into a perfect aviary.

I look across the Gasse at our opposite neighbour, as he dandles his baby about, and occasionally takes a spoonful or two of some pale slimy nastiness that looks like *dead porridge*, if you can take the conception. These two are his only occupations. All day long you can hear him singing over the brat when he is not eating; or see him eating when he is not keeping baby. Besides which, there comes into his house a continual round of visitors that puts me in mind of the luncheon hour at home. As he has thus no ostensible avocation, we have named him 'the W.S.' to give a flavour of respectability to the street.

Enough of the Gasse. The weather is here much colder. It rained a good deal yesterday; and though it is fair and sunshiny again to-day, and we can still sit, of course, with our windows open, yet there is no more excuse for the siesta; and the bathe in the river, except for cleanliness, is no longer a necessity of life. The Main is very swift. In one part of the baths it is next door to impossible to swim against it, and I suspect that, out in the open, it would be quite impossible.—Adieu, my dear mother, and believe me, ever your affectionate son,

ROBERT LOUIS STEVENSON
(*Rentier*).

1873.
AET. 23.

TO CHARLES BAXTER

In the winter of 1872-73 Stevenson was out of health again; and by the beginning of spring there began the trouble which for the next twelve months clouded his home life. The following, which is the only one of many letters on the subject I shall print, shows exactly in what spirit he took it:—

17 *Heriot Row, Edinburgh, Sunday, February* 2, 1873.

MY DEAR BAXTER,—The thunderbolt has fallen with a vengeance now. On Friday night after leaving you, in the course of conversation, my father put me one or two questions as to beliefs, which I candidly answered. I really hate all lying so much now—a new found honesty that has somehow come out of my late illness—that I could not so much as hesitate at the time; but if I had foreseen the real hell of everything since, I think I should have lied, as I have done so often before. I so far thought of my father, but I had forgotten my mother. And now! they are both ill, both silent, both as down in the mouth as if—I can find no simile. You may fancy how happy it is for me. If it were not too late, I think I could almost find it in my heart to retract, but it is too late; and again, am I to live my whole life as one falsehood? Of course, it is rougher than hell upon my father, but can I help it? They don't see either that my game is not the light-hearted scoffer; that I am not (as they call me) a careless infidel. I believe as much as they do, only generally in the inverse ratio: I am, I think, as honest as they can be in what I hold. I have not come hastily to my views. I reserve (as I told them) many points until I acquire fuller information, and do not think I am thus justly to be called 'horrible atheist.'

Now, what is to take place? What a curse I am to my parents! O Lord, what a pleasant thing it is to have just *damned* the happiness of (probably) the only two people who care a damn about you in the world.

What is my life to be at this rate? What, you rascal?

Answer—I have a pistol at your throat. If all that I hold true and most desire to spread is to be such death, and worse than death, in the eyes of my father and mother, what the *devil* am I to do?

Here is a good heavy cross with a vengeance, and all rough with rusty nails that tear your fingers, only it is not I that have to carry it alone; I hold the light end, but the heavy burden falls on these two.

Don't—I don't know what I was going to say. I am an abject idiot, which, all things considered, is not remarkable. —Ever your affectionate and horrible atheist,

R. L. STEVENSON.

II

STUDENT DAYS—*Continued*

ORDERED SOUTH

SEPTEMBER 1873—JULY 1875

It was in the summer of 1873 that I first met Stevenson, in the house of my kind friend and colleague, Professor Churchill Babington, formerly of St. John's College, Cambridge, and then resident at his country living of Cockfield, near Bury St. Edmunds, Suffolk. Professor Babington was married to a grand-daughter of the Rev. Lewis Balfour of Colinton, and Louis Stevenson was accordingly a first cousin of his hostess (see above, p. 24). It needed no conjurer to recognise, in this very un-academical type of Scottish youth, a spirit the most interesting and full of promise. His social charm was already at its height, and quite irresistible; but inwardly he was full of trouble and self-doubt. If he could steer himself or be steered safely through the difficulties of youth, and if he could learn to write with half the charm and genius that shone from his presence and conversation, there seemed room to hope for the highest from him. He had not long before this made friends in the same house with the lady, a connection by marriage of his hostess, to whom so many of the letters in the present section are addressed; had found in her sympathy a strong encouragement; and under her influence had begun for the first time to believe hopefully and manfully in his own powers and future. To encourage such hopes further, and to lend what hand one could towards their fulfilment, became quickly one of the first of cares and pleasures. He attached himself to me, almost from our first acquaintance, with the winning and eager warmth of heart that was natural to him, and I was able to help him with introductions to editors, who were glad, of course, to welcome so promising a recruit, and with such hints and criticisms concerning his work as a beginner may in most cases profitably take from a senior of a certain training and experience. He went back to Edinburgh in the beginning of September full of new hope and heart. It had been agreed that while still reading, as his parents desired, for the bar, he should try seriously to get ready for publication some essays which he had already on hand—one on Walt Whitman, one on John Knox, one on Roads and the Spirit of the Road, and should so far as possible avoid topics of dispute in the home circle.

But after a while the news of him was not favourable. Those differences with his father, which had been weighing almost morbidly upon his high-strung nature, were renewed. By mid-October his letters told of failing health; and coming to consult the late Sir Andrew Clark in London, he was found to be suffering from acute nerve exhaustion, with some threat of danger to the lungs. He was ordered to break at once with Edinburgh for a time, and to spend the winter in a more soothing climate and surroundings. He went accordingly to Mentone, a place he had delighted in as a boy ten years before, and during a stay of six months made a slow, but for the time being a pretty complete recovery. I visited him twice during the winter, and the second time found him coming fairly to himself again in the southern peace and sunshine. He was busy with the essay 'Ordered South,' and with that on Victor Hugo's Romances, which was afterwards his first contribution to the *Cornhill Magazine*; was full of a thousand dreams and projects for future work; and was passing his invalid days pleasantly meanwhile in the companionship of two kind and accomplished Russian ladies, who took to him warmly, and of their children. Returning to Edinburgh in May 1874, he went to live with his parents at Swanston and Edinburgh, and resumed his reading for the bar. Illness and absence had done their work, and the old harmony of the home was henceforth quite re-established. In his spare time, during the next year, he worked hard at his chosen art, trying his hand at essays, short stories, criticisms, and prose poems. In all this experimental writing he had neither the aims nor the facility of the journalist, but strove always after the higher qualities of literature, and accordingly was never satisfied with what he had done. In the course of this summer his excursions included a week or two spent with me at Hampstead, during which he joined the Savile Club and made some acquaintance with London literary society; a yachting excursion with his friend Sir Walter Simpson in the western islands of Scotland; a trip to the west of England with his parents by way of the English lakes and Chester; and in the late autumn a walking tour in Buckinghamshire. The Scottish winter (1874-75) tried him severely, as Scottish winters always did, but was enlivened by a new and what was destined to be an extremely fruitful and intimate friendship, the origin of which is described in the following letters; namely that with Mr. W. E. Henley. In April 1875 he made his first visit, in the company of his painter cousin, Mr. R. A. M. Stevenson, to the artist haunts of the forest of Fontainebleau, whence he returned to finish his reading for the Scottish bar and face the examination which was before him in July.

His letters to his friends in general in these days were few and scrappy, those to myself pretty numerous, but concerned almost entirely with the technicalities of literature. Those which I shall quote below were written, with few exceptions, either to his parents, or to the lady already mentioned; who was his chief correspondent in these years, and whom he was accustomed to keep acquainted with his moods and doings by means of journal-letters made up almost weekly.

1873.
AET. 23.

TO MRS. THOMAS STEVENSON

This is from his cousin's house in Suffolk. Some of the impressions then received of the contrasts between Scotland and England were later worked out in the essay 'The Foreigner at Home,' printed at the head of *Memories and Portraits*:—

Cockfield Rectory, Sudbury, Suffolk,
Tuesday, July 28, 1873.

MY DEAR MOTHER,—I am too happy to be much of a correspondent. Yesterday we were away to Melford and Lavenham, both exceptionally placid, beautiful old English towns. Melford scattered all round a big green, with an Elizabethan Hall and Park, great screens of trees that seem twice as high as trees should seem, and everything else like what ought to be in a novel, and what one never expects to see in reality, made me cry out how good we were to live in Scotland, for the many hundredth time. I cannot get over my astonishment—indeed, it increases every day—at the hopeless gulf that there is between England and Scotland, and English and Scotch. Nothing is the same; and I feel as strange and outlandish here as I do in France or Germany. Everything by the wayside, in the houses, or about the people, strikes me with an unexpected unfamiliarity: I walk among surprises, for just where you think you have them, something wrong turns up.

1873.
AET. 23.

I got a little Law read yesterday, and some German this morning, but on the whole there are too many amusements going for much work; as for correspondence, I have neither heart nor time for it to-day.   R. L. S.

TO MRS. SITWELL

17 *Heriot Row, Edinburgh*,
Saturday, September 6, 1873.

I HAVE been to-day a very long walk with my father through some of the most beautiful ways hereabouts; the day was cold with an iron, windy sky, and only glorified now and then with autumn sunlight. For it is fully autumn with us, with a blight already over the greens, and a keen wind in the morning that makes one rather timid of one's tub when it finds its way indoors.

I was out this evening to call on a friend, and, coming back through the wet, crowded, lamp-lit streets, was singing after my own fashion, *Du hast Diamanten und Perlen*, when I heard a poor cripple man in the gutter wailing over a pitiful Scotch air, his club-foot supported on the other knee, and his whole woebegone body propped sideways against a crutch. The nearest lamp threw a strong light on his worn, sordid face and the three boxes of lucifer matches that he held for sale. My own false notes stuck in my chest. How well off I am! is the burthen of my songs all day long—*Drum ist so wohl mir in der Welt!* and the ugly reality of the cripple man was an intrusion on the beautiful world in which I was walking. He could no more sing than I could; and his voice was cracked and rusty, and altogether perished. To think that that wreck may have walked the streets some night years ago, as glad at heart as I was, and promising himself a future as golden and honourable!

Sunday, 11.20 *a.m.*—I wonder what you are doing now? —in church likely, at the *Te Deum*. Everything here is utterly silent. I can hear men's footfalls streets away; the whole life of Edinburgh has been sucked into sundry pious edifices; the gardens below my windows are steeped in a diffused sunlight, and every tree seems standing on tiptoes, strained and silent, as though to get its head above its neighbour's and *listen*. You know what I mean, don't you? How trees do seem silently to assert themselves on an occasion! I have been trying to write *Roads* until I feel as if I were standing on my head; but I mean *Roads*, and shall do something to them.

I wish I could make you feel the hush that is over everything, only made the more perfect by rare interruptions; and the rich, placid light, and the still, autumnal foliage. Houses, you know, stand all about our gardens: solid, steady blocks of houses; all look empty and asleep.

Monday night.—The drums and fifes up in the Castle are sounding the guard-call through the dark, and there is a great rattle of carriages without. I have had (I must tell you) my bed taken out of this room, so that I am alone in it with my books and two tables, and two chairs, and a coal-skuttle (or *scuttle*)(?) and a *débris* of broken pipes in a corner, and my old school play-box, so full of papers and books that the lid will not shut down, standing reproachfully in the midst. There is something in it that is still a little gaunt and vacant; it needs a little populous disorder over it to give it the feel of homeliness, and perhaps a bit more furniture, just to take the edge off the sense of illimitable space, eternity, and a future state, and the like, that is brought home to one, even in this small attic, by the wide, empty floor. 1873. AET. 23.

You would require to know, what only I can ever know, many grim and many maudlin passages out of my past life to feel how great a change has been made for me by this past summer. Let me be ever so poor and threadpaper a soul, I am going to try for the best.

These good booksellers of mine have at last got a *Werther* without illustrations. I want you to like Charlotte. Werther himself has every feebleness and vice that could tend to make his suicide a most virtuous and commendable action; and yet I like Werther too—I don't know why, except that he has written the most delightful letters in the world. Note, by the way, the passage under date June 21st not far from the beginning; it finds a voice for a great deal of dumb, uneasy, pleasurable longing that we have all had, times without number. I looked that up the other day for *Roads*, so I know the reference; but you will find it a garden of flowers from beginning to end. All through the passion keeps steadily rising, from the thunderstorm at the country-house—there was thunder in that story too—up to the last wild delirious interview; either Lotte was no good at all, or else Werther should have remained alive after that; either he knew his woman too well, or else he was precipitate. But an idiot like that is hopeless; and yet, he wasn't an idiot—I make reparation, and will offer eighteen pounds of best wax at his tomb. Poor devil! he was only the weakest—or, at least, a very weak strong man. R. L. S.

TO MRS. SITWELL

17 Heriot Row, Edinburgh,
Friday, September 12, 1873.

. . . I WAS over last night, contrary to my own wish, in Leven, Fife; and this morning I had a conversation of which, I think, some account might interest you. I was up with a cousin who was fishing in a mill-lade, and a shower of rain drove me for shelter into a tumbledown steading attached to the mill. There I found a labourer cleaning a byre, with whom I fell into talk. The man was to all appearance as heavy, as *hébété*, as any English clodhopper; but I knew I was in Scotland, and launched out forthright into Education and Politics and the aims of one's life. I told him how I had found the peasantry in Suffolk, and added that their state had made me feel quite pained and down-hearted. 'It but to do that,' he said, 'to onybody that thinks at a'!' Then, again, he said that he could not conceive how anything could daunt or cast down a man who had an aim in life. 'They that have had a guid schoolin' and do nae mair, whatever they do, they have done; but him that has aye something ayont need never be weary.' I have had to mutilate the dialect much, so that it might be comprehensible to you; but I think the sentiment will keep, even through a change of words, something of the heartsome ring of encouragement that it had for me: and that from a man cleaning a byre! You see what John Knox and his schools have done.

Saturday.—This has been a charming day for me from morning to now (5 P.M.). First, I found your letter, and went down and read it on a seat in those Public Gardens of which you have heard already. After lunch, my father and I went down to the coast and walked a little way along the shore between Granton and Cramond. This has always been with me a very favourite walk. The Firth closes gradually together before you, the coast runs in a series of the most beautifully moulded bays, hill after hill, wooded and softly outlined, trends away in front till the two shores join together. When the tide is out there are great, gleaming flats of wet sand, over which the gulls go flying and crying; and every cape runs down into them with its little spit of wall and trees. We lay together a long time on the beach; the sea just babbled among the stones; and at one time we heard the hollow, sturdy beat of the paddles of an unseen steamer somewhere round the cape. I am glad to say that the peace of the day and scenery was not marred by any unpleasantness between us two.

1873.
AET. 23.

I am, unhappily, off my style, and can do nothing well; indeed, I fear I have marred *Roads* finally by patching at it when I was out of the humour. Only, I am beginning to see something great about John Knox and Queen Mary: I like them both so much, that I feel as if I could write the history fairly.

I have finished *Roads* to-day, and send it off to you to see. The Lord knows whether it is worth anything!—some of it pleases me a good deal, but I fear it is quite unfit for any possible magazine. However, I wish you to see it, as you know the humour in which it was conceived, walking alone and very happily about the Suffolk highways and byeways on several splendid sunny afternoons. —Believe me, ever your faithful friend,

ROBERT LOUIS STEVENSON.

Monday.—I have looked over *Roads* again, and I am aghast at its feebleness. It is the trial of a very ''prentice hand' indeed. Shall I ever learn to do anything *well*? However, it shall go to you, for the reasons given above.

TO MRS. SITWELL

After an outpouring about difficulties at home.

Edinburgh, Tuesday, September 16, 1873.

... I MUST be very strong to have all this vexation and still to be well. I was weighed the other day, and the gross weight of my large person was eight stone six!

1873.
AET. 23.

Does it not seem surprising that I can keep the lamp alight, through all this gusty weather, in so frail a lantern? And yet it burns cheerily.

My mother is leaving for the country this morning, and my father and I will be alone for the best part of the week in this house. Then on Friday I go south to Dumfries till Monday. I must write small, or I shall have a tremendous budget by then.

7.20 *p.m.*—I must tell you a thing I saw to-day. I was going down to Portobello in the train, when there came into the next compartment (third class) an artisan, strongly marked with smallpox, and with sunken, heavy eyes—a face hard and unkind, and without anything lovely. There was a woman on the platform seeing him off. At first sight, with her one eye blind and the whole cast of her features strongly plebeian, and even vicious, she seemed as unpleasant as the man; but there was something beautifully soft, a sort of light of tenderness, as on some Dutch Madonna, that came over her face when she looked at the man. They talked for a while together through the window; the man seemed to have been asking money. 'Ye ken the last time,' she said, 'I gave ye two shillin's for your ludgin', and ye said——' it died off into whisper. Plainly Falstaff and Dame Quickly over again. The man laughed unpleasantly, even cruelly, and said something; and the woman turned her back on the carriage and stood a long while so, and, do what I might, I could catch no glimpse of her expression, although I thought I saw the heave of a sob in her shoulders. At last, after the train was already in motion, she turned round and put two shillings into his hand. I saw her stand and look after us with a perfect heaven of love on her face—this poor one-eyed Madonna—until the train was out of sight; but the man, sordidly happy with his gains, did not put himself to the inconvenience of one glance to thank her for her ill-deserved kindness.

I have been up at the Spec. and looked out a reference
I wanted. The whole town is drowned in white, wet
vapour off the sea. Everything drips and soaks. The
very statues seem wet to the skin. I cannot pretend to
be very cheerful; I did not see one contented face in the
streets; and the poor did look so helplessly chill and
dripping, without a stitch to change, or so much as a fire
to dry themselves at, or perhaps money to buy a meal, or
perhaps even a bed. My heart shivers for them.

Dumfries, Friday.—All my thirst for a little warmth, a
little sun, a little corner of blue sky avails nothing.
Without, the rain falls with a long drawn *swish*, and the
night is as dark as a vault. There is no wind indeed, and
that is a blessed change after the unruly, bedlamite gusts
that have been charging against one round street corners
and utterly abolishing and destroying all that is peaceful
in life. Nothing sours my temper like these coarse
termagant winds. I hate practical joking; and your
vulgarest practical joker is your flaw of wind.

I have tried to write some verses; but I find I have
nothing to say that has not been already perfectly said
and perfectly sung in *Adelaïde*. I have so perfect an
idea out of that song! The great Alps, a wonder in the
starlight—the river, strong from the hills, and turbulent,
and loudly audible at night—the country, a scented
Frühlingsgarten of orchards and deep wood where the
nightingales harbour—a sort of German flavour over all—
and this love-drunken man, wandering on by sleeping
village and silent town, pours out of his full heart, *Einst,
O Wunder, einst*, etc. I wonder if I am wrong about this
being the most beautiful and perfect thing in the world
— the only marriage of really accordant words and
music—both drunk with the same poignant, unutterable
sentiment.

To-day in Glasgow my father went off on some business,
and my mother and I wandered about for two hours. We

had lunch together, and were very merry over what the people at the restaurant would think of us—mother and son they could not suppose us to be.

Saturday.—And to-day it came—warmth, sunlight, and a strong, hearty living wind among the trees. I found myself a new being. My father and I went off a long walk, through a country most beautifully wooded and various, under a range of hills. You should have seen one place where the wood suddenly fell away in front of us down a long, steep hill between a double row of trees, with one small fair-haired child framed in shadow in the foreground; and when we got to the foot there was the little kirk and kirkyard of Irongray, among broken fields and woods by the side of the bright, rapid river. In the kirkyard there was a wonderful congregation of tombstones, upright and recumbent on four legs (after our Scotch fashion), and of flat-armed fir-trees. One gravestone was erected by Scott (at a cost, I learn, of £70) to the poor woman who served him as heroine in the *Heart of Midlothian*, and the inscription in its stiff, Jedediah Cleishbotham fashion is not without something touching.[1] We went up the stream a little further to where two Covenanters lie buried in an oakwood; the tombstone (as the custom is) containing the details of their grim little tragedy in funnily bad rhyme, one verse of which sticks in my memory :—

'We died, their furious rage to stay,
Near to the kirk of Iron-gray.'

We then fetched a long compass round about through Holywood Kirk and Lincluden ruins to Dumfries. But the walk came sadly to grief as a pleasure excursion before our return . . .

[1] See Scott himself in the preface to the Author's edition.

Sunday.—Another beautiful day. My father and I 1873.
walked into Dumfries to church. When the service was AET. 23.
done I noted the two halberts laid against the pillar of
the churchyard gate; and as I had not seen the little
weekly pomp of civic dignitaries in our Scotch country
towns for some years, I made my father wait. You
should have seen the provost and three bailies going
stately away down the sunlit street, and the two town
servants strutting in front of them, in red coats and
cocked hats, and with the halberts most conspicuously
shouldered. We saw Burns's house—a place that made
me deeply sad—and spent the afternoon down the banks
of the Nith. I had not spent a day by a river since we
lunched in the meadows near Sudbury. The air was as
pure and clear and sparkling as spring water; beautiful,
graceful outlines of hill and wood shut us in on every
side; and the swift, brown river fled smoothly away from
before our eyes, rippled over with oily eddies and dimples.
White gulls had come up from the sea to fish, and hovered
and flew hither and thither among the loops of the stream.
By good fortune, too, it was a dead calm between my
father and me.   R. L. S.

TO MRS. SITWELL

On the question of the authorship of the *Ode to the Cuckoo*,
which Burke thought the most beautiful lyric in our language,
the debate is between the claims of John Logan, minister of
South Leith (1745-1785), and his friend and fellow-worker
Michael Bruce. Those of Logan have, I believe, been now
vindicated past doubt.

[*Edinburgh*]*, Saturday, October* 4, 1873.

IT is a little sharp to-day; but bright and sunny with a
sparkle in the air, which is delightful after four days of
unintermitting rain. In the streets I saw two men meet
after a long separation, it was plain. They came forward

with a little run and *leaped* at each other's hands. You never saw such bright eyes as they both had. It put one in a good humour to see it.

8 *p.m.*—I made a little more out of my work than I have made for a long while back; though even now I cannot make things fall into sentences—they only sprawl over the paper in bald orphan clauses. Then I was about in the afternoon with Baxter; and we had a good deal of fun, first rhyming on the names of all the shops we passed, and afterwards buying needles and quack drugs from open-air vendors, and taking much pleasure in their inexhaustible eloquence. Every now and then as we went, Arthur's Seat showed its head at the end of a street. Now, to-day the blue sky and the sunshine were both entirely wintry; and there was about the hill, in these glimpses, a sort of thin, unreal, crystalline distinctness that I have not often seen excelled. As the sun began to go down over the valley between the new town and the old, the evening grew resplendent; all the gardens and low-lying buildings sank back and became almost invisible in a mist of wonderful sun, and the Castle stood up against the sky, as thin and sharp in outline as a castle cut out of paper. Baxter made a good remark about Princes Street, that it was the most elastic street for length that he knew; sometimes it looks, as it looked to-night, interminable, a way leading right into the heart of the red sundown; sometimes, again, it shrinks together, as if for warmth, on one of the withering, clear east-windy days, until it seems to lie underneath your feet.

I want to let you see these verses from an *Ode to the Cuckoo*, written by one of the ministers of Leith in the middle of last century—the palmy days of Edinburgh—who was a friend of Hume and Adam Smith and the whole constellation. The authorship of these beautiful verses has been most truculently fought about; but whoever wrote them (and it seems as if this Logan had) they are lovely—

> 'What time the pea puts on the bloom,
>   Thou fliest the vocal vale,
> An annual guest, in other lands
>   Another spring to hail.
>
> Sweet bird! thy bower is ever green,
>   Thy sky is ever clear;
> Thou hast no sorrow in thy song,
>   No winter in thy year.
>
> O could I fly, I'd fly with thee!
>   We'd make on joyful wing
> Our annual visit o'er the globe,
>   Companions of the spring.'

Sunday. — I have been at church with my mother, where we heard 'Arise, shine,' sung excellently well, and my mother was so much upset with it that she nearly had to leave church. This was the antidote, however, to fifty minutes of solid sermon, varra heavy. I have been sticking in to Walt Whitman; nor do I think I have ever laboured so hard to attain so small a success. Still, the thing is taking shape, I think; I know a little better what I want to say all through; and in process of time, possibly I shall manage to say it. I must say I am a very bad workman, *mais j'ai du courage*; I am indefatigable at rewriting and lettering, and surely that humble quality should get me on a little.

Monday, October 6. — It is a magnificent glimmering moonlight night, with a wild, great west wind abroad, flapping above one like an immense banner, and every now and again swooping furiously against my windows. The wind is too strong perhaps, and the trees are certainly too leafless for much of that wide rustle that we both

1873.
AET. 23.

remember; there is only a sharp, angry, sibilant hiss, like breath drawn with the strength of the elements through shut teeth, that one hears between the gusts only. I am in excellent humour with myself, for I have worked hard and not altogether fruitlessly; and I wished before I turned in just to tell you that things were so. My dear friend, I feel so happy when I think that you remember me kindly. I have been up to-night lecturing to a friend on life and duties and what a man could do; a coal off the altar had been laid on my lips, and I talked quite above my average, and hope I spread, what you would wish to see spread, into one person's heart; and with a new light upon it.

I shall tell you a story. Last Friday I went down to Portobello, in the heavy rain, with an uneasy wind blowing *par rafales* off the sea (or '*en rafales*' should it be? or what?). As I got down near the beach a poor woman, oldish, and seemingly, lately at least, respectable, followed me and made signs. She was drenched to the skin, and looked wretched below wretchedness. You know, I did not like to look back at her; it seemed as if she might misunderstand and be terribly hurt and slighted; so I stood at the end of the street—there was no one else within sight in the wet—and lifted up my hand very high with some money in it. I heard her steps draw heavily near behind me, and, when she was near enough to see, I let the money fall in the mud and went off at my best walk without ever turning round. There is nothing in the story; and yet you will understand how much there is, if one chose to set it forth. You see, she was so ugly; and you know there is something terribly, miserably pathetic in a certain smile, a certain sodden aspect of invitation on such faces. It is so terrible, that it is in a way sacred; it means the outside of degradation and (what is worst of all in life) false position. I hope you understand me rightly.—Ever your faithful friend,

ROBERT LOUIS STEVENSON.

TO MRS. SITWELL

1873.
AET. 23.

[*Edinburgh*], *Tuesday, October* 14, 1873.

MY father has returned in better health, and I am more delighted than I can well tell you. The one trouble that I can see no way through is that his health, or my mother's, should give way. To-night, as I was walking along Princes Street, I heard the bugles sound the recall. I do not think I had ever remarked it before; there is something of unspeakable appeal in the cadence. I felt as if something yearningly cried to me out of the darkness overhead to come thither and find rest; one felt as if there must be warm hearts and bright fires waiting for one up there, where the buglers stood on the damp pavement and sounded their friendly invitation forth into the night.

Wednesday.—I may as well tell you exactly about my health. I am not at all ill; have quite recovered; only I am what *MM. les médecins* call below par; which, in plain English, is that I am weak. With tonics, decent weather, and a little cheerfulness, that will go away in its turn, and I shall be all right again.

I am glad to hear what you say about the Exam.; until quite lately I have treated that pretty cavalierly, for I say honestly that I do not mind being plucked; I shall just have to go up again. We travelled with the Lord Advocate the other day, and he strongly advised me in my father's hearing to go to the English Bar; and the Lord Advocate's advice goes a long way in Scotland. It is a sort of special legal revelation. Don't misunderstand me. I don't, of course, want to be plucked; but so far as my style of knowledge suits them, I cannot make much betterment on it in a month. If they wish scholarship more exact, I must take a new lease altogether.

Thursday.—My head and eyes both gave in this morning, and I had to take a day of complete idleness. I was in the open air all day, and did no thought that I could avoid, and I think I have got my head between my shoulders again; however, I am not going to do much. I don't want you to run away with any fancy about my being ill. Given a person weak and in some trouble, and working longer hours than he is used to, and you have the matter in a nutshell. You should have seen the sunshine on the hill to-day; it has lost now that crystalline clearness, as if the medium were spring-water (you see, I am stupid!); but it retains that wonderful thinness of outline that makes the delicate shape and hue savour better in one's mouth, like fine wine out of a finely-blown glass. The birds are all silent now but the crows. I sat a long time on the stairs that lead down to Duddingston Loch—a place as busy as a great town during frost, but now solitary and silent; and when I shut my eyes I heard nothing but the wind in the trees; and you know all that went through me, I dare say, without my saying it.

11.—I am now all right. I do not expect any tic to-night, and shall be at work again to-morrow. I have had a day of open air, only a little modified by *Le Capitaine Fracasse* before the dining-room fire. I must write no more, for I am sleepy after two nights, and to quote my book, '*sinon blanches, du moins grises*'; and so I must go to bed and faithfully, hoggishly slumber. —Your faithful

ROBERT LOUIS STEVENSON.

TO MRS. THOMAS STEVENSON

A week later Stevenson came to London, it having been agreed that he should present himself for the entrance examination at one of the London Inns of Court. But he was obviously much run down in health; it was before the physicians and not the lawyers that he must present himself; and the result of an examination by Dr. Andrew Clark was his prompt and peremptory despatch to Mentone for a winter's rest and sunshine. This episode of his life gave occasion to the essay *Ordered South*, the only one of his writings in which he ever took the invalid point of view, or allowed his health troubles in any degree to colour his work.

Mentone, November 13, 1873.

MY DEAR MOTHER,—The *Place* is not where I thought; it is about where the old Post Office was. The Hotel de Londres is no more an hotel. I have found a charming room in the Hotel du Pavillon, just across the road from the Prince's Villa; it has one window to the south and one to the east, with a superb view of Mentone and the hills, to which I move this afternoon. In the old great *Place* there is a kiosque for the sale of newspapers; a string of omnibuses (perhaps thirty) go up and down under the plane-trees of the Turin Road on the occasion of each train; the Promenade has crossed both streams, and bids fair to reach the Cap St. Martin. The old chapel near Freeman's house at the entrance to the Gorbio valley is now entirely submerged under a shining new villa, with Pavilion annexed; over which, in all the pride of oak and chestnut and divers coloured marbles, I was shown this morning by the obliging proprietor. The Prince's Palace itself is rehabilitated, and shines afar with white window-curtains from the midst of a garden, all trim borders and greenhouses and carefully kept walks. On the other side, the villas are more thronged together, and they have arranged themselves, shelf after shelf, behind each other. I see the glimmer of new buildings, too, as far eastward as Grimaldi; and a viaduct carries (I suppose) the railway past the mouth of the bone caves. F. Bacon (Lord Chancellor) made the remark that 'Time was the greatest innovator'; it is perhaps as meaningless a remark as was ever made; but as Bacon made it, I suppose it is better than any that I could make. Does it not seem as if things were fluid? They are displaced and altered in ten years so that one has difficulty, even

1873.
AET. 23.

with a memory so very vivid and retentive for that sort of thing as mine, in identifying places where one lived a long while in the past, and which one has kept piously in mind during all the interval. Nevertheless, the hills, I am glad to say, are unaltered; though I dare say the torrents have given them many a shrewd scar, and the rains and thaws dislodged many a boulder from their heights, if one were only keen enough to perceive it. The sea makes the same noise in the shingle; and the lemon and orange gardens still discharge in the still air their fresh perfume; and the people have still brown comely faces; and the Pharmacie Gros still dispenses English medicines; and the invalids (eheu!) still sit on the promenade and trifle with their fingers in the fringes of shawls and wrappers; and the shop of Pascal Amarante still, in its present bright consummate flower of aggrandisement and new paint, offers everything that it has entered into people's hearts to wish for in the idleness of a sanatorium; and the 'Château des Morts' is still at the top of the town; and the fort and the jetty are still at the foot, only there are now two jetties; and —I am out of breath. (To be continued in our next.)

For myself, I have come famously through the journey; and as I have written this letter (for the first time for ever so long) with ease and even pleasure, I think my head must be better. I am still no good at coming down hills or stairs; and my feet are more consistently cold than is quite comfortable. But, these apart, I feel well; and in good spirits all round.

I have written to Nice for letters, and hope to get them to-night. Continue to address Poste Restante. Take care of yourselves.

This is my birthday, by the way — O, I said that before. Adieu.—Ever your affectionate son,

R. L. STEVENSON.

TO MRS. SITWELL

1873.
AET. 23.

In the latter part of this letter will be found the germ of the essay *Ordered South.*

Mentone, Sunday, November 1873.

MY DEAR FRIEND,—I sat a long while up among the olive yards to-day at a favourite corner, where one has a fair view down the valley and on to the blue floor of the sea. I had a Horace with me, and read a little; but Horace, when you try to read him fairly under the open heaven, sounds urban, and you find something of the escaped townsman in his descriptions of the country, just as somebody said that Morris's sea-pieces were all taken from the coast. I tried for long to hit upon some language that might catch ever so faintly the indefinable shifting colour of olive leaves; and, above all, the changes and little silverings that pass over them, like blushes over a face, when the wind tosses great branches to and fro; but the Muse was not favourable. A few birds scattered here and there at wide intervals on either side of the valley sang the little broken songs of late autumn; and there was a great stir of insect life in the grass at my feet. The path up to this coign of vantage, where I think I shall make it a habit to ensconce myself a while of a morning, is for a little while common to the peasant and a little clear brooklet. It is pleasant, in the tempered grey daylight of the olive shadows, to see the people picking their way among the stones and the water and the brambles; the women especially, with the weights poised on their heads and walking all from the hips with a certain graceful deliberation.

Tuesday.—I have been to Nice to-day to see Dr. Bennet; he agrees with Clark that there is no disease; but I finished up my day with a lamentable exhibition of weakness. I could not remember French, or at least I was afraid to go into any place lest I should not be able to remember it, and so could not tell when the train went. At last I crawled up to the station and sat down on the steps, and just steeped myself there in the sunshine until the evening began to fall and the air to grow chilly. This long rest put me all right; and I came home here triumphantly and ate dinner well. There is the full, true, and particular account of the worst day I have had since I left London. I shall not go to Nice again for some time to come.

Thursday.—I am to-day quite recovered, and got into Mentone to-day for a book, which is quite a creditable walk. As an intellectual being I have not yet begun to re-exist; my immortal soul is still very nearly extinct; but we must hope the best. Now, do take warning by me. I am set up by a beneficent providence at the corner of the road, to warn you to flee from the hebetude that is to follow. Being sent to the South is not much good unless you take your soul with you, you see; and my soul is rarely with me here. I don't see much beauty. I have lost the key; I can only be placid and inert, and see the bright days go past uselessly one after another; therefore don't talk foolishly with your mouth any more about getting liberty by being ill and going south *viâ* the sickbed. It is not the old free-born bird that gets thus to freedom; but I know not what manacled and hidebound spirit, incapable of pleasure, the clay of a man. Go south! Why, I saw more beauty with my eyes healthfully alert to see in two wet windy February afternoons in Scotland than I can see in my beautiful olive gardens and grey hills in a whole week in my low and lost estate, as the Shorter Catechism puts it somewhere. It is a pitiable blindness, this blindness of the soul; I hope it may not be long with me. So remember to keep well; and remember rather anything than not to keep well; and again I say, *anything* rather than not to keep well.

Not that I am unhappy, mind you. I have found the words already—placid and inert, that is what I am. I sit in the sun and enjoy the tingle all over me, and I am cheerfully ready to concur with any one who says that this is a beautiful place, and I have a sneaking partiality for the newspapers, which would be all very well, if one had not fallen from heaven and were not troubled with some reminiscence of the *ineffable aurore*.

To sit by the sea and to be conscious of nothing but the sound of the waves, and the sunshine over all your body, is not unpleasant; but I was an Archangel once.

Friday.—If you knew how old I felt! I am sure this is what age brings with it—this carelessness, this disenchantment, this continual bodily weariness. I am a man of seventy: O Medea, kill me, or make me young again!!¹

To-day has been cloudy and mild; and I have lain a great while on a bench outside the garden wall (my usual place now) and looked at the dove-coloured sea and the broken roof of cloud, but there was no seeing in my eye. Let us hope to-morrow will be more profitable.

R. L. S.

TO MRS. THOMAS STEVENSON

Soon after the date of this letter I went out to join my friend for a part of the Christmas vacation, and found him without tangible disease, but very weak and ailing; ill-health and anxiety, however, neither then nor ever at all diminished his charm as a companion. After spending two or three weeks between the old town of Monaco and Monte Carlo, we returned to Mentone, to a hotel—now, I believe, defunct—at the eastern extremity of the town, where I presently left him, cheered by congenial society in the shape of an American family, two kind and accomplished Russian ladies from Georgia, with their children (one of whom, as will be seen, became his especial playmate and sweetheart), and a French landscape painter. In the intimacy of these friends he passed the winter, until he had recovered sufficient strength to return to his family in Scotland. The 'M'Laren' herein mentioned is, of course, the distinguished

---

¹ Compare the paragraph in 'Ordered South' describing the state of mind of the invalid doubtful of recovery, and ending: 'He will pray for Medea; when she comes, let her either rejuvenate or slay.'

1874.
AET. 24.
Scotch politician and social reformer, the late Duncan M'Laren, for sixteen years M.P. for Edinburgh.

Hotel Mirabeau, Mentone, Sunday, January 4, 1874.

MY DEAR MOTHER,—We have here fallen on the very pink of hotels. I do not say that it is more pleasantly conducted than the Pavillon, for that were impossible; but the rooms are so cheery and bright and new, and then the food! I never, I think, so fully appreciated the phrase 'the fat of the land' as I have done since I have been here installed. There was a dish of eggs at *déjeûner* the other day, over the memory of which I lick my lips in the silent watches.

Now that the cold has gone again, I continue to keep well in body, and already I begin to walk a little more. My head is still a very feeble implement, and easily set a-spinning; and I can do nothing in the way of work beyond reading books that may, I hope, be of some use to me afterwards.

I was very glad to see that M'Laren was sat upon, and principally for the reason why. Deploring as I do much of the action of the Trades Unions, these conspiracy clauses and the whole partiality of the Master and Servant Act are a disgrace to our equal laws. Equal laws become a byeword when what is legal for one class becomes a criminal offence for another. It did my heart good to hear that man tell M'Laren how, as he had talked much of getting the franchise for working men, he must now be content to see them use it now they had got it. This is a smooth stone well planted in the foreheads of certain dilettanti radicals, after M'Laren's fashion, who are willing to give the working men words and wind, and votes and the like, and yet think to keep all the advantages, just or unjust, of the wealthier classes without abatement. I do hope wise men will not attempt to fight the working men on the head of this notorious injustice. Any such step will only precipitate the action of the newly enfranchised classes, and irritate them into acting hastily; when what we ought to desire should be that they should act warily and little for many years to come, until education and habit may make them the more fit.

All this (intended for my father) is much after the fashion of his own correspondence. I confess it has left my own head exhausted; I hope it may not produce the same effect on yours. But I want him to look really into this question (both sides of it, and not the representations of rabid middle-class newspapers, sworn to support all the little tyrannies of wealth), and I know he will be convinced that this is a case of unjust law; and that, however desirable the end may seem to him, he will not be Jesuit enough to think that any end will justify an unjust law.

Here ends the political sermon of your affectionate (and somewhat dogmatical) son,

ROBERT LOUIS STEVENSON.

TO MRS. THOMAS STEVENSON

Mentone, January 7, 1874.

MY DEAR MOTHER,—I received yesterday two most charming letters—the nicest I have had since I left—December 26th and January 1st: this morning I got January 3rd.

Into the bargain with Marie, the American girl, who is grace itself, and comes leaping and dancing simply like a wave—like nothing else, and who yesterday was Queen out of the Epiphany cake and chose Robinet (the French painter) as her *favori* with the most pretty confusion possible—into the bargain with Marie, we have two little Russian girls, with the youngest of whom, a little polyglot button of a three-year old, I had the most laughable little scene at lunch to-day. I was watching her being fed with great amusement, her face being as broad as it is long, and her mouth capable of unlimited extension; when suddenly, her eye catching mine, the fashion of her countenance was changed, and regarding me with a really admirable appearance of offended dignity, she said something in Italian which made everybody laugh much. It was explained to me that she had said I was very *polisson* to stare at her. After this she was somewhat taken up with me, and after some examination she announced emphatically to the whole table, in German, that I was a *Mädchen*; which word she repeated with shrill emphasis, as though fearing that her proposition would be called in question—*Mädchen, Mädchen, Mädchen, Mädchen.* This hasty conclusion as to my sex she was led afterwards to revise, I am informed; but her new opinion (which seems to have been something nearer the truth) was announced in a third language quite unknown to me, and probably Russian. To complete the scroll of her accomplishments, she was brought round the table after the meal was over, and said good-bye to me in very commendable English.

The weather I shall say nothing about, as I am incapable of explaining my sentiments upon that subject before a lady. But my health is really greatly improved: I begin to recognise myself occasionally now and again, not without satisfaction.

Please remember me very kindly to Professor Swan; I wish I had a story to send him; but story, Lord bless you, I have none to tell, sir, unless it is the foregoing adventure with the little polyglot. The best of that depends on the significance of *polisson*, which is beautifully out of place.

Saturday, 10th January.—The little Russian kid is only two and a half: she speaks six languages. She and her sister (æt. 8) and May Johnstone (æt. 8) are the delight of my life. Last night I saw them all dancing—O it was jolly; kids are what is the matter with me. After the dancing, we all—that is the two Russian ladies, Robinet the French painter, Mr. and Mrs. Johnstone, two governesses, and fitful kids joining us at intervals—played a game of the stool of repentance in the Gallic idiom.

O—I have not told you that Colvin is gone; however, he is coming back again; he has left clothes in pawn to me.—Ever your affectionate son,

ROBERT LOUIS STEVENSON.

TO MRS. SITWELL

Mentone, Tuesday, 13th January 1874.

... I LOST a Philipine to little Mary Johnstone last night; so to-day I sent her a rubbishing doll's toilet, and a little note with it, with some verses telling how happy children made every one near them happy also, and advising her to keep the lines, and some day, when she was 'grown a stately demoiselle,' it would make her 'glad to know she gave pleasure long ago,' all in a very lame fashion, with just a note of prose at the end, telling her to mind her doll and the dog, and not trouble her little head just now to understand the bad verses; for some time when she was ill, as I am now, they would be plain to her and make her happy. She has just been here to thank me, and has left me very happy. Children are certainly too good to be true.

Yesterday I walked too far, and spent all the afternoon on the outside of my bed; went finally to rest at nine, and slept nearly twelve hours on the stretch. Bennet (the doctor), when told of it this morning, augured well for my recovery; he said youth must be putting in strong; of course I ought not to have slept at all. As it was, I dreamed *horridly*; but not my usual dreams of social miseries and misunderstandings and all sorts of crucifixions of the spirit; but of good, cheery, physical things —of long successions of vaulted, dimly lit cellars full of black water, in which I went swimming among toads and unutterable, cold, blind fishes. Now and then these cellars opened up into sort of domed music-hall places, where one could land for a little on the slope of the orchestra, but a sort of horror prevented one from staying long, and made one plunge back again into the dead waters. Then my dream changed, and I was a sort of Siamese pirate, on a very high deck with several others. The ship was almost captured, and we were fighting desperately. The hideous engines we used and the perfectly incredible carnage that we effected by means of them kept me cheery, as you may imagine; especially as I felt all the time my sympathy with the boarders, and knew that I was only a prisoner with these horrid Malays. Then I saw a signal being given, and knew they were going to blow up the ship. I leaped right off, and heard my captors splash in the water after me as thick as pebbles when a bit of river bank has given way beneath the foot. I never heard the ship blow up; but I spent the rest of the night swimming about some piles with the whole sea full of Malays, searching for me with knives in their mouths. They could swim any distance under water, and every now and again, just as I was beginning to reckon myself safe, a cold hand would be laid on my ankle—ugh!

However, my long sleep, troubled as it was, put me all right again, and I was able to work acceptably this morning and be very jolly all day. This evening I have had a great deal of talk with both the Russian ladies; they talked very nicely, and are bright, likable women both. They come from Georgia.

Wednesday, 10.30.—We have all been to tea to-night at the Russians' villa. Tea was made out of a samovar, which is something like a small steam engine, and whose principal advantage is that it burns the fingers of all who lay their profane touch upon it. After tea Madame Z. played Russian airs, very plaintive and pretty; so the evening was Muscovite from beginning to end. Madame G.'s daughter danced a tarantella, which was very pretty.

Whenever Nelitchka cries—and she never cries except

from pain—all that one has to do is to start 'Malbrook s'en va-t-en guerre.' She cannot resist the attraction; she is drawn through her sobs into the air; and in a moment there is Nelly singing, with the glad look that comes into her face always when she sings, and all the tears and pain forgotten.

It is wonderful, before I shut this up, how that child remains ever interesting to me. Nothing can stale her infinite variety; and yet it is not very various. You see her thinking what she is to do or to say next, with a funny grave air of reserve, and then the face breaks up into a smile, and it is probably 'Berecchino!' said with that sudden little jump of the voice that one knows in children, as the escape of a jack-in-the-box, and, somehow, I am quite happy after that! R. L. S.

TO MRS. SITWELL

[*Mentone, January* 1874.]

... LAST night I had a quarrel with the American on politics. It is odd how it irritates you to hear certain political statements made. He was excited, and he began suddenly to abuse our conduct to America. I, of course, admitted right and left that we had behaved disgracefully (as we had); until somehow I got tired of turning alternate cheeks and getting duly buffeted; and when he said that the Alabama money had not wiped out the injury, I suggested, in language (I remember) of admirable directness and force, that it was a pity they had taken the money in that case. He lost his temper at once, and cried out that his dearest wish was a war with England; whereupon I also lost my temper, and, thundering at the pitch of my voice, I left him and went away by myself to another part of the garden. A very tender reconciliation took place, and I think there will come no more harm out of it. We are both of us nervous people, and he had had a very long walk and a good deal of beer at dinner: that explains the scene a little. But I regret having employed so much of the voice with which I have been endowed, as I fear every person in the hotel was taken into confidence as to my sentiments, just at the very juncture when neither the sentiments nor (perhaps) the language had been sufficiently considered.

Friday.—You have not yet heard of my book?—*Four Great Scotsmen*—John Knox, David Hume, Robert Burns, Walter Scott. These, their lives, their work, the social media in which they lived and worked, with, if I can so make it, the strong current of the race making itself felt underneath and throughout—this is my idea. You must tell me what you think of it. The Knox will really be new matter, as his life hitherto has been disgracefully written, and the events are romantic and rapid; the character very strong, salient, and worthy; much interest as to the future of Scotland, and as to that part of him which was truly modern under his Hebrew disguise. Hume, of course, the urbane, cheerful, gentlemanly, letter-writing eighteenth century, full of attraction, and much that I don't yet know as to his work. Burns, the sentimental side that there is in most Scotsmen, his poor troubled existence, how far his poems were his personally, and how far national, the question of the framework of society in Scotland, and its fatal effect upon the finest natures. Scott again, the ever delightful man, sane, courageous, admirable; the birth of Romance, in a dawn that was a sunset; snobbery, conservatism, the wrong thread in History, and notably in that of his own land. *Voilà, madame, le menu. Comment le trouvez-vous? Il y a de la bonne viande, si on parvient à la cuire convenablement.*
R. L. S.

TO MRS. THOMAS STEVENSON

This describes another member of the Russian party, recently arrived at Mentone, who did his best, very nearly with success, to persuade Stevenson to join him in the study of law for some terms at Göttingen.

[*Mentone, March* 28, 1874.]

MY DEAR MOTHER,—Beautiful weather, perfect weather; sun, pleasant cooling winds; health very good; only incapacity to write.

The only new cloud on my horizon (I mean this in no menacing sense) is the Prince. I have philosophical and artistic discussions with the Prince. He is capable of talking for two hours upon end, developing his theory of everything under Heaven from his first position, which is that there is no straight line. Doesn't that sound like a game of my father's—I beg your pardon, you haven't read it—I don't mean *my* father, I mean Tristram Shandy's. He is very clever, and it is an immense joke to hear him unrolling all the problems of life—philosophy, science, what you will—in this charmingly cut-and-dry, here-we-are-again kind of manner. He is better to listen to than to argue withal. When you differ from him, he lifts up his voice and thunders; and you know that the thunder of an excited foreigner often miscarries. One stands aghast, marvelling how such a colossus of a man, in such a great commotion of spirit, can open his mouth so much and emit such a still small voice at the hinder end of it all. All this while he walks about the room, smokes cigarettes, occupies divers chairs for divers brief spaces, and casts his huge arms to the four winds like the sails of a mill. He is a most sportive Prince.   R. L. S.

TO MRS. SITWELL

This and the following letters were written after Stevenson's return to Scotland. The essay *Ordered South* appeared in *Macmillan's Magazine* at this date: that on Victor Hugo's romances in the *Cornhill* a little later.

[*Swanston*], *May* 1874, *Monday.*

WE are now at Swanston Cottage, Lothianburn, Edinburgh. The garden is but little clothed yet, for, you

1874.
AET. 24.

know, here we are six hundred feet above the sea. It is very cold, and has sleeted this morning. Everything wintry. I am very jolly, however, having finished Victor Hugo, and just looking round to see what I should next take up. I have been reading Roman Law and Calvin this morning.

Evening.—I went up the hill a little this afternoon. The air was invigorating, but it was so cold that my scalp was sore. With this high wintry wind, and the grey sky, and faint northern daylight, it was quite wonderful to hear such a clamour of blackbirds coming up to me out of the woods, and the bleating of sheep being shorn in a field near the garden, and to see golden patches of blossom already on the furze, and delicate green shoots upright and beginning to frond out, among last year's russet bracken. Flights of crows were passing continually between the wintry leaden sky and the wintry cold-looking hills. It was the oddest conflict of seasons. A wee rabbit—this year's making, beyond question—ran out from under my feet, and was in a pretty perturbation, until he hit upon a lucky juniper and blotted himself there promptly. Evidently this gentleman had not had much experience of life.

I have made an arrangement with my people: I am to have £84 a year—I only asked for £80 on mature reflection—and as I should soon make a good bit by my pen, I shall be very comfortable. We are all as jolly as can be together, so that is a great thing gained.

Wednesday.—Yesterday I received a letter that gave me much pleasure from a poor fellow-student of mine, who has been all winter very ill, and seems to be but little better even now. He seems very much pleased with *Ordered South.* 'A month ago,' he says, 'I could scarcely have ventured to read it; to-day I felt on reading it as I did on the first day that I was able to sun myself a little

in the open air.' And much more to the like effect. It is very gratifying.—Ever your faithful friend,
ROBERT LOUIS STEVENSON.

TO MRS. SITWELL

Mr. John Morley had asked for a notice by R. L. S. for the *Fortnightly Review* of Lord Lytton's *Fables in Song*.

Swanston, Wednesday, May 1874.

STRUGGLING away at *Fables in Song*. I am much afraid I am going to make a real failure; the time is so short, and I am so out of the humour. Otherwise very calm and jolly: cold still *impossible*.

Thursday.—I feel happier about the *Fables*, and it is warmer a bit; but my body is most decrepit, and I can just manage to be cheery and tread down hypochondria under foot by work. I lead such a funny life, utterly without interest or pleasure outside of my work: nothing, indeed, but work all day long, except a short walk alone on the cold hills, and meals, and a couple of pipes with my father in the evening. It is surprising how it suits me, and how happy I keep.

Saturday.—I have received such a nice long letter (four sides) from Leslie Stephen to-day about my Victor Hugo. It is accepted. This ought to have made me gay, but it hasn't. I am not likely to be much of a tonic to-night. I have been very cynical over myself to-day, partly, perhaps, because I have just finished some of the deedest rubbish about Lord Lytton's fables that an intelligent editor ever shot into his wastepaper basket. If Morley prints it I shall be glad, but my respect for him will be shaken.

Tuesday.—Another cold day; yet I have been along the hillside, wondering much at idiotic sheep, and raising partridges at every second step. One little plover is the

1874.
AET. 24.

object of my firm adherence. I pass his nest every day, and if you saw how he flies by me, and almost into my face, crying and flapping his wings, to direct my attention from his little treasure, you would have as kind a heart to him as I. To-day I saw him not, although I took my usual way; and I am afraid that some person has abused his simple wiliness and harried (as we say in Scotland) the nest. I feel much righteous indignation against such imaginary aggressor. However, one must not be too chary of the lower forms. To-day I sat down on a tree-stump at the skirt of a little strip of planting, and thoughtlessly began to dig out the touchwood with an end of twig. I found I had carried ruin, death, and universal consternation into a little community of ants; and this set me a-thinking of how close we are environed with frail lives, so that we can do nothing without spreading havoc over all manner of perishable homes and interests and affections; and so on to my favourite mood of an holy terror for all action and all inaction equally—a sort of shuddering revulsion from the necessary responsibilities of life. We must not be too scrupulous of others, or we shall die. Conscientiousness is a sort of moral opium; an excitant in small doses, perhaps, but at bottom a strong narcotic.

Saturday.—I have been two days in Edinburgh, and so had not the occasion to write to you. Morley has accepted the *Fables*, and I have seen it in proof, and think less of it than ever. However, of course, I shall send you a copy of the *Magazine* without fail, and you can be as disappointed as you like, or the reverse if you can. I would willingly recall it if I could.

Try, by way of change, Byron's *Mazeppa*; you will be astonished. It is grand and no mistake, and one sees through it a fire, and a passion, and a rapid intuition of genius, that makes one rather sorry for one's own generation of better writers, and—I don't know what to say; I was going to say 'smaller men'; but that's not right; read it, and you will feel what I cannot express. Don't be put out by the beginning; persevere, and you will find yourself thrilled before you are at an end with it.— Ever your faithful friend,

1874.
AET. 24.

      ROBERT LOUIS STEVENSON.

TO MRS. SITWELL

Written on an expedition to the west of England with his parents.

Train between Edinburgh and Chester, August 8, 1874.

MY father and mother reading. I think I shall talk to you for a moment or two. This morning at Swanston, the birds, poor creatures, had the most troubled hour or two; evidently there was a hawk in the neighbourhood; not one sang; and the whole garden thrilled with little notes of warning and terror. I did not know before that the voice of birds could be so tragically expressive. I had always heard them before express their trivial satisfaction with the blue sky and the return of daylight. Really, they almost frightened me; I could hear mothers and wives in terror for those who were dear to them; it was easy to translate, I wish it were as easy to write; but it is very hard in this flying train, or I would write you more.

Chester.—I like this place much; but somehow I feel glad when I get among the quiet eighteenth century buildings, in cosy places with some elbow room about them, after the older architecture. This other is bedevilled and furtive; it seems to stoop; I am afraid of trap-doors, and could not go pleasantly into such houses. I don't know how much of this is legitimately the effect of the architecture; little enough possibly; possibly far the most part of it comes from bad historical novels and the disquieting statuary that garnishes some façades.

On the way, to-day, I passed through my dear Cumberland country. Nowhere to as great a degree can one find

1874.
AET. 24.

the combination of lowland and highland beauties; the outline of the blue hills is broken by the outline of many tumultuous tree-clumps; and the broad spaces of moorland are balanced by a network of deep hedgerows that might rival Suffolk, in the foreground.—How a railway journey shakes and discomposes one, mind and body! I grow blacker and blacker in humour as the day goes on; and when at last I am let out, and have the fresh air about me, it is as though I were born again, and the sick fancies flee away from my mind like swans in spring.

I want to come back on what I have said about eighteenth century and middle-age houses: I do not know if I have yet explained to you the sort of loyalty, of urbanity, that there is about the one to my mind; the spirit of a country orderly and prosperous, a flavour of the presence of magistrates and well-to-do merchants in bag-wigs, the clink of glasses at night in fire-lit parlours, something certain and civic and domestic, is all about these quiet, staid, shapely houses, with no character but their exceeding shapeliness, and the comely external utterance that they make of their internal comfort. Now the others are, as I have said, both furtive and bedevilled; they are sly and grotesque; they combine their sort of feverish grandeur with their sort of secretive baseness, after the manner of a Charles the Ninth. They are peopled for me with persons of the same fashion. Dwarfs and sinister people in cloaks are about them; and I seem to divine crypts, and, as I said, trap-doors. O God be praised that we live in this good daylight and this good peace.

Barmouth, August 9th.—To-day we saw the cathedral at Chester; and, far more delightful, saw and heard a certain inimitable verger who took us round. He was full of a certain recondite, far-away humour that did not quite make you laugh at the time, but was somehow laughable to recollect. Moreover, he had so far a just imagination, and could put one in the right humour for seeing an old place, very much as, according to my favourite text, Scott's novels and poems do for one. His account of the monks in the Scriptorium, with their cowls over their heads, in a certain sheltered angle of the cloister where the big Cathedral building kept the sun off the parchments, was all that could be wished; and so too was what he added of the others pacing solemnly behind them and dropping, ever and again, on their knees before a little shrine there is in the wall, 'to keep 'em in the frame of mind.' You will begin to think me unduly biassed in this verger's favour if I go on to tell you his opinion of me. We got into a little side chapel, whence we could hear the choir children at practice, and I stopped a moment listening to them, with, I dare say, a very bright face, for the sound was delightful to me. 'Ah,' says he, 'you're *very* fond of music.' I said I was. 'Yes, I could tell that by your head,' he answered. 'There's a deal in that head.' And he shook his own solemnly. I said it might be so, but I found it hard, at least, to get it out. Then my father cut in brutally, said anyway I had no ear, and left the verger so distressed and shaken in the foundations of his creed that, I hear, he got my father aside afterwards and said he was sure there was something in my face, and wanted to know what it was, if not music. He was relieved when he heard that I occupied myself with litterature (which word, note here, I do not spell correctly). Good-night, and here's the verger's health! R. L. S.

1874.
AET. 24.

TO MRS. SITWELL

'John Knox' and 'J. K.' herein mentioned are the two papers on 'John Knox and his Relations with Women,' first printed in *Macmillan's Magazine* and afterwards in *Familiar Studies*.

Swanston, Wednesday, [*Autumn*] 1874.

I HAVE been hard at work all yesterday, and besides had to write a long letter to Bob, so I found no time until quite late, and then was sleepy. Last night it blew a fearful gale; I was kept awake about a couple of hours, and could not get to sleep for the horror of the wind's noise; the whole house shook; and, mind you, our house *is* a house, a great castle of jointed stone that would weigh up a street of English houses; so that when it quakes, as it did last night, it means something. But the quaking was not what put me about; it was the horrible howl of the wind round the corner; the audible haunting of an incarnate anger about the house; the evil spirit that was abroad; and, above all, the shuddering silent pauses when the storm's heart stands dreadfully still for a moment. O how I hate a storm at night! They have been a great influence in my life, I am sure; for I can remember them so far back—long before I was six at least, for we left the house in which I remember listening to them times without number when I was six. And in those days the storm had for me a perfect impersonation, as durable and unvarying as any heathen deity. I always heard it, as a horseman riding past with his cloak about his head, and somehow always carried away, and riding past again, and being baffled yet once more, *ad infinitum*, all night long. I think I wanted him to get past, but I am not sure; I know only that I had some interest either for or against in the matter; and I used to lie and hold my breath, not quite frightened, but in a state of miserable exaltation.

My first John Knox is in proof, and my second is on the anvil. It is very good of me so to do; for I want so much to get to my real tour and my sham tour, the real tour first: it is always working in my head, and if I can only turn on the right sort of style at the right moment, I am not much afraid of it. One thing bothers me; what with hammering at this J. K., and writing necessary letters, and taking necessary exercise (that even not enough, the weather is so repulsive to me, cold and windy), I find I have no time for reading except times of fatigue, when I wish merely to relax myself. O—and I read over again for this purpose Flaubert's *Tentation de St. Antoine*; it struck me a good deal at first, but this second time it has fetched me immensely. I am but just done with it, so you will know the large proportion of salt to take with my present statement, that it's the finest thing I ever read! Of course, it isn't that, it's full of *longueurs*, and is not quite 'redd up,' as we say in Scotland, not quite articulated; but there are splendid things in it.

I say, *do* take your maccaroni with oil: *do, please.* It's *beastly* with butter.—Ever your faithful friend,
ROBERT LOUIS STEVENSON.

TO MRS. SITWELL
[*Edinburgh*], *December* 23, 1874.

Monday.—I have come from a concert, and the concert was rather a disappointment. Not so my afternoon skating—Duddingston, our big loch, is bearing; and I wish you could have seen it this afternoon, covered with people, in thin driving snow flurries, the big hill grim and white and alpine overhead in the thick air, and the road up the gorge, as it were into the heart of it, dotted black with traffic. Moreover, I *can* skate a little bit; and what one can do is always pleasant to do.

Tuesday.—I got your letter to-day, and was so glad thereof. It was of good omen to me also. I worked from ten to one (my classes are suspended now for Xmas holidays), and wrote four or five Portfolio pages of my Buckinghamshire affair. Then I went to Duddingston and skated all afternoon. If you had seen the moon rising, a perfect sphere of smoky gold, in the dark air above the trees, and the white loch thick with skaters, and the great hill, snow-sprinkled, overhead! It was a sight for a king.

Wednesday.—I stayed on Duddingston to-day till after nightfall. The little booths that hucksters set up round the edge were marked each one by its little lamp. There were some fires too; and the light, and the shadows of the people who stood round them to warm themselves, made a strange pattern all round on the snow-covered ice. A few people with torches began to travel up and down the ice, a lit circle travelling along with them over the snow. A gigantic moon rose, meanwhile, over the trees and the kirk on the promontory, among perturbed and vacillating clouds.

The walk home was very solemn and strange. Once, through a broken gorge, we had a glimpse of a little space of mackerel sky, moon-litten, on the other side of the hill; the broken ridges standing grey and spectral between; and the hilltop over all, snow-white, and strangely magnified in size.

This must go to you to-morrow, so that you may read it on Christmas Day for company. I hope it may be good company to you.

Thursday.—Outside, it snows thick and steadily. The gardens before our house are now a wonderful fairy forest. And O, this whiteness of things, how I love it, how it sends the blood about my body! Maurice de Guérin hated snow; what a fool he must have been! Somebody tried to put me out of conceit with it by saying that people were lost in it. As if people don't get lost in love, too, and die of devotion to art; as if everything worth were not an occasion to some people's end.

What a wintry letter this is! Only I think it is winter seen from the inside of a warm greatcoat. And there is, at least, a warm heart about it somewhere. Do you know, what they say in Xmas stories is true? I think one loves their friends more dearly at this season.—Ever your faithful friend, ROBERT LOUIS STEVENSON.

TO SIDNEY COLVIN

17 *Heriot Row, Edinburgh* [*January* 1875].

MY DEAR COLVIN,—I have worked too hard; I have given myself one day of rest, and that was not enough;

so I am giving myself another. I shall go to bed again likewise so soon as this is done, and slumber most potently.

1875.
AET. 25.

9 P.M., slept all afternoon like a lamb.

About my coming south, I think the still small unanswerable voice of coins will make it impossible until the session is over (end of March); but for all that, I think I shall hold out jolly. I do not want you to come and bother yourself; indeed, it is still not quite certain whether my father will be quite fit for you, although I have now no fear of that really. Now don't take up this wrongly; I wish you could come; and I do not know anything that would make me happier, but I see that it is wrong to expect it, and so I resign myself: some time after. I offered Appleton a series of papers on the modern French school—the Parnassiens, I think they call them—de Banville, Coppée, Soulary, and Sully Prudhomme. But he has not deigned to answer my letter.

I shall have another Portfolio paper so soon as I am done with this story, that has played me out; the story is to be called *When the Devil was well*: scene, Italy, Renaissance; colour, purely imaginary of course, my own unregenerate idea of what Italy then was. O, when shall I find the story of my dreams, that shall never halt nor wander nor step aside, but go ever before its face, and ever swifter and louder, until the pit receives it, roaring? The Portfolio paper will be about Scotland and England.
—Ever yours, R. L. STEVENSON.

TO MRS. SITWELL

In the following is related Stevenson's first introduction to Mr. W. E. Henley. The acquaintance thus formed ripened quickly, as is well known, into a close and stimulating literary friendship:—

Edinburgh, Tuesday [January 1875].

I GOT your nice long gossiping letter to-day—I mean by that that there was more news in it than usual—and so, of course, I am pretty jolly. I am in the house, however, with such a beastly cold in the head. Our east winds begin already to be very cold.

O, I have such a longing for children of my own; and yet I do not think I could bear it if I had one. I fancy I must feel more like a woman than like a man about that. I sometimes hate the children I see on the street—you know what I mean by hate—wish they were somewhere else, and not there to mock me; and sometimes, again, I don't know how to go by them for the love of them, especially the very wee ones.

Thursday.—I have been still in the house since I wrote, and I *have* worked. I finished the Italian story; not well, but as well as I can just now; I must go all over it again, some time soon, when I feel in the humour to better and perfect it. And now I have taken up an old story, begun years ago; and I have now re-written all I had written of it then, and mean to finish it. What I have lost and gained is odd. As far as regards simple writing, of course, I am in another world now; but in some things, though more clumsy, I seem to have been freer and more plucky: this is a lesson I have taken to heart. I have got a jolly new name for my old story. I am going to call it *A Country Dance*; the two heroes keep changing places, you know; and the chapter where the most of this changing goes on is to be called ' Up the middle, down the middle.' It will be in six, or (perhaps) seven chapters. I have never worked harder in my life than these last four days. If I can only keep it up.

Saturday.—Yesterday, Leslie Stephen, who was down here to lecture, called on me and took me up to see a poor fellow, a poet who writes for him, and who has been eighteen months in our infirmary, and may be, for all I know, eighteen months more. It was very sad to see him there, in a little room with two beds, and a couple of sick children in the other bed; a girl came in to visit the children, and played dominoes on the counterpane with them; the gas flared and crackled, the fire burned in a dull economical way; Stephen and I sat on a couple of chairs, and the poor fellow sat up in his bed with his hair and beard all tangled, and talked as cheerfully as if he had been in a King's palace, or the great King's palace of the blue air. He has taught himself two languages since he has been lying there. I shall try to be of use to him.

We have had two beautiful spring days, mild as milk, windy withal, and the sun hot. I dreamed last night I was walking by moonlight round the place where the scene of my story is laid; it was all so quiet and sweet, and the blackbirds were singing as if it was day; it made my heart very cool and happy.—Ever yours,

. ROBERT LOUIS STEVENSON.

TO SIDNEY COLVIN

February 8, 1875.

MY DEAR COLVIN,—Forgive my bothering you. Here is the proof of my second *Knox*. Glance it over, like a good fellow, and if there's anything very flagrant send it to me marked. I have no confidence in myself; I feel such an ass. What have I been doing? As near as I can calculate, nothing. And yet I have worked all this month from three to five hours a day, that is to say, from one to three hours more than my doctor allows me; positively no result.

No, I can write no article just now; I am *pioching*, like a madman, at my stories, and can make nothing of them; my simplicity is tame and dull—my passion tinsel, boyish, hysterical. Never mind—ten years hence, if I live, I shall have learned, so help me God. I know one must work, in the meantime (so says Balzac) *comme le mineur enfoui sous un éboulement.*

J'y parviendrai, nom de nom de nom! But it's a long look forward.—Ever yours, R. L. S.

1875.
AET. 25.

TO MRS. SITWELL

As the spring advanced Stevenson had again been much out of sorts, and had been gone for a change, in the company of Mr. R. A. M. Stevenson, on his first visit to the artist haunts of Fontainebleau, which were afterwards so much endeared to him.

[*Barbizon, April* 1875.]

MY DEAR FRIEND,—This is just a line to say I am well and happy. I am here in my dear forest all day in the open air. It is very be—no, not beautiful exactly, just now, but very bright and living. There are one or two song birds and a cuckoo; all the fruit-trees are in flower, and the beeches make sunshine in a shady place. I begin to go all right; you need not be vexed about my health; I really was ill at first, as bad as I have been for nearly a year; but the forest begins to work, and the air, and the sun, and the smell of the pines. If I could stay a month here, I should be as right as possible. Thanks for your letter.—Your faithful   R. L. S.

TO MRS. SITWELL

On his way through town after his return to Scotland from Fontainebleau he had been given a photograph of the Three Fates of the Elgin Marbles, who are the 'three women' discussed in the second part of this letter.

17 *Heriot Row, Edinburgh, Sunday* [*April* 1875].

HERE is my long story: yesterday night, after having supped, I grew so restless that I was obliged to go out in search of some excitement. There was a half-moon lying over on its back, and incredibly bright in the midst of a faint grey sky set with faint stars: a very inartistic moon, that would have damned a picture.

At the most populous place of the city I found a little boy, three years old perhaps, half frantic with terror, and crying to every one for his 'Mammy.' This was about eleven, mark you. People stopped and spoke to him, and then went on, leaving him more frightened than before.

But I and a good-humoured mechanic came up together; and I instantly developed a latent faculty for setting the hearts of children at rest. Master Tommy Murphy (such was his name) soon stopped crying, and allowed me to take him up and carry him; and the mechanic and I trudged away along Princes Street to find his parents. I was soon so tired that I had to ask the mechanic to carry the bairn; and you should have seen the puzzled contempt with which he looked at me, for knocking in so soon. He was a good fellow, however, although very impracticable and sentimental; and he soon bethought him that Master Murphy might catch cold after his excitement, so we wrapped him up in my greatcoat. 'Tobauga (Tobago) Street' was the address he gave us; and we deposited him in a little grocer's shop and went through all the houses in the street without being able to find any one of the name of Murphy. Then I set off to the head police office, leaving my greatcoat in pawn about Master Murphy's person. As I went down one of the lowest streets in the town, I saw a little bit of life that struck me. It was now half-past twelve, a little shop stood still half-open, and a boy of four or five years old was walking up and down before it imitating cockcrow. He was the only living creature within sight.

At the police offices no word of Master Murphy's parents; so I went back empty-handed. The good groceress, who had kept her shop open all this time, could keep the child no longer; her father, bad with bronchitis, said he must forth. So I got a large scone with currants in it, wrapped my coat about Tommy, got him up on my arm, and away to the police office with him: not very easy in my mind, for the poor child, young as he was—he could scarce speak—was full of terror for the 'office,' as he called it. He was now very grave and quiet and communicative with me; told me how his father thrashed him, and divers household matters. Whenever he saw a woman on our way he looked after

1875.
AET. 25.

her over my shoulder and then gave his judgment: 'That's no *her*,' adding sometimes, 'She has a wean wi' her.' Meantime I was telling him how I was going to take him to a gentleman who would find out his mother for him quicker than ever I could, and how he must not be afraid of him, but be brave, as he had been with me. We had just arrived at our destination—we were just under the lamp—when he looked me in the face and said appealingly, 'He'll no put me in the office?' And I had to assure him that he would not, even as I pushed open the door and took him in.

The serjeant was very nice, and I got Tommy comfortably seated on a bench, and spirited him up with good words and the scone with the currants in it; and then, telling him I was just going out to look for Mammy, I got my greatcoat and slipped away.

Poor little boy! he was not called for, I learn, until ten this morning. This is very ill written, and I've missed half that was picturesque in it; but to say truth, I am very tired and sleepy: it was two before I got to bed. However, you see, I had my excitement.

Monday.—I have written nothing all morning; I cannot settle to it. Yes—I *will* though.

10.45.—And I did. I want to say something more to you about the three women. I wonder so much why they should have been *women*, and halt between two opinions in the matter. Sometimes I think it is because they were made by a man for men; sometimes, again, I think there is an abstract reason for it, and there is something more substantive about a woman than ever there can be about a man. I can conceive a great mythical woman, living alone among inaccessible mountain-tops or in some lost island in the pagan seas, and ask no more. Whereas if I hear of a Hercules, I ask after Iole or Dejanira. I cannot think him a man without women. But I can think of these three deep-breasted women, living out all their days on remote hilltops, seeing the white dawn and the purple even, and the world outspread before them for ever, and no more to them for ever than a sight of the eyes, a hearing of the ears, a far-away interest of the inflexible heart, not pausing, not pitying, but austere with a holy austerity, rigid with a calm and passionless rigidity; and I find them none the less women to the end.

1875.
AET. 25.

And think, if one could love a woman like that once, see her once grow pale with passion, and once wring your lips out upon hers, would it not be a small thing to die? Not that there is not a passion of a quite other sort, much less epic, far more dramatic and intimate, that comes out of the very frailty of perishable women; out of the lines of suffering that we see written about their eyes, and that we may wipe out if it were but for a moment; out of the thin hands, wrought and tempered in agony to a fineness of perception, that the indifferent or the merely happy cannot know; out of the tragedy that lies about such a love, and the pathetic incompleteness. This is another thing, and perhaps it is a higher. I look over my shoulder at the three great headless Madonnas, and they look back at me and do not move; see me, and through and over me, the foul life of the city dying to its embers already as the night draws on; and over miles and miles of silent country, set here and there with lit towns, thundered through here and there with night expresses scattering fire and smoke; and away to the ends of the earth, and the furthest star, and the blank regions of nothing; and they are not moved. My quiet, great-kneed, deep-breasted, well-draped ladies of Necessity, I give my heart to you!   R. L. S.

TO MRS. SITWELL

[*Swanston, Tuesday, April* 1875.]

MY DEAR FRIEND,—I have been so busy, away to Bridge of Allan with my father first, and then with Simpson and

1875.
AET. 25.

Baxter out here from Saturday till Monday. I had no time to write, and, as it is, am strangely incapable. Thanks for your letter. I have been reading such lots of law, and it seems to take away the power of writing from me. From morning to night, so often as I have a spare moment, I am in the embrace of a law book—barren embraces. I am in good spirits; and my heart smites me as usual, when I am in good spirits, about my parents. If I get a bit dull, I am away to London without a scruple; but so long as my heart keeps up, I am all for my parents.

What do you think of Henley's hospital verses? They were to have been dedicated to me, but Stephen wouldn't allow it—said it would be pretentious.

Wednesday.—I meant to have made this quite a decent letter this morning, but listen. I had pain all last night, and did not sleep well, and now am cold and sickish, and strung up ever and again with another flash of pain. Will you remember me to everybody? My principal characteristics are cold, poverty, and Scots Law—three very bad things. Oo, how the rain falls! The mist is quite low on the hill. The birds are twittering to each other about the indifferent season. O, here's a gem for you. An old godly woman predicted the end of the world, because the seasons were becoming indistinguishable; my cousin Dora objected that last winter had been pretty well marked. 'Yes, my dear,' replied the soothsayeress; 'but I think you'll find the summer will be rather coamplicated.' —Ever your faithful   R. L. S.

TO MRS. SITWELL

The rehearsals were those of Shakespeare's *Twelfth Night* for amateur theatricals at Professor Fleeming Jenkin's, in which Stevenson played the part of Orsino.

[*Edinburgh, Saturday, April* 1875.]

I AM getting on with my rehearsals, but I find the part very hard. I rehearsed yesterday from a quarter to seven, and to-day from four (with interval for dinner) to eleven. You see the sad strait I am in for ink.—*À demain.*

Sunday.—This is the third ink-bottle I have tried, and still it's nothing to boast of. My journey went off all right, and I have kept ever in good spirits. Last night, indeed, I did think my little bit of gaiety was going away down the wind like a whiff of tobacco smoke, but to-day it has come back to me a little. The influence of this place is assuredly all that can be worst against one; *mais il faut lutter.* I was haunted last night when I was in bed by the most cold, desolate recollections of my past life here; I was glad to try and think of the forest, and warm my hands at the thought of it. O the quiet, grey thickets, and the yellow butterflies, and the woodpeckers, and the outlook over the plain as it were over a sea! O for the good, fleshly stupidity of the woods, the body conscious of itself all over and the mind forgotten, the clean air nestling next your skin as though your clothes were gossamer, the eye filled and content, the whole MAN HAPPY! Whereas here it takes a pull to hold yourself together; it needs both hands, and a book of stoical maxims, and a sort of bitterness at the heart by way of armour.—Ever your faithful   R. L. S.

Wednesday.—I am so played out with a cold in my eye that I cannot see to write or read without difficulty. It is swollen *horrible*; so how I shall look as Orsino, God knows! I have my fine clothes tho'. Henley's sonnets have been taken for the *Cornhill.* He is out of hospital now, and dressed, but still not too much to brag of in health, poor fellow, I am afraid.

Sunday.—So. I have still rather bad eyes, and a nasty sore throat. I play Orsino every day, in all the pomp of Solomon, splendid Francis the First clothes, heavy with gold and stage jewellery. I play it ill enough, I believe; but me and the clothes, and the wedding wherewith the clothes and me are reconciled, produce every night a thrill

1875.
AET. 25.

of admiration. Our cook told my mother (there is a servants' night, you know) that she and the housemaid were 'just prood to be able to say it waś oor young gentleman.' To sup afterwards with these clothes on, and a wonderful lot of gaiety and Shakespearean jokes about the table, is something to live for. It is so nice to feel you have been dead three hundred years, and the sound of your laughter is faint and far off in the centuries.—Ever your faithful ROBERT LOUIS STEVENSON.

Wednesday.—A moment at last. These last few days have been as jolly as days could be, and by good fortune I leave to-morrow for Swanston, so that I shall not feel the whole fall back to habitual self. The pride of life could scarce go further. To live in splendid clothes, velvet and gold and fur, upon principally champagne and lobster salad, with a company of people nearly all of whom are exceptionally good talkers; when your days began about eleven and ended about four—I have lost that sentence; I give it up; it is very admirable sport, any way. Then both my afternoons have been so pleasantly occupied—taking Henley drives. I had a business to carry him down the long stair, and more of a business to get him up again, but while he was in the carriage it was splendid. It is now just the top of spring with us. The whole country is mad with green. To see the cherry-blossom bitten out upon the black firs, and the black firs bitten out of the blue sky, was a sight to set before a king. You may imagine what it was to a man who has been eighteen months in an hospital ward. The look of his face was a wine to me.

I shall send this off to-day to let you know of my new address—Swanston Cottage, Lothianburn, Edinburgh. Salute the faithful in my name. Salute Priscilla, salute Barnabas, salute Ebenezer—O no, he's too much, I withdraw Ebenezer; enough of early Christians.—Ever your faithful ROBERT LOUIS STEVENSON.

TO MRS. SITWELL

1875.
AET. 25.

'Burns' means the article on Burns which R. L. S. had been commissioned to write for the *Encyclopædia Britannica*. The 'awfully nice man' was Mr. Seed, Premier of New Zealand; and it was from his conversation that the notion of the Samoan Islands as a place of refuge for the sick and world-worn first entered Stevenson's mind, to lie dormant (I never heard him speak of it) and be revived fifteen years later.

[*Edinburgh, June* 1875.]

SIMPLY a scratch. All right, jolly, well, and through with the difficulty. My father pleased about the Burns. Never travel in the same carriage with three able-bodied seamen and a fruiterer from Kent; the A.-B.'s speak all night as though they were hailing vessels at sea; and the fruiterer as if he were crying fruit in a noisy market-place —such, at least, is my *funeste* experience. I wonder if a fruiterer from some place else—say Worcestershire— would offer the same phenomena? insoluble doubt.

R. L. S.

Later.—Forgive me, couldn't get it off. Awfully nice man here to-night. Public servant—New Zealand. Telling us all about the South Sea Islands till I was sick with desire to go there: beautiful places, green for ever; perfect climate; perfect shapes of men and women, with red flowers in their hair; and nothing to do but to study oratory and etiquette, sit in the sun, and pick up the fruits as they fall. Navigator's Island is the place; absolute balm for the weary.—Ever your faithful friend,

R. L. S.

TO MRS. SITWELL

The examination for the Bar at Edinburgh was approaching. 'Fontainebleau' is the paper called 'Forest Notes,' afterwards printed in the *Cornhill Magazine*. The church is Glencorse Church in the Pentlands, to the thoughts of which Stevenson

1875. reverted in his last days with so much emotion (see *Weir of*
AET. 25. *Hermiston*, chap. v.).

Swanston. End of June, 1875.

Thursday.—This day fortnight I shall fall or conquer. Outside the rain still soaks; but now and again the hill-top looks through the mist vaguely. I am very comfortable, very sleepy, and very much satisfied with the arrangements of Providence.

Saturday—no, Sunday, 12.45.—Just been—not grinding, alas!—I couldn't—but doing a bit of Fontainebleau. I don't think I'll be plucked. I am not sure though—I am so busy, what with this d—d law, and this Fontainebleau always at my elbow, and three plays (three, think of that!) and a story, all crying out to me, 'Finish, finish, make an entire end, make us strong, shapely, viable creatures!' It's enough to put a man crazy. Moreover, I have my thesis given out now, which is a fifth (is it fifth? I can't count) incumbrance.

Sunday.—I've been to church, and am not depressed—a great step. I was at that beautiful church my *petit poëme en prose* was about. It is a little cruciform place, with heavy cornices and string course to match, and a steep slate roof. The small kirkyard is full of old gravestones. One of a Frenchman from Dunkerque—I suppose he died prisoner in the military prison hard by—and one, the most pathetic memorial I ever saw, a poor school-slate, in a wooden frame, with the inscription cut into it evidently by the father's own hand. In church, old Mr. Torrence preached—over eighty, and a relic of times forgotten, with his black thread gloves and mild old foolish face. One of the nicest parts of it was to see John Inglis, the greatest man in Scotland, our Justice-General, and the only born lawyer I ever heard, listening to the piping old body, as though it had all been a revelation, grave and respectful.—Ever your faithful   R. L. S.

III

ADVOCATE AND AUTHOR

EDINBURGH—PARIS—FONTAINEBLEAU

JULY 1875—JULY 1879

ON the 14th of July 1875, Stevenson passed with credit his examination for the Bar at Edinburgh, and thenceforth enjoyed whatever status and consideration attaches to the title of Advocate. But he made no serious attempt to practise, and by the 25th of the same month had started with Sir Walter Simpson for France. Here he lived and tramped for several weeks among the artist haunts of Fontainebleau and the neighbourhood, occupying himself chiefly with studies of the French poets and poetry of the fifteenth century, which afterwards bore fruit in his papers on Charles of Orleans and François Villon. Thence he travelled to join his parents at Wiesbaden and Homburg, and, returning in the autumn to Scotland, made, to please them, an effort to live the ordinary life of an Edinburgh advocate—attending trials, and spending his mornings in wig and gown at the Parliament House. But this attempt was before long abandoned as tending to waste of time and being incompatible with his real occupation of literature. Through the next winter and spring he remained in Edinburgh, except for a winter's walking tour in Ayrshire and Galloway, and a month spent among his friends in London. In the late summer of 1876, after a visit to the West Highlands, he made the canoe trip with Sir

Walter Simpson, which furnished the subject of the *Inland Voyage*, followed by a prolonged autumn stay at Grez and Barbizon. The life, atmosphere, and scenery of these forest haunts had charmed and soothed him, as we have seen, since he was first introduced to them by his cousin, Mr. R. A. M. Stevenson, in the spring of 1875. An unfettered, unconventional, open-air existence, passed face to face with nature and in the company of congenial people engaged, like himself, in grappling with the problems and difficulties of an art, had been what he had longed for most consistently through all the agitations of his youth. And now he had found just such an existence, and with it, as he thought, peace of mind, health, and the spirit of unimpeded work.

What indeed awaited him in the forest was something very different and more momentous, namely his fate; the romance which decided his life, and the companion whom he resolved to make his own at all hazards. But of this hereafter. To continue briefly the annals of the time: the year 1877 was again spent between Edinburgh, London, the Fontainebleau region, and the artist's quarter in Paris, with an excursion in the company of his parents to the Land's End in August. In 1878 a similar general mode of life was varied by a visit with his parents in March to Burford Bridge, where he made warm friends with a senior to whom he had long looked up from a distance, Mr. George Meredith; by a spell of secretarial work under Professor Fleeming Jenkin, who was serving as a juror on the Paris Exhibition; and lastly, by the autumn tramp through the Cévennes, afterwards recounted with so much charm in *Travels with a Donkey*. The first half of 1879 was again spent between London, Scotland, and Paris.

During these four years, it should be added, Stevenson's health was very passable. It often, indeed, threatened to give way after any prolonged residence in Edinburgh, but was generally soon restored by open-air excursions (during which he was capable of fairly vigorous and sustained daily exercise), or by a spell of life among the woods of Fontainebleau. They were also the years in which he settled for good into his chosen profession of letters. He worked rather desultorily for the first twelve months after his call to the bar, but afterwards with ever-growing industry and success, winning from the critical a full measure of recognition, though relatively little, so far, from the general public. In 1876 he contributed as a journalist, though not frequently, to the *Academy* and *Vanity Fair*, and in 1877 more abundantly to *London*, a weekly review newly founded under the editorship of Mr. Glasgow Brown, an acquaintance of Edinburgh Speculative days. But he had no great gift or liking for journalism, or for any work not calling for the best literary form and finish he could give. Where he found special scope for such work was in the *Cornhill Magazine* under the editorship of Mr. Leslie Stephen. Here he continued his critical papers on men and books, already begun in 1874 with *Victor Hugo*, and began in 1876 the series of papers afterwards collected in *Virginibus Puerisque*, in which he preaches, with such captivating gaiety and vigour, his gospel of courage and of contempt for the bourgeois timidities and petty respectabilities of life. They were continued in 1877, and in greater number throughout 1878. His first published stories appeared as follows:—'A Lodging for the Night,' *Temple Bar*, October 1877; 'The Sire de Malétroit's Door,' *Temple Bar*, January 1878; and 'Will o' the Mill,' *Cornhill Magazine*, January 1878. The first two of these were inspired by the studies of fifteenth century France which he had made in the autumn of 1875, and by their energy of vision and vividness of presentment seemed to justify the best hopes his friends had formed of him as a story-teller; while the third, admirable at once as parable—the parable of the hanger-back—and as idyll of the Alpine road and river, showed a quality still rarer and more poetical. In May 1878 followed his first travel book, *The Inland Voyage*, containing the account of his canoe trip from Antwerp to Grez. This was to Stevenson a year of great and various productiveness. Besides six or eight characteristic essays of the 'Virginibus Puerisque' series, there appeared in *London* (now edited by Mr. Henley) the set of fantastic modern tales called the 'New Arabian Nights,' conceived and written in an entirely different key from any of his previous work, as well as the kindly, sentimental comedy of French artist life, 'Providence and the Guitar'; and in the *Portfolio* the 'Picturesque Notes on Edinburgh,' republished at the end of the year in book form. During the autumn and winter of this year he wrote *Travels with a Donkey in the Cévennes*, and was much engaged in the planning of plays in collaboration with Mr. Henley; of which one, *Deacon Brodie*, was finished in the spring of 1879. This was also the date of the much debated essay 'On some Aspects of Burns.' In the same spring he drafted in Edinburgh, but afterwards laid by, four chapters on ethics, a study of which he once spoke as being always his 'veiled mistress,' under the name of *Lay Morals*.

But abounding in good work as this period was, and momentous as it was in regard to Stevenson's future life, it is a period which figures hardly at all in his correspondence, and in this book must fill quite a disproportionately scanty space. Partly his increasing absorption in the interests of his life and work left him little time or inclination for letter-writing; partly his greater freedom of movement made it unnecessary. On his way backwards and forwards between Scotland and France, his friends in London had the chance of seeing him much more frequently than of yore. His visits were always a delight, and the charm of his talk and presence unequalled. He avoided formal and dress-coated society; but in the company of congenial friends, whether men or women, and in places like the Savile Club (his favourite haunt), he won and kept all hearts by that mixture which was his own of the most inexhaustible, far-ranging brilliancy and gaiety in discourse with the most sympathetic humanity of feeling and affectionateness of nature. But I am letting myself lapse too much into biography, and it is time that the meagre correspondence of these years should speak for itself.

1875.
AET. 25.

TO MRS. THOMAS STEVENSON

[*Chez Siron, Barbizon, Seine et Marne, August* 1875.]

MY DEAR MOTHER,—I have been three days at a place called Grez, a pretty and very melancholy village on the plain. A low bridge of many arches choked with sedge; great fields of white and yellow water-lilies; poplars and willows innumerable; and about it all such an atmosphere of sadness and slackness, one could do nothing but get into the boat and out of it again, and yawn for bedtime.

Yesterday Bob and I walked home; it came on a very creditable thunderstorm; we were soon wet through; sometimes the rain was so heavy that one could only see by holding the hand over the eyes; and to crown all, we lost our way and wandered all over the place, and into the artillery range, among broken trees, with big shot lying about among the rocks. It was near dinner-time when we got to Barbizon; and it is supposed that we walked from twenty-three to twenty-five miles, which is not bad for the Advocate, who is not tired this morning. I was very glad to be back again in this dear place, and smell the wet forest in the morning.

Simpson and the rest drove back in a carriage, and got about as wet as we did.

Why don't you write? I have no more to say.—Ever your affectionate son,

ROBERT LOUIS STEVENSON.

TO MRS. SITWELL

At this time Stevenson was much occupied, as were several young writers his contemporaries, with imitating the artificial forms of early French verse. None of his attempts, I believe, have been preserved, except the two contained in this letter. The second is of course a translation.

Château Renard, Loiret, August 1875.

... I HAVE been walking these last days from place to place; and it does make it hot for walking with a sack in this weather. I am burned in horrid patches of red; my nose, I fear, is going to take the lead in colour; Simpson is all flushed, as if he were seen by a sunset. I send you here two rondeaux; I don't suppose they will amuse anybody but me; but this measure, short and yet intricate, is just what I desire; and I have had some good times walking along the glaring roads, or down the poplar alley of the great canal, pitting my own humour to this old verse.

Far have you come, my lady, from the town,
And far from all your sorrows, if you please,
To smell the good sea-winds and hear the seas,
And in green meadows lay your body down.

To find your pale face grow from pale to brown,
Your sad eyes growing brighter by degrees;
Far have you come, my lady, from the town,
And far from all your sorrows, if you please.

Here in this seaboard land of old renown,
In meadow grass go wading to the knees;
Bathe your whole soul a while in simple ease;
There is no sorrow but the sea can drown;
Far have you come, my lady, from the town.

Nous n'irons plus au bois.

We'll walk the woods no more,
But stay beside the fire,
To weep for old desire
And things that are no more.

1875.
AET. 25.

>The woods are spoiled and hoar,
>The ways are full of mire;
>We'll walk the woods no more,
>But stay beside the fire.
>We loved, in days of yore,
>Love, laughter, and the lyre.
>Ah God, but death is dire,
>And death is at the door—
>We'll walk the woods no more.
>
>ROBERT LOUIS STEVENSON.

TO SIDNEY COLVIN

The 'Burns' herein mentioned is an article undertaken in the early summer of the same year for the *Encyclopædia Britannica*. In the end Stevenson's work was thought to convey a view of the poet too frankly critical, and too little in accordance with the accepted Scotch tradition; and the publishers, duly paying him for his labours, transferred the task to Professor Shairp. The volume here announced on the three Scottish eighteenth-century poets unfortunately never came into being. The 'Charles of Orleans' essay appeared in the *Cornhill Magazine* for December of the following year; that on Villon (with the story on the same theme, 'A Lodging for the Night') not until the autumn of 1887. The essay on Béranger referred to at the end of the letter was one commissioned and used by the editor of the *Encyclopædia*; that on 'Spring' was a prose poem, of which the manuscript, sent to me at Cambridge, was unluckily lost in the confusion of a change of rooms.

Edinburgh, [*Autumn*] 1875.

MY DEAR COLVIN,—Thanks for your letter and news. No—my *Burns* is not done yet, it has led me so far afield that I cannot finish it; every time I think I see my way to an end, some new game (or perhaps wild goose) starts up, and away I go. And then, again, to be plain, I shirk the work of the critical part, shirk it as a man shirks a long jump. It is awful to have to express and differentiate *Burns* in a column or two. O golly, I say, you know, it *can't* be done at the money. All the more as I'm going to write a book about it. *Ramsay, Fergusson,* and *Burns: an Essay* (or *a critical essay*? but then I'm going to give lives of the three gentlemen, only the gist of the book is the criticism) *by Robert Louis Stevenson, Advocate.* How's that for cut and dry? And I *could* write this book. Unless I deceive myself, I could even write it pretty adequately. I feel as if I was really in it, and knew the game thoroughly. You see what comes of trying to write an essay on *Burns* in ten columns.

1875.
AET. 25.

Meantime, when I have done Burns, I shall finish Charles of Orleans (who is in a good way, about the fifth month, I should think, and promises to be a fine healthy child, better than any of his elder brothers for a while); and then perhaps a Villon, for Villon is a very essential part of my *Ramsay-Fergusson-Burns*; I mean, is a note in it, and will recur again and again for comparison and illustration; then, perhaps, I may try Fontainebleau, by the way. But so soon as Charles of Orleans is polished off, and immortalised for ever, he and his pipings, in a solid imperishable shrine of R. L. S., my true aim and end will be this little book. Suppose I could jerk you out 100 Cornhill pages; that would easy make 200 pages of decent form; and then thickish paper—eh? would that do? I dare say it could be made bigger; but I know what 100 pages of copy, bright consummate copy, imply behind the scenes of weary manuscribing; I think if I put another nothing to it, I should not be outside the mark; and 100 Cornhill pages of 500 words means, I fancy (but I never was good at figures), means 500,000 words. There's a prospect for an idle young gentleman who lives at home at ease! The future is thick with inky fingers. And then perhaps nobody would publish. *Ah nom de dieu !* What do you think of all this? will it paddle, think you?

I hope this pen will write; it is the third I have tried.

About coming up, no, that's impossible; for I am worse than a bankrupt. I have at the present six shillings and a penny; I have a sounding lot of bills for Christmas; new dress suit, for instance, the old one having gone for Parliament House; and new white shirts to live up to my new profession; I'm as gay and swell and gummy as can be; only all my boots leak; one pair water, and the other two simple black mud; so that my rig is more for the eye, than a very solid comfort to myself. That is my budget. Dismal enough, and no prospect of any coin coming in; at least for months. So that here I am, I almost fear, for the winter; certainly till after Christmas, and then it depends on how my bills 'turn out' whether it shall not be till spring. So, meantime, I must whistle in my cage. My cage is better by one thing; I am an Advocate now. If you ask me why that makes it better, I would remind you that in the most distressing circumstances a little consequence goes a long way, and even bereaved relatives stand on precedence round the coffin. I idle finely. I read Boswell's *Life of Johnson*, Martin's *History of France*, *Allan Ramsay*, *Olivier Bosselin*, all sorts of rubbish *àpropos* of *Burns*, *Commines*, *Juvénal des Ursins*, etc. I walk about the Parliament House five forenoons a week, in wig and gown; I have either a five or six mile walk, or an hour or two hard skating on the rink, every afternoon, without fail.

I have not written much; but, like the seaman's parrot in the tale, I have thought a deal. You have never, by the way, returned me either *Spring* or *Béranger*, which is certainly a d—d shame. I always comforted myself with that when my conscience pricked me about a letter to you. 'Thus conscience'—O no, that's not appropriate in this connection.—Ever yours,

                        ROBERT LOUIS STEVENSON.

I say, is there any chance of your coming north this year? Mind you that promise is now more respectable for age than is becoming.   R. L. S.

TO CHARLES BAXTER

1875.
AET. 25.

The following epistle in verse, with its mixed flavour of Burns and Horace, gives a lively picture of winter forenoons spent in the Parliament House:—

[*Edinburgh, October* 1875.]

Noo lyart leaves blaw ower the green,
Red are the bonny woods o' Dean,
An' here we're back in Embro, freen',
    To pass the winter.
Whilk noo, wi' frosts afore, draws in,
    An' snaws ahint her.

I've seen 's hae days to fricht us a',
The Pentlands poothered weel wi' snaw,
The ways half-smoored wi' liquid thaw,
    An' half-congealin',
The snell an' scowtherin' norther blaw
    Frae blae Brunteelan'.

I've seen 's been unco sweir to sally,
And at the door-cheeks daff an' dally
Seen 's daidle thus an' shilly-shally
    For near a minute—
Sae cauld the wind blew up the valley,
    The deil was in it!—

Syne spread the silk an' tak the gate,
In blast an' blaudin' rain, deil hae't!
The hale toon glintin', stane an' slate,
    Wi' cauld an' weet,
An' to the Court, gin we'se be late,
    Bicker oor feet.

And at the Court, tae, aft I saw
Whaur Advocates by twa an' twa
Gang gesterin' end to end the ha'
    In weeg an' goon,
To crack o' what ye wull but Law
    The hale forenoon.

That muckle ha,' maist like a kirk,
I've kent at braid mid-day sae mirk
Ye'd seen white weegs an' faces lurk
    Like ghaists frae Hell,
But whether Christian ghaists or Turk
    Deil ane could tell.

The three fires lunted in the gloom,
The wind blew like the blast o' doom,
The rain upo' the roof abune
    Played Peter Dick—
Ye wad nae'd licht enough i' the room
    Your teeth to pick!

But, freend, ye ken how me an' you,
The ling-lang lanely winter through,
Keep'd a guid speerit up, an' true
    To lore Horatian,
We aye the ither bottle drew
    To inclination.

Sae let us in the comin' days
Stand sicker on our aunceint ways—
The strauchtest road in a' the maze
    Since Eve ate apples;
An' let the winter weet our cla'es—
    We'll weet oor thrapples.

TO SIDNEY COLVIN

This recurs to the lost MS. of the essay on 'Spring.' 'P.P.P.'s' are *petits poëmes en prose*, attempts in the form, though not in the spirit, of Baudelaire.

[Edinburgh, Autumn 1875.]

MY DEAR COLVIN,—*Fous ne me gombrennez pas.* Angry with you? No. Is the thing lost? Well, so be it. There is one masterpiece fewer in the world. The world can ill spare it, but I, sir, I (and here I strike my hollow bosom so that it resounds) I am full of this sort of bauble; I am made of it; it comes to me, sir, as the desire to sneeze comes upon poor ordinary devils on cold days, when they should be getting out of bed and into their horrid cold tubs by the light of a seven o'clock candle, with the dismal seven o'clock frost-flowers all over the window.

Show Stephen what you please; if you could show him how to give me money, you would oblige, sincerely yours, R. L. S.

I have a scroll of *Springtime* somewhere, but I know that it is not in very good order, and do not feel myself up to very much grind over it. I am damped about *Springtime,* that's the truth of it. It might have been four or five quid!

Sir, I shall shave my head, if this goes on. All men take a pleasure to gird at me. The laws of nature are in open war with me. The wheel of a dog-cart took the toes off my new boots. Gout has set in with extreme rigour, and cut me out of the cheap refreshment of beer. I leant my back against an oak, I thought it was a trusty tree, but first it bent, and syne—it lost the Spirit of Springtime, and so did Professor Sidney Colvin, Trinity College, to me.—Ever yours,

ROBERT LOUIS STEVENSON.

Along with this, I send you some P.P.P's; if you lose them, you need not seek to look upon my face again. Do, for God's sake, answer me about them also; it is a horrid thing for a fond architect to find his monuments received in silence.—Yours, R. L. S.

TO MRS. SITWELL

[Edinburgh, November 12, 1875.]

MY DEAR FRIEND,—Since I got your letter I have been able to do a little more work, and I have been much better contented with myself; but I can't get away, that is absolutely prevented by the state of my purse and my debts, which, I may say, are red like crimson. I don't know how I am to clear my hands of them, nor when, not before Christmas anyway. Yesterday I was twenty-five; so please wish me many happy returns—directly. This one was not *un*happy anyway. I have got back a good deal into my old random, little-thought way of life, and do not care whether I read, write, speak, or walk, so long as I do something. I have a great delight in this wheel-skating; I have made great advance in it of late, can do a good many amusing things (I mean amusing in *my* sense—amusing to do). You know, I lose all my forenoons at Court! So it is, but the time passes; it is a great pleasure to sit and hear cases argued or advised. This is quite autobiographical, but I feel as if it was some time since we met, and I can tell you, I am glad to meet you again. In every way, you see, but that of work the world goes well with me. My health is better than ever it was before; I get on without any jar, nay, as if there never had been a jar, with my parents. If it weren't about that work, I'd be happy. But the fact is, I don't think—the fact is, I'm going to trust in Providence about work. If I could get one or two pieces I hate out of my way all would be well, I think; but these obstacles disgust me, and as I know I ought to do them first, I don't do anything. I must finish this off, or I'll just lose another day. I'll try to write again soon.—Ever your faithful friend, R. L. S.

TO MRS. DE MATTOS

In the following letter to a favourite cousin Stevenson unbosoms himself of one of the moods of depression to which he was sometimes subject in Edinburgh winters:—

Edinburgh, January 1876.

MY DEAR KATHARINE,—The prisoner reserved his defence. He has been seedy, however; principally sick of the family evil, despondency; the sun is gone out utterly; and the breath of the people of this city lies about as a sort of damp, unwholesome fog, in which we go walking with bowed hearts. If I understand what is a contrite spirit, I have one; it is to feel that you are a small jar, or rather, as I feel myself, a very large jar, of pottery work rather *mal réussi*, and to make every allowance for the potter (I beg pardon; Potter with a capital P.) on his ill-success, and rather wish he would reduce you as soon as possible to potsherds. However, there are many things to do yet before we go

> *Grossir la pâte universelle*
> *Faite des formes que Dieu fond.*

For instance, I have never been in a revolution yet. I pray God I may be in one at the end, if I am to make a mucker. The best way to make a mucker is to have your back set against a wall and a few lead pellets whiffed into you in a moment, while yet you are all in a heat and a fury of combat, with drums sounding on all sides, and people crying, and a general smash like the infernal orchestration at the end of the *Huguenots*. . . .

Please pardon me for having been so long of writing, and show your pardon by writing soon to me; it will be a kindness, for I am sometimes very dull. Edinburgh is much changed for the worse by the absence of Bob; and this damned weather weighs on me like a curse. Yesterday, or the day before, there came so black a rain squall that I was frightened—what a child would call frightened, you know, for want of a better word—although in reality it has nothing to do with fright. I lit the gas and sat cowering in my chair until it went away again.—Ever yours, R. L. S.

O I am trying my hand at a novel just now; it may interest you to know, I am bound to say I do not think it will be a success. However, it's an amusement for the

VOL. I.—H

moment, and work, work is your only ally against the 'bearded people' that squat upon their hams in the dark places of life and embrace people horribly as they go by. God save us from the bearded people! to think that the sun is still shining in some happy places!   R. L. S.

To Mrs Sitwell

[Edinburgh, January 1876.]

... OUR weather continues as it was, bitterly cold, and raining often. There is not much pleasure in life certainly as it stands at present. *Nous n'irons plus au bois, hélas!*

I meant to write some more last night, but my father was ill and it put it out of my way. He is better this morning.

If I had written last night, I should have written a lot. But this morning I am so dreadfully tired and stupid that I can say nothing. I was down at Leith in the afternoon. God bless me, what horrid women I saw; I never knew what a plain-looking race it was before. I was sick at heart with the looks of them. And the children, filthy and ragged! And the smells! And the fat black mud!

My soul was full of disgust ere I got back. And yet the ships were beautiful to see, as they are always; and on the pier there was a clean cold wind that smelt a little of the sea, though it came down the Firth, and the sunset had a certain *éclat* and warmth. Perhaps if I could get more work done, I should be in a better trim to enjoy filthy streets and people and cold grim weather; but I don't much feel as if it was what I would have chosen. I am tempted every day of my life to go off on another walking tour. I like that better than anything else that I know.—Ever your faithful friend,

ROBERT LOUIS STEVENSON.

To Sidney Colvin

1876.
AET. 26.

'Fontainebleau' is the paper called 'Forest Notes' which appeared in the *Cornhill Magazine* in May of this year (reprinted Edinburgh edition *Miscellanies*, vol. iv.). The 'Winter's Walk,' as far as it goes one of the most charming of his essays of the *Road*, was for some reason never finished; it was first printed from the MS. in the Edinburgh edition *Miscellanies*, vol. iv.

[Edinburgh, February 1876.]

MY DEAR COLVIN,—1*st.* I have sent 'Fontainebleau' long ago, long ago. And Leslie Stephen is worse than tepid about it—liked 'some parts' of it 'very well,' the son of Belial. Moreover, he proposes to shorten it; and I, who want *money*, and money soon, and not glory and the illustration of the English language, I feel as if my poverty were going to consent.

2*nd.* I'm as fit as a fiddle after my walk. I am four inches bigger about the waist than last July! There, that's your prophecy did that. I am on 'Charles of Orleans' now, but I don't know where to send him. Stephen obviously spews me out of his mouth, and I spew him out of mine, so help me! A man who doesn't like my 'Fontainebleau'! His head must be turned.

3*rd.* If ever you do come across my 'Spring' (I beg your pardon for referring to it again, but I don't want you to forget) send it off at once.

4*th.* I went to Ayr, Maybole, Girvan, Ballantrae, Stranraer, Glenluce, and Wigton. I shall make an article of it some day soon, 'A Winter's Walk in Carrick and Galloway.' I had a good time.—Yours,   R. L. S.

To Sidney Colvin

'Baynes' in the following is Stevenson's good friend and mine, the late Professor Spencer Baynes, who was just relinquishing the editorship of the *Encyclopædia Britannica* by reason of ill health.

[Swanston Cottage, Lothianburn, July 1876.]

HERE I am, here, and very well too. I am glad you liked 'Walking Tours'; I like it, too; I think it's prose;

1876.
AET. 26.

and I own with contrition that I have not always written prose. However, I am 'endeavouring after new obedience' (Scot. Shorter Catechism). You don't say aught of 'Forest Notes,' which is kind. There is one, if you will, that was too sweet to be wholesome.

I am at 'Charles d'Orléans.' About fifteen *Cornhill* pages have already coulé'd from under my facile plume—no, I mean eleven, fifteen of MS.—and we are not much more than half-way through, 'Charles' and I; but he's a pleasant companion. My health is very well; I am in a fine exercisy state. Baynes is gone to London; if you see him, inquire about my 'Burns.' They have sent me £5, 5s. for it, which has mollified me horrid. £5, 5s. is a good deal to pay for a read of it in MS.; I can't complain.—Yours, R. L. S.

TO MRS. SITWELL

This dates from just before the canoeing trip recounted in the *Inland Voyage*.

[*Swanston Cottage, Lothianburn, July* 1876.]

... I HAVE the strangest repugnance for writing; indeed, I have nearly got myself persuaded into the notion that letters don't arrive, in order to salve my conscience for never sending them off. I'm reading a great deal of fifteenth century: *Trial of Joan of Arc, Paston Letters, Basin*, etc., also *Boswell* daily by way of a Bible; I mean to read *Boswell* now until the day I die. And now and again a bit of *Pilgrim's Progress*. Is that all? Yes, I think that's all. I have a thing in proof for the *Cornhill* called *Virginibus Puerisque*. 'Charles of Orleans' is again laid aside, but in a good state of furtherance this time. A paper called 'A Defence of Idlers' (which is really a defence of R. L. S.) is in a good way. So, you see, I am busy in a tumultuous, knotless sort of fashion; and as I say, I take lots of exercise, and I'm as brown as a berry.

This is the first letter I've written for—O I don't know how long.

July 30th.—This is, I suppose, three weeks after I began. Do, please, forgive me.

To the Highlands, first, to the Jenkins', then to Antwerp; thence, by canoe with Simpson, to Paris and Grez (on the Loing, and an old acquaintance of mine on the skirts of Fontainebleau) to complete our cruise next spring (if we're all alive and jolly) by Loing and Loire, Saone and Rhone to the Mediterranean. It should make a jolly book of gossip, I imagine.

God bless you. ROBERT LOUIS STEVENSON.

P.S.—Virginibus Puerisque is in August *Cornhill.* 'Charles of Orleans' is finished, and sent to Stephen; 'Idlers' ditto, and sent to Grove; but I've no word of either. So I've not been idle. R. L. S.

TO W. E. HENLEY

In a well-known passage of the *Inland Voyage* the following incident is related to the same purport, but in another style:—

Chauny, Aisne [September 1876].

MY DEAR HENLEY,—Here I am, you see; and if you will take to a map, you will observe I am already more than two doors from Antwerp, whence I started. I have fought it through under the worst weather I ever saw in France; I have been wet through nearly every day of travel since the second (inclusive); besides this, I have had to fight against pretty mouldy health; so that, on the whole, the essayist and reviewer has shown, I think, some pluck. Four days ago I was not a hundred miles from being miserably drowned, to the immense regret of a large circle of friends and the permanent impoverishment of British Essayism and Reviewery. My boat culbutted me under a fallen tree in a very rapid current; and I was a good while before I got on to the outside of that fallen

1877.
AET. 27.

tree; rather a better while than I cared about. When I got up, I lay some time on my belly, panting, and exuded fluid. All my symptoms *jusqu' ici* are trifling. But I've a damned sore throat.—Yours ever, R. L. S.

TO MRS. SITWELL

The 'Hair Trunk' still exists in MS. It contains some tolerable fooling, but is chiefly interesting from the fact that the seat of the proposed Bohemian colony from Cambridge is to be in the Navigator Islands; showing the direction which had been given to Stevenson's thoughts by the conversation of the New Zealand Premier, Mr. Seed, two years before.

17 *Heriot Row, Edinburgh, May* 1877.

... A PERFECT chorus of repudiation is sounding in my ears; and although you say nothing, I know you must be repudiating me, all the same. Write I cannot—there's no good mincing matters, a letter frightens me worse than the devil; and I am just as unfit for correspondence as if I had never learned the three R.'s.

Let me give my news quickly before I relapse into my usual idleness. I have a terror lest I should relapse before I get this finished. Courage, R. L. S.! On Leslie Stephen's advice, I gave up the idea of a book of essays. He said he didn't imagine I was rich enough for such an amusement; and moreover, whatever was worth publication was worth republication. So the best of those I had ready: 'An Apology for Idlers' is in proof for the *Cornhill*. I have 'Villon' to do for the same magazine, but God knows when I'll get it done, for drums, trumpets—I'm engaged upon—trumpets, drums—a novel! 'THE HAIR TRUNK; OR, THE IDEAL COMMONWEALTH.' It is a most absurd story of a lot of young Cambridge fellows who are going to found a new society, with no ideas on the subject, and nothing but Bohemian tastes in the place of ideas; and who are—well, I can't explain about the trunk—it would take too long—but the trunk is the fun of it—everybody steals it; burglary, marine fight, life on desert island on west coast of Scotland, sloops, etc. The first scene where they make their grand schemes and get drunk is supposed to be very funny, by Henley. I really saw him laugh over it until he cried.

Please write to me, although I deserve it so little, and show a Christian spirit.—Ever your faithful friend,
ROBERT LOUIS STEVENSON.

TO SIDNEY COLVIN

[*Edinburgh, August* 1877.]

MY DEAR COLVIN,—I'm to be whipped away to-morrow to Penzance, where at the post-office a letter will find me glad and grateful. I am well, but somewhat tired out with overwork. I have only been home a fortnight this morning, and I have already written to the tune of forty-five *Cornhill* pages and upwards. The most of it was only very laborious re-casting and re-modelling, it is true; but it took it out of me famously, all the same.

Temple Bar appears to like my 'Villon,' so I may count on another market there in the future, I hope. At least, I am going to put it to the proof at once, and send another story, 'The Sire de Malétroit's Mousetrap': a true novel, in the old sense; all unities preserved moreover, if that's anything, and I believe with some little merits; not so *clever* perhaps as the last, but sounder and more natural.

My 'Villon' is out this month; I should so much like to know what you think of it. Stephen has written to me apropos of 'Idlers,' that something more in that vein would be agreeable to his views. From Stephen I count that a devil of a lot.

I am honestly so tired this morning that I hope you will take this for what it's worth and give me an answer in peace.—Ever yours, LOUIS STEVENSON.

1877.
AET. 27.

TO MRS. SITWELL

[*Penzance, August* 1877.]

... You will do well to stick to your burn, that is a delightful life you sketch, and a very fountain of health. I wish I could live like that, but, alas! it is just as well I got my 'Idlers' written and done with, for I have quite lost all power of resting. I have a goad in my flesh continually, pushing me to work, work, work. I have an essay pretty well through for Stephen; a story, 'The Sire de Malétroit's Mousetrap,' with which I shall try *Temple Bar*; another story, in the clouds, 'The Stepfather's Story,' most pathetic work of a high morality or immorality, according to point of view; and lastly, also in the clouds, or perhaps a little farther away, an essay on the 'Two St. Michael's Mounts,' historical and picturesque; perhaps if it didn't come too long, I might throw in the 'Bass Rock,' and call it 'Three Sea Fortalices,' or something of that kind. You see how work keeps bubbling in my mind. Then I shall do another fifteenth century paper this autumn—La Sale and *Petit Jehan de Saintré*, which is a kind of fifteenth century *Sandford and Merton*, ending in horrid immoral cynicism, as if the author had got tired of being didactic, and just had a good wallow in the mire to wind up with and indemnify himself for so much restraint.

Cornwall is not much to my taste, being as bleak as the bleakest parts of Scotland, and nothing like so pointed and characteristic. It has a flavour of its own, though, which I may try and catch, if I find the space, in the proposed article. 'Will o' the Mill' I sent, red hot, to Stephen in a fit of haste, and have not yet had an answer. I am quite prepared for a refusal. But I begin to have more hope in the story line, and that should improve my income anyway. I am glad you liked 'Villon'; some of it was not as good as it ought to be, but on the whole it seems pretty vivid, and the features strongly marked. Vividness and not style is now my line; style is all very well, but vividness is the real line of country; if a thing is meant to be read, it seems just as well to try and make it readable. I am such a dull person now, I cannot keep off my own immortal works. Indeed, they are scarcely ever out of my head. And yet I value them less and less every day. But occupation is the great thing; so that a man should have his life in his own pocket, and never be thrown out of work by anything. I am glad to hear you are better. I must stop—going to Land's End.—Always your faithful friend,

1877.
AET. 27.

ROBERT LOUIS STEVENSON.

TO A. PATCHETT MARTIN

This correspondent, living at the time in Australia, was, I believe, the first to write and seek Stevenson's acquaintance from admiration of his work, meaning especially the *Cornhill* essays of the *Virginibus Puerisque* series so far as they had yet appeared. The 'present' herein referred to is Mr. Martin's volume called *A Sweet Girl Graduate and other Poems*, Melbourne, 1876.

[1877.]

DEAR SIR,—It would not be very easy for me to give you any idea of the pleasure I found in your present. People who write for the magazines (probably from a guilty conscience) are apt to suppose their works practically unpublished. It seems unlikely that any one would take the trouble to read a little paper buried among so many others; and reading it, read it with any attention or pleasure. And so, I can assure you, your little book, coming from so far, gave me all the pleasure and encouragement in the world.

I suppose you know and remember Charles Lamb's essay on distant correspondents? Well, I was somewhat of his way of thinking about my mild productions. I did not indeed imagine they were read, and (I suppose I may say) enjoyed right round upon the other side of the

1877.
AET. 27.

big Football we have the honour to inhabit. And as your present was the first sign to the contrary, I feel I have been very ungrateful in not writing earlier to acknowledge the receipt. I dare say, however, you hate writing letters as much as I can do myself (for if you like my article, I may presume other points of sympathy between us); and on this hypothesis you will be ready to forgive me the delay.

I may mention with regard to the piece of verses called 'Such is Life,' that I am not the only one on this side of the Football aforesaid to think it a good and bright piece of work, and recognised a link of sympathy with the poets who 'play in hostelries at euchre.'—Believe me, dear sir, yours truly, R. L. S.

TO A. PATCHETT MARTIN

17 *Heriot Row, Edinburgh* [*December* 1877].

MY DEAR SIR,—I am afraid you must already have condemned me for a very idle fellow truly. Here it is more than two months since I received your letter; I had no fewer than three journals to acknowledge; and never a sign upon my part. If you have seen a *Cornhill* paper of mine upon idling, you will be inclined to set it all down to that. But you will not be doing me justice. Indeed, I have had a summer so troubled that I have had little leisure and still less inclination to write letters. I was keeping the devil at bay with all my disposable activities; and more than once I thought he had me by the throat. The odd conditions of our acquaintance enable me to say more to you than I would to a person who lived at my elbow. And besides, I am too much pleased and flattered at our correspondence not to go as far as I can to set myself right in your eyes.

In this damnable confusion (I beg pardon) I have lost all my possessions, or near about, and quite lost all my wits. I wish I could lay my hands on the numbers of the

Review, for I know I wished to say something on that head more particularly than I can from memory; but where they have escaped to, only time or chance can show. However, I can tell you so far, that I was very much pleased with the article on Bret Harte; it seemed to me just, clear, and to the point. I agreed pretty well with all you said about George Eliot: a high, but, may we not add?—a rather dry lady. Did you—I forget—did you have a kick at the stern works of that melancholy puppy and humbug Daniel Deronda himself?—the Prince of Prigs; the literary abomination of desolation in the way of manhood; a type which is enough to make a man forswear the love of women, if that is how it must be gained. ... Hats off all the same, you understand: a woman of genius.

Of your poems I have myself a kindness for 'Noll and Nell,' although I don't think you have made it as good as you ought: verse five is surely not *quite melodious*. I confess I like the Sonnet in the last number of the *Review*— the Sonnet to England.

Please, if you have not, and I don't suppose you have, already read it, institute a search in all Melbourne for one of the rarest and certainly one of the best of books— *Clarissa Harlowe*. For any man who takes an interest in the problems of the two sexes, that book is a perfect mine of documents. And it is written, sir, with the pen of an angel. Miss Howe and Lovelace, words cannot tell how good they are! And the scene where Clarissa beards her family, with her fan going all the while; and some of the quarrel scenes between her and Lovelace; and the scene where Colonel Marden goes to Mr. Hall, with Lord M. trying to compose matters, and the Colonel with his eternal 'finest woman in the world,' and the inimitable affirmation of Mowbray — nothing, nothing could be better! You will bless me when you read it for this recommendation; but, indeed, I can do nothing but recommend Clarissa. I am like that Frenchman of the

1877.
AET. 27.

eighteenth century who discovered Habakkuk, and would give no one peace about that respectable Hebrew. For my part, I never was able to get over his eminently respectable name; Isaiah is the boy, if you must have a prophet, no less. About Clarissa, I meditate a choice work: *A Dialogue on Man, Woman, and 'Clarissa Harlowe.'* It is to be so clever that no array of terms can give you any idea; and very likely that particular array in which I shall finally embody it, less than any other.

Do you know, my dear sir, what I like best in your letter? The egotism for which you thought necessary to apologise. I am a rogue at egotism myself; and to be plain, I have rarely or never liked any man who was not. The first step to discovering the beauties of God's universe is usually a (perhaps partial) apprehension of such of them as adorn our own characters. When I see a man who does not think pretty well of himself, I always suspect him of being in the right. And besides, if he does not like himself, whom he has seen, how is he ever to like one whom he never can see but in dim and artificial presentments?

I cordially reciprocate your offer of a welcome; it shall be at least a warm one. Are you not my first, my only, admirer—a dear tie? Besides, you are a man of sense, and you treat me as one by writing to me as you do, and that gives me pleasure also. Please continue to let me see your work. I have one or two things coming out in the *Cornhill*: a story called 'The Sire de Malétroit's Door' in *Temple Bar*; and a series of articles on Edinburgh in the *Portfolio*; but I don't know if these last fly all the way to Melbourne.—Yours very truly,

ROBERT LOUIS STEVENSON.

TO SIDNEY COLVIN

The *Inland Voyage*, it must be remembered, at this time just put into the publisher's hands, was the author's first book. The 'Crane sketch' mentioned in the second of the following notes to me was the well-known frontispiece to that book on which Mr. Walter Crane was then at work. The essay on 'Pan's Pipes,' reprinted in *Virginibus Puerisque*, was written about this time:—

Hôtel des Etrangers, Dieppe, January 1, 1878.

MY DEAR COLVIN,—I am at the *Inland Voyage* again: have finished another section, and have only two more to execute. But one at least of these will be very long—the longest in the book—being a great digression on French artistic tramps. I only hope Paul may take the thing; I want coin so badly, and besides it would be something done —something put outside of me and off my conscience; and I should not feel such a muff as I do, if once I saw the thing in boards with a ticket on its back. I think I shall frequent circulating libraries a good deal. The Preface shall stand over, as you suggest, until the last, and then, sir, we shall see. This to be read with a big voice.

This is New Year's Day: let me, my dear Colvin, wish you a very good year, free of all misunderstanding and bereavement, and full of good weather and good work. You know best what you have done for me, and so you will know best how heartily I mean this.—Ever yours,

ROBERT LOUIS STEVENSON.

TO SIDNEY COLVIN

[*Paris, January or February* 1878.]

MY DEAR COLVIN,—Many thanks for your letter. I was much interested by all the Edinburgh gossip. Most likely I shall arrive in London next week. I think you know all about the Crane sketch; but it should be a river, not a canal, you know, and the look should be 'cruel, lewd, and kindly,' all at once. There is more sense in that Greek myth of Pan than in any other that I recollect except the luminous Hebrew one of the Fall: one of the biggest things done. If people would remember that all religions are no more than representations of life, they would find them, as they are, the best representations, licking Shakespeare.

1878.
AET. 28.

What an inconceivable cheese is Alfred de Musset! His comedies are, to my view, the best work of France this century: a large order. Did you ever read them? They are real, clear, living work.—Ever yours,

R. L. S.

TO MR. AND MRS. THOMAS STEVENSON

Paris, 44 *Bd. Haussmann, Friday, February* 21, 1878.

MY DEAR PEOPLE,—Do you know who is my favourite author just now? How are the mighty fallen! Anthony Trollope. I batten on him; he is so nearly wearying you, and yet he never does; or rather, he never does, until he gets near the end, when he begins to wean you from him, so that you're as pleased to be done with him as you thought you would be sorry. I wonder if it's old age? It is a little, I am sure. A young person would get sickened by the dead level of meanness and cowardliness; you require to be a little spoiled and cynical before you can enjoy it. I have just finished the *Way of the World*; there is only one person in it—no, there are three—who are nice: the wild American woman, and two of the dissipated young men, Dolly and Lord Nidderdale. All the heroes and heroines are just ghastly. But what a triumph is Lady Carbury! That is real, sound, strong, genuine work: the man who could do that, if he had had courage, might have written a fine book; he has preferred to write many readable ones. I meant to write such a long, nice letter, but I cannot hold the pen. R. L. S.

TO MRS. THOMAS STEVENSON

The following refers to the newspaper criticisms on the *Inland Voyage*:—

Hotel du Val de Grâce, Rue St. Jacques,
Paris, Sunday [*June* 1878].

MY DEAR MOTHER,—About criticisms, I was more surprised at the tone of the critics than I suppose any one else. And the effect it has produced in me is one of shame. If they liked that so much, I ought to have given them something better, that's all. And I shall try to do so. Still, it strikes me as odd; and I don't understand the vogue. It should sell the thing.—Ever your affectionate son, ROBERT LOUIS STEVENSON.

1878.
AET. 28.

TO MRS. THOMAS STEVENSON
This and the two following letters tell of the preparations for the walking tour narrated in *Travels with a Donkey*.

Monastier, September 1878.

MY DEAR MOTHER,—You must not expect to hear much from me for the next two weeks; for I am near starting. Donkey purchased—a love—price, 65 francs and a glass of brandy. My route is all pretty well laid out; I shall go near no town till I get to Alais. Remember, Poste Restante, Alais, Gard. Greyfriars will be in October. You did not say whether you liked September; you might tell me that at Alais. The other No.'s of Edinburgh are: Parliament Close, Villa Quarters (which perhaps may not appear), Calton Hill, Winter and New Year, and to the Pentland Hills. 'Tis a kind of book nobody would ever care to read; but none of the young men could have done it better than I have, which is always a consolation. I read *Inland Voyage* the other day: what rubbish these reviewers did talk! It is not badly written, thin, mildly cheery, and strained. *Selon moi.* I mean to visit Hamerton on my return journey; otherwise, I should come by sea from Marseilles. I am very well known here now; indeed, quite a feature of the place. —Your affectionate son, R. L. S.

The Engineer is the Conductor of Roads and Bridges; then I have the Receiver of Registrations, the First Clerk of Excise, and the Perceiver of the Impost. That is our dinner party. I am a sort of hovering government official, as you see. But away—away from these great companions!

TO W. E. HENLEY

[*Monastier, September* 1878.]

DEAR HENLEY,—I hope to leave Monastier this day (Saturday) week; thenceforward Poste Restante, Alais, Gard, is my address. 'Travels with a Donkey in the French Highlands.' I am no good to-day. I cannot work, nor even write letters. A colossal breakfast yesterday at Puy has, I think, done for me for ever; I certainly ate more than ever I ate before in my life—a big slice of melon, some ham and jelly, a *filet*, a helping of gudgeons, the breast and leg of a partridge, some green peas, eight crayfish, some Mont d'Or cheese, a peach, and a handful of biscuits, macaroons, and things. It sounds Gargantuan; it cost three francs a head. So that it was inexpensive to the pocket, although I fear it may prove extravagant to the fleshly tabernacle. I can't think how I did it or why. It is a new form of excess for me; but I think it pays less than any of them.   R. L. S.

TO CHARLES BAXTER

Monastier, at Morel's [*September* 1878].

Lud knows about date, *vide* postmark.

MY DEAR CHARLES,—Yours (with enclosures) of the 16th to hand. All work done. I go to Le Puy to-morrow to dispatch baggage, get cash, stand lunch to engineer, who has been very jolly and useful to me, and hope by five o'clock on Saturday morning to be driving Modestine towards the Gévaudan. Modestine is my ânesse; a darling, mouse-colour, about the size of a Newfoundland dog (bigger, between you and me), the colour of a mouse, costing 65 francs and a glass of brandy. Glad you sent on all the coin; was half afraid I might come to a stick in the mountains, donkey and all, which would have been the devil. Have finished *Arabian Nights* and Edinburgh book, and am a free man. Next address, Poste Restante,

Alais, Gard. Give my servilities to the family. Health bad; spirits, I think, looking up.—Ever yours,

R. L. S.

To Mrs. Thomas Stevenson

On his way home from the Cévennes country, Stevenson had paid a brief, but to both parties extremely pleasant, visit to the late Mr. P. G. Hamerton in his country home near Autun.

October 1878.

MY DEAR MOTHER,—I have seen Hamerton; he was very kind, all his family seemed pleased to see an *Inland Voyage*, and the book seemed to be quite a household word with them. P. G. himself promised to help me in my bargains with publishers, which, said he, and I doubt not very truthfully, he could manage to much greater advantage than I. He is also to read an *Inland Voyage* over again, and send me his cuts and cuffs in private, after having liberally administered his kisses *coram publico*. I liked him very much. Of all the pleasant parts of my profession, I think the spirit of other men of letters makes the pleasantest.

Do you know, your sunset was very good? The 'attack' (to speak learnedly) was so plucky and odd. I have thought of it repeatedly since. I have just made a delightful dinner by myself in the Café Félix, where I am an old established beggar, and am just smoking a cigar over my coffee. I came last night from Autun, and I am muddled about my plans. The world is such a dance!—Ever your affectionate son,

ROBERT LOUIS STEVENSON.

To W. E. Henley

Stevenson, hard at work upon *Providence and the Guitar* and *Travels with a Donkey*, was at this time occupying for a few days my rooms at Trinity in my absence. The college buildings and gardens, the ideal setting and careful tutelage of

1878. English academic life—in these respects so strongly contrasted
AET. 28. with the Scotch—affected him always with a sense of unreality.

[*Trinity College, Cambridge, Autumn* 1878.]

MY DEAR HENLEY,—Here I am living like a fighting-cock, and have not spoken to a real person for about sixty hours. Those who wait on me are not real. The man I know to be a myth, because I have seen him acting so often in the Palais Royal. He plays the Duke in *Tricoche et Cacolet*; I knew his nose at once. The part he plays here is very dull for him, but conscientious. As for the bedmaker, she's a dream, a kind of cheerful, innocent nightmare; I never saw so poor an imitation of humanity. I cannot work—*cannot*. Even the *Guitar* is still undone; I can only write ditch-water. 'Tis ghastly; but I am quite cheerful, and that is more important. Do you think you could prepare the printers for a possible breakdown this week? I shall try all I know on Monday; but if I can get nothing better than I got this morning, I prefer to drop a week. Telegraph to me if you think it necessary. I shall not leave till Wednesday at soonest. Shall write again.   R. L. S.

TO EDMUND GOSSE

The matter of the loan and its repayment, here touched on, comes up again in Stevenson's last letter of all, that which closes the book. Stevenson and Mr. Gosse had planned a joint book of old murder stories retold, and had been to visit the scene of one famous murder together.

[17 *Heriot Row, Edinburgh, April* 16, 1879].
Pool of Siloam, by El Dorado,
Delectable Mountains, Arcadia.

MY DEAR GOSSE,—Herewith of the dibbs—a homely fiver. How, and why, do you continue to exist? I do so ill, but for a variety of reasons. First, I wait an angel to come down and trouble the waters; second, more angels; third—well, more angels. The waters are sluggish; the angels—well, the angels won't come, that's about all. But I sit waiting and waiting, and people bring me meals, which help to pass time (I'm sure it's very kind of them), and sometimes I whistle to myself; and as there's a very pretty echo at my pool of Siloam, the thing's agreeable to hear. The sun continues to rise every day, to my growing wonder. 'The moon by night thee shall not smite.' And the stars are all doing as well as can be expected. The air of Arcady is very brisk and pure, and we command many enchanting prospects in space and time. I do not yet know much about my situation; for, to tell the truth, I only came here by the run since I began to write this letter; I had to go back to date it; and I am grateful to you for having been the occasion of this little outing. What good travellers we are, if we had only faith; no man need stay in Edinburgh but by unbelief; my religious organ has been ailing for a while past, and I have lain a great deal in Edinburgh, a sheer hulk in consequence. But I got out my wings, and have taken a change of air.

I read your book with great interest, and ought long ago to have told you so. An ordinary man would say that he had been waiting till he could pay his debts. . . . The book is good reading. Your personal notes of those you saw struck me as perhaps most sharp and 'best held.' See as many people as you can, and make a book of them before you die. That will be a living book, upon my word. You have the touch required. I ask you to put hands to it in private already. Think of what Carlyle's caricature of old Coleridge is to us who never saw S. T. C. With that and Kubla Khan, we have the man in the fact. Carlyle's picture, of course, is not of the author of *Kubla*, but of the author of that surprising *Friend* which has knocked the breath out of two generations of hopeful youth. Your portraits would be milder, sweeter, more true perhaps, and perhaps not so truth-*telling*—if you will take my meaning.

I have to thank you for an introduction to that beautiful

1879.
AET. 29.
—no, that's not the word—that jolly, with an Arcadian jollity—thing of Vogelweide's. Also for your preface. Some day I want to read a whole book in the same picked dialect as that preface. I think it must be one E. W. Gosse who must write it. He has got himself into a fix with me by writing the preface; I look for a great deal, and will not be easily pleased.

I never thought of it, but my new book, which should soon be out, contains a visit to a murder scene, but not done as we should like to see them, for, of course, I was running another hare.

If you do not answer this in four pages, I shall stop the enclosed fiver at the bank, a step which will lead to your incarceration for life. As my visits to Arcady are somewhat uncertain, you had better address 17 Heriot Row, Edinburgh, as usual. I shall walk over for the note if I am not yet home.—Believe me, very really yours,
ROBERT LOUIS STEVENSON.

I charge extra for a flourish when it is successful; this isn't, so you have it gratis. Is there any news in Babylon the Great? My fellow-creatures are electing school boards here in the midst of the ages. It is very composed of them. I can't think why they do it. Nor why I have written a real letter. If you write a real letter back, damme, I'll try to *correspond* with you. A thing unknown in this age. It is a consequence of the decay of faith; we cannot believe that the fellow will be at the pains to read us.

TO W. E. HENLEY

This is in reply to some technical criticisms of his correspondent on the poem 'Our Lady of the Snows,' referring to the Trappist monastery in the Cévennes so called, and afterwards published in *Underwoods*.

17 *Heriot Row, Edinburgh* [*April* 1879].

MY DEAR HENLEY,—Heavens! have I done the like? 'Clarify and strain,' indeed? 'Make it like Marvell,' no less. I'll tell you what—you may go to the devil; that's what I think. 'Be eloquent' is another of your pregnant suggestions. I cannot sufficiently thank you for that one. Portrait of a person about to be eloquent at the request of a literary friend. You seem to forget sir, that rhyme is rhyme, sir, and—go to the devil.

I'll try to improve it, but I shan't be able to—O go to the devil.

Seriously, you're a cool hand. And then you have the brass to ask me *why* 'my steps went one by one'? Why? Powers of man! to rhyme with *sun*, to be sure. Why else could it be? And you yourself have been a poet! G-r-r-r-r-r! I'll never be a poet any more. Men are so d—d ungrateful and captious, I declare I could weep.

> O Henley, in my hours of ease
> You may say anything you please,
> But when I join the Muse's revel,
> Begad, I wish you at the devil!
> In vain my verse I plane and bevel,
> Like Banville's rhyming devotees;
> In vain by many an artful swivel
> Lug in my meaning by degrees;
> I'm sure to hear my Henley cavil;
> And grovelling prostrate on my knees,
> Devote his body to the seas,
> His correspondence to the devil!

Impromptu poem.

I'm going to Shandon Hydropathic *cum parentibus*. Write here. I heard from Lang. Ferrier prayeth to be remembered; he means to write, likes his Tourgenieff greatly. Also likes my 'What was on the Slate,' which, under a new title, yet unfound, and with a new and, on the whole, kindly *dénouement*, is going to shoot up and become a star. . . .

I see I must write some more to you about my

1879.
AET. 29.

Monastery. I am a weak brother in verse. You ask me to re-write things that I have already managed just to write with the skin of my teeth. If I don't re-write them, it's because I don't see how to write them better, not because I don't think they should be. But, curiously enough, you condemn two of my favourite passages, one of which is J. W. Ferrier's favourite of the whole. Here I shall think it's you who are wrong. You see, I did not try to make good verse, but to say what I wanted as well as verse would let me. I don't like the rhyme 'ear' and 'hear.' But the couplet, 'My undissuaded heart I hear Whisper courage in my ear,' is exactly what I want for the thought, and to me seems very energetic as speech, if not as verse. Would 'daring' be better than 'courage'? *Je me le demande.* No, it would be ambiguous, as though I had used it licentiously for 'daringly,' and that would cloak the sense.

In short, your suggestions have broken the heart of the scald. He doesn't agree with them all; and those he does agree with, the spirit indeed is willing, but the d—d flesh cannot, cannot, cannot, see its way to profit by. I think I'll lay it by for nine years, like Horace. I think the well of Castaly's run out. No more the Muses round my pillow haunt. I am fallen once more to the mere proser. God bless you.   R. L. S.

TO EDMUND GOSSE

This letter is contemporary with the much debated Cornhill essay 'On some Aspects of Burns,' afterwards published in *Familiar Studies of Men and Books.*

Swanston, Lothianburn, Edinburgh, July 24, 1879.

MY DEAR GOSSE,—I have greatly enjoyed your article, which seems to me handsome in tone, and written like a fine old English gentleman. But is there not a hitch in the sentence at foot of page 153? I get lost in it.

Chapters VIII. and IX. of Meredith's story are very good, I think. But who wrote the review of my book? Whoever he was, he cannot write; he is humane, but a duffer; I could weep when I think of him; for surely to be virtuous and incompetent is a hard lot. I should prefer to be a bold pirate, the gay sailor-boy of immorality, and a publisher at once. My mind is extinct; my appetite is expiring; I have fallen altogether into a hollow-eyed, yawning way of life, like the parties in Burne Jones's pictures. . . . Talking of Burns. (Is this not sad, Weg? I use the term of reproach not because I am angry with you this time, but because I am angry with myself and desire to give pain.) Talking, I say, of Robert Burns, the inspired poet is a very gay subject for study. I made a kind of chronological table of his various loves and lusts, and have been comparatively speechless ever since. I am sorry to say it, but there was something in him of the vulgar, bagmanlike, professional seducer.—Oblige me by taking down and reading, for the hundredth time I hope, his 'Twa Dogs' and his 'Address to the Unco Guid.' I am only a Scotchman, after all, you see; and when I have beaten Burns, I am driven at once, by my parental feelings, to console him with a sugar-plum. But hang me if I know anything I like so well as the 'Twa Dogs.' Even a common Englishman may have a glimpse, as it were from Pisgah, of its extraordinary merits.

1879.
AET. 29.

'*English, The*:—a dull people, incapable of comprehending the Scottish tongue. Their history is so intimately connected with that of Scotland, that we must refer our readers to that heading. Their literature is principally the work of venal Scots.'—Stevenson's *Handy Cyclopædia*. Glescow: Blaikie & Bannock.

Remember me in suitable fashion to Mrs. Gosse, the offspring, and the cat.—And believe me ever yours,

ROBERT LOUIS STEVENSON.

1879.
AET. 29.

TO SIDNEY COLVIN

'Bummkopf' was Stevenson's name for the typical pedant, German or other, who cannot clear his edifice of its scaffolding, nor set forth the results of research without intruding on the reader all its processes, evidences, and supports. 'Burns' is the Cornhill Essay reprinted in *Familiar Studies*: not the rejected Encyclopædic article.

17 *Heriot Row, Edinburgh* [*July* 28, 1879].

MY DEAR COLVIN,—I am just in the middle of your Rembrandt. The taste for Bummkopf and his works is agreeably dissembled so far as I have gone; and the reins have never for an instant been thrown upon the neck of that wooden Pegasus; he only perks up a learned snout from a footnote in the cellarage of a paragraph; just, in short, where he ought to be, to inspire confidence in a wicked and adulterous generation. But, mind you, Bummkopf is not human; he is Dagon the fish god, and down he will come, sprawling on his belly or his behind, with his hands broken from his helpless carcase, and his head rolling off into a corner. Up will rise on the other side, sane, pleasurable, human knowledge: a thing of beauty and a joy, etc.

I'm three parts through Burns; long, dry, unsympathetic, but sound and, I think, in its dry way, interesting. Next I shall finish the story, and then perhaps Thoreau. Meredith has been staying with Morley, who is about, it is believed, to write to me on a literary scheme. Is it Keats, hope you? My heart leaps at the thought.—Yours ever,
R. L. S.

TO EDMUND GOSSE

With reference to the 'term of reproach,' it must be explained that Mr. Gosse, who now signs with only one initial, used in these days to sign with two, E. W. G. The nickname Weg was fastened on him by Stevenson, partly under a false impression as to the order of these initials, partly in friendly derision of a passing fit of lameness, which called up the memory of Silas

Wegg, the immortal literary gentleman '*with* a wooden leg' of   1879.
Our *Mutual Friend*.   AET. 29.

17 *Heriot Row, Edinburgh* [*July* 29, 1879].

MY DEAR GOSSE,—Yours was delicious; you are a young person of wit; one of the last of them; wit being quite out of date, and humour confined to the Scotch Church and the *Spectator* in unconscious survival. You will probably be glad to hear that I am up again in the world; I have breathed again, and had a frolic on the strength of it. The frolic was yesterday, Sawbath; the scene, the Royal Hotel, Bathgate; I went there with a humorous friend to lunch. The maid soon showed herself a lass of character. She was looking out of window. On being asked what she was after, 'I'm lookin' for my lad,' says she. 'Is that him?' 'Weel, I've been lookin' for him a' my life, and I've never seen him yet,' was the response. I wrote her some verses in the vernacular; she read them. 'They're no bad for a beginner,' said she. The landlord's daughter, Miss Stewart, was present in oil colour; so I wrote her a declaration in verse, and sent it by the hand-maid. She (Miss S.) was present on the stair to witness our departure, in a warm, suffused condition. Damn it, Gosse, you needn't suppose that you're the only poet in the world.

Your statement about your initials, it will be seen, I pass over in contempt and silence. When once I have made up my mind, let me tell you, sir, there lives no pock-pudding who can change it. Your anger I defy. Your unmanly reference to a well-known statesman I puff from me, sir, like so much vapour. Weg is your name; Weg. W E G.

My enthusiasm has kind of dropped from me. I envy you your wife, your home, your child—I was going to say your cat. There would be cats in my home too if I could but get it. I may seem to you 'the impersonation of life,'

1879.
AET. 29.

but my life is the impersonation of waiting, and that's a poor creature. God help us all, and the deil be kind to the hindmost! Upon my word, we are a brave, cheery crew, we human beings, and my admiration increases daily—primarily for myself, but by a roundabout process for the whole crowd; for I dare say they have all their poor little secrets and anxieties. And here am I, for instance, writing to you as if you were in the seventh heaven, and yet I know you are in a sad anxiety yourself. I hope earnestly it will soon be over, and a fine pink Gosse sprawling in a tub, and a mother in the best of health and spirits, glad and tired, and with another interest in life. Man, you are out of the trouble when this is through. A first child is a rival, but a second is only a rival to the first; and the husband stands his ground and may keep married all his life—a consummation heartily to be desired. Good-bye, Gosse. Write me a witty letter with good news of the mistress.

R. L. S.

IV

THE AMATEUR EMIGRANT

MONTEREY AND SAN FRANCISCO

JULY 1879—JULY 1880

IN France, as has been already indicated, Stevenson had met the American lady, Mrs. Osbourne, who was afterwards to become his wife. Almost from their first meeting, soon after the canoe voyage of 1876, Stevenson had conceived for her a devotion which never swerved nor faltered. Her domestic circumstances had not been fortunate, and on her return to America with her children in the autumn of 1878, she determined to seek a divorce from her husband. Hearing of her intention, together with very disquieting news of her health, Stevenson suddenly started for California at the beginning of August 1879.

For what he knew must seem to his friends so wild an errand, he would ask for no supplies from home; but resolved, risking his whole future on the issue, to test during this adventure his power of supporting himself, and eventually others, by his own labours in literature. In order from the outset to save as much as possible, he made the journey in the steerage and the emigrant train. With this prime motive of economy was combined a second—that of learning for himself the pinch of life as it is felt by the unprivileged and the poor (he had long ago disclaimed for himself the character of a 'consistent first-class passenger in life')—and also, it should be added, a third, that of turning his experiences to literary account. On board ship he took daily notes with this intent, and wrote moreover *The Story of a Lie* for an English magazine. Arrived at his destination, he found his health, as was natural, badly shaken by the hardships of the journey; tried his favourite open-air cure for three weeks at an Angora goat-ranche some twenty miles from Monterey; and then lived from September to December in that old Californian coast-town itself, under the conditions set forth in the earlier of the following letters, and under a heavy combined strain of personal anxiety and literary effort. From the notes taken on board ship and in the emigrant train he drafted an account of his journey, intending to make a volume matching in form, though in contents much unlike, the earlier *Inland Voyage* and *Travels with a Donkey*. He wrote also the essays on Thoreau and the Japanese reformer, Yoshida Torajiro, afterwards published in *Familiar Studies of Men and Books*; one of the most vivid of his shorter tales, 'The Pavilion on the Links,' as well as a great part of another and longer story drawn from his new experiences and called 'A Vendetta in the West'; but this did not satisfy him, and was never finished. He planned at the same time that tale in the spirit of romantic comedy, which took final shape four years later as *Prince Otto*. Towards the end of December 1879 Stevenson moved to San Francisco, where he lived for three months in a workman's lodging, leading a life of frugality amounting, it will be seen, to self-imposed penury, and working always with the same intensity of application, until his health utterly broke down. One of the causes which contributed to his illness was the fatigue he underwent in helping to watch beside the sickbed of a child, the son of his landlady. During March and a part of April he lay at death's door—his first really dangerous sickness since childhood—and was slowly tended back to life by the joint ministrations of his future wife and the physician to whom his letter of thanks will be found below. His marriage ensued in May 1880; immediately afterwards, to try and consolidate his recovery, he moved to a deserted mining-camp in the Californian coast range; and has recorded the aspects and humours of his life there with a master's touch in *The Silverado Squatters*.

The news of his dangerous illness and approaching marriage had in the meantime unlocked the parental heart and purse; supplies were sent insuring his present comfort, with the promise of their continuance for the future, and of a cordial welcome for the new daughter-in-law in his father's house. The following letters, chosen from among those written during the period in question, depict his way of life, and reflect at once the anxiety of his friends and the strain of the time upon himself.

1879.
AET. 29.

TO SIDNEY COLVIN

On board ss. 'Devonia,' an hour or two out of New York
[*August* 1879].

MY DEAR COLVIN,—I have finished my story.[1] The handwriting is not good because of the ship's misconduct: thirty-one pages in ten days at sea is not bad.

I shall write a general procuration about this story on another bit of paper. I am not very well; bad food, bad air, and hard work have brought me down. But the spirits keep good. The voyage has been most interesting, and will make, if not a series of *Pall Mall* articles, at least the first part of a new book. The last weight on me has been trying to keep notes for this purpose. Indeed, I have worked like a horse, and am now as tired as a donkey. If I should have to push on far by rail, I shall bring nothing but my fine bones to port.

Good-bye to you all. I suppose it is now late afternoon with you and all across the seas. What shall I find over there? I dare not wonder.—Ever yours,

R. L. S.

P.S.—I go on my way to-night, if I can; if not, to-morrow: emigrant train ten to fourteen days' journey; warranted extreme discomfort. The only American institution which has yet won my respect is the rain. One sees it is a new country, they are so free with their water. I have been steadily drenched for twenty-four hours; water-proof wet through; immortal spirit fitfully blinking up in spite. Bought a copy of my own work, and the man said 'by Stevenson.'—'Indeed,' says I.—'Yes, sir,' says he.—Scene closes.

TO SIDNEY COLVIN

[*In the Emigrant Train from New York to San Francisco, August* 1879.]

DEAR COLVIN,—I am in the cars between Pittsburgh and Chicago, just now bowling through Ohio. I am

[1] 'The Story of a Lie.'

taking charge of a kid, whose mother is asleep, with one eye, while I write you this with the other. I reached N. Y. Sunday night; and by five o'clock Monday was under way for the West. It is now about ten on Wednesday morning, so I have already been about forty hours in the cars. It is impossible to lie down in them, which must end by being very wearying.

I had no idea how easy it was to commit suicide. There seems nothing left of me; I died a while ago; I do not know who it is that is travelling.

> Of where or how, I nothing know;
> And why, I do not care;
> Enough if, even so,
> My travelling eyes, my travelling mind
> can go
> By flood and field and hill, by wood
> and meadow fair,
> Beside the Susquehannah and along the
> Delaware.
>
> I think, I hope, I dream no more
> The dreams of otherwhere,
> The cherished thoughts of yore;
> I have been changed from what I was before;
> And drunk too deep perchance the lotus
> of the air
> Beside the Susquehannah and along the
> Delaware.
>
> Unweary God me yet shall bring
> To lands of brighter air,
> Where I, now half a king,
> Shall with enfranchised spirit loudlier
> sing,
> And wear a bolder front than that which
> now I wear
> Beside the Susquehannah and along the
> Delaware.

1879.
AET. 29.

Exit Muse, hurried by child's games. . . .

Have at you again, being now well through Indiana. In America you eat better than anywhere else: fact. The food is heavenly.

No man is any use until he has dared everything; I feel just now as if I had, and so might become a man. 'If ye have faith like a grain of mustard seed.' That is so true! Just now I have faith as big as a cigar-case; I will not say die, and do not fear man nor fortune. ·R. L. S.

TO W. E. HENLEY

Crossing Nebraska [1879].

MY DEAR HENLEY,—I am sitting on the top of the cars with a mill party from Missouri going west for his health. Desolate flat prairie upon all hands. Here and there a herd of cattle, a yellow butterfly or two; a patch of wild sunflowers; a wooden house or two; then a wooden church alone in miles of waste; then a windmill to pump water. When we stop, which we do often, for emigrants and freight travel together, the kine first, the men after, the whole plain is heard singing with cicadae. This is a pause, as you may see from the writing. What happened to the old pedestrian emigrants, what was the tedium suffered by the Indians and trappers of our youth, the imagination trembles to conceive. This is now Saturday, 23rd, and I have been steadily travelling since I parted from you at St. Pancras. It is a strange vicissitude from the Savile Club to this; I sleep with a man from Pennsylvania who has been in the States Navy, and mess with him and the Missouri bird already alluded to. We have a tin wash-bowl among four. I wear nothing but a shirt and a pair of trousers, and never button my shirt. When I land for a meal, I pass my coat and feel dressed. This life is to last till Friday, Saturday, or Sunday next. It is a strange affair to be an emigrant, as I hope you shall see in a future work. I wonder if this will be legible; my present station on the waggon roof, though airy compared to the cars, is both dirty and insecure. I can see the track straight before and straight behind me to either horizon. Peace of mind I enjoy with extreme serenity; I am doing right; I know no one will think so; and don't care. My body, however, is all to whistles; I don't eat; but, man, I can sleep. The car in front of mine is chock full of Chinese.

1879.
AET. 29.

Monday.—What it is to be ill in an emigrant train let those declare who know. I slept none till late in the morning, overcome with laudanum, of which I had luckily a little bottle. All to-day I have eaten nothing, and only drunk two cups of tea, for each of which, on the pretext that the one was breakfast, and the other dinner, I was charged fifty cents. Our journey is through ghostly deserts, sage brush and alkali, and rocks, without form or colour, a sad corner of the world. I confess I am not jolly, but mighty calm, in my distresses. My illness is a subject of great mirth to some of my fellow-travellers, and I smile rather sickly at their jests.

We are going along Bitter Creek just now, a place infamous in the history of emigration, a place I shall remember myself among the blackest. I hope I may get this posted at Ogden, Utah.   R. L. S.

TO SIDNEY COLVIN

[*Coast Line Mountains, California, September* 1879.]

HERE is another curious start in my life. I am living at an Angora goat-ranche, in the Coast Line Mountains, eighteen miles from Monterey. I was camping out, but got so sick that the two rancheros took me in and tended me. One is an old bear-hunter, seventy-two years old, and a captain from the Mexican war; the other a pilgrim, and one who was out with the bear flag and under Fremont when California was taken by the States. They are both true frontiersmen, and most kind and pleasant. Captain Smith, the bear-hunter, is my physician, and I obey him like an oracle.

The business of my life stands pretty nigh still. I work at my notes of the voyage. It will not be very like a book of mine; but perhaps none the less successful for that. I will not deny that I feel lonely to-day; but I do not fear to go on, for I am doing right. I have not yet had a word from England, partly, I suppose, because I have not yet written for my letters to New York; do not blame me for this neglect; if you knew all I have been through, you would wonder I had done so much as I have. I teach the ranche children reading in the morning, for the mother is from home sick.—Ever your affectionate friend, R. L. S.

TO SIDNEY COLVIN

Monterey, Ditto Co., California, 21st October [1879].

MY DEAR COLVIN,—Although you have absolutely disregarded my plaintive appeals for correspondence, and written only once as against God knows how many notes and notikins of mine—here goes again. I am now all alone in Monterey, a real inhabitant, with a box of my own at the P. O. I have splendid rooms at the doctor's, where I get coffee in the morning (the doctor is French), and I mess with another jolly old Frenchman, the stranded fifty-eight-year-old wreck of a good-hearted, dissipated, and once wealthy Nantais tradesman. My health goes on better; as for work, the draft of my book was laid aside at p. 68 or so; and I have now, by way of change, more than seventy pages of a novel, a one-volume novel, alas! to be called either *A Chapter in the Experi-*

ence of Arizona Breckonridge or *A Vendetta in the West*, or a combination of the two. The scene from Chapter IV. to the end lies in Monterey and the adjacent country; of course, with my usual luck, the plot of the story is somewhat scandalous, containing an illegitimate father for piece of resistance. . . . Ever yours,   R. L. S.

1879.
AET. 29.

To Sidney Colvin

Monterey, California, September 1879.

MY DEAR COLVIN,—I received your letter with delight; it was the first word that reached me from the old country. I am in good health now; I have been pretty seedy, for I was exhausted by the journey and anxiety below even my point of keeping up; I am still a little weak, but that is all; I begin to ingrease,[1] it seems, already. My book is about half drafted: the *Amateur Emigrant*, that is. Can you find a better name? I believe it will be more popular than any of my others; the canvas is so much more popular and larger too. Fancy, it is my fourth. That voluminous writer. I was vexed to hear about the last chapter of 'The Lie,' and pleased to hear about the rest; it would have been odd if it had no birthmark, born where and how it was. It should by rights have been called the *Devonia*, for that is the habit with all children born in a steerage.

I write to you, hoping for more. Give me news of all who concern me, near or far, or big or little. Here, sir, in California you have a willing hearer.

Monterey is a place where there is no summer or winter, and pines and sand and distant hills and a bay all filled with real water from the Pacific. You will perceive that no expense has been spared. I now live with a little French doctor; I take one of my meals in a little French restaurant; for the other two, I sponge. The population

[1] *Engraisser*, grow fat.

of Monterey is about that of a dissenting chapel on a wet Sunday in a strong church neighbourhood. They are mostly Mexican and Indian—mixed.—Ever yours,

R. L. S.

TO EDMUND GOSSE

Monterey, Monterey Co., California, 8th October 1879.

MY DEAR WEG,—I know I am a rogue and the son of a dog. Yet let me tell you, when I came here I had a week's misery and a fortnight's illness, and since then I have been more or less busy in being content. This is a kind of excuse for my laziness. I hope you will not excuse yourself. My plans are still very uncertain, and it is not likely that anything will happen before Christmas. In the meanwhile, I believe I shall live on here 'between the sandhills and the sea,' as I think Mr. Swinburne hath it. I was pretty nearly slain; my spirit lay down and kicked for three days; I was up at an Angora goat-ranche in the Santa Lucia Mountains, nursed by an old frontiersman, a mighty hunter of bears, and I scarcely slept, or ate, or thought for four days. Two nights I lay out under a tree in a sort of stupor, doing nothing but fetch water for myself and horse, light a fire and make coffee, and all night awake hearing the goat-bells ringing and the tree-frogs singing when each new noise was enough to set me mad. Then the bear-hunter came round, pronounced me 'real sick,' and ordered me up to the ranche.

It was an odd, miserable piece of my life; and according to all rule, it should have been my death; but after a while my spirit got up again in a divine frenzy, and has since kicked and spurred my vile body forward with great emphasis and success.

My new book, *The Amateur Emigrant*, is about half drafted. I don't know if it will be good, but I think it ought to sell in spite of the deil and the publishers; for it tells an odd enough experience, and one, I think, never yet told before. Look for my 'Burns' in the *Cornhill*, and for my 'Story of a Lie' in Paul's withered babe, the *New Quarterly*. You may have seen the latter ere this reaches you: tell me if it has any interest, like a good boy, and remember that it was written at sea in great anxiety of mind. What is your news? Send me your works, like an angel, *au fur et à mesure* of their apparition, for I am naturally short of literature, and I do not wish to rust.

1879.
AET. 29.

I fear this can hardly be called a letter. To say truth, I feel already a difficulty of approach; I do not know if I am the same man I was in Europe, perhaps I can hardly claim acquaintance with you. My head went round and looks another way now; for when I found myself over here in a new land, and all the past uprooted in the one tug, and I neither feeling glad nor sorry, I got my last lesson about mankind; I mean my latest lesson, for of course I do not know what surprises there are yet in store for me. But that I could have so felt astonished me beyond description. There is a wonderful callousness in human nature which enables us to live. I had no feeling one way or another, from New York to California, until, at Dutch Flat, a mining camp in the Sierra, I heard a cock crowing with a home voice; and then I fell to hope and regret both in the same moment.

Is there a boy or a girl? and how is your wife? I thought of you more than once, to put it mildly.

I live here comfortably enough; but I shall soon be left all alone, perhaps till Christmas. Then you may hope for correspondence—and may not I?—Your friend,

R. L. S.

TO W. E. HENLEY

[*Monterey, California, October* 1879.]

MY DEAR HENLEY,—Herewith the *Pavilion on the Links*, grand carpentry story in nine chapters, and I should hesitate to say how many tableaux. Where is it to go? God knows. It is the dibbs that are wanted. It is not

1879.
AET. 29.

bad, though I say it; carpentry, of course, but not bad at that; and who else can carpenter in England, now that Wilkie Collins is played out? It might be broken for magazine purposes at the end of Chapter IV. I send it to you, as I dare say Payn may help, if all else fails. Dibbs and speed are my mottoes.

Do acknowledge the *Pavilion* by return. I shall be so nervous till I hear, as of course I have no copy except of one or two places where the vein would not run. God prosper it, poor *Pavilion*! May it bring me money for myself and my sick one, who may read it, I do not know how soon.

Love to your wife, Anthony and all. I shall write to Colvin to-day or to-morrow.—Yours ever, R. L. S.

TO W. E. HENLEY

[*Monterey, California, October* 1879.]

MY DEAR HENLEY,—Many thanks for your good letter, which is the best way to forgive you for your previous silence. I hope Colvin or somebody has sent me the *Cornhill* and the *New Quarterly*, though I am trying to get them in San Francisco. I think you might have sent me (1) some of your articles in the P. M. G.; (2) a paper with the announcement of second edition; and (3) the announcement of the essays in *Athenæum*. This to prick you in the future. Again, choose, in your head, the best volume of Labiche there is, and post it to Jules Simoneau, Monterey, Monterey Co., California: do this at once, as he is my restaurant man, a most pleasant old boy with whom I discuss the universe and play chess daily. He has been out of France for thirty-five years, and never heard of Labiche. I have eighty-three pages written of a story called a *Vendetta in the West*, and about sixty pages of the first draft of the *Amateur Emigrant*. They should each cover from 130 to 150 pages when done. That is all my literary news. Do keep me posted, won't you?

Your letter and Bob's made the fifth and sixth I have had from Europe in three months.

At times I get terribly frightened about my work, which seems to advance too slowly. I hope soon to have a greater burthen to support, and must make money a great deal quicker than I used. I may get nothing for the *Vendetta*; I may only get some forty quid for the *Emigrant*; I cannot hope to have them both done much before the end of November.

O, and look here, why did you not send me the *Spectator* which slanged me? Rogues and rascals, is that all you are worth?

Yesterday I set fire to the forest, for which, had I been caught, I should have been hung out of hand to the nearest tree, Judge Lynch being an active person hereaway. You should have seen my retreat (which was entirely for strategical purposes). I ran like hell. It was a fine sight. At night I went out again to see it; it was a good fire, though I say it that should not. I had a near escape for my life with a revolver: I fired six charges, and the six bullets all remained in the barrel, which was choked from end to end, from muzzle to breach, with solid lead; it took a man three hours to drill them out. Another shot, and I'd have gone to kingdom come.

This is a lovely place, which I am growing to love. The Pacific licks all other oceans out of hand; there is no place but the Pacific Coast to hear eternal roaring surf. When I get to the top of the woods behind Monterey, I can hear the seas breaking all round over ten or twelve miles of coast from near Carmel on my left, out to Point Pinas in front, and away to the right along the sands of Monterey to Castroville and the mouth of the Salinas. I was wishing yesterday that the world could get—no, what I mean was that you should be kept in suspense like Mahomet's coffin until the world had made half a revolution, then dropped here at the station as though you had stepped from the cars; you would then comfortably enter

1879.
AET. 29.
Walter's waggon (the sun has just gone down, the moon beginning to throw shadows, you hear the surf rolling, and smell the sea and the pines). That shall deposit you at Sanchez's saloon, where we take a drink; you are introduced to Bronson, the local editor ('I have no brain music,' he says; 'I'm a mechanic, you see,' but he's a nice fellow); to Adolpho Sanchez, who is delightful. Meantime I go to the P. O. for my mail; thence we walk up Alvarado Street together, you now floundering in the sand, now merrily stumping on the wooden sidewalks; I call at Hadsell's for my paper; at length behold us installed in Simoneau's little white-washed back-room, round a dirty tablecloth, with François the baker, perhaps an Italian fisherman, perhaps Augustin Dutra, and Simoneau himself. Simoneau, François, and I are the three sure cards; the others mere waifs. Then home to my great airy rooms with five windows opening on a balcony; I sleep on the floor in my camp blankets; you instal yourself abed; in the morning coffee with the little doctor and his little wife; we hire a waggon and make a day of it; and by night, I should let you up again into the air, to be returned to Mrs. Henley in the forenoon following. By God, you would enjoy yourself. So should I. I have tales enough to keep you going till five in the morning, and then they would not be at an end. I forget if you asked me any questions, and I sent your letter up to the city to one who will like to read it. I expect other letters now steadily. If I have to wait another two months, I shall begin to be happy. Will you remember me most affectionately to your wife? Shake hands with Anthony from me; and God bless your mother.

God bless Stephen! Does he not know that I am a man, and cannot live by bread alone, but must have guineas into the bargain. Burns, I believe, in my own mind, is one of my high-water marks; Meiklejohn flames me a letter about it, which is so complimentary that I must keep it or get it published in the *Monterey Californian*. Some of these days I shall send an exemplaire of that paper; it is huge.—Ever your affectionate friend,

ROBERT LOUIS STEVENSON.

1879.
AET. 29.

TO P. G. HAMERTON

The following refers to Mr. Hamerton's candidature, which was not successful, for the Professorship of Fine Art at Edinburgh:—

Monterey, California [*November* 1879].

MY DEAR MR. HAMERTON,—Your letter to my father was forwarded to me by mistake, and by mistake I opened it. The letter to myself has not yet reached me. This must explain my own and my father's silence. I shall write by this or next post to the only friends I have who, I think, would have an influence, as they are both professors. I regret exceedingly that I am not in Edinburgh, as I could perhaps have done more, and I need not tell you that what I might do for you in the matter of the election is neither from friendship nor gratitude, but because you are the only man (I beg your pardon) worth a damn. I shall write to a third friend, now I think of it, whose father will have great influence.

I find here (of all places in the world) your *Essays on Art*, which I have read with signal interest. I believe I shall dig an essay of my own out of one of them, for it set me thinking; if mine could only produce yet another in reply, we could have the marrow out between us.

I hope, my dear sir, you will not think badly of me for my long silence. My head has scarce been on my shoulders. I had scarce recovered from a long fit of useless ill-health than I was whirled over here double-quick time and by cheapest conveyance.

I have been since pretty ill, but pick up, though still somewhat of a mossy ruin. If you would view my countenance aright, come—view it by the pale moonlight. But that is on the mend. I believe I have now a distant claim to tan.

A letter will be more than welcome in this distant clime, where I have a box at the post-office—generally, I regret to say, empty. Could your recommendation introduce me to an American publisher? My next book I should really try to get hold of here, as its interest is international, and the more I am in this country the more I understand the weight of your influence. It is pleasant to be thus most at home abroad, above all, when the prophet is still not without honour in his own land ...

TO EDMUND GOSSE

Monterey, California, 15*th November* 1879.

MY DEAR GOSSE,—Your letter was to me such a bright spot that I answer it right away to the prejudice of other correspondents or -dants (don't know how to spell it) who have prior claims. ... It is the history of our kindnesses that alone makes this world tolerable. If it were not for that, for the effect of kind words, kind looks, kind letters, multiplying, spreading, making one happy through another and bringing forth benefits, some thirty, some fifty, some a thousandfold, I should be tempted to think our life a practical jest in the worst possible spirit. So your four pages have confirmed my philosophy as well as consoled my heart in these ill hours.

Yes, you are right; Monterey is a pleasant place; but I see I can write no more to-night. I am tired and sad, and being already in bed, have no more to do but turn out the light.—Your affectionate friend, R. L. S.

I try it again by daylight. Once more in bed however; for to-day it is *mucho piro*, as we Spaniards say; and I had no other means of keeping warm for my work. I have done a good spell, $9\frac{1}{2}$ foolscap pages; at least 8 of *Cornhill*; ah, if I thought that I could get eight guineas for it. My trouble is that I am all too ambitious just now. A book whereof 70 out of 120 are scrolled. A novel whereof 85 out of, say, 140 are pretty well nigh done. A short story of 50 pp., which shall be finished to-morrow, or I'll know the reason why. This may bring in a lot of money: but I dread to think that it is all on three chances. If the three were to fail, I am in a bog. The novel is called *A Vendetta in the West*. I see I am in a grasping, dismal humour, and should, as we Americans put it, quit writing. In truth, I am so haunted by anxieties that one or other is sure to come up in all that I write.

I will send you herewith a Monterey paper where the works of R. L. S. appear, nor only that, but all my life on studying the advertisements will become clear. I lodge with Dr. Heintz; take my meals with Simoneau; have been only two days ago shaved by the tonsorial artist Michaels; drink daily at the Bohemia saloon; get my daily paper from Hadsel's; was stood a drink to-day by Albano Rodriguez; in short, there is scarce a person advertised in that paper but I know him, and I may add scarce a person in Monterey but is there advertised. The paper is the marrow of the place. Its bones—pooh, I am tired of writing so sillily.   R. L. S.

TO SIDNEY COLVIN

[*Monterey, December* 1879.]

TO-DAY, my dear Colvin, I send you the first part of the *Amateur Emigrant*, 71 pp., by far the longest and the best of the whole. It is not a monument of eloquence; indeed, I have sought to be prosaic in view of the nature of the subject; but I almost think it is interesting.

Whatever is done about any book publication, two things remember: I must keep a royalty; and, second, I must have all my books advertised, in the French manner,

1879.
AET. 29.

on the leaf opposite the title. I know from my own experience how much good this does an author with book buyers.

The entire A. E. will be a little longer than the two others, but not very much. Here and there, I fancy, you will laugh as you read it; but it seems to me rather a *clever* book than anything else: the book of a man, that is, who has paid a great deal of attention to contemporary life, and not through the newspapers.

I have never seen my Burns! the darling of my heart! I await your promised letter. Papers, magazines, articles by friends; reviews of myself, all would be very welcome. I am reporter for the *Monterey Californian*, at a salary of two dollars a week! *Comment trouvez-vous ça?* I am also in a conspiracy with the American editor, a French restaurant-man, and an Italian fisherman against the Padre. The enclosed poster is my last literary appearance. It was put up to the number of 200 exemplaires at the witching hour; and they were almost all destroyed by eight in the morning. But I think the nickname will stick. Dos Reales; deux réaux; two bits; twenty-five cents; about a shilling; but in practice it is worth from ninepence to threepence: thus two glasses of beer would cost two bits. The Italian fisherman, an old Garibaldian, is a splendid fellow.　　　　　　　　　　R. L. S.

TO EDMUND GOSSE

The following is in acknowledgment of Mr. Gosse's volume called *New Poems*:—

Monterey, Monterey Co., California, Dec. 8, 1879.

MY DEAR WEG,—I received your book last night as I lay abed with a pleurisy, the result, I fear, of overwork, gradual decline of appetite, etc. You know what a wooden-hearted curmudgeon I am about contemporary verse. I like none of it, except some of my own. (I look back on that sentence with pleasure; it comes from an honest heart.) Hence you will be kind enough to take this from me in a kindly spirit; the piece ' To my daughter' is delicious. And yet even here I am going to pick holes. I am a *beastly* curmudgeon. It is the last verse. 'Newly budded' is off the venue; and haven't you gone ahead to make a poetry daybreak instead of sticking to your muttons, and comparing with the mysterious light of stars the plain, friendly, perspicuous, human day? But this is to be a beast. The little poem is eminently pleasant, human, and original.

1879.
AET. 29.

I have read nearly the whole volume, and shall read it nearly all over again; you have no rivals!

Bancroft's *History of the United States*, even in a centenary edition, is essentially heavy fare; a little goes a long way; I respect Bancroft, but I do not love him; he has moments when he feels himself inspired to open up his improvisations upon universal history and the designs of God; but I flatter myself I am more nearly acquainted with the latter than Mr. Bancroft. A man, in the words of my Plymouth Brother, 'who knows the Lord,' must needs, from time to time, write less emphatically. It is a fetter dance to the music of minute guns— not at sea, but in a region not a thousand miles from the Sahara. Still, I am half-way through volume three, and shall count myself unworthy of the name of an Englishman if I do not see the back of volume six. The countryman of Livingstone, Burton, Speke, Drake, Cook, etc.!

I have been sweated not only out of my pleuritic fever, but out of all my eating cares, and the better part of my brains (strange coincidence!), by aconite. I have that peculiar and delicious sense of being born again in an expurgated edition which belongs to convalescence. It will not be for long; I hear the breakers roar; I shall be steering head first for another rapid before many days; *nitor aquis*, said a certain Eton boy, translating for his sins a part of the *Inland Voyage* into Latin elegiacs; and from the hour I saw it, or rather a friend of mine, the admirable Jenkin, saw and recognised its absurd appropriateness, I took it for my device in life. I am going for thirty now; and unless I can snatch a little rest before long, I have, I may tell you in confidence, no hope of seeing thirty-one. My health began to break last winter, and has given me but fitful times since then. This pleurisy, though but a slight affair in itself, was a huge disappointment to me, and marked an epoch. To start a pleurisy about nothing, while leading a dull, regular life in a mild climate, was not my habit in past days; and it is six years, all but a few months, since I was obliged to spend twenty-four hours in bed. I may be wrong, but if the niting is to continue, I believe I must go. It is a pity in one sense, for I believe the class of work I *might* yet give out is better and more real and solid than people fancy. But death is no bad friend; a few aches and gasps, and we are done; like the truant child, I am beginning to grow weary and timid in this big jostling city, and could run to my nurse, even although she should have to whip me before putting me to bed.

Will you kiss your little daughter from me, and tell her that her father has written a delightful poem about her? Remember me, please, to Mrs. Gosse, to Middlemore, to whom some of these days I will write, to——, to ——, yes, to ——, and to——. I know you will gnash your teeth at some of these; wicked, grim, catlike old poet. If I were God, I would sort you—as we say in Scotland.—Your sincere friend, R. L. S.

'Too young to be our child': blooming good.

TO SIDNEY COLVIN

608 *Bush Street*, San Francisco [*December* 26, 1879].

MY DEAR COLVIN,—I am now writing to you in a café waiting for some music to begin. For four days I have spoken to no one but to my landlady or landlord or to restaurant waiters. This is not a gay way to pass Christmas, is it? and I must own the guts are a little knocked out of me. If I could work, I could worry through better. But I have no style at command for the moment, with the second part of the *Emigrant*, the last of the novel, the essay on Thoreau, and God knows all, waiting for me. But I trust something can be done with the first part, or, by God, I'll starve here. . . .[1]

O Colvin, you don't know how much good I have done myself. I feared to think this out by myself. I have made a base use of you, and it comes out so much better than I had dreamed. But I have to stick to work now; and here's December gone pretty near useless. But, Lord love you, October and November saw a great harvest. It might have affected the price of paper on the Pacific coast. As for ink, they haven't any, not what I call ink; only stuff to write cookery-books with, or the works of Hayley, or the pallid perambulations of the—I can find nobody to beat Hayley. I like good, knock-me-down black-strap to write with; that makes a mark and done with it.—By the way, I have tried to read the *Spectator*, which they all say I imitate, and—it's very wrong of me, I know—but I can't. It's all very fine, you know, and all that, but it's vapid. They have just played the overture to *Norma*, and I know it's a good one, for I bitterly wanted the opera to go on; I had just got thoroughly interested—and then no curtain to rise.

I have written myself into a kind of spirits, bless your dear heart, by your leave. But this is wild work for me, nearly nine and me not back! What will Mrs. Carson think of me! Quite a night-hawk, I do declare. You are the worst correspondent in the world—no, not that, Henley is that—well, I don't know, I leave the pair of you to Him that made you—surely with small attention. But here's my service, and I'll away home to my den O! much the better for this crack, Professor Colvin.   R. L. S.

1879.
AET. 29.

[1] Here follows a long calculation of ways and means.

1880.
AET. 30.

TO SIDNEY COLVIN

608 *Bush Street, San Francisco* [*January* 10, 1880].

MY DEAR COLVIN,—This is a circular letter to tell my estate fully. You have no right to it, being the worst of correspondents; but I wish to efface the impression of my last, so to you it goes.

Any time between eight and half-past nine in the morning, a slender gentleman in an ulster, with a volume buttoned into the breast of it, may be observed leaving No. 608 Bush and descending Powell with an active step. The gentleman is R. L. S.; the volume relates to Benjamin Franklin, on whom he meditates one of his charming essays. He descends Powell, crosses Market, and descends in Sixth on a branch of the original Pine Street Coffee House, no less; I believe he would be capable of going to the original itself, if he could only find it. In the branch he seats himself at a table covered with waxcloth, and a pampered menial, of High-Dutch extraction and, indeed, as yet only partially extracted, lays before him a cup of coffee, a roll and a pat of butter, all, to quote the deity, very good. A while ago, and R. L. S. used to find the supply of butter insufficient; but he has now learned the art to exactitude, and butter and roll expire at the same moment. For this refection he pays ten cents., or five pence sterling (£0, 0s. 5d.).

Half an hour later, the inhabitants of Bush Street observe the same slender gentleman armed, like George Washington, with his little hatchet, splitting, kindling, and breaking coal for his fire. He does this quasi-publicly upon the window-sill; but this is not to be attributed to any love of notoriety, though he is indeed vain of his prowess with the hatchet (which he persists in calling an axe), and daily surprised at the perpetuation of his fingers. The reason is this: that the sill is a strong, supporting beam, and that blows of the same emphasis in other parts of his room might knock the entire shanty into hell. Thenceforth, for from three to four hours, he is engaged darkly with an inkbottle. Yet he is not blacking his boots, for the only pair that he possesses are innocent of lustre and wear the natural hue of the material turned up with caked and venerable slush. The youngest child of his landlady remarks several times a day, as this strange occupant enters or quits the house, 'Dere's de author.' Can it be that this bright-haired innocent has found the true clue to the mystery? The being in question is, at least, poor enough to belong to that honourable craft.

1880.
AET. 30.

His next appearance is at the restaurant of one Donadieu, in Bush Street, between Dupont and Kearney, where a copious meal, half a bottle of wine, coffee and brandy may be procured for the sum of four bits, *alias* fifty cents., £0, 2s. 2d. sterling. The wine is put down in a whole bottleful, and it is strange and painful to observe the greed with which the gentleman in question seeks to secure the last drop of his allotted half, and the scrupulousness with which he seeks to avoid taking the first drop of the other. This is partly explained by the fact that if he were to go over the mark—bang would go a tenpence. He is again armed with a book, but his best friends will learn with pain that he seems at this hour to have deserted the more serious studies of the morning. When last observed, he was studying with apparent zest the exploits of one Rocambole by the late Viscomte Ponson du Terrail. This work, originally of prodigious dimensions, he had cut into liths or thicknesses apparently for convenience of carriage.

Then the being walks, where is not certain. But by about half-past four, a light beams from the windows of 608 Bush, and he may be observed sometimes engaged in correspondence, sometimes once again plunged in the mysterious rites of the forenoon. About six he returns to the Branch Original, where he once more imbrues himself to the worth of fivepence in coffee and roll. The

1880.
AET. 30.

evening is devoted to writing and reading, and by eleven or half-past darkness closes over this weird and truculent existence.

As for coin, you see I don't spend much, only you and Henley both seem to think my work rather bosh nowadays, and I do want to make as much as I was making, that is £200; if I can do that, I can swim: last year, with my ill health I touched only £109, that would not do, I could not fight it through on that; but on £200, as I say, I am good for the world, and can even in this quiet way save a little, and that I must do. The worst is my health; it is suspected I had an ague chill yesterday; I shall know by to-morrow, and you know if I am to be laid down with ague the game is pretty well lost. But I don't know; I managed to write a good deal down in Monterey, when I was pretty sickly most of the time, and, by God, I'll try, ague and all. I have to ask you frankly, when you write, to give me any good news you can, and chat a little, but *just in the meantime*, give me no bad. If I could get *Thoreau*, *Emigrant* and *Vendetta* all finished and out of my hand, I should feel like a man who had made half a year's income in a half year; but until the two last are *finished*, you see, they don't fairly count.

I am afraid I bore you sadly with this perpetual talk about my affairs; I will try and stow it; but you see, it touches me nearly. I'm the miser in earnest now: last night, when I felt so ill, the supposed ague chill, it seemed strange not to be able to afford a drink. I would have walked half a mile, tired as I felt, for a brandy and soda. —Ever yours, R. L. S.

TO CHARLES BAXTER

608 Bush Street, San Francisco, Jan. 26, '80.

MY DEAR CHARLES,—I have to drop from a 50 cent. to a 25 cent. dinner; to-day begins my fall. That brings down my outlay in food and drink to 45 cents., or 1s. 10½d. per day. How are the mighty fallen! Luckily, this is such a cheap place for food; I used to pay as much as that for my first breakfast in the Savile in the grand old palmy days of yore. I regret nothing, and do not even dislike these straits, though the flesh will rebel on occasion. It is to-day bitter cold, after weeks of lovely warm weather, and I am all in a chitter. I am about to issue for my little shilling and halfpenny meal, taken in the middle of the day, the poor man's hour; and I shall eat and drink to your prosperity.—Ever yours, R. L. S.

To Sidney Colvin

With reference to the following, it must be explained that the first draft of the first part of the *Amateur Emigrant*, when it reached me about Christmas, had seemed to me, compared to his previous travel papers, but a spiritless record of squalid experiences, little likely to advance his still only half-established reputation; and I had written to him to that effect, inopportunely enough, with a fuller measure even than usual of the frankness which always marked our intercourse.

608 *Bush Street, San Francisco, California* [*January* 1880].

MY DEAR COLVIN,—I received this morning your long letter from Paris. Well, God's will be done; if it's dull, it's dull; it was a fair fight, and it's lost, and there's an end. But, fortunately, dulness is not a fault the public hates; perhaps they may like this vein of dulness. If they don't, damn them, we'll try them with another. I sat down on the back of your letter, and wrote twelve Cornhill pages this day as ever was of that same despised *Emigrant*; so you see my moral courage has not gone down with my intellect. Only, frankly, Colvin, do you think it a good plan to be so eminently descriptive, and even eloquent in dispraise? You rolled such a lot of polysyllables over me that a better man than I might have been disheartened.—However, I was not, as you see, and am not. The *Emigrant* shall be finished and leave in the course of next week. And then, I'll stick to stories. I am not frightened. I know my mind is changing; I have been telling you so for long; and I suppose I am fumbling for the new vein. Well, I'll find it.

The *Vendetta* you will not much like, I dare say: and that must be finished next; but I'll knock you with *The Forest State: A Romance.*

I'm vexed about my letters; I know it is painful to get these unsatisfactory things; but at least I have written often enough. And not one soul ever gives me any *news*, about people or things; everybody writes me sermons; it's good for me, but hardly the food necessary for a man who lives all alone on forty-five cents. a day, and sometimes less, with quantities of hard work and many heavy thoughts. If one of you could write me a letter with a jest in it, a letter like what is written to real people in this world—I am still flesh and blood—I should enjoy it. Simpson did, the other day, and it did me as much good as a bottle of wine. A lonely man gets to feel like a pariah after awhile—or no, not that, but like a saint and martyr, or a kind of macerated clergyman with pebbles in his boots, a pillared Simeon, I'm damned if I know what, but, man alive, I want gossip.

My health is better, my spirits steadier, I am not the least cast down. If the *Emigrant* was a failure, the *Pavilion*, by your leave, was not: it was a story quite adequately and rightly done, I contend; and when I find Stephen, for whom certainly I did not mean it, taking it in, I am better pleased with it than before. I know I shall do better work than ever I have done before; but, mind you, it will not be like it. My sympathies and interests are changed. There shall be no more books of travel for me. I care for nothing but the moral and the dramatic, not a jot for the picturesque or the beautiful, other than about people. It bored me hellishly to write the *Emigrant*; well, it's going to bore others to read it; that's only fair.

I should also write to others; but indeed I am jack-tired, and must go to bed to a French novel to compose myself for slumber.—Ever your affectionate friend,

1880.
AET. 30.

R. L. S.

TO W. E. HENLEY

608 Bush Street, San Francisco, Cal., February 1880.

MY DEAR HENLEY,—Before my work or anything I sit down to answer your long and kind letter.

I am well, cheerful, busy, hopeful; I cannot be knocked down; I do not mind about the *Emigrant*. I never thought it a masterpiece. It was written to sell, and I believe it will sell; and if it does not, the next will. You need not be uneasy about my work; I am only beginning to see my true method.

(1) As to *Studies*. There are two more already gone to Stephen. *Yoshida Torajiro*, which I think temperate and adequate; and *Thoreau*, which will want a really Balzacian effort over the proofs. But I want *Benjamin Franklin and the Art of Virtue* to follow; and perhaps also *William Penn*, but this last may be perhaps delayed for another volume—I think not, though. The *Studies* will be an intelligent volume, and in their latter numbers more like what I mean to be my style, or I mean what my style means to be, for I am passive. (2) The *Essays*. Good news indeed. I think *Ordered South* must be thrown in. It always swells the volume, and it will never find a more appropriate place. It was May 1874, Macmillan, I believe. (3) *Plays*. I did not understand you meant to try the draft. I shall make you a full scenario as soon as the *Emigrant* is done. (4) *Emigrant*. He shall be sent off next week. (5) Stories. You need not be alarmed that I am going to imitate Meredith. You know I was a Story-teller ingrain; did not that reassure you? The *Vendetta*, which falls next to be finished, is not entirely pleasant. But it has points. *The Forest State* or *The*

1880.
AET. 30.

Greenwood State: A Romance, is another pair of shoes. It is my old Semiramis, our half-seen Duke and Duchess, which suddenly sprang into sunshine clearness as a story the other day. The kind, happy *dénouement* is unfortunately absolutely undramatic, which will be our only trouble in quarrying out the play. I mean we shall quarry from it. *Characters*—Otto Frederick John, hereditary Prince of Grünwald; Amelia Seraphina, Princess; Conrad, Baron Gondremarck, Prime Minister; Cancellarius Greisengesang; Killian Gottesacker, Steward of the River Farm; Ottilie, his daughter; the Countess von Rosen. Seven in all. A brave story, I swear; and a brave play too, if we can find the trick to make the end. The play, I fear, will have to end darkly, and that spoils the quality as I now see it of a kind of crockery, eighteenth century, high-life-below-stairs life, breaking up like ice in spring before the nature and the certain modicum of manhood of my poor, clever, feather-headed Prince, whom I love already. I see Seraphina too. Gondremarck is not quite so clear. The Countess von Rosen, I have; I'll never tell you who she is; it's a secret; but I have known the countess; well, I will tell you; it's my old Russian friend, Madame Z. Certain scenes are, in conception, the best I have ever made, except for *Hester Noble*. Those at the end, Von Rosen and the Princess, the Prince and Princess, and the Princess and Gondremarck, as I now see them from here, should be nuts, Henley, nuts. It irks me not to go to them straight. But the *Emigrant* stops the way; then a reassured scenario for *Hester*; then the *Vendetta*; then two (or three) Essays—Benjamin Franklin, Thoughts on Literature as an Art, Dialogue on Character and Destiny between two Puppets, The Human Compromise; and then, at length—come to me, my Prince. O Lord, it's going to be courtly! And there is not an ugly person nor an ugly scene in it. The *Slate* both Fanny and I have damned utterly; it is too morbid, ugly, and unkind; better starvation.
                                                                R. L. S.

TO SIDNEY COLVIN

608 Bush Street, San Francisco, [*March* 1880].

1880.
AET. 30.

MY DEAR COLVIN,—My landlord and landlady's little four-year-old child is dying in the house; and O, what he has suffered. It has really affected my health. O never, never any family for me! I am cured of that.

I have taken a long holiday—have not worked for three days, and will not for a week; for I was really weary. Excuse this scratch; for the child weighs on me, dear Colvin. I did all I could to help; but all seems little, to the point of crime, when one of these poor innocents lies in such misery.—Ever yours,   R. L. S.

TO EDMUND GOSSE

In the interval between this letter and the last, the writer had been down with the dangerous illness already referred to. A poetical counterpart to this letter will be found in the piece beginning 'Not yet, my soul, these friendly fields desert,' which was composed at the same time and is printed in *Underwoods*, p. 30.

San Francisco, Cal., April 16 [1880].

MY DEAR GOSSE,—You have not answered my last; and I know you will repent when you hear how near I have been to another world. For about six weeks I have been in utter doubt; it was a toss-up for life or death all that time; but I won the toss, sir, and Hades went off once more discomfited. This is not the first time, nor will it be the last, that I have a friendly game with that gentleman. I know he will end by cleaning me out; but the rogue is insidious, and the habit of that sort of gambling seems to be a part of my nature; it was, I suspect, too much indulged in youth; break your children of this tendency, my dear Gosse, from the first. It is, when once formed, a habit more fatal than opium—I speak, as St. Paul says, like a fool. I have been very very sick; on the verge of a galloping consumption, cold sweats, prostrating attacks of cough, sinking fits in which I lost the power of speech, fever, and all the ugliest circumstances of the disease;

1880.
AET. 30.
and I have cause to bless God, my wife that is to be, and one Dr. Bamford (a name the Muse repels), that I have come out of all this, and got my feet once more upon a little hilltop, with a fair prospect of life and some new desire of living. Yet I did not wish to die, neither; only I felt unable to go on farther with that rough horseplay of human life: a man must be pretty well to take the business in good part. Yet I felt all the time that I had done nothing to entitle me to an honourable discharge; that I had taken up many obligations and begun many friendships which I had no right to put away from me; and that for me to die was to play the cur and slinking sybarite, and desert the colours on the eve of the decisive fight. Of course I have done no work for I do not know how long; and here you can triumph. I have been reduced to writing verses for amusement. A fact. The whirligig of time brings in its revenges, after all. But I'll have them buried with me, I think, for I have not the heart to burn them while I live. Do write. I shall go to the mountains as soon as the weather clears; on the way thither, I marry myself; then I set up my family altar among the pinewoods, 3000 feet, sir, from the disputatious sea.—I am, dear Weg, most truly yours, R. L. S.

TO DR. W. BAMFORD

With a copy of *Travels with a Donkey*.

[*San Francisco, April* 1880.]

MY DEAR SIR,—Will you let me offer you this little book? If I had anything better, it should be yours. May you not dislike it, for it will be your own handiwork if there are other fruits from the same tree! But for your kindness and skill, this would have been my last book, and now I am in hopes that it will be neither my last nor my best.

You doctors have a serious responsibility. You recall a man from the gates of death, you give him health and strength once more to use or to abuse. I hope I shall feel

your responsibility added to my own, and seek in the future to make a better profit of the life you have renewed to me.—I am, my dear sir, gratefully yours,
 ROBERT LOUIS STEVENSON.

TO SIDNEY COLVIN

[*San Francisco, April* 1880.]

MY DEAR COLVIN,—You must be sick indeed of my demand for books, for you have seemingly not yet sent me one. Still, I live on promises: waiting for Penn, for H. James's *Hawthorne*, for my *Burns*, etc.; and now, to make matters worse, pending your *Centuries*, etc., I do earnestly desire the best book about mythology (if it be German, so much the worse; send a bunctionary along with it, and pray for me). This is why. If I recover, I feel called on to write a volume of gods and demi-gods in exile: Pan, Jove, Cybele, Venus, Charon, etc.; and though I should like to take them very free, I should like to know a little about 'em to begin with. For two days, till last night, I had no night sweats, and my cough is almost gone, and I digest well; so all looks hopeful. However, I was near the other side of Jordan. I send the proof of *Thoreau* to you, so that you may correct and fill up the quotation from Goethe. It is a pity I was ill, as, for matter, I think I prefer that to any of my essays except Burns; but the style, though quite manly, never attains any melody or lenity. So much for consumption: I begin to appreciate what the *Emigrant* must be. As soon as I have done the last few pages of the *Emigrant* they shall go to you. But when will that be? I know not quite yet—I have to be so careful.—Ever yours, R. L. S.

TO SIDNEY COLVIN

[*San Francisco, April* 1880.]

MY DEAR COLVIN,—My dear people telegraphed me in these words: 'Count on 250 pounds annually.' You

1880.
AET. 30.

may imagine what a blessed business this was. And so now recover the sheets of the *Emigrant*, and post them registered to me. And now please give me all your venom against it; say your worst, and most incisively, for now it will be a help, and I'll make it right or perish in the attempt. Now, do you understand why I protested against your depressing eloquence on the subject? When I *had* to go on any way, for dear life, I thought it a kind of pity and not much good to discourage me. Now all's changed. God only knows how much courage and suffering is buried in that MS. The second part was written in a circle of hell unknown to Dante—that of the penniless and dying author. For dying I was, although now saved. Another week, the doctor said, and I should have been past salvation. I think I shall always think of it as my best work. There is one page in Part II., about having got to shore, and sich, which must have cost me altogether six hours of work as miserable as ever I went through. I feel sick even to think of it.—Ever your friend,

R. L. S.

TO SIDNEY COLVIN

[*San Francisco, May* 1880.]

MY DEAR COLVIN,—I received your letter and proof to-day, and was greatly delighted with the last.

I am now out of danger; in but a short while (*i.e.* as soon as the weather is settled), F. and I marry and go up to the hills to look for a place; 'I to the hills will lift mine eyes, from whence doth come mine aid': once the place found, the furniture will follow. There, sir, in, I hope, a ranche among the pine-trees and hard by a running brook, we are to fish, hunt, sketch, study Spanish, French, Latin, Euclid, and History; and, if possible, not quarrel. Far from man, sir, in the virgin forest. Thence, as my strength returns, you may expect works of genius. I always feel as if I must write a work of genius some time or other; and when is it more likely to come off, than just after I have paid a visit to Styx and go thence to the eternal mountains? Such a revolution in a man's affairs, as I have somewhere written, would set anybody singing. When we get installed, Lloyd and I are going to print my poetical works; so all those who have been poetically addressed shall receive copies of their addresses. They are, I believe, pretty correct literary exercises, or will be, with a few filings; but they are not remarkable for white-hot vehemence of inspiration; tepid works! respectable versifications of very proper and even original sentiments: kind of Hayleyistic, I fear—but no, this is morbid self-depreciation. The family is all very shaky in health, but our motto is now 'Al Monte!' in the words of Don Lope, in the play the sister and I are just beating through with two bad dictionaries and an insane grammar. I to the hills.—Yours ever, R. L. S.

1880.
AET. 30.

TO C. W. STODDARD

This correspondent is Mr. Charles Warren Stoddard, author of *Summer Cruising in the South Seas*, etc., with whom Stevenson had made friends in the manner and amid the scenes faithfully described in *The Wrecker*, in the chapter called 'Faces on the City Front.'

East Oakland, Cal., May 1880.

MY DEAR STODDARD,—I am guilty in thy sight and the sight of God. However, I swore a great oath that you should see some of my manuscript at last; and though I have long delayed to keep it, yet it was to be. You re-read your story and were disgusted; that is the cold fit following the hot. I don't say you did wrong to be disgusted, yet I am sure you did wrong to be disgusted altogether. There was, you may depend upon it, some reason for your previous vanity, as well as your present mortification. I shall hear you, years from now, timidly begin to retrim your feathers for a little self-laudation, and trot out this misdespised novelette as not the worst of your performances. I read the album extracts with sincere interest; but I regret that you spared to give the paper more development; and I conceive that you might do a great deal worse than expand each of its paragraphs into an essay or sketch, the excuse being in each case your personal intercourse; the bulk, when that would not be sufficient, to be made up from their own works and stories. Three at least—Menken, Yelverton, and Keeler —could not fail of a vivid human interest. Let me press upon you this plan; should any document be wanted from Europe, let me offer my services to procure it. I am persuaded that there is stuff in the idea.

Are you coming over again to see me some day soon? I keep returning, and now hand over fist, from the realms of Hades: I saw that gentleman between the eyes, and fear him less after each visit. Only Charon, and his rough boatmanship, I somewhat fear.

I have a desire to write some verses for your album; so, if you will give me the entry among your gods, goddesses, and godlets, there will be nothing wanting but the Muse. I think of the verses like Mark Twain; sometimes I wish fulsomely to belaud you; sometimes to insult your city and fellow-citizens; sometimes to sit down quietly, with the slender reed, and troll a few staves of Panic ecstasy—but fy! fy! as my ancestors observed, the last is too easy for a man of my feet and inches.

At least, Stoddard, you now see that, although so costive, when I once begin I am a copious letter-writer. I thank you, and *au revoir*.

ROBERT LOUIS STEVENSON.

TO SIDNEY COLVIN

[*San Francisco, May* 1880.]

MY DEAR COLVIN,—It is a long while since I have heard from you; nearly a month, I believe; and I begin to grow very uneasy. At first I was tempted to suppose that I had been myself to blame in some way; but now I have grown to fear lest some sickness or trouble among those whom you love may not be the impediment. I believe I shall soon hear; so I wait as best I can. I am, beyond a doubt, greatly stronger, and yet still useless for any work, and, I may say, for any pleasure. My affairs and the bad weather still keep me here unmarried; but not, I earnestly hope, for long. Whenever I get into the mountain, I trust I shall rapidly pick up. Until I get away from these sea fogs and my imprisonment in the house, I do not hope to do much more than keep from active harm. My doctor took a desponding fit about me, and scared Fanny into blue fits; but I have talked her over again. It is the change I want, and the blessed sun, and a gentle air in which I can sit out and see the trees and running water: these mere defensive hygienics cannot advance one, though they may prevent evil. I do nothing now, but try to possess my soul in peace, and continue to possess my body on any terms.

Calistoga, Napa County, California.

All which is a fortnight old and not much to the point nowadays. Here we are, Fanny and I, and a certain hound, in a lovely valley under Mount Saint Helena, looking around, or rather wondering when we shall begin to look around, for a house of our own. I have received the first sheets of the *Amateur Emigrant*; not yet the second bunch, as announced. It is a pretty heavy, emphatic piece of pedantry; but I don't care; the public, I verily believe, will like it. I have excised all you proposed and more on my own movement. But I have not yet been able to rewrite the two special pieces which, as you said, so badly wanted it; it is hard work to rewrite passages in proof; and the easiest work is still hard to me. But I am certainly recovering fast; a married and convalescent being.

1880.
AET. 30.
Received James's *Hawthorne*, on which I meditate a blast, Miss Bird, Dixon's *Penn*, a *wrong Cornhill* (like my luck) and *Coquelin*: for all which, and especially the last, I tender my best thanks. I have opened only James; it is very clever, very well written, and out of sight the most inside-out thing in the world; I have dug up the hatchet; a scalp shall flutter at my belt ere long. I think my new book should be good; it will contain our adventures for the summer, so far as these are worth narrating; and I have already a few pages of diary which should make up bright. I am going to repeat my old experiment, after buckling-to a while to write more correctly, lie down and have a wallow. Whether I shall get any of my novels done this summer I do not know; I wish to finish the *Vendetta* first, for it really could not come after *Prince Otto*. Lewis Campbell has made some noble work in that Agamemnon; it surprised me. We hope to get a house at Silverado, a deserted mining-camp eight miles up the mountain, now solely inhabited by a mighty hunter answering to the name of Rufe Hansome, who slew last year a hundred and fifty deer. This is the motto I propose for the new volume: '*Vixerunt nonnulli in agris, delectati re sua familiari. His idem propositum fuit quod regibus, ut ne qua re egerent, ne cui parerent, libertate uterentur; cujus proprium est sic vivere ut velis.*' I always have a terror lest the wish should have been father to the translation, when I come to quote; but that seems too plain sailing. I should put *regibus* in capitals for the pleasantry's sake. We are in the Coast Range, that being so much cheaper to reach; the family, I hope, will soon follow.—Love to all, ever yours, R. L. S.

V

ALPINE WINTERS
AND HIGHLAND SUMMERS

AUGUST 1880—OCTOBER 1882

AFTER spending the months of June and July 1880 in the rough Californian mountain quarters described in *The Silverado Squatters*, Stevenson took passage with his wife and young stepson from New York on the 7th of August, and arrived on the 17th at Liverpool, where his parents and I were waiting to meet him. Of her new family, the Mrs. Robert Louis Stevenson brought thus strangely and from far into their midst made an immediate conquest. To her husband's especial happiness, there sprang up between her and his father the closest possible affection and confidence. Parents and friends—if it is permissible to one of the latter to say as much—rejoiced to recognise in Stevenson's wife a character as strong, interesting, and romantic almost as his own; an inseparable sharer of all his thoughts, and staunch companion of all his adventures; the most open-hearted of friends to all who loved him; the most shrewd and stimulating critic of his work; and in sickness, despite her own precarious health, the most devoted and most efficient of nurses. But there must be limits to the praise of the living; and what his wife was to him Stevenson has himself expressed, in words which are the fittest, and than which none ever came more truly from the heart.

From Liverpool the Stevenson party went on to make a

stay in Scotland, first at Edinburgh, and afterwards for a few weeks at Strathpeffer, resting at Blair Athol on the way. It was now, in his thirtieth year, among the woods of Tummelside and under the shoulder of Ben Wyvis, that Stevenson acknowledged for the first time the full power and beauty of the Highland scenery, which in youth, with his longings fixed ever upon the South, he had been accustomed to think too bleak and desolate. In the history of the country and its clans, on the other hand, and especially of their political and social transformation during the eighteenth century, he had been always keenly interested. In conversations with Principal Tulloch at Strathpeffer this interest was now revived, and he resolved to attempt a book on the subject, his father undertaking to keep him supplied with books and authorities; for it had quickly become apparent that he could not winter in Scotland. The state of his health continued to be very threatening. He suffered from acute chronic catarrh, accompanied by disquieting lung symptoms and great weakness; and was told accordingly that he must go for the winter, and probably for several succeeding winters, to the mountain valley of Davos in Switzerland, which within the last few years had been coming into repute as a place of recovery, or at least of arrested mischief, for lung patients. Thither he and his wife and stepson travelled accordingly at the end of October. Nor must another member of the party be forgotten, a black thoroughbred Skye terrier, the gift of Sir Walter Simpson (Stevenson's companion on the Inland Voyage). This creature was named, after his giver, Walter—a name subsequently corrupted into Wattie, Woggie, Wogg, Woggin, Bogie, Bogue, and a number of other affectionate diminutives which will be found occurring often enough in the following pages. He was a remarkably pretty, engaging, excitable, capricious little specimen of his race, the occasion of infinite anxiety and laughing care to his devoted master and mistress until his death six years later.

The Davos of 1880, approached by an eight hours' laborious drive up the valley of the Prättigau, was a very different place from the extended and embellished Davos of to-day, which to many readers is doubtless familiar, with its railway, its modern shops, its electric lighting, and its crowd of winter visitors bent on outdoor and indoor entertainment. The Stevensons' quarters for the first winter were at the Hotel Belvedere, then a mere nucleus of the huge establishment it has since become. Besides the usual society of an invalid hotel, with its mingled tragedies and comedies, they had there the great advantage of the presence, in a neighbouring house, of an accomplished man of letters and one of the most charming of companions, John Addington Symonds, with his family. Mr. Symonds, whose health had been desperate before he tried the place, was a living testimony to its virtues, and was at this time engaged in building the chalet which became his home until he died fourteen years later. During Stevenson's first season at Davos, though his mind was full of literary enterprises, he was too ill to do much actual work. For the Highland history he read much, but composed little or nothing, and eventually this history went to swell the long list of his unwritten books. He saw through the press his first volume of collected essays, *Virginibus Puerisque*, which came out early in 1881; and wrote the essay on Pepys afterwards published in *Familiar Studies of Men and Books*. Beyond this, he only amused himself with verses. Leaving the Alps at the end of April 1881, he returned, after a short stay in France (at Fontainebleau, Paris, and St. Germain), to his family in Edinburgh. Thence the whole party again went to the Highlands, this time to Pitlochry and Braemar.

During the summer Stevenson heard of the intended retirement of Professor Æneas Mackay from the chair of History and Constitutional Law at Edinburgh University. He determined, with the encouragement of the outgoing professor and of several of his literary friends, to become a candidate for the post, which had to be filled by the Faculty of Advocates from among their own number. The duties were limited to the delivery of a short course of lectures in the summer term, and Stevenson thought that he might be equal to them, and might prove, though certainly a new, yet perhaps a stimulating, type of Professor. But knowing the nature of his public reputation, especially in Edinburgh, where the recollection of his daft student days was as yet stronger than the impression made by his recent performances in literature, he was well aware that his candidature must seem paradoxical, and stood little chance of success. The election took place in the late autumn of the same year, and he was defeated, receiving only three votes.

At Pitlochry Stevenson was for a while able to enjoy his life and to work well, writing two of the strongest of his short stories of Scottish life and superstition, *Thrawn Janet* and *The Merry Men*, originally designed to form part of a volume to be written by himself and his wife in collaboration. At Braemar he made a beginning of the nursery verses which afterwards grew into the volume called *The Child's Garden*, and conceived and half executed the fortunate project of *Treasure Island*, the book which was destined first to make him famous. But one of the most inclement of Scottish summers had before long undone all the good gained in the previous winter at Davos, and in the autumn of the year 1881 he repaired thither again.

This time his quarters were in a small chalet belonging to the proprietors of the Buol Hotel, the Chalet am Stein, in the near neighbourhood of the Symonds's house. The beginning of his second stay was darkened by the serious illness of his wife; nevertheless, the winter was one of much greater literary activity than the last. A Life of Hazlitt was projected, and studies were made for it, but for some reason the project was never carried out. *Treasure Island* was finished; the greater part of the *Silverado Squatters* written; so were the Essays *Talk and Talkers*, *A Gossip on Romance*, and several other of his best papers for magazines. By way of whim and pastime he occupied himself, to his own and his stepson's delight, with the little set of woodcuts and verses printed by the latter at his toy press—'The Davos Press,' as they called it—as well as with mimic campaigns carried on between the man and boy with armies of lead soldiers in the spacious loft which filled the upper floor of the chalet. For the first and almost the only time in his life there awoke in him during these winters in Davos the spirit of lampoon; and he poured forth sets of verses, not without touches of a Swiftean fire, against commercial frauds in general, and those of certain local tradesmen in particular, as well as others in memory of a defunct publican of Edinburgh who had been one of his butts in youth. Finally, much revived in health by the beneficent air of the Alpine valley, he left it again in mid-spring of 1882, to return once more to Scotland, and to be once more thrown back to, or below, the point where he had started. After a short excursion from Edinburgh into the Appin country, where he made inquiries on the spot into the traditions concerning the murder of Campbell of Glenure, his three resting-places in Scotland during this summer were Stobo Manse, near Peebles, Lochearnhead, and Kingussie. At Stobo the dampness of the season and the place quickly threw him again into a very low state of health, from which three subsequent weeks of brilliant sunshine in Speyside did but little to restore him. In spite of this renewed breakdown, when autumn came he would not face the idea of returning for a third season to Davos. He had himself felt deeply the austerity and monotony of the white Alpine world in winter; and though he had unquestionably gained in health there, his wife on her part had suffered much. So he made up his mind once again to try the Mediterranean coast of France, and Davos knew him no more.

To A. G. Dew-Smith

1880.
AET. 30.

I print at the head of the first winter's letters from the Alps some verses from one in rhyme which he addressed by way of thanks to a friend at Cambridge, Mr. A. G. Dew-Smith, who had sent him a present of a box of cigarettes. It gives his first general impressions of the place, some of which he presently found cause to modify; and is very characteristic in its comments on the tame behaviour of the valley stream, the Landwasser, at this part of its course.

[*Hotel Belvedere, Davos, November* 1880.]

Figure me to yourself, I pray—
   A man of my peculiar cut—
Apart from dancing and deray,[1]
   Into an Alpine valley shut;

Shut in a kind of damned Hotel,
   Discountenanced by God and man;
The food?—Sir, you would do as well
   To cram your belly full of bran.

The company? Alas, the day
   That I should dwell with such a crew,
With devil anything to say,
   Nor any one to say it to!

The place? Although they call it Platz,
   I will be bold and state my view;
It's not a place at all—and that's
   The bottom verity, my Dew.

There are, as I will not deny,
   Innumerable inns; a road;
Several Alps indifferent high;
   The snow's inviolable abode;

Eleven English parsons, all
   Entirely inoffensive; four
True human beings—what I call
   Human—the deuce a cipher more;

---

[1] 'The whole front of the house was lighted, and there were pipes and fiddles, and as much dancing and deray within as used to be in Sir Robert's house at Pace and Yule, and such high seasons.'—From 'Wandering Willie's Tale' in *Redgauntlet*.

1880.
AET. 30.

A climate of surprising worth;
   Innumerable dogs that bark;
Some air, some weather, and some earth;
   A native race—God save the mark!—

A race that works, yet cannot work,
   Yodels, but cannot yodel right,
Such as, unhelp'd, with rusty dirk,
   I vow that I could wholly smite.

A river that from morn to night
   Down all the valley plays the fool;
Not once she pauses in her flight,
   Nor knows the comfort of a pool;

But still keeps up, by straight or bend,
   The selfsame pace she hath begun—
Still hurry, hurry, to the end—
   Good God, is that the way to run?

If I a river were, I hope
   That I should better realise
The opportunities and scope
   Of that romantic enterprise.

I should not ape the merely strange,
   But aim besides at the divine;
And continuity and change
   I still should labour to combine.

Here should I gallop down the race,
   Here charge the sterling[1] like a bull;
There, as a man might wipe his face,
   Lie, pleased and panting, in a pool.

But what, my Dew, in idle mood,
   What prate I, minding not my debt?
What do I talk of bad or good?
   The best is still a cigarette.

[1] In architecture, a series of piles to defend the pier of a bridge.

Me whether evil fate assault,
  Or smiling providences crown—
Whether on high the eternal vault
  Be blue, or crash with thunder down—

I judge the best, whate'er befall,
  Is still to sit on one's behind,
And, having duly moistened all,
  Smoke with an unperturbèd mind.
R. L. S.

TO THOMAS STEVENSON

R. L. S. here sketches for his father the plan of the work on Highland History which they had discussed together in the preceding summer, and which Principal Tulloch had urged him to attempt.

[Hotel Belvedere], Davos, December 12 [1880

MY DEAR FATHER,—Here is the scheme as well as I can foresee. I begin the book immediately after the '15, as then began the attempt to suppress the Highlands.

I. THIRTY YEARS' INTERVAL

(1) Rob Roy.
(2) The Independent Companies: the Watches.
(3) Story of Lady Grange.
(4) The Military Roads, and Disarmament: Wade and
(5) Burt.

II. THE HEROIC AGE

(1) Duncan Forbes of Culloden.
(2) Flora Macdonald.
(3) The Forfeited Estates; including Hereditary Jurisdictions; and the admirable conduct of the tenants.

1880.
AET. 30.

III. LITERATURE HERE INTERVENES
(1) The Ossianic Controversy.
(2) Boswell and Johnson.
(3) Mrs. Grant of Laggan.

IV. ECONOMY
(1) Highland Economics.
(2) The Reinstatement of the Proprietors.
(3) The Evictions.
(4) Emigration.
(5) Present State.

V. RELIGION
(1) The Catholics, Episcopals, and Kirk, and Soc. Prop. Christ. Knowledge.
(2) The Men.
(3) The Disruption.

All this, of course, will greatly change in form, scope, and order; this is just a bird's-eye glance. Thank you for *Burt*, which came, and for your Union notes. I have read one-half (about 900 pages) of Wodrow's *Correspondence*, with some improvement, but great fatigue. The doctor thinks well of my recovery, which puts me in good hope for the future. I should certainly be able to make a fine history of this.

My Essays are going through the press, and should be out in January or February.—Ever affectionate son,

R. L. S.

TO EDMUND GOSSE

The suggestions contained in the following letters to Mr. Gosse refer to the collection of English Odes which that gentleman was then engaged in editing (Kegan Paul, 1881).

Hotel Belvedere, Davos Platz [*Dec.* 6, 1880].

MY DEAR WEG,—I have many letters that I ought to write in preference to this; but a duty to letters and to you prevails over any private consideration. You are going to collect odes; I could not wish a better man to do so; but I tremble lest you should commit two sins of omission. You will not, I am sure, be so far left to yourself as to give us no more of Dryden than the hackneyed St. Cecilia; I know you will give us some others of those surprising masterpieces where there is more sustained eloquence and harmony of English numbers than in all that has been written since; there is a machine about a poetical young lady, and another about either Charles or James, I know not which; and they are both indescribably fine. (Is Marvell's Horatian Ode good enough? I half think so.) But my great point is a fear that you are one of those who are unjust to our old Tennyson's Duke of Wellington. I have just been talking it over with Symonds; and we agreed that whether for its metrical effects, for its brief, plain, stirring words of portraiture, as—he 'that never lost an English gun,' or—the soldier salute; or for the heroic apostrophe to Nelson; that ode has never been surpassed in any tongue or time. Grant me the Duke, O Weg! I suppose you must not put in yours about the warship; you will have to admit worse ones, however.—Ever yours, R. L. S.

TO EDMUND GOSSE

[*Hotel Belvedere*], *Davos, Dec.* 19, 1880.

This letter is a report of a long sederunt, also steterunt in small committee at Davos Platz, Dec. 15, 1880. Its results are unhesitatingly shot at your head.

MY DEAR WEG,—We both insist on the Duke of Wellington. Really it cannot be left out. Symonds said you would cover yourself with shame, and I add, your friends with confusion, if you leave it out. Really, you know it is the only thing you have, since Dryden, where that irregular odic, odal, odous (?) verse is used with mastery

1880.
AET. 30.
and sense. And it's one of our few English blood-boilers.

(2) Byron: if anything: *Prometheus*.

(3) Shelley (1) *The world's great age* from *Hellas*; we are both dead on. After that you have, of course, *The West Wind* thing. But we think (1) would maybe be enough; no more than two any way.

(4) Herrick. *Meddowes* and *Come, my Corinna*. After that *Mr. Wickes*: two any way.

(5) Leave out stanza 3rd of Congreve's thing, like a dear; we can't stand the 'sigh' nor the 'peruke.'

(6) Milton. *Time* and the *Solemn Music*. We both agree we would rather go without L'Allegro and Il Penseroso than these; for the reason that these are not so well known to the brutish herd.

(7) Is the *Royal George* an ode, or only an elegy? It's so good.

(8) We leave Campbell to you.

(9) If you take anything from Clough, but we don't either of us fancy you will, let it be *Come back*.

(10) Quite right about Dryden. I had a hankering after *Threnodia Augustalis*; but I find it long and with very prosaic holes: though, O! what fine stuff between whiles.

(11) Right with Collins.

(12) Right about Pope's Ode. But what can you give? *The Dying Christian*? or one of his inimitable courtesies? These last are fairly odes, by the Horatian model, just as my dear *Meddowes* is an ode in the name and for the sake of Bandusia.

(13) Whatever you do, you'll give us the Greek Vase.

(14) Do you like Johnson's 'loathèd stage'? Verses 2, 3, and 4 are so bad, also the last line. But there is a fine movement and feeling in the rest.

We will have the Duke of Wellington by God. Pro Symonds and Stevenson.   R. L. S.

1880.
AET. 30.

TO CHARLES WARREN STODDARD

The prospect here alluded to of a cheap edition of the little travel-books did not get realised. The volume of essays in the printer's hands was *Virginibus Puerisque*. I do not know what were the pages in broad Scotch copied by way of enclosure.

Hotel Belvedere, Davos Platz, Switzerland [*December* 1880].

DEAR CHARLES WARREN STODDARD,—Many thanks to you for the letter and the photograph. Will you think it mean if I ask you to wait till there appears a promised cheap edition? Possibly the canny Scot does feel pleasure in the superior cheapness; but the true reason is this, that I think to put a few words, by way of notes, to each book in its new form, because that will be the Standard Edition, without which no g.'s l.[1] will be complete. The edition, briefly, *sine qua non*. Before that, I shall hope to send you my essays, which are in the printer's hands. I look to get yours soon. I am sorry to hear that the Custom House has proved fallible, like all other human houses and customs. Life consists of that sort of business, and I fear that there is a class of man, of which you offer no inapt type, doomed to a kind of mild, general disappointment through life. I do not believe that a man is the more unhappy for that. Disappointment, except with one's self, is not a very capital affair; and the sham beatitude, 'Blessed is he that expecteth little,' one of the truest, and in a sense, the most Christlike things in literature.

Alongside of you, I have been all my days a red cannon ball of dissipated effort; here I am by the heels in this Alpine valley, with just so much of a prospect of future restoration as shall make my present caged estate easily tolerable to me—shall or should, I would not swear to the word before the trial's done. I miss all my objects

[1] Gentleman's library.

1880.
AET. 30.

in the meantime; and, thank God, I have enough of my old, and maybe somewhat base philosophy, to keep me on a good understanding with myself and Providence.

The mere extent of a man's travels has in it something consolatory. That he should have left friends and enemies in many different and distant quarters gives a sort of earthly dignity to his existence. And I think the better of myself for the belief that I have left some in California interested in me and my successes. Let me assure you, you who have made friends already among such various and distant races, that there is a certain phthisical Scot who will always be pleased to hear good news of you, and would be better pleased by nothing than to learn that you had thrown off your present incubus, largely consisting of letters I believe, and had sailed into some square work by way of change.

And by way of change in itself, let me copy on the other pages some broad Scotch I wrote for you when I was ill last spring in Oakland. It is no muckle worth: but ye should na look a gien horse in the moo'.—Yours ever,
R. L. STEVENSON.

TO MR. AND MRS. THOMAS STEVENSON

The verses, here mentioned, to John Brown (the admired author of *Rab and his Friends*) were meant as a reply to a letter of congratulation on the *Inland Voyage* received from him the year before. They are printed in *Underwoods*, p. 166.

December 21, 1880. *Davos.*

MY DEAR PEOPLE,—I do not understand these reproaches. The letters come between seven and nine in the evening; and every one about the books was answered that same night, and the answer left Davos by seven o'clock next morning. Perhaps the snow delayed them; if so, 'tis a good hint to you not to be uneasy at apparent silences. There is no hurry about my father's notes; I shall not be writing anything till I get home again, I believe. Only I want to be able to keep reading *ad hoc* all winter, as it seems about all I shall be fit for. About John Brown, I have been breaking my heart to finish a Scotch poem to him. Some of it is not really bad, but the rest will not come, and I mean to get it right before I do anything else.

The bazaar is over, £160 gained, and everybody's health lost: altogether, I never had a more uncomfortable time; apply to Fanny for further details of the discomfort.

We have our Wogg in somewhat better trim now, and vastly better spirits. The weather has been bad—for Davos, but indeed it is a wonderful climate. It never feels cold; yesterday, with a little, chill, small, northerly draught, for the first time, it was pinching. Usually, it may freeze, or snow, or do what it pleases, you feel it not, or hardly any.

Thanks for your notes; that fishery question will come in, as you notice, in the Highland Book, as well as under the Union; it is very important. I hear no word of Hugh Miller's *Evictions*; I count on that. What you say about the old and new Statistical is odd. It seems to me very much as if I were gingerly embarking on a *History of Modern Scotland*. Probably Tulloch will never carry it out. And, you see, once I have studied and written these two vols., *The Transformation of the Scottish Highlands* and *Scotland and the Union*, I shall have a good ground to go upon. The effect on my mind of what I have read has been to awaken a livelier sympathy for the Irish; although they never had the remarkable virtues, I fear they have suffered many of the injustices, of the Scottish Highlanders. Ruedi has seen me this morning; he says the disease is at a standstill, and I am to profit by it to take more exercise. Altogether, he seemed quite hopeful and pleased.—I am your ever affectionate son, R. L. S.

1880.
AET. 30.

TO SIDNEY COLVIN

[*Hotel Belvedere, Davos, Christmas* 1880.]

MY DEAR COLVIN,—Thanks for yours; I waited, as I said I would. I now expect no answer from you, regarding you as a mere dumb cock-shy, or a target, at which we fire our arrows diligently all day long, with no anticipation it will bring them back to us. We are both sadly mortified you are not coming, but health comes first; alas, that man should be so crazy. What fun we could have, if we were all well, what work we could do, what a happy place we could make it for each other! If I were able to do what I want; but then I am not, and may leave that vein.

No. I do not think I shall require to know the Gaelic; few things are written in that language, or ever were; if you come to that, the number of those who could write, or even read it, through almost all my period, must, by all accounts, have been incredibly small. Of course, until the book is done, I must live as much as possible in the Highlands, and that suits my book as to health. It is a most interesting and sad story, and from the '45 it is all to be written for the first time. This, of course, will cause me a far greater difficulty about authorities; but I have already learned much, and where to look for more. One pleasant feature is the vast number of delightful writers I shall have to deal with: Burt, Johnson, Boswell, Mrs. Grant of Laggan, Scott. There will be interesting sections on the Ossianic controversy and the growth of the taste for Highland scenery. I have to touch upon Rob Roy, Flora Macdonald, the strange story of Lady Grange, the beautiful story of the tenants on the Forfeited Estates, and the odd, inhuman problem of the great evictions. The religious conditions are wild, unknown, very surprising. And three out of my five parts remain hitherto entirely unwritten. Smack!—Yours ever,   R. L. S.

TO MRS. THOMAS STEVENSON

1880.
AET. 30.

Christmas Sermon.

[*Hotel Belvedere, Davos, December* 26, 1880.]

MY DEAR MOTHER,—I was very tired yesterday and could not write; tobogganed so furiously all morning; we had a delightful day, crowned by an incredible dinner —more courses than I have fingers on my hands. Your letter arrived duly at night, and I thank you for it as I should. You need not suppose I am at all insensible to my father's extraordinary kindness about this book; he is a brick; I vote for him freely.

... The assurance you speak of is what we all ought to have, and might have, and should not consent to live without. That people do not have it more than they do is, I believe, because persons speak so much in large-drawn, theological similitudes, and won't say out what they mean about life, and man, and God, in fair and square human language. I wonder if you or my father ever thought of the obscurities that lie upon human duty from the negative form in which the Ten Commandments are stated, or of how Christ was so continually substituting affirmations. 'Thou shalt not' is but an example; 'Thou shalt' is the law of God. It was this that seems meant in the phrase that 'not one jot nor tittle of the law should pass.' But what led me to the remark is this: A kind of black, angry look goes with that statement of the law of negatives. 'To love one's neighbour as oneself' is certainly much harder, but states life so much more actively, gladly, and kindly, that you can begin to see some pleasure in it; and till you can see pleasure in these hard choices and bitter necessities, where is there any Good News to men? It is much more important to do right than not to do wrong; further, the one is possible, the other has always been and will ever be impossible; and the faithful *design to do right* is accepted by God; that seems to me to be the Gospel, and that was how Christ delivered us from the Law. After people are told that, surely they might hear more encouraging sermons. To blow the trumpet for good would seem the Parson's business; and since it is not in our own strength, but by faith and perseverance (no account made of slips), that we are to run the race, I do not see where they get the material for their gloomy discourses. Faith is not to believe the Bible, but to believe in God; if you believe in God (or, for it's the same thing, have that assurance you speak about), where is there any more room for terror? There are only three possible attitudes—Optimism, which has gone to smash; Pessimism, which is on the rising hand, and very popular with many clergymen who seem to think they are Christians. And this Faith, which is the Gospel. Once you hold the last, it is your business (1) to find out what is right in any given case, and (2) to try to do it; if you fail in the last, that is by commission, Christ tells you to hope; if you fail in the first, that is by omission, his picture of the last day gives you but a black lookout. The whole necessary morality is kindness; and it should spring, of itself, from the one fundamental doctrine, Faith. If you are sure that God, in the long run, means kindness by you, you should be happy; and if happy, surely you should be kind.

I beg your pardon for this long discourse; it is not all right, of course, but I am sure there is something in it. One thing I have not got clearly; that about the omission and the commission; but there is truth somewhere about it, and I have no time to clear it just now. Do you know, you have had about a Cornhill page of sermon? It is, however, true.

Lloyd heard with dismay Fanny was not going to give me a present; so F. and I had to go and buy things for ourselves, and go through a representation of surprise when they were presented next morning. It gave us both quite a Santa Claus feeling on Xmas Eve to see him so excited and hopeful; I enjoyed it hugely.—Your affectionate son, ROBERT LOUIS STEVENSON.

1881.
AET. 31.

TO SIDNEY COLVIN

I did go out to my friend after all in January; found him apparently little improved in health, and depressed by a sad turn of destiny which had brought out to the same place, at the same time, his old friend of Suffolk and Edinburgh days to watch beside the deathbed of her son—the youth commemorated in the verses headed *F. A. S., In Memoriam*, afterwards published in *Underwoods*. The following letter refers to a copy of Carlyle's *Reminiscences* which I had sent out to him some time after I came back to England.

[*Hotel Belvedere, Davos, Spring* 1881.]

MY DEAR COLVIN.—My health is not just what it should be; I have lost weight, pulse, respiration, etc., and gained nothing in the way of my old bellows. But these last few days, with tonic, cod-liver oil, better wine (there is some better now), and perpetual beef-tea, I think I have progressed. To say truth, I have been here a little over long. I was reckoning up, and since I have known you, already quite a while, I have not, I believe, remained so long in any one place as here in Davos. That tells on my old gipsy nature; like a violin hung up, I begin to lose what music there was in me; and with the music, I do not know what besides, or do not know what to call it, but something radically part of life, a rhythm, perhaps, in one's old and so brutally over-ridden nerves, or perhaps a kind of variety of blood that the heart has come to look for.

I purposely knocked myself off first. As to F. A. S., I believe I am no sound authority; I alternate between a stiff disregard and a kind of horror. In neither mood can a man judge at all. I know the thing to be terribly perilous, I fear it to be now altogether

1881.
AET. 31.

hopeless. Luck has failed; the weather has not been favourable; and in her true heart, the mother hopes no more. But—well, I feel a great deal, that I either cannot or will not say, as you well know. It has helped to make me more conscious of the wolverine on my own shoulders, and that also makes me a poor judge and poor adviser. Perhaps, if we were all marched out in a row, and a piece of platoon firing to the drums performed, it would be well for us; although, I suppose—and yet I wonder!—so ill for the poor mother and for the dear wife. But you can see this makes me morbid. *Sufficit*; *explicit*.

You are right about the Carlyle book; F. and I are in a world not ours; but pardon me, as far as sending on goes, we take another view: the first volume, *à la bonne heure!* but not—never—the second. Two hours of hysterics can be no good matter for a sick nurse, and the strange, hard, old being in so lamentable and yet human a desolation—crying out like a burnt child, and yet always wisely and beautifully—how can that end, as a piece of reading, even to the strong—but on the brink of the most cruel kind of weeping? I observe the old man's style is stronger on me than ever it was, and by rights, too, since I have just laid down his most attaching book. God rest the baith o' them! But even if they do not meet again, how we should all be strengthened to be kind, and not only in act, in speech also, that so much more important part. See what this apostle of silence most regrets, not speaking out his heart.

I was struck as you were by the admirable, sudden, clear sunshine upon Southey—even on his works. Symonds, to whom I repeated it, remarked at once, a man who was thus respected by both Carlyle and Landor must have had more in him than we can trace. So I feel with true humility.

It was to save my brain that Symonds proposed reviewing. He and, it appears, Leslie Stephen fear a little some eclipse; I am not quite without sharing the fear. I know my own languor as no one else does; it is a dead down-draught, a heavy fardel. Yet if I could shake off the wolverine aforesaid, and his fangs are lighter, though perhaps I feel them more, I believe I could be myself again a while. I have not written any letter for a great time; none saying what I feel, since you were here, I fancy. Be duly obliged for it, and take my most earnest thanks not only for the books but for your letter. Your affectionate, R. L. S.

1881.
AET. 31.

The effect of reading this on Fanny shows me I must tell you I am very happy, peaceful, and jolly, except for questions of work and the states of other people.
Woggin sends his love.

TO HORATIO F. BROWN

A close intimate of J. A. Symonds, and frequent visitor at Davos, was Mr. Horatio F. Brown, author of *Life on the Lagoons*, etc. He took warmly, as did every one, to Stevenson. The following two notes are from a copy of Penn's *Fruits of Solitude*, printed at Philadelphia, which Stevenson sent him as a gift this winter after his return to Venice.

Davos, 1881.

MY DEAR BROWN.—Here it is, with the mark of a San Francisco *bouquiniste*. And if ever in all my 'human conduct' I have done a better thing to any fellow-creature than handing on to you this sweet, dignified, and wholesome book, I know I shall hear of it on the last day. To write a book like this were impossible; at least one can hand it on—with a wrench—one to another. My wife cries out and my own heart misgives me, but still here it is. I could scarcely better prove myself—Yours affectionately, R. L. STEVENSON.

1881.
AET. 31.

TO HORATIO F. BROWN

Davos, 1881.

MY DEAR BROWN.—I hope, if you get thus far, you will know what an invaluable present I have made you. Even the copy was dear to me, printed in the colony that Penn established, and carried in my pocket all about the San Francisco streets, read in street cars and ferry-boats, when I was sick unto death, and found in all times and places a peaceful and sweet companion. But I hope, when you shall have reached this note, my gift will not have been in vain; for while just now we are so busy and intelligent, there is not the man living, no, nor recently dead, that could put, with so lovely a spirit, so much honest, kind wisdom into words. — R. L. S.

TO HORATIO F. BROWN

The following experiment in English alcaics was suggested by conversations with Mr. Brown and J. A. Symonds on metrical forms, followed by the despatch of some translations from old Venetian boat-songs by the former after his return to Venice. There is evidently something wrong with stanza ii., line 3, but I print it as written:—

[*Hotel Belvedere, Davos, Spring* 1881.

MY DEAR BROWN,—Nine years I have conded them.

> Brave lads in olden musical centuries
> Sang, night by night, adorable choruses,
>   Sat late by alehouse doors in April
>   Chaunting in joy as the moon was rising:

> Moon-seen and merry, under the trellises,
> Flush-faced they played with old polysyllables;
>   Spring scents inspired, old wine diluted,
>   Love and Apollo were there to chorus.

> Now these, the songs, remain to eternity,
> Those, only those, the bountiful choristers
>   Gone—those are gone, those unremembered
>   Sleep and are silent in earth for ever.

So man himself appears and evanishes,
So smiles and goes; as wanderers halting at
    Some green-embowered house, play their music,
    Play and are gone on the windy highway;

Yet dwells the strain enshrined in the memory
Long after they departed eternally,
    Forth-faring tow'rd far mountain summits,
    Cities of men on the sounding Ocean.

Youth sang the song in years immemorial;
Brave chanticleer, he sang and was beautiful;
    Bird-haunted, green tree-tops in springtime
    Heard and were pleased by the voice of singing;

Youth goes, and leaves behind him a prodigy—
Songs sent by thee afar from Venetian
    Sea-grey lagunes, sea-paven highways,
    Dear to me here in my Alpine exile.

Please, my dear Brown, forgive my horrid delay. Symonds overworked and knocked up. I off my sleep; my wife gone to Paris. Weather lovely.—Yours ever,
                ROBERT LOUIS STEVENSON.

Monte Generoso in May; here, I think, till the end of April; write again, to prove you are forgiving.

TO MR. AND MRS. THOMAS STEVENSON

Monte Generoso was given up; and on the way home to Scotland Stevenson had stopped for a while at Fontainebleau, and then in Paris; whence, finding himself unpleasantly affected by the climate, he presently took refuge at St. Germain.

Hotel du Pavillon Henry IV.,
St. Germain-en-Laye, Sunday, May 1st, 1881.

MY DEAR PEOPLE,—A week in Paris reduced me to the limpness and lack of appetite peculiar to a kid glove, and gave Fanny a jumping sore throat. It's my belief there is death in the kettle there; a pestilence or the like. We came out here, pitched on the *Star and Garter* (they call

1881.
AET. 31.

it Somebody's pavilion), found the place a bed of lilacs and nightingales (first time I ever heard one), and also of a bird called the *piasseur*, cheerfulest of sylvan creatures, an ideal comic opera in itself. 'Come along, what fun, here's Pan in the next glade at picnic, and this-yer's Arcadia, and it's awful fun, and I've had a glass, I will not deny, but not to see it on me,' that is his meaning as near as I can gather. Well, the place (forest of beeches all new-fledged, grass like velvet, fleets of hyacinth) pleased us and did us good. We tried all ways to find a cheaper place, but could find nothing safe; cold, damp, brick-floored rooms and sich; we could not leave Paris till your seven days' sight on draft expired; we dared not go back to be miasmatised in these homes of putridity; so here we are till Tuesday in the *Star and Garter*. My throat is quite cured, appetite and strength on the mend. Fanny seems also picking up.

If we are to come to Scotland, I *will* have fir-trees, and I want a burn, the firs for my physical, the water for my moral health.—Ever affectionate son,   R. L. S.

TO EDMUND GOSSE

At Pitlochry, Stevenson was for some weeks in good health and working order. The inquiries about the later life of Jean Cavalier, the Protestant leader in the Cévennes, refer to a literary scheme, whether of romance or history I forget, which had been in his mind ever since the *Travels with a Donkey*.

Pitlochry, Perthshire, June 6, 1881.

MY DEAR WEG,—Here I am in my native land, being gently blown and hailed upon, and sitting nearer and nearer to the fire. A cottage near a moor is soon to receive our human forms; it is also near a burn to which Professor Blackie (no less!) has written some verses in his hot old age, and near a farm from whence we shall draw cream and fatness. Should I be moved to join Blackie,

I shall go upon my knees and pray hard against tempta- 1881.
tion; although, since the new Version, I do not know the AET. 31.
proper form of words. The swollen, childish, and pedantic
vanity that moved the said revisers to put 'bring' for
'lead,' is a sort of literary fault that calls for an eternal
hell; it may be quite a small place, a star of the least
magnitude, and shabbily furnished; there shall ——, ——,
the revisers of the Bible and other absolutely loathsome
literary lepers, dwell among broken pens, bad, *groundy*
ink and ruled blotting-paper made in France—all eagerly
burning to write, and all inflicted with incurable aphasia.
I should not have thought upon that torture had I not
suffered it in moderation myself, but it is too horrid even
for a hell; let's let 'em off with an eternal toothache.

All this talk is partly to persuade you that I write to
you out of good feeling only, which is not the case. I am
a beggar: ask Dobson, Saintsbury, yourself, and any
other of these cheeses who know something of the eighteenth century, what became of Jean Cavalier between his
coming to England and his death in 1740. Is anything
interesting known about him? Whom did he marry?
The happy French, smilingly following one another in a
long procession headed by the loud and empty Napoleon
Peyrat, say, Olympe Dunoyer, Voltaire's old flame.
Vacquerie even thinks that they were rivals, and is very
French and very literary and very silly in his comments.
Now I may almost say it consists with my knowledge
that all this has not a shadow to rest upon. It is very
odd and very annoying; I have splendid materials for
Cavalier till he comes to my own country; and there,
though he continues to advance in the service, he becomes
entirely invisible to me. Any information about him will
be greatly welcome: I may mention that I know as much
as I desire about the other prophets, Marion, Fage,
Cavalier (de Sonne), my Cavalier's cousin, the unhappy
Lions, and the idiotic Mr. Lacy; so if any erudite starts
upon that track, you may choke him off. If you can find

1881.
AET. 31.

aught for me, or if you will but try, count on my undying gratitude. Lang's 'Library' is very pleasant reading. My book *will* reach you soon, for I write about it to-day.
—Yours ever, ROBERT LOUIS STEVENSON.

TO SIDNEY COLVIN

Work on a series of tales of terror, or, as he called them, 'crawlers,' planned in collaboration with his wife, soon superseded for the moment other literary interests in his mind.

Kinnaird Cottage, Pitlochry, Perthshire, June 1881.

MY DEAR COLVIN,—*The Black Man and Other Tales.*

The Black Man:
   I. Thrawn Janet.
   II. The Devil on Cramond Sands.
The Shadow on the Bed.
The Body Snatchers.
The Case Bottle.
The King's Horn.
The Actor's Wife.
The Wreck of the *Susanna*.

This is the new work on which I am engaged with Fanny; they are all supernatural. 'Thrawn Janet' is off to Stephen, but as it is all in Scotch he cannot take it, I know. It was *so good*, I could not help sending it. My health improves. We have a lovely spot here: a little green glen with a burn, a wonderful burn, gold and green and snow-white, singing loud and low in different steps of its career, now pouring over miniature crags, now fretting itself to death in a maze of rocky stairs and pots; never was so sweet a little river. Behind, great purple moorlands reaching to Ben Vrackie. Hunger lives here, alone with larks and sheep. Sweet spot, sweet spot.

Write me a word about Bob's professoriate and Landor, and what you think of *The Black Man*. The tales are all ghastly. 'Thrawn Janet' frightened me to death. There will maybe be another—'The Dead Man's Letter.' I believe I shall recover; and I am, in this blessed hope, yours exuberantly, R. L. S.

1881.
AET. 31.

TO PROFESSOR ÆNEAS MACKAY

This and the next four or five letters refer to the candidature of R. L. S. for the Edinburgh Chair.

Kinnaird Cottage, Pitlochry, Wednesday, June 21, 1881.

MY DEAR MACKAY,—What is this I hear?—that you are retiring from your chair. It is not, I hope, from ill-health?

But if you are retiring, may I ask if you have promised your support to any successor? I have a great mind to try. The summer session would suit me; the chair would suit me—if only I would suit it; I certainly should work it hard: that I can promise. I only wish it were a few years from now, when I hope to have something more substantial to show for myself. Up to the present time, all that I have published, even bordering on history, has been in an occasional form, and I fear this is much against me.

Please let me hear a word in answer, and believe me, yours very sincerely, ROBERT LOUIS STEVENSON.

TO PROFESSOR ÆNEAS MACKAY

Kinnaird Cottage, Pitlochry, Perthshire [June 1881].

MY DEAR MACKAY,—Thank you very much for your kind letter, and still more for your good opinion. You are not the only one who has regretted my absence from your lectures; but you were to me, then, only a part of a mangle through which I was being slowly and unwillingly dragged—part of a course which I had not chosen —part, in a word, of an organised boredom.

I am glad to have your reasons for giving up the chair;

1881.
AET. 31.

they are partly pleasant, and partly honourable to you. And I think one may say that every man who publicly declines a plurality of offices, makes it perceptibly more difficult for the next man to accept them.

Every one tells me that I come too late upon the field, every one being pledged, which, seeing it is yet too early for any one to come upon the field, I must regard as a polite evasion. Yet all advise me to stand, as it might serve me against the next vacancy. So stand I shall, unless things are changed. As it is, with my health this summer class is a great attraction; it is perhaps the only hope I may have of a permanent income. I had supposed the needs of the chair might be met by choosing every year some period of history in which questions of Constitutional Law were involved; but this is to look too far forward.

I understand (1st) that no overt steps can be taken till your resignation is accepted; and (2nd) that in the meantime I may, without offence, mention my design to stand.

If I am mistaken about these, please correct me, as I do not wish to appear where I should not.

Again thanking you very heartily for your coals of fire, I remain yours very sincerely,

ROBERT LOUIS STEVENSON.

TO EDMUND GOSSE

Kinnaird Cottage, Pitlochry, June 24, 1881.

MY DEAR GOSSE,—I wonder if I misdirected my last to you. I begin to fear it. I hope, however, this will go right. I am in act to do a mad thing—to stand for the Edinburgh Chair of History; it is elected for by the advocates, *quorum pars*; I am told that I am too late this year; but advised on all hands to go on, as it is likely soon to be once more vacant; and I shall have done myself good for the next time. Now, if I got the thing (which I cannot, it appears), I believe, in spite of all my imperfections, I could be decently effectual. If you can think so also, do put it in a testimonial.

Heavens! *Je me sauve*, I have something else to say to you, but after that (which is not a joke) I shall keep it for another shoot.—Yours testimonially,

ROBERT LOUIS STEVENSON.

I surely need not add, dear lad, that if you don't feel like it, you will only have to pacify me by a long letter on general subjects, when I shall hasten to respond in recompense for my assault upon the postal highway.

TO EDMUND GOSSE

Kinnaird Cottage, Pitlochry [*July* 1881].

MY DEAR WEG,—Many thanks for the testimonial; many thanks for your blind, wondering letter; many wishes, lastly, for your swift recovery. Insomnia is the opposite pole from my complaint; which brings with it a nervous lethargy, an unkind, unwholesome, and ungentle somnolence, fruitful in heavy heads and heavy eyes at morning. You cannot sleep; well, I can best explain my state thus: I cannot wake. Sleep, like the lees of a posset, lingers all day, lead-heavy, in my knees and ankles. Weight on the shoulders, torpor on the brain. And there is more than too much of that from an ungrateful hound who is now enjoying his first decently competent and peaceful weeks for close upon two years; happy in a big brown moor behind him, and an incomparable burn by his side; happy, above all, in some work —for at last I am at work with that appetite and confidence that alone makes work supportable.

I told you I had something else to say. I am very tedious—it is another request. In August and a good part of September we shall be in Braemar, in a house with some accommodation. Now Braemar is a place

1881.
AET. 31.
patronised by the royalty of the Sister Kingdoms—Victoria and the Cairngorms, sir, honouring that countryside by their conjunct presence. This seems to me the spot for A Bard. Now can you come to see us for a little while? I can promise you, you must like my father, because you are a human being; you ought to like Braemar, because of your avocation; and you ought to like me, because I like you; and again, you must like my wife, because she likes cats; and as for my mother—well, come and see, what do you think? that is best. Mrs. Gosse, my wife tells me, will have other fish to fry; and to be plain, I should not like to ask her till I had seen the house. But a lone man I know we shall be equal to. *Qu'en dis tu? Viens.*—Yours, R. L. S.

TO P. G. HAMERTON

Kinnaird Cottage, Pitlochry [*July* 1881].

MY DEAR MR. HAMMERTON,—(There goes the second M.; it is a certainty.) Thank you for your prompt and kind answer, little as I deserved it, though I hope to show you I was less undeserving than I seemed. But just might I delete two words in your testimonial? The two words 'and legal' were unfortunately winged by chance against my weakest spot, and would go far to damn me.

It was not my bliss that I was interested in when I was married; it was a sort of marriage *in extremis*; and if I am where I am, it is thanks to the care of that lady who married me when I was a mere complication of cough and bones, much fitter for an emblem of mortality than a bridegroom.

I had a fair experience of that kind of illness when all the women (God bless them!) turn round upon the streets and look after you with a look that is only too kind not to be cruel. I have had nearly two years of more or less prostration. I have done no work whatever since the

February before last until quite of late. To be precise, until the beginning of last month, exactly two essays. All last winter I was at Davos; and indeed I am home here just now against the doctor's orders, and must soon be back again to that unkindly haunt 'upon the mountains visitant'—there goes no angel there but the angel of death.[1] The deaths of last winter are still sore spots to me. . . . So, you see, I am not very likely to go on a 'wild expedition,' cis-Stygian at least. The truth is, I am scarce justified in standing for the chair, though I hope you will not mention this; and yet my health is one of my reasons, for the class is in summer.

I hope this statement of my case will make my long neglect appear less unkind. It was certainly not because I ever forgot you, or your unwonted kindness; and it was not because I was in any sense rioting in pleasures.

I am glad to hear the catamaran is on her legs again; you have my warmest wishes for a good cruise down the Saône; and yet there comes some envy to that wish, for when shall I go cruising? Here a sheer hulk, alas! lies R. L. S. But I will continue to hope for a better time, canoes that will sail better to the wind, and a river grander than the Saône.

I heard, by the way, in a letter of counsel from a well-wisher, one reason of my town's absurdity about the chair of Art: I fear it is characteristic of her manners. It was because you did not call upon the electors!

Will you remember me to Mrs. Hamerton and your son?—And believe me, etc., etc.,

ROBERT LOUIS STEVENSON.

TO SIDNEY COLVIN

Kinnaird Cottage, Pitlochry, [*July* 1881].

MY DEAR COLVIN,—I do believe I am better, mind and body; I am tired just now, for I have just been up

---

[1] The reference is of course to Wordsworth's *Song at the Feast of Brougham Castle*.

1881.
AET. 31.

the burn with Wogg, daily growing better and boo'f'ler; so do not judge my state by my style in this. I am working steady, four Cornhill pages scrolled every day, besides the correspondence about this chair, which is heavy in itself. My first story, 'Thrawn Janet,' all in Scotch, is accepted by Stephen; my second, 'The Body Snatchers,' is laid aside in a justifiable disgust, the tale being horrid; my third, 'The Merry Men,' I am more than half through, and think real well of. It is a fantastic sonata about the sea and wrecks; and I like it much above all my other attempts at story-telling; I think it is strange; if ever I shall make a hit, I have the line now, as I believe.

Fanny has finished one of hers, 'The Shadow on the Bed,' and is now hammering at a second, for which we have 'no name' as yet—not by Wilkie Collins.

Tales for Winter Nights. Yes, that, I think, we will call the lot of them when republished.

Why have you not sent me a testimonial? Everybody else but you has responded, and Symonds, but I'm afraid he's ill. Do think, too, if anybody else would write me a testimonial. I am told quantity goes far. I have good ones from Rev. Professor Campbell, Professor Meiklejohn, Leslie Stephen, Lang, Gosse, and a very shaky one from Hamerton.

Grant is an elector, so can't, but has written me kindly. From Tulloch I have not yet heard. Do help me with suggestions. This old chair, with its £250 and its light work, would make me.

It looks as if we should take Cater's chalet[1] after all; but O! to go back to that place, it seems cruel. I have not yet received the Landor; but it may be at home, detained by my mother, who returns to-morrow.

Believe me, dear Colvin, ever yours,   R. L. S.

Yours came; the class is in summer; many thanks for the testimonial, it is bully; arrived along with it another

[1] At Davos-Platz.

from Symonds, also bully; he is ill, but not lungs, thank God—fever got in Italy. We *have* taken Cater's chalet; so we are now the aristo.'s of the valley. There is no hope for me, but if there were, you would hear sweetness and light streaming from my lips.

'The Merry Men'
    Chap. I. Eilean Aros.
        II. What the Wreck had brought to Aros.
        III. Past and Present in Sandag Bay.
        IV. The Gale.
        V. A Man out of the Sea.

} Tip Top Tale.

TO W. E. HENLEY

Kinnaird Cottage, Pitlochry, July 1881.

MY DEAR HENLEY,—I hope, then, to have a visit from you. If before August, here; if later, at Braemar. Tupe!

And now, *mon bon*, I must babble about 'The Merry Men,' my favourite work. It is a fantastic sonata about the sea and wrecks. Chapter I. 'Eilean Aros'—the island, the roost, the 'merry men,' the three people there living—sea superstitions. Chapter II. 'What the Wreck had brought to Aros.' Eh, boy? what had it? Silver and clocks and brocades, and what a conscience, what a mad brain! Chapter III. 'Past and Present in Sandag Bay'—the new wreck and the old—so old—the Armada treasure-ship, Sant^{ma} Trini^d—the grave in the heather—strangers there. Chapter IV. 'The Gale'—the doomed ship—the storm—the drunken madman on the head—cries in the night. Chapter V. 'A Man out of the Sea.' But I must not breathe to you my plot. It is, I fancy, my first real shoot at a story; an odd thing, sir, but, I believe, my own, though there is a little of Scott's *Pirate* in it, as how should there not? He had the root of romance in such places. Aros is Earraid, where I lived lang syne; the Ross of Grisapol is the Ross of Mull; Ben Ryan, Ben More. I have written to the middle of Chapter IV. Like enough, when it is finished I shall discard all chapterings; for the thing is written straight through. It must, unhappily, be re-written—too well written not to be.

The chair is only three months in summer; that is why I try for it. If I get it, which I shall not, I should be independent at once. Sweet thought. I liked your Byron well; your Berlioz better. No one would remark these cuts; even I, who was looking for it, knew it not at all to be a *torso*. The paper strengthens me in my recommendation to you to follow Colvin's hint. Give us an 1830; you will do it well, and the subject smiles widely on the world:—

1830: *A Chapter of Artistic History*, by William Ernest Henley (or *of Social and Artistic History*, as the thing might grow to you). Sir, you might be in the Athenæum yet with that; and, believe me, you might and would be far better, the author of a readable book.—Yours ever,

R. L. S.

The following names have been invented for Wogg by his dear papa:—

Grunty-pig (when he is scratched),

Rose-mouth (when he comes flying up with his rose-leaf tongue depending), and

Hoofen-boots (when he has had his foots wet).

How would *Tales for Winter Nights* do?

TO W. E. HENLEY

The spell of good health did not last long, and with a break of the weather came a return of catarrhal troubles and hemorrhage. This letter answers some criticisms made by his correspondent on *The Merry Men* as drafted in MS.

Pitlochry, if you please, [*August*] 1881.

DEAR HENLEY,—To answer a point or two. First, the Spanish ship was sloop-rigged and clumsy, because she was fitted out by some private adventurers, not over wealthy, and glad to take what they could get. Is that not right? Tell me if you think not. That, at least, was how I meant it. As for the boat-cloaks, I am afraid they are, as you say, false imagination; but I love the name, nature, and being of them so dearly, that I feel as if I would almost rather ruin a story than omit the reference. The proudest moments of my life have been passed in the stern-sheets of a boat with that romantic garment over my shoulders. This, without prejudice to one glorious day when standing upon some water stairs at Lerwick I signalled with my pocket-handkerchief for a boat to come ashore for me. I was then aged fifteen or sixteen; conceive my glory.

Several of the phrases you object to are proper nautical, or long-shore phrases, and therefore, I think, not out of place in this long-shore story. As for the two members which you thought at first so ill-united; I confess they seem perfectly so to me. I have chosen to sacrifice a long-projected story of adventure because the sentiment of that is identical with the sentiment of 'My uncle.' My uncle himself is not the story as I see it, only the leading episode of that story. It's really a story of wrecks, as they appear to the dweller on the coast. It's a view of the sea. Goodness knows when I shall be able to re-write; I must first get over this copper-headed cold.

R. L. S.

TO SIDNEY COLVIN

The reference to Landor in the following is to a volume of mine in Mr. Morley's series of 'English Men of Letters.' This and the next two or three years were those of the Fenian dynamite outrages at Clerkenwell Prison, the Tower of London, the House of Lords, etc.

Pitlochry, August 1881.

MY DEAR COLVIN,—This is the first letter I have written this good while. I have had a brutal cold, not

1881.
AET. 31.

perhaps very wisely treated; lots of blood—for me, I mean. I was so well, however, before, that I seem to be sailing through with it splendidly. My appetite never failed; indeed, as I got worse, it sharpened—a sort of reparatory instinct. Now I feel in a fair way to get round soon.

Monday, August (2*nd*, is it ?).—We set out for the Spital of Glenshee, and reach Braemar on Tuesday. The Braemar address we cannot learn; it looks as if 'Braemar' were all that was necessary; if particular, you can address 17 Heriot Row. We shall be delighted to see you whenever, and as soon as ever, you can make it possible.

. . . I hope heartily you will survive me, and do not doubt it. There are seven or eight people it is no part of my scheme in life to survive—yet if I could but heal me of my bellowses, I could have a jolly life—have it, even now, when I can work and stroll a little, as I have been doing till this cold. I have so many things to make life sweet to me, it seems a pity I cannot have that other one thing—health. But though you will be angry to hear it, I believe, for myself at least, what is is best. I believed it all through my worst days, and I am not ashamed to profess it now.

Landor has just turned up; but I had read him already. I like him extremely; I wonder if the 'cuts' were perhaps not advantageous. It seems quite full enough; but then you know I am a compressionist.

If I am to criticise, it is a little staid; but the classical is apt to look so. It is in curious contrast to that inexpressive, unplanned wilderness of Forster's; clear, readable, precise, and sufficiently human. I see nothing lost in it, though I could have wished, in my Scotch capacity, a trifle clearer and fuller exposition of his moral attitude, which is not quite clear 'from here.'

He and his tyrannicide! I am in a mad fury about these explosions. If that is the new world! Damn

O'Donovan Rossa; damn him behind and before, above, below, and roundabout; damn, deracinate, and destroy him, root and branch, self and company, world without end. Amen. I write that for sport if you like, but I will pray in earnest, O Lord, if you cannot convert, kindly delete him!

Stories naturally at—halt. Henley has seen one and approves. I believe it to be good myself, even real good. He has also seen and approved one of Fanny's. It will make a good volume. We have now

    Thrawn Janet (with Stephen), proof to-day.
    The Shadow on the Bed (Fanny's copying).
    The Merry Men (scrolled).
    The Body Snatchers (scrolled).

In germis

    The Travelling Companion.
    The Torn Surplice (*not final title*).

Yours ever,   R. L. S.

TO DR. ALEXANDER JAPP

Dr. Japp had written to R. L. S. criticising statements of fact and opinion in his essay on 'Thoreau,' and expressing the hope that they might meet and discuss their differences. In the interval between the last letter and this Stevenson with all his family had moved to Braemar.

The Cottage, Castleton of Braemar, Sunday, August 1881.

MY DEAR SIR,—I should long ago have written to thank you for your kind and frank letter; but in my state of health papers are apt to get mislaid, and your letter has been vainly hunted for until this (Sunday) morning.

I regret I shall not be able to see you in Edinburgh; one visit to Edinburgh has already cost me too dear in that invaluable particular health; but if it should be at all possible for you to push on as far as Braemar, I believe you would find an attentive listener, and I can offer you a bed, a drive, and necessary food, etc.

If, however, you should not be able to come thus far, I

can promise you two things: First, I shall religiously revise what I have written, and bring out more clearly the point of view from which I regarded Thoreau; second, I shall in the Preface record your objection.

The point of view (and I must ask you not to forget that any such short paper is essentially only a *section through* a man) was this: I desired to look at the man through his books. Thus, for instance, when I mentioned his return to the pencil-making, I did it only in passing (perhaps I was wrong), because it seemed to me not an illustration of his principles, but a brave departure from them. Thousands of such there were I do not doubt; still, they might be hardly to my purpose, though, as you say so, some of them would be.

Our difference as to pity I suspect was a logomachy of my making. No pitiful acts on his part would surprise me; I know he would be more pitiful in practice than most of the whiners; but the spirit of that practice would still seem to be unjustly described by the word pity.

When I try to be measured, I find myself usually suspected of a sneaking unkindness for my subject; but you may be sure, sir, I would give up most other things to be so good a man as Thoreau. Even my knowledge of him leads me thus far.

Should you find yourself able to push on to Braemar—it may even be on your way—believe me, your visit will be most welcome. The weather is cruel, but the place is, as I dare say you know, the very 'wale' of Scotland—bar Tummelside.—Yours very sincerely,

ROBERT LOUIS STEVENSON.

TO MRS. SITWELL

The Cottage, Castleton of Braemar, August 1881.

... WELL, I have been pretty mean, but I have not yet got over my cold so completely as to have recovered much energy. It is really extraordinary that I should have recovered as well as I have in this blighting weather; the wind pipes, the rain comes in squalls, great black clouds are continually overhead, and it is as cold as March. The country is delightful, more cannot be said; it is very beautiful, a perfect joy when we get a blink of sun to see it in. The Queen knows a thing or two, I perceive; she has picked out the finest habitable spot in Britain.

I have done no work, and scarce written a letter for three weeks, but I think I should soon begin again; my cough is now very trifling. I eat well, and seem to have lost but little flesh in the meanwhile. I was *wonderfully* well before I caught this horrid cold. I never thought I should have been as well again; I really enjoyed life and work; and, of course, I now have a good hope that this may return.

I suppose you heard of our ghost stories. They are somewhat delayed by my cold and a bad attack of laziness, embroidery, etc., under which Fanny had been some time prostrate. It is horrid that we can get no better weather. I did not get such good accounts of you as might have been. You must imitate me. I am now one of the most conscientious people at trying to get better you ever saw. I have a white hat, it is much admired; also a plaid, and a heavy stoop; so I take my walks abroad, witching the world.

Last night I was beaten at chess, and am still grinding under the blow.—Ever your faithful friend,   R. L. S.

TO EDMUND GOSSE

*The Cottage (late the late Miss M'Gregor's),
Castleton of Braemar, August 10, 1881.*

MY DEAR GOSSE,—Come on the 24th, there is a dear fellow. Everybody else wants to come later, and it will be a godsend for, sir—Yours sincerely,

You can stay as long as you behave decently, and are not sick of, sir—Your obedient, humble servant.

We have family worship in the home of, sir—Yours respectfully.

Braemar is a fine country, but nothing to (what you will also see) the maps of, sir—Yours in the Lord.

A carriage and two spanking hacks draw up daily at the hour of two before the house of, sir—Yours truly.

The rain rains and the winds do beat upon the cottage of the late Miss Macgregor and of, sir—Yours affectionately.

It is to be trusted that the weather may improve ere you know the halls of, sir—Yours emphatically.

All will be glad to welcome you, not excepting, sir—Yours ever.

You will now have gathered the lamentable intellectual collapse of, sir—Yours indeed.

And nothing remains for me but to sign myself, sir—Yours, ROBERT LOUIS STEVENSON.

N.B.—Each of these clauses has to be read with extreme glibness, coming down whack upon the 'Sir.' This is very important. The fine stylistic inspiration will else be lost.

I commit the man who made, the man who sold, and the woman who supplied me with my present excruciating gilt nib to that place where the worm never dies.

The reference to a deceased Highland lady (tending as it does to foster unavailing sorrow) may be with advantage omitted from the address, which would therefore run—The Cottage, Castleton of Braemar.

TO EDMUND GOSSE

The Cottage, Castleton of Braemar, August 19, 1881.

IF you had an uncle who was a sea captain and went to the North Pole, you had better bring his outfit. *Verbum Sapientibus.* I look towards you.

R. L. STEVENSON.

TO EDMUND GOSSE

1881.
AET. 31.

[*Braemar*], *August* 19, 1881.

MY DEAR WEG,—I have by an extraordinary drollery of Fortune sent off to you by this day's post a P. C. inviting you to appear in sealskin. But this had reference to the weather, and not at all, as you may have been led to fancy, to our rustic raiment of an evening.

As to that question, I would deal, in so far as in me lies, fairly with all men. We are not dressy people by nature; but it sometimes occurs to us to entertain angels. In the country, I believe, even angels may be decently welcomed in tweed; I have faced many great personages, for my own part, in a tasteful suit of sea-cloth with an end of carpet pending from my gullet. Still, we do maybe twice a summer burst out in the direction of blacks ... and yet we do it seldom.... In short, let your own heart decide, and the capacity of your portmanteau. If you came in camel's hair, you would still, although conspicuous, be welcome.

The sooner the better after Tuesday.—Yours ever,

ROBERT LOUIS STEVENSON.

TO W. E. HENLEY

The following records the beginning of work upon *Treasure Island*, the name originally proposed for which was the *Sea-Cook*:—

Braemar, August 1881.

MY DEAR HENLEY,—Of course I am a rogue. Why, Lord, it's known, man; but you should remember I have had a horrid cold. Now, I'm better, I think; and see here —nobody, not you, nor Lang, nor the devil, will hurry me with our crawlers. They are coming. Four of them are as good as done, and the rest will come when ripe; but I am now on another lay for the moment, purely owing to Lloyd, this one; but I believe there's more coin in it than in any amount of crawlers: now, see here, 'The Sea Cook, or Treasure Island: A Story for Boys.'

If this don't fetch the kids, why, they have gone rotten since my day. Will you be surprised to learn that it is about Buccaneers, that it begins in the *Admiral Benbow* public-house on Devon coast, that it's all about a map, and a treasure, and a mutiny, and a derelict ship, and a current, and a fine old Squire Trelawney (the real Tre, purged of literature and sin, to suit the infant mind), and a doctor, and another doctor, and a sea-cook with one leg, and a sea-song with the chorus 'Yo-ho-ho-and a bottle of rum' (at the third Ho you heave at the capstan bars), which is a real buccaneer's song, only known to the crew of the late Captain Flint (died of rum at Key West, much regretted, friends will please accept this intimation); and lastly, would you be surprised to hear, in this connection, the name of *Routledge*? That's the kind of man I am, blast your eyes. Two chapters are written, and have been tried on Lloyd with great success; the trouble is to work it off without oaths. Buccaneers without oaths—bricks without straw. But youth and the fond parient have to be consulted.

And now look here—this is next day—and three chapters are written and read. (Chapter I. The Old Sea-dog at the *Admiral Benbow*. Chapter II. Black Dog appears and disappears. Chapter III. The Black Spot.) All now heard by Lloyd, F., and my father and mother, with high approval. It's quite silly and horrid fun, and what I want is the *best* book about the Buccaneers that can be had—the latter B's above all, Blackbeard and sich, and get Nutt or Bain to send it skimming by the fastest post. And now I know you'll write to me, for 'The Sea Cook's' sake.

Your 'Admiral Guinea' is curiously near my line, but of course I'm fooling; and your Admiral sounds like a shublime gent. Stick to him like wax—he'll do. My Trelawney is, as I indicate, several thousand sea-miles off the lie of the original or your Admiral Guinea; and besides, I have no more about him yet but one mention of his name, and I think it likely he may turn yet farther from the model in the course of handling. A chapter a day I mean to do; they are short; and perhaps in a month the 'Sea Cook' may to Routledge go, yo-ho-ho and a bottle of rum! My Trelawney has a strong dash of Landor, as I see him from here. No women in the story, Lloyd's orders; and who so blithe to obey? It's awful fun boys' stories; you just indulge the pleasure of your heart, that's all; no trouble, no strain. The only stiff thing is to get it ended—that I don't see, but I look to a volcano. O sweet, O generous, O human toils. You would like my blind beggar in Chapter III. I believe; no writing, just drive along as the words come and the pen will scratch!

1881.
AET. 31.

R. L. S.,
Author of *Boys' Stories.*

TO DR. ALEXANDER JAPP

This correspondent had paid his visit as proposed, discussed the Thoreau differences, listened delightedly to the first chapters of *Treasure Island*, and proposed to offer the story for publication to his friend Mr. Henderson, proprietor and editor of *Young Folks.*

Braemar, 1881.

MY DEAR DR. JAPP,—My father has gone, but I think I may take it upon me to ask you to keep the book. Of all things you could do to endear yourself to me, you have done the best, for my father and you have taken a fancy to each other.

I do not know how to thank you for all your kind trouble in the matter of 'The Sea-Cook,' but I am not unmindful. My health is still poorly, and I have added intercostal rheumatism—a new attraction—which sewed me up nearly double for two days, and still gives me a list to starboard—let us be ever nautical!

1881.
AET. 31.

I do not think with the start I have there will be any difficulty in letting Mr. Henderson go ahead whenever he likes. I will write my story up to its legitimate conclusion; and then we shall be in a position to judge whether a sequel would be desirable, and I would then myself know better about its practicability from the story-teller's point of view.—Yours ever very sincerely,

R. L. STEVENSON.

TO W. E. HENLEY

This tells of the farther progress of Treasure Island, *of the price paid for it, and of the modest hopes with which it was launched. 'The poet' is Mr. Gosse. The project of a highway story,* Jerry Abershaw, *remained a favourite one with Stevenson, until it was superseded three or four years later by another, that of the* Great North Road, *which in its turn had to be abandoned, from lack of health and leisure, after some six or eight chapters had been written.*

Braemar, September 1881.

MY DEAR HENLEY,—Thanks for your last. The £100 fell through, or dwindled at least into somewhere about £30. However, that I've taken as a mouthful, so you may look out for 'The Sea Cook, or Treasure Island: A Tale of the Buccaneers,' in *Young Folks*. (The terms are £2, 10s. a page of 4500 words; that's not noble, is it? But I have my copyright safe. I don't get illustrated—a blessing; that's the price I have to pay for my copyright.)

I'll make this boys' book business pay; but I have to make a beginning. When I'm done with *Young Folks*, I'll try Routledge or some one. I feel pretty sure the 'Sea Cook' will do to reprint, and bring something decent at that.

Japp is a good soul. The poet was very gay and pleasant. He told me much: he is simply the most active young man in England, and one of the most intelligent.

'He shall o'er Europe, shall o'er earth extend.'[1] He is now extending over adjacent parts of Scotland.

1881.
AET. 31.

I propose to follow up the 'Sea Cook' at proper intervals by 'Jerry Abershaw: A Tale of Putney Heath' (which or its site I must visit), 'The Leading Light: A Tale of the Coast,' 'The Squaw Men: or the Wild West,' and other instructive and entertaining work. 'Jerry Abershaw' should be good, eh? I love writing boys' books. This first is only an experiment; wait till you see what I can make 'em with my hand in. I'll be the Harrison Ainsworth of the future; and a chalk better by St. Christopher; or at least as good. You'll see that even by the 'Sea Cook.'

Jerry Abershaw—O what a title! Jerry Abershaw: d—n it, sir, it's a poem. The two most lovely words in English; and what a sentiment! Hark you, how the hoofs ring! Is this a blacksmith's? No, it's a wayside inn. Jerry Abershaw. 'It was a clear, frosty evening, not 100 miles from Putney,' etc. Jerry Abershaw. Jerry Abershaw. Jerry Abershaw. The 'Sea Cook' is now in its sixteenth chapter, and bids for well up in the thirties. Each three chapters is worth £2, 10s. So we've £12, 10s. already.

Don't read Marryat's '*Pirate* anyhow; it is written in sand with a salt-spoon: arid, feeble, vain, tottering production. But then we're not always all there. *He* was *all* somewhere else that trip. It's *damnable*, Henley. I don't go much on the 'Sea Cook'; but, Lord, it's a little fruitier than the *Pirate* by Cap'n. Marryat.

Since this was written 'The Cook' is in his nineteenth chapter. Yo-heave ho! R. L. S.

TO THOMAS STEVENSON

With all his throat and lung troubles actively renewed, Stevenson fled to Davos again in October. This time he and his wife

---

[1] From Landor's *Gebir*: the line refers to Napoleon Bonaparte.

1881.
AET. 31.

and stepson occupied a small house by themselves, the Chalet am Stein, near the Buol Hotel. The election to the Edinburgh Professorship was still pending, and the following note to his father shows that he thought for a moment of giving the electors a specimen of his qualifications in the shape of a magazine article on the Appin murder—a theme afterwards turned to so much more vital account in the tales of *Kidnapped* and *Catriona*.

[*Chalet am Stein, Davos, Autumn* 1881.]

MY DEAR FATHER,—It occurred to me last night in bed that I could write

The Murder of Red Colin,
A Story of the Forfeited Estates.

This I have all that is necessary for, with the following exceptions:—

Trials of the Sons of Roy Rob with Anecdotes: Edinburgh, 1818, and

The second volume of *Blackwood's Magazine*.

You might also look in Arnot's *Criminal Trials* up in my room, and see what observations he has on the case (Trial of James Stewart in Appin for murder of Campbell of Glenure, 1752); if he has none, perhaps you could see —O yes, see if Burton has it in his two vols. of trial stories. I hope he hasn't; but care not; do it over again anyway.

The two named authorities I must see. With these, I could soon pull off this article; and it shall be my first for the electors.—Ever affectionate son, R. L. S.

TO P. G. HAMERTON

The volume of republished essays here mentioned is *Familiar Studies of Men and Books*. 'The silly story of the election' refers to his correspondent's failure as a candidate for the Edinburgh Chair of Fine Arts.

Châlet am Stein, Davos, Autumn [1881].

MY DEAR MR. HAMERTON,—My conscience has long been smiting me, till it became nearly chronic. My excuses, however, are many and not pleasant. Almost immediately after I last wrote to you, I had a hemorreage (I can't spell it), was badly treated by a doctor in the country, and have been a long while picking up—still, in fact, have much to desire on that side. Next, as soon as I got here, my wife took ill; she is, I fear, seriously so; and this combination of two invalids very much depresses both.

1881.
AET. 31.

I have a volume of republished essays coming out with Chatto and Windus; I wish they would come, that my wife might have the reviews to divert her. Otherwise my news is *nil.* I am up here in a little chalet, on the borders of a pinewood, overlooking a great part of the Davos Thal, a beautiful scene at night, with the moon upon the snowy mountains, and the lights warmly shining in the village. J. A. Symonds is next door to me, just at the foot of my Hill Difficulty (this you will please regard as the House Beautiful), and his society is my great stand-by.

Did you see I had joined the band of the rejected? ' Hardly one of us,' said my *confrères* at the bar.

I was blamed by a common friend for asking you to give me a testimonial; in the circumstances he thought it was indelicate. Lest, by some calamity, you should ever have felt the same way, I must say in two words how the matter appeared to me. That silly story of the election altered in no tittle the value of your testimony: so much for that. On the other hand, it led me to take quite a particular pleasure in asking you to give it; and so much for the other. I trust, even if you cannot share it, you will understand my view.

I am in treaty with Bentley for a life of Hazlitt; I hope it will not fall through, as I love the subject, and appear to have found a publisher who loves it also. That, I think, makes things more pleasant. You know I am a fervent Hazlittite; I mean regarding him as *the* English writer who has had the scantiest justice. Besides which,

1881.
AET. 31.

I am anxious to write biography; really, if I understand myself in quest of profit, I think it must be good to live with another man from birth to death. You have tried it, and know.

How has the cruising gone? Pray remember me to Mrs. Hamerton and your son, and believe me, yours very sincerely, ROBERT LOUIS STEVENSON.

TO CHARLES BAXTER

[*Chalet am Stein*], *Davos, December* 5, 1881.

MY DEAR CHARLES,—We have been in miserable case here; my wife worse and worse; and now sent away with Lloyd for sick nurse, I not being allowed to go down. I do not know what is to become of us; and you may imagine how rotten I have been feeling, and feel now, alone with my weasel-dog and my German maid, on the top of a hill here, heavy mist and thin snow all about me, and the devil to pay in general. I don't care so much for solitude as I used to; results, I suppose, of marriage.

Pray write me something cheery. A little Edinburgh gossip, in Heaven's name. Ah! what would I not give to steal this evening with you through the big, echoing, college archway, and away south under the street lamps, and away to dear Brash's, now defunct! But the old time is dead also, never, never to revive. It was a sad time too, but so gay and so hopeful, and we had such sport with all our low spirits and all our distresses, that it looks like a kind of lamplit fairyland behind me. O for ten Edinburgh minutes—sixpence between us, and the ever-glorious Lothian Road, or dear mysterious Leith Walk! But here, a sheer hulk, lies poor Tom Bowling; here in this strange place, whose very strangeness would have been heaven to him then; and aspires, yes, C. B., with tears, after the past. See what comes of being left alone. Do you remember Brash? the sheet of glass that we followed along George Street? Granton? the night at Bonny mainhead? the compass near the sign of the *Twinkling Eye*? the night I lay on the pavement in misery?

>I swear it by the eternal sky
>Johnson—nor Thomson—ne'er shall die!

Yet I fancy they are dead too; dead like Brash.

R. L. S.

TO MRS. THOMAS STEVENSON

The next is after going down to meet his wife and stepson, after the former had left the doctor's hands at Berne.

Chalet Buol, Davos-Platz, December 26, 1881.

MY DEAR MOTHER,—Yesterday, Sunday and Christmas, we finished this eventful journey by a drive in an *open* sleigh—none others were to be had—seven hours on end through whole forests of Christmas trees. The cold was beyond belief. I have often suffered less at a dentist's. It was a clear, sunny day, but the sun even at noon falls, at this season, only here and there into the Prättigau. I kept up as long as I could in an imitation of a street singer:—

Away, ye gay landscapes, ye gardens of roses, etc.

At last Lloyd remarked, a blue mouth speaking from a corpse-coloured face, 'You seem to be the only one with any courage left?' And, do you know, with that word my courage disappeared, and I made the rest of the stage in the same dumb wretchedness as the others. My only terror was lest Fanny should ask for brandy, or laudanum, or something. So awful was the idea of putting my hands out, that I half thought I would refuse.

Well, none of us are a penny the worse, Lloyd's cold better; I, with a twinge of the rheumatiz; and Fanny better than her ordinary.

1882.
AET. 32.

General conclusion between Lloyd and me as to the journey: A prolonged visit to the dentist's, complicated with the fear of death.

Never, O never, do you get me there again.—Ever affectionate son,
R. L. S.

TO ALISON CUNNINGHAM

[Chalet am Stein, Davos-Platz, February 1882.]

MY DEAR CUMMY,—My wife and I are very much vexed to hear you are still unwell. We are both keeping far better; she especially seems quite to have taken a turn—*the* turn, we shall hope. Please let us know how you get on, and what has been the matter with you; Braemar I believe—the vile hole. You know what a lazy rascal I am, so you won't be surprised at a short letter, I know; indeed, you will be much more surprised at my having had the decency to write at all. We have got rid of our young, pretty, and incompetent maid; and now we have a fine, canny, twinkling, shrewd, auld-farrant peasant body, who gives us good food and keeps us in good spirits. If we could only understand what she says! But she speaks Davos language, which is to German what Aberdeen-awa' is to English, so it comes heavy. God bless you, my dear Cummy; and so says Fanny forbye. —Ever your affectionate,
ROBERT LOUIS STEVENSON.

TO CHARLES BAXTER

[Chalet am Stein, Davos], 22*nd February* '82.

MY DEAR CHARLES,—Your most welcome letter has raised clouds of sulphur from my horizon. . . .

I am glad you have gone back to your music. Life is a poor thing, I am more and more convinced, without an art, that always waits for us and is always new. Art and marriage are two very good stand-by's.

In an article which will appear sometime in the *Cornhill*, 'Talk and Talkers,' and where I have full-lengthened the conversation of Bob, Henley, Jenkin, Simpson, Symonds, and Gosse, I have at the end one single word about yourself. It may amuse you to see it.

1882.
AET. 32.

We are coming to Scotland after all, so we shall meet, which pleases me, and I do believe I am strong enough to stand it this time. My knee is still quite lame.

My wife is better again. . . . But we take it by turns; it is the dog that is ill now.—Ever yours,   R. L. S.

To W. E. HENLEY

Mr. Henley was at this time and for some years following editor of the *Magazine of Art*, and had enrolled R. L. S. among his contributors: this is the meaning of the words below about 'San Francisco.' In the early months of this year a hurt knee kept Stevenson more indoors than was good for him.

[*Chalet am Stein, Davos-Platz, February* 1882.]

MY DEAR HENLEY,—Here comes the letter as promised last night. And first two requests: Pray send the enclosed to c/o Blackmore's publisher, 'tis from Fanny; second, pray send us Routledge's shilling book, Edward Mayhew's *Dogs*, by return if it can be managed.

Our dog is very ill again, poor fellow, looks very ill too, only sleeps at night because of morphine; and we do not know what ails him, only fear it to be canker of the ear. He makes a bad, black spot in our life, poor, selfish, silly, little tangle; and my wife is wretched. Otherwise she is better, steadily and slowly moving up through all her relapses. My knee never gets the least better; it hurts to-night, which it has not done for long. I do not suppose my doctor knows any least thing about it. He says it is a nerve that I struck, but I assure you he does not know.

I have just finished a paper, 'A Gossip on Romance,'

1882.
AET. 32.

in which I have tried to do, very popularly, about one-half of the matter you wanted me to try. In a way, I have found an answer to the question. But the subject was hardly fit for so chatty a paper, and it is all loose ends. If ever I do my book on the Art of Literature, I shall gather them together and be clear.

To-morrow, having once finished off the touches still due on this, I shall tackle *San Francisco* for you. Then the tide of work will fairly bury me, lost to view and hope. You have no idea what it costs me to wring out my work now. I have certainly been a fortnight over this Romance, sometimes five hours a day; and yet it is about my usual length—eight pages or so, and would be a d—d sight the better for another curry. But I do not think I can honestly re-write it all; so I call it done, and shall only straighten words in a revision currently.

I had meant to go on for a great while, and say all manner of entertaining things. But all's gone. I am now an idiot.—Yours ever,   R. L. S.

TO W. E. HENLEY

The following flight of fancy refers to supposed errors of judgment on the part of an eminent firm of publishers, with whom Stevenson had at this time no connection. Very soon afterwards, it should be noted, he entered into relations with them which proved equally pleasant and profitable to both parties, and were continued on the most cordial terms until his death.

[*Chalet am Stein, Davos, Spring* 1882.]

MY DEAR HENLEY,—. . . Last night we had a dinner-party, consisting of the John Addington, curry, onions (lovely onions), and beefsteak. So unusual is any excitement, that F. and I feel this morning as if we had been to a coronation. However I must, I suppose, write.

I was sorry about your female contributor squabble. 'Tis very comic, but really unpleasant. But what care I?

Now that I illustrate my own books, I can always offer you a situation in our house—S. L. Osbourne and Co. As an author gets a halfpenny a copy of verses, and an artist a penny a cut, perhaps a proof-reader might get several pounds a year.

1882.
AET. 32.

O that Coronation! What a shouting crowd there was! I obviously got a firework in each eye. The king looked very magnificent, to be sure; and that great hall where we feasted on seven hundred delicate foods, and drank fifty royal wines—*quel coup d'œil!* but was it not overdone, even for a coronation—almost a vulgar luxury? And eleven is certainly too late to begin dinner. (It was really 6.30 instead of 5.30.)

Your list of books that Cassells have refused in these weeks is not quite complete; they also refused:—

1. Six undiscovered Tragedies, one romantic Comedy, a fragment of Journal extending over six years, and an unfinished Autobiography reaching up to the first performance of King John. By William Shakespeare.

2. The Journals and Private Correspondence of David, King of Israel.

3. Poetical Works of Arthur, Iron Dook of Wellington, including a Monody on Napoleon.

4. Eight books of an unfinished novel, *Solomon Crabb.* By Henry Fielding.

5. Stevenson's Moral Emblems.

You also neglected to mention, as *per contra*, that they had during the same time accepted and triumphantly published Brown's *Handbook to Cricket*, Jones's *First French Reader*, and Robinson's *Picturesque Cheshire*, uniform with the same author's *Stately Homes of Salop*.

O if that list could come true! How we would tear at Solomon Crabb! O what a bully, bully, bully business. Which would you read first—Shakespeare's autobiography, or his journals? What sport the monody on Napoleon would be—what wooden verse, what stucco ornament! I should read both the autobiography and the journals before I looked at one of the plays, beyond the names of them, which shows that Saintsbury was right, and I do care more for life than for poetry. No—I take it back. Do you know one of the tragedies —a Bible tragedy too—*David*—was written in his third period — much about the same time as Lear? The comedy, *April Rain*, is also a late work. *Beckett* is a fine ranting piece, like *Richard II.*, but very fine for the stage. Irving is to play it this autumn when I'm in town; the part rather suits him—but who is to play Henry—a tremendous creation, sir. Betterton in his private journal seems to have seen this piece; and he says distinctly that Henry is the best part in any play. 'Though,' he adds, 'how it be with the ancient plays I know not. But in this I have ever feared to do ill, and indeed will not be persuaded to that undertaking.' So says Betterton. *Rufus* is not so good; I am not pleased with *Rufus*; plainly a *rifaccimento* of some inferior work; but there are some damned fine lines. As for the purely satiric ill-minded *Abelard and Heloise*, another *Troilus, quoi!* it is not pleasant, truly, but what strength, what verve, what knowledge of life, and the Canon! What a finished, humorous, rich picture is the Canon! Ah, there was nobody like Shakespeare. But what I like is the David and Absalom business: Absalom is so well felt—you love him as David did; David's speech is one roll of royal music from the first act to the fifth.

I am enjoying *Solomon Crabb* extremely; Solomon's capital adventure with the two highwaymen and Squire Trecothick and Parson Vance; it is as good, I think, as anything in Joseph Andrews. I have just come to the part where the highwayman with the black patch over his eye has tricked poor Solomon into his place, and the squire and the parson are hearing the evidence. Parson Vance is splendid. How good, too, is old Mrs. Crabb and the coastguardsman in the third chapter, or her delightful quarrel with the sexton of Seaham; Lord Conybeare is surely a little overdone; but I don't know either; he's such damned fine sport. Do you like Sally Barnes? I'm in love with her. Constable Muddon is as good as Dogberry and Verges put together; when he takes Solomon to the cage, and the highwayman gives him Solomon's own guinea for his pains, and kisses Mrs. Muddon, and just then up drives Lord Conybeare, and instead of helping Solomon, calls him all the rascals in Christendom—O Henry Fielding, Henry Fielding! Yet perhaps the scenes at Seaham are the best. But I'm bewildered among all these excellences.

Stay, cried a voice that made the welkin crack—
This here's a dream, return and study BLACK!

—Ever yours, R. L. S.

TO ALEXANDER IRELAND

The following is in reply to a letter Stevenson had received on some questions connected with his proposed Life of Hazlitt from the veteran critic and bibliographer since deceased, Mr. Alexander Ireland. At the foot is to be found the first reference to his new amusement of wood engraving for the Davos Press:—

[*Chalet am Stein, Davos, March* 1882.]

MY DEAR SIR,—This formidable paper need not alarm you; it argues nothing beyond penury of other sorts, and is not at all likely to lead me into a long letter. If I were at all grateful it would, for yours has just passed for me a considerable part of a stormy evening. And speaking of gratitude, let me at once and with becoming eagerness accept your kind invitation to Bowdon. I shall hope, if we can agree as to dates when I am nearer hand, to come to you sometime in the month of May. I was pleased to hear you were a Scot; I feel more at home with my compatriots always; perhaps the more we are away, the stronger we feel that bond.

You ask about Davos; I have discoursed about it

1882.
AET. 32.

already, rather sillily I think, in the *Pall Mall*, and I mean to say no more, but the ways of the Muse are dubious and obscure, and who knows? I may be wiled again. As a place of residence, beyond a splendid climate, it has to my eyes but one advantage—the neighbourhood of J. A. Symonds—I dare say you know his work, but the man is far more interesting. It has done me, in my two winters' Alpine exile, much good; so much, that I hope to leave it now for ever, but would not be understood to boast. In my present unpardonably crazy state, any cold might send me skipping, either back to Davos, or further off. Let us hope not. It is dear; a little dreary; very far from many things that both my taste and my needs prompt me to seek; and altogether not the place that I should choose of my free will.

I am chilled by your description of the man in question, though I had almost argued so much from his cold and undigested volume. If the republication does not interfere with my publisher, it will not interfere with me; but there, of course, comes the hitch. I do not know Mr. Bentley, and I fear all publishers like the devil from legend and experience both. However, when I come to town, we shall, I hope, meet and understand each other as well as author and publisher ever do. I liked his letters; they seemed hearty, kind, and personal. Still—I am notedly suspicious of the trade—your news of this republication alarms me.

The best of the present French novelists seems to me, incomparably, Daudet. *Les Rois en Exil* comes very near being a masterpiece. For Zola I have no toleration, though the curious, eminently bourgeois, and eminently French creature has power of a kind. But I would he were deleted. I would not give a chapter of old Dumas (meaning himself, not his collaborators) for the whole boiling of the Zolas. Romance with the smallpox—as the great one: diseased anyway and blackhearted and fundamentally at enmity with joy.

I trust that Mrs. Ireland does not object to smoking; and if you are a teetotaller, I beg you to mention it before I come—I have all the vices; some of the virtues also, let us hope—that, at least, of being a Scotchman, and yours very sincerely,

ROBERT LOUIS STEVENSON.

P.S.—My father was in the old High School the last year, and walked in the procession to the new. I blush to own I am an Academy boy; it seems modern, and smacks not of the soil.

P.P.S.—I enclose a good joke—at least, I think so—my first efforts at wood engraving printed by my stepson, a boy of thirteen. I will put in also one of my later attempts. I have been nine days at the art—observe my progress. R. L. S.

TO EDMUND GOSSE.

Stevenson and Mr. Gosse had been planning a volume in which some of the famous historical murder cases should be retold.

Davos, March 23, 1882.

MY DEAR WEG,—And I had just written the best note to Mrs. Gosse that was in my power. Most blameable.

I now send (for Mrs. Gosse).

BLACK CANYON.

Also an advertisement of my new appearance as poet (bard, rather) and hartis on wood. The cut represents the Hero and the Eagle, and is emblematic of Cortez first viewing the Pacific Ocean, which (according to the bard Keats) it took place in Darien. The cut is much admired for the sentiment of discovery, the manly proportions of the voyager, and the fine impression of tropical scenes and the untrodden WASTE, so aptly rendered by the hartis.

I would send you the book; but I declare I'm ruined.

1882.
AET. 32.

I got a penny a cut and a halfpenny a set of verses from the flint-hearted publisher, and only one specimen copy, as I'm a sinner. —— was apostolic alongside of Osbourne.

I hope you will be able to decipher this, written at steam speed with a breaking pen, the hotfast postman at my heels. No excuse, says you. None, sir, says I, and touches my 'at most civil (extraordinary evolution of pen, now quite doomed—to resume—) I have not put pen to the Bloody Murder yet. But it is early on my list; and when once I get to it, three weeks should see the last bloodstain—maybe a fortnight. For I am beginning to combine an extraordinary laborious slowness while at work, with the most surprisingly quick results in the way of finished manuscripts. How goes Gray? Colvin is to do Keats. My wife is still not well.—Yours ever,

R. L. S.

TO DR. ALEXANDER JAPP

[*Chalet am Stein, Davos, March* 1882.]

MY DEAR DR. JAPP,—You must think me a forgetful rogue, as indeed I am; for I have but now told my publisher to send you a copy of the *Familiar Studies*. However, I own I have delayed this letter till I could send you the enclosed. Remembering the nights at Braemar when we visited the Picture Gallery, I hoped they might amuse you. You see, we do some publishing hereaway. I shall hope to see you in town in May.—Always yours faithfully, ROBERT LOUIS STEVENSON.

TO DR. ALEXANDER JAPP

The references in the first paragraph are to the volume *Familiar Studies of Men and Books*.

Châlet Buol, Davos, April 1, 1882.

MY DEAR DR. JAPP,—A good day to date this letter, which is in fact a confession of incapacity. During my wife's illness I somewhat lost my head, and entirely lost a great quire of corrected proofs. This is one of the results; I hope there are none more serious. I was never so sick of any volume as I was of that; I was continually receiving fresh proofs with fresh infinitesimal difficulties. I was ill—I did really fear my wife was worse than ill. Well, it's out now; and though I have observed several carelessnesses myself, and now here's another of your finding—of which, indeed, I ought to be ashamed—it will only justify the sweeping humility of the Preface.

Symonds was actually dining with us when your letter came, and I communicated your remarks.... He is a far better and more interesting thing than any of his books.

The Elephant was my wife's; so she is proportionately elate you should have picked it out for praise—from a collection, let me add, so replete with the highest qualities of art.

My wicked carcase, as John Knox calls it, holds together wonderfully. In addition to many other things, and a volume of travel, I find I have written, since December, 90 *Cornhill* pages of magazine work—essays and stories: 40,000 words, and I am none the worse—I am the better. I begin to hope I may, if not outlive this wolverine upon my shoulders, at least carry him bravely like Symonds and Alexander Pope. I begin to take a pride in that hope.

I shall be much interested to see your criticisms; you might perhaps send them to me. I believe you know that is not dangerous; one folly I have not—I am not touchy under criticism.

Lloyd and my wife both beg to be remembered; and Lloyd sends as a present a work of his own. I hope you feel flattered; for this is *simply the first time he has ever given one away.* I have to buy my own works, I can tell you.—Yours very sincerely,

      ROBERT LOUIS STEVENSON.

1882.
AET. 32.

TO W. E. HENLEY

From about this time until 1885 Mr. Henley acted in an informal way as agent for R. L. S. in most of his dealings with publishers in London. 'Both' in the second paragraph means, I think, Treasure Island and Silverado Squatters.

[*Chalet am Stein, Davos, April* 1882.]

MY DEAR HENLEY,—I hope and hope for a long letter—soon I hope to be superseded by long talks—and it comes not. I remember I have never formally thanked you for that hundred quid, nor in general for the introduction to Chatto and Windus, and continue to bury you in copy as if you were my private secretary. Well, I am not unconscious of it all; but I think least said is often best, generally best; gratitude is a tedious sentiment, it's not ductile, not dramatic.

If Chatto should take both, *cui dedicare*? I am running out of dedikees; if I do, the whole fun of writing is stranded. *Treasure Island*, if it comes out, and I mean it shall, of course goes to Lloyd. Lemme see, I have now dedicated to

W. E. H. [William Ernest Henley].
S. C. [Sidney Colvin].
T. S. [Thomas Stevenson].
Simp. [Sir Walter Simpson].

There remain: C. B., the Williamses—you know they were the parties who stuck up for us about our marriage, and Mrs. W. was my guardian angel, and our Best Man and Bridesmaid rolled in one, and the only third of the wedding party—my sister-in-law, who is booked for *Prince Otto*—Jenkin I suppose sometime—George Meredith, the only man of genius of my acquaintance, and then I believe I'll have to take to the dead, the immortal memory business.

Talking of Meredith, I have just re-read for the third and fourth time *The Egoist*. When I shall have read it the sixth or seventh, I begin to see I shall know about it.

You will be astonished when you come to re-read it; I had no idea of the matter—human, red matter he has contrived to plug and pack into that strange and admirable book. Willoughby is, of course, a pure discovery; a complete set of nerves, not heretofore examined, and yet running all over the human body—a suit of nerves. Clara is the best girl ever I saw anywhere. Vernon is almost as good. The manner and the faults of the book greatly justify themselves on further study. Only Dr. Middleton does not hang together; and Ladies Busshe and Culmer *sont des monstruosités*. Vernon's conduct makes a wonderful odd contrast with Daniel Deronda's. I see more and more that Meredith is built for immortality.

1882.
AET. 32.

Talking of which, Heywood, as a small immortal, an immortalet, claims some attention. *The Woman killed with Kindness* is one of the most striking novels—not plays, though it's more of a play than anything else of his —I ever read. He had such a sweet, sound soul, the old boy. The death of the two pirates in *Fortune by Sea and Land* is a document. He had obviously been present, and heard Purser and Clinton take death by the beard with similar braggadocios. Purser and Clinton, names of pirates; Scarlet and Bobbington, names of highwaymen. He had the touch of names, I think. No man I ever knew had such a sense, such a tact, for English nomenclature: Rainsforth, Lacy, Audley, Forrest, Acton, Spencer, Frankford—so his names run.

Byron not only wrote *Don Juan*; he called Joan of Arc 'a fanatical strumpet.' These are his words. I think the double shame, first to a great poet, second to an English noble, passes words.

Here is a strange gossip.—I am yours loquaciously,

R. L. S.

My lungs are said to be in a splendid state. A cruel examination, an exa*nim*ation I may call it, had this brave result. *Taïaut!* Hillo! Hey! Stand by! Avast! Hurrah!

1882.
AET. 32.

TO MRS. T. STEVENSON

[*Chalet am Stein, Davos, April* 9, 1882.]

MY DEAR MOTHER,—Herewith please find belated birthday present. Fanny has another.

Cockshot = Jenkin.	But
Jack = Bob.	pray
Burly = Henley.	regard
Athelred = Simpson.	these
Opalstein = Symonds.	as
Purcel = Gosse.	secrets.

My dear mother, how can I keep up with your breathless changes? Innerleithen, Cramond, Bridge of Allan, Dunblane, Selkirk. I lean to Cramond, but I shall be pleased anywhere, any respite from Davos; never mind, it has been a good, though a dear lesson. Now, with my improved health, if I can pass the summer, I believe I shall be able no more to exceed, no more to draw on you. It is time I sufficed for myself indeed. And I believe I can.

I am still far from satisfied about Fanny; she is certainly better, but it is by fits a good deal, and the symptoms continue, which should not be. I had her persuaded to leave without me this very day (Saturday 8th), but the disclosure of my mismanagement broke up that plan; she would not leave me lest I should mismanage more. I think this an unfair revenge; but I have been so bothered that I cannot struggle. All Davos has been drinking our wine. During the month of March, three litres a day were drunk—O it is too sickening—and that is only a specimen. It is enough to make any one a misanthrope, but the right thing is to hate the donkey that was duped—which I devoutly do.

I have this winter finished *Treasure Island*, written the preface to the *Studies*, a small book about the *Inland*

Voyage size, *The Silverado Squatters*, and over and above that upwards of ninety (90) *Cornhill* pages of magazine work. No man can say I have been idle.—Your affectionate son, R. L. STEVENSON.

TO EDMUND GOSSE

The few remaining letters of this period are dated from Edinburgh and from Stobo Manse, near Peebles. This, in the matter of weather and health, was the most disappointing of all Stevenson's attempts at summer residence in Scotland. In despair he moved on to the Highlands in July; first with his father for a short while to Lochearnhead, and then in my company to Kingussie; whence he wrote no letters worth preserving.

[Edinburgh] Sunday [June 1882].

... NOTE turned up, but no gray opuscule, which, however, will probably turn up to-morrow in time to go out with me to Stobo Manse, Peeblesshire, where, if you can make it out, you will be a good soul to pay a visit. I shall write again about the opuscule; and about Stobo, which I have not seen since I was thirteen, though my memory speaks delightfully of it.

I have been very tired and seedy, or I should have written before, *inter alia*, to tell you that I had visited my murder place and found *living traditions* not yet in any printed book; most startling. I also got photographs taken, but the negatives have not yet turned up. I lie on the sofa to write this, whence the pencil; having slept yesterday—$1 + 4 + 7\frac{1}{2} = 12\frac{1}{2}$ hours and being (9 A.M.) very anxious to sleep again. The arms of Porpus, quoi! A poppy gules, etc.

From Stobo you can conquer Peebles and Selkirk, or to give them their old decent names, Tweeddale and Ettrick. Think of having been called Tweeddale, and being called PEEBLES! Did I ever tell you my skit on my own travel books? We understand that Mr. Stevenson has in the press another volume of unconventional

1882.
AET. 32.

travels: *Personal Adventures in Peeblesshire. Je la trouve méchante.*—Yours affectionately, R. L. S.

Did I say I had seen a verse on two of the Buccaneers? I did, and *ça-y-est.*

To Edmund Gosse

Mr. Gosse had mistaken the name of the Peeblesshire manse, and is reproached accordingly. 'Gray' is Mr. Gosse's volume on that poet in Mr. Morley's series of *English Men of Letters.*

Stobo Manse, Peeblesshire [*July* 1882].

I would shoot you, but I have no bow:
The place is not called Stobs, but Stobo.
As Gallic Kids complain of 'Bobo,'
I mourn for your mistake of Stobo.

First, we shall be gone in September. But if you think of coming in August, my mother will hunt for you with pleasure. We should all be overjoyed—though Stobo it could not be, as it is but a kirk and manse, but possibly somewhere within reach. Let us know.

Second, I have read your Gray with care. A more difficult subject I can scarce fancy; it is crushing; yet I think you have managed to shadow forth a man, and a good man too; and honestly, I doubt if I could have done the same. This may seem egoistic; but you are not such a fool as to think so. It is the natural expression of real praise. The book as a whole is readable; your subject peeps every here and there out of the crannies like a shy violet—he could do no more—and his aroma hangs there.

I write to catch a minion of the post. Hence brevity. Answer about the house.—Yours affectionately,

R. L. S.

To W. E. Henley

In the heat of conversation Stevenson was accustomed to invent any number of fictitious personages, generally Scottish, and to give them names and to set them playing their imaginary parts in life, reputable or otherwise. Many of these inventions, of whom Mr. Pirbright Smith and Mr. Pegfurth Bannatyne were two, assumed for himself and his friends a kind of substantial existence; and constantly in talk, and occasionally in writing, he would keep up the play of reporting their sayings and doings quite gravely, as in the following:—

[*Stobo Manse, July* 1882.]

DEAR HENLEY, . . . I am not worth an old damn. I am also crushed by bad news of Symonds; his good lung going; I cannot help reading it as a personal hint; God help us all! Really I am not very fit for work; but I try, try, and nothing comes of it.

I believe we shall have to leave this place; it is low, damp, and *mauchy*; the rain it raineth every day; and the glass goes tol-de-rol-de riddle.

Yet it's a bonny bit; I wish I could live in it, but doubt. I wish I was well away somewhere else. I feel like flight some days; honour bright.

Pirbright Smith is well. Old Mr. Pegfurth Bannatyne is here staying at a country inn. His whole baggage is a pair of socks and a book in a fishing-basket; and he borrows even a rod from the landlord. He walked here over the hills from Sanquhar, 'singin', he says, 'like a mavis.' I naturally asked him about Hazlitt. 'He wouldnae take his drink,' he said, 'a queer, queer fellow.' But did not seem further communicative. He says he has become 'releegious,' but still swears like a trooper. I asked him if he had no headquarters. 'No likely,' said he. He says he is writing his memoirs, which will be interesting. He once met Borrow; they boxed; 'and Geordie,' says the old man chuckling, 'gave me the damnedest hiding.' Of Wordsworth he remarked, 'He wasnae sound in the faith, sir, and a milk-blooded, blue-spectacled bitch forbye. But his po'mes are grand—there's no denying that.' I asked him what his book was. 'I havenae mind,' said he—that was his only book! On turning it out, I found it was one of my own, and on showing it to him, he remembered it at once. 'O aye,' he said, 'I mind now. It's pretty bad; ye'll have to do better than that, chieldy,' and chuckled, chuckled. He is a strange old figure, to be sure. He cannot endure Pirbright Smith—'a mere æsth*a*tic,' he said. 'Pooh!' 'Fishin' and releegion—these are my aysthatics,' he wound up.

I thought this would interest you, so scribbled it down. I still hope to get more out of him about Hazlitt, though he utterly pooh-poohed the idea of writing H.'s life. 'Ma life now,' he said, 'there's been queer things in *it*.' He is seventy-nine! but may well last to a hundred!—Yours ever, R. L. S.

VI

MARSEILLES AND HYÈRES

OCTOBER 1882—AUGUST 1884

IN the two years and odd months since his return from California, Stevenson had made no solid gain of health. His winters, and especially his second winter, at Davos had seemed to do him much temporary good; but during the summers in Scotland he had lost as much as he had gained, or more. Loving Provence and the Mediterranean shore from of old, he now made up his mind to try them once again.

As the ways and restrictions of a settled invalid were repugnant to Stevenson's character and instincts, so were the life and society of a regular invalid station depressing and uncongenial to him. He determined, accordingly, to avoid settling in one of these, and hoped to find a suitable climate and habitation that should be near, though not in, some centre of the active and ordinary life of man, with accessible markets, libraries, and other resources. In September 1883 he started with his cousin Mr. R. A. M. Stevenson in search of a new home, and thought first of Western Provence, a region new to him. Arriving at Montpellier, he was laid up again with a bad bout of his lung troubles; and, the doctor not recommending him to stay, returned to Marseilles. Here he was rejoined by his wife, and after a few days' exploration in the neighbourhood they lighted on what seemed exactly the domicile they wanted. This was a roomy and attractive enough house and garden called the Campagne Defli, near the manufacturing suburb of St. Marcel, in a sheltered position in full view of the shapely coastward hills. By the third week in October they were installed, and in eager hopes of pleasant days to come and a return to working health. These hopes were not realised. Week after week went on, and the hemorrhages and fits of fever and exhaustion did not diminish. Work, except occasional verses, and a part of the story called *The Treasure of Franchard*, would not flow, and the time had to be whiled away with games of patience and other resources of the sick man. Nearly two months were thus passed; during the whole of one of them Stevenson had not been able to go beyond the garden; and by Christmas he had to face the fact that the air of the place was tainted. An epidemic of fever, due to some defect of drainage, broke out, and it became clear that this could be no home for Stevenson. Accordingly, at his wife's instance, though having scarce the strength to travel, he left suddenly for Nice, she staying behind to pack their chattels and wind up their affairs and responsibilities as well as might be. Various misadventures, miscarriages of telegrams, journeys taken at cross purposes and the like, making existence uncomfortably dramatic at the moment, but not needful to be recounted here, caused the couple to believe for a while that they had fairly lost each other. They came together, however, at Marseilles in the course of January.

Next they made a few weeks' stay together at Nice, where Stevenson's health quickly mended, and thence returned as far as Hyères. Staying here through the greater part of February, at the Hôtel des Îles d'Or, and finding the place to their liking, they cast about once more for a resting-place, and were this time successful.

The house chosen by the Stevensons at Hyères was not near the sea, but inland, on the road above the old town and beneath the ruins of the castle. The Chalet La Solitude it was called; a cramped but habitable cottage built in the Swiss manner, with a pleasant strip of garden, and a view and situation hardly to be bettered. Here he and his family lived for the next sixteen months (March 1883 to July 1884). To the first part of this period he often afterwards referred as the happiest time of his life. His malady remained quiescent enough to afford, at least to his own buoyant spirit, a strong hope of ultimate recovery. He delighted in his surroundings, and realised for the first time the joys of a true home of his own. The last shadow of a cloud between himself and his parents had long passed away; and towards his father, now in declining health, and often suffering from moods of constitutional depression, the son begins on his part to assume, how touchingly and tenderly will be seen from the following letters, a quasi-paternal attitude of encouragement and monition. At the same time his work on the completion of the *Silverado Squatters*, on *Prince Otto*, the *Child's Garden of Verses* (for which his own name was *Penny Whistles*), on the *Black Arrow*, (designated hereinafter, on account of its Old English dialect, as 'tushery'), and other undertakings prospered well. In the autumn the publication of *Treasure Island* in book form brought with it the first breath of popular applause. The reader will see how modest a price Stevenson was content, nay, delighted, to receive for this classic. It was two or three years yet before he could earn enough to support himself and his family by literature: a thing he had always been earnestly bent on doing, regarding it as the only justification for his chosen way of life. In the meantime, it must be understood, whatever help he needed from his father was from the hour of his marriage always amply and ungrudgingly given.

In September of the same year, 1883, Stevenson had felt deeply the death of his old friend James Walter Ferrier (see the essay 'Old Mortality' and the references in the following letters). But still his health held out fairly, until, in January 1884, on a visit to Nice, he was unexpectedly prostrated anew by an acute congestion of the internal organs, which for the time being brought him to death's door. Returning to his home, his recovery had been only partial when, after four months (May 1884), a recurrence of violent hemorrhages from the lung once more prostrated him completely; soon after which he quitted Hyères, and the epidemic of cholera which broke out there the same summer prevented all thoughts of his return.

The time, both during the happy and hard-working months of March-December 1883, and the semi-convalescence of February-May 1884, was a prolific one in the way of correspondence; and there is perhaps no period of his life when his letters reflect so fully the variety of his moods and the eagerness of his occupations.

TO THE EDITOR OF THE 'NEW YORK TRIBUNE' 1882. AET. 32.

At Marseilles, while waiting to occupy the house which he had leased in the suburbs of that city, Stevenson learned that his old friend and kind adviser, Mr. James Payn, with whom he had been intimate as sub-editor of the *Cornhill Magazine* under Mr. Leslie Stephen in the '70's, had been inadvertently represented in the columns of the *New York Tribune* as a plagiarist of R. L. S. In order to put matters right, he at once sent the following letter both to the *Tribune* and to the London *Athenæum*:—

Terminus Hotel, Marseilles, October 16, 1882.

SIR,—It has come to my ears that you have lent the authority of your columns to an error.

More than half in pleasantry—and I now think the pleasantry ill-judged—I complained in a note to my *New Arabian Nights* that some one, who shall remain nameless for me, had borrowed the idea of a story from one of mine. As if I had not borrowed the ideas of the half of my own! As if any one who had written a story ill had a right to complain of any other who should have written it better! I am indeed thoroughly ashamed of the note, and of the principle which it implies.

But it is no mere abstract penitence which leads me to beg a corner of your paper—it is the desire to defend the honour of a man of letters equally known in America and England, of a man who could afford to lend to me and yet be none the poorer; and who, if he would so far condescend, has my free permission to borrow from me all that he can find worth borrowing.

1882.
AET. 32.

Indeed, sir, I am doubly surprised at your correspondent's error. That James Payn should have borrowed from me is already a strange conception. The author of *Lost Sir Massingberd* and *By Proxy* may be trusted to invent his own stories. The author of *A Grape from a Thorn* knows enough, in his own right, of the humorous and pathetic sides of human nature.

But what is far more monstrous—what argues total ignorance of the man in question—is the idea that James Payn could ever have transgressed the limits of professional propriety. I may tell his thousands of readers on your side of the Atlantic that there breathes no man of letters more inspired by kindness and generosity to his brethren of the profession, and, to put an end to any possibility of error, I may be allowed to add that I often have recourse, and that I had recourse once more but a few weeks ago, to the valuable practical help which he makes it his pleasure to extend to younger men.

I send a duplicate of this letter to a London weekly; for the mistake, first set forth in your columns, has already reached England, and my wanderings have made me perhaps last of the persons interested to hear a word of it.—I am, etc., ROBERT LOUIS STEVENSON.

TO R. A. M. STEVENSON

Terminus Hotel, Marseille, Saturday (October 1882).

MY DEAR BOB,—We have found a house!—at Saint Marcel, Banlieue de Marseille. In a lovely valley between hills part wooded, part white cliffs; a house of a dining-room, of a fine salon—one side lined with a long divan—three good bedrooms (two of them with dressing-rooms), three small rooms (chambers of *bonne* and sich), a large kitchen, a lumber room, many cupboards, a back court, a large, large olive yard, cultivated by a resident *paysan*, a well, a berceau, a good deal of rockery, a little pine shrubbery, a railway station in front, two lines of omnibus to Marseille.

£48 per annum.

It is called Campagne Defli! query Campagne Debug? The Campagne Demosquito goes on here nightly, and is very deadly. Ere we can get installed, we shall be beggared to the door, I see.

I vote for separations; F.'s arrival here, after our separation, was better fun to me than being married was by far. A separation completed is a most valuable property; worth piles.—Ever your affectionate cousin,

R. L. S.

TO THOMAS STEVENSON

Terminus Hotel, Marseille, le 17th October 1882.

MY DEAR FATHER,—. . . We grow, every time we see it, more delighted with our house. It is five miles out of Marseilles, in a lovely spot, among lovely wooded and cliffy hills—most mountainous in line—far lovelier, to my eyes, than any Alps. To-day we have been out inventorying; and though a mistral blew, it was delightful in an open cab, and our house with the windows open was heavenly, soft, dry, sunny, southern. I fear there are fleas—it is called Campagne Defli—and I look forward to tons of insecticide being employed.

I have had to write a letter to the *New York Tribune* and the *Athenæum*. Payn was accused of stealing my stories! I think I have put things handsomely for him.

Just got a servant ! ! !—Ever affectionate son,

R. L. STEVENSON.

Our servant is a Muckle Hash of a Weedy!

TO MRS. THOMAS STEVENSON

The next two months' letters had perforce to consist of little save bulletins of back-going health, and consequent disappointment and incapacity for work.

Campagne Defli, St. Marcel,
Banlieue de Marseille, November 13, 1882.

MY DEAR MOTHER,—Your delightful letters duly arrived this morning. They were the only good feature of the day, which was not a success. Fanny was in bed—she begged I would not split upon her, she felt so guilty; but as I believe she is better this evening, and has a good chance to be right again in a day or two, I will disregard her orders. I do not go back, but do not go forward—or not much. It is, in one way, miserable—for I can do no work; a very little wood-cutting, the newspapers, and a note about every two days to write, completely exhausts my surplus energy; even Patience I have to cultivate with parsimony. I see, if I could only get to work, that we could live here with comfort, almost with luxury. Even as it is, we should be able to get through a considerable time of idleness. I like the place immensely, though I have seen so little of it—I have only been once outside the gate since I was here! It puts me in mind of a summer at Prestonpans and a sickly child you once told me of.

Thirty-two years now finished! My twenty-ninth was in San Francisco, I remember—rather a bleak birthday. The twenty-eighth was not much better; but the rest have been usually pleasant days in pleasant circumstances.

Love to you and to my father and to Cummy.
From me and Fanny and Wogg.   R. L. S.

TO CHARLES BAXTER

After his Christmas flight to Marseilles, and thence to Nice, Stevenson began to mend quickly. In this letter to Mr. Baxter he acknowledges the receipt of a specimen proof, set up for their private amusement, of *Brashiana*, the series of burlesque sonnets he had written at Davos in memory of the Edinburgh publican already mentioned. It should be explained that in their correspondence Stevenson and Mr. Baxter were accustomed to merge their identities in those of two fictitious personages, Thomson and Johnson, imaginary types of Edinburgh character, and ex-elders of the Scottish Kirk. The Pile-on is, of course, the Paillon.

Grand Hotel, Nice, 12th January '83.

DEAR CHARLES,—Thanks for your good letter. It is true, man, God's trüth, what ye say about the body Stevison. The deil himsel, it's my belief, couldnae get the soul harled oot o' the creature's wame, or he had seen the hinder end o' they proofs. Ye crack o' Mæcenas, he's naebody by you! He gied the lad Horace a rax forrit by all accounts; but he never gied him proofs like yon. Horace may hae been a better hand at the clink than Stevison—mind, I'm no sayin' 't—but onyway he was never sae weel prentit. Damned, but it's bonny! Hoo mony pages will there be, think ye? Stevison maun hae sent ye the feck o' twenty sangs— fifteen I'se warrant. Weel, that'll can make thretty pages, gin ye were to prent on ae side only, whilk wad be perhaps what a man o' your *great* idees would be ettlin' at, man Johnson. Then there wad be -the Pre-face, an' prose ye ken prents oot langer than po'try at the hinder end, for ye hae to say things in't. An' then there'll be a title-page and a dedication and an index wi' the first lines like, and the deil an' a'. Man, it'll be grand. Nae copies to be given to the Liberys.

I am alane myself, in Nice, they ca't, but damned, I think they micht as well ca't Nesty. The Pile-on, 's they ca't, 's aboot as big as the river Tay at Perth; and it's rainin' maist like Greenock. Dod, I've seen 's had mair o' what they ca' the I-talian at Muttonhole. I-talian! I haenae seen the sun for eicht and forty hours. Thomson's better, I believe. But the body's fair attenyated. He's

1883.
AET. 33.

doon to seeven stane eleeven, an' he sooks awa' at cod liver ile, till it's a fair disgrace. Ye see he tak's it on a drap brandy; and it's my belief, it's just an excuse for a dram. He an' Stevison gang aboot their lane, maistly; they're company to either, like, an' whiles they'll speak o' Johnson. But *he's* far awa', losh me! Stevison's last book's in a third edeetion; an' it's bein' translated (like the psaulms o' David, nae less) into French; and an eediot they ca' Asher—a kind o' rival of Tauchnitz—is bringin' him oot in a paper book for the Frenchies and the German folk in twa volumes. Sae he's in luck, ye see.—Yours, THOMSON.

TO ALISON CUNNINGHAM

The verses referred to in the following are those of the *Child's Garden*.

[*Nice, February* 1883.]

MY DEAR CUMMY,—You must think, and quite justly, that I am one of the meanest rogues in creation. But though I do not write (which is a thing I hate), it by no means follows that people are out of my mind. It is natural that I should always think more or less about you, and still more natural that I should think of you when I went back to Nice. But the real reason why you have been more in my mind than usual is because of some little verses that I have been writing, and that I mean to make a book of; and the real reason of this letter (although I ought to have written to you anyway) is that I have just seen that the book in question must be dedicated to

ALISON CUNNINGHAM,

the only person who will really understand it. I don't know when it may be ready, for it has to be illustrated, but I hope in the meantime you may like the idea of what is to be; and when the time comes, I shall try to make the dedication as pretty as I can make it. Of course, this is only a flourish, like taking off one's hat; but still, a person who has taken the trouble to write things does not dedicate them to any one without meaning it; and you must just try to take this dedication in place of a great many things that I might have said, and that I ought to have done, to prove that I am not altogether unconscious of the great debt of gratitude I owe you. This little book, which is all about my childhood, should indeed go to no other person but you, who did so much to make that childhood happy.

Do you know, we came very near sending for you this winter. If we had not had news that you were ill too, I almost believe we should have done so, we were so much in trouble.

I am now very well; but my wife has had a very, very bad spell, through overwork and anxiety, when I was *lost*! I suppose you heard of that. She sends you her love, and hopes you will write to her, though she no more than I deserves it. She would add a word herself, but she is too played out.—I am, ever your old boy,

R. L. S.

TO W. E. HENLEY

Stevenson was by this time beginning to send home some of the MS. of the *Child's Garden*, the title of which had not yet been settled. The pieces as first numbered are in a different order from that afterwards adopted, but the reader will easily identify the references.

[*Nice, March* 1883.]

MY DEAR LAD,—This is to announce to you the MS. of Nursery Verses, now numbering XLVIII. pieces or 599 verses, which, of course, one might augment *ad infinitum*.

But here is my notion to make all clear.

I do not want a big ugly quarto; my soul sickens at the look of a quarto. I want a refined octavo, not large —not *larger* than the *Donkey Book*, at any price.

I think the full page might hold four verses of four

1883.
AET. 33.

lines, that is to say, counting their blanks at two, of twenty-two lines in height. The first page of each number would only hold two verses or ten lines, the title being low down. At this rate, we should have seventy-eight or eighty pages of letterpress.

The designs should not be in the text, but facing the poem; so that if the artist liked, he might give two pages of design to every poem that turned the leaf, *i.e.* longer than eight lines, *i.e.* to twenty-eight out of the forty-six. I should say he would not use this privilege (?) above five times, and some he might scorn to illustrate at all, so we may say fifty drawings. I shall come to the drawings next.

But now you see my book of the thickness, since the drawings count two pages, of 180 pages; and since the paper will perhaps be thicker, of near two hundred by bulk. It is bound in a quiet green with the words in thin gilt. Its shape is a slender, tall octavo. And it sells for the publisher's fancy, and it will be a darling to look at; in short, it would be like one of the original Heine books in type and spacing.

Now for the pictures. I take another sheet and begin to jot notes for them when my imagination serves: I will run through the book, writing when I have an idea. There, I have jotted enough to give the artist a notion. Of course, I don't do more than contribute ideas, but I will be happy to help in any and every way. I may as well add another idea; when the artist finds nothing much to illustrate, a good drawing of any *object* mentioned in the text, were it only a loaf of bread or a candlestick, is a most delightful thing to a young child. I remember this keenly.

Of course, if the artist insists on a larger form, I must, I suppose, bow my head. But my idea I am convinced is the best, and would make the book truly, not fashionably, pretty.

I forgot to mention that I shall have a dedication; I

am going to dedicate 'em to Cummy; it will please her, and lighten a little my burthen of ingratitude. A low affair is the Muse business.

I will add no more to this lest you should want to communicate with the artist; try another sheet. I wonder how many I'll keep wandering to.

O I forgot. As for the title, I think 'Nursery Verses' the best. Poetry is not the strong point of the text, and I shrink from any title that might seem to claim that quality; otherwise we might have 'Nursery Muses' or 'New Songs of Innocence' (but that were a blasphemy), or 'Rimes of Innocence': the last not bad, or—an idea —'The Jews' Harp,' or—now I have it—'The Penny Whistle.'

THE PENNY WHISTLE:

NURSERY VERSES

BY

ROBERT LOUIS STEVENSON.

ILLUSTRATED BY —— —— ——

And here we have an excellent frontispiece, of a party playing on a P. W. to a little ring of dancing children.

THE PENNY WHISTLE
is the name for me.

Fool! this is all wrong, here is the true name:—

PENNY WHISTLES

FOR SMALL WHISTLERS.

The second title is queried, it is perhaps better, as simply PENNY WHISTLES.

> Nor you, O Penny Whistler, grudge
> That I your instrument debase:
> By worse performers still we judge,
> And give that fife a second place!

Crossed penny whistles on the cover, or else a sheaf of 'em.

SUGGESTIONS.

IV. The procession—the child running behind it. The procession tailing off through the gates of a cloudy city.

IX. *Foreign Lands.*—This will, I think, want two plates—the child climbing, his first glimpse over the garden wall, with what he sees—the tree shooting higher and higher like the beanstalk, and the view widening. The river slipping in. The road arriving in Fairyland.

X. *Windy Nights.*—The child in bed listening—the horseman galloping.

XII. The child helplessly watching his ship—then he gets smaller, and the doll joyfully comes alive—the pair landing on the island—the ship's deck with the doll steering and the child firing the penny canon. Query two plates? The doll should never come properly alive.

XV. Building of the ship—storing her—Navigation—Tom's accident, the other child paying no attention.

XXXI. *The Wind.*—I sent you my notion of already.

XXXVII. *Foreign Children.*—The foreign types dancing in a jing-a-ring, with the English child pushing in the middle. The foreign children looking at and showing each other marvels. The English child at the leeside of a roast of beef. The English child sitting thinking with his picture-books all round him, and the jing-a-ring of the foreign children in miniature dancing over the picture-books.

XXXIX. Dear artist, can you do me that?

XLII. The child being started off—the bed sailing, curtains and all, upon the sea—the child waking and finding himself at home; the corner of toilette might be worked in to look like the pier.

XLVII. The lighted part of the room, to be carefully distinguished from my child's dark hunting grounds. A shaded lamp. R. L. S.

TO MRS. THOMAS STEVENSON

Hotel des Iles d'Or, Hyères, Var, March 2, [1883].

MY DEAR MOTHER,—It must be at least a fortnight since we have had a scratch of a pen from you; and if it had not been for Cummy's letter, I should have feared you were worse again: as it is, I hope we shall hear from you to-day or to-morrow at latest.

Health.

Our news is good: Fanny never got so bad as we feared, and we hope now that this attack may pass off in threatenings. I am greatly better, have gained flesh, strength, spirits; eat well, walk a good deal, and do some work without fatigue. I am off the sick list.

Lodging.

We have found a house up the hill, close to the town, an excellent place though very, very little. If I can get the landlord to agree to let us take it by the month just now, and let our month's rent count for the year in case we take it on, you may expect to hear we are again installed, and to receive a letter dated thus:—

> La Solitude,
> Hyères-les-Palmiers,
> Var.

If the man won't agree to that, of course I must just give it up, as the house would be dear enough anyway at 2000 f. However, I hope we may get it, as it is healthy, cheerful, and close to shops, and society, and civilisation. The garden, which is above, is lovely, and will be cool in summer. There are two rooms below with a kitchen, and four rooms above, all told.—Ever your affectionate son, R. L. STEVENSON.

1883.
AET. 33.

TO THOMAS STEVENSON

'Cassandra' was a nickname of the elder Mr. Stevenson for his daughter-in-law. The scheme of a play to be founded on *Great Expectations* was one of a hundred formed in these days and afterwards given up.

Hotel des Iles d'Or, but my address will be Chalet la Solitude, Hyères-les-Palmiers, Var, France, March 17, 1883.

DEAR SIR,—Your undated favour from Eastbourne came to hand in course of post, and I now hasten to acknowledge its receipt. We must ask you in future, for the convenience of our business arrangements, to struggle with and tread below your feet this most unsatisfactory and uncommercial habit. Our Mr. Cassandra is better; our Mr. Wogg expresses himself dissatisfied with our new place of business; when left alone in the front shop, he bawled like a parrot; it is supposed the offices are haunted.

To turn to the matter of your letter, your remarks on *Great Expectations* are very good. We have both re-read it this winter, and I, in a manner, twice. The object being a play; the play, in its rough outline, I now see; and it is extraordinary how much of Dickens had to be discarded as unhuman, impossible, and ineffective: all that really remains is the loan of a file (but from a grown-up young man who knows what he was doing, and to a convict who, although he does not know it is his father—the father knows it is his son), and the fact of the convict-father's return and disclosure of himself to the son whom he has made rich. Everything else has been thrown aside; and the position has had to be explained by a prologue which is pretty strong. I have great hopes of this piece, which is very amiable and, in places, very strong indeed: but it was curious how Dickens had to be rolled away; he had made his story turn on such improbabilities, such fantastic trifles, not on a good human basis, such as I recognised. You are right about the casts, they were a capital idea; a good description of them at first, and then afterwards, say second, for the lawyer to have illustrated points out of the history of the originals, dusting the particular bust—that was all the development the thing would bear. Dickens killed them. The only really well *executed* scenes are the riverside ones; the escape in particular is excellent; and I may add, the capture of the two convicts at the beginning. Miss Havisham is, probably, the worst thing in human fiction. But Wemmick I like; and I like Trabb's boy; and Mr. Wopsle as Hamlet is splendid.

The weather here is greatly improved, and I hope in three days to be in the chalet. That is, if I get some money to float me there.

I hope you are all right again, and will keep better. The month of March is past its mid career; it must soon begin to turn toward the lamb; here it has already begun to do so; and I hope milder weather will pick you up. Wogg has eaten a forpet of rice and milk, his beard is streaming, his eyes wild. I am besieged by demands of work from America.

The £50 has just arrived; many thanks; I am now at ease.—Ever your affectionate son, *pro* Cassandra, Wogg and Co., R. L. S.

TO MRS. SITWELL

Chalet la Solitude, Hyères, [April 1883].

MY DEAR FRIEND,—I am one of the lowest of the—but that's understood. I received the copy,[1] excellently written, with I think only one slip from first to last. I have struck out two, and added five or six; so they now number forty-five; when they are fifty, they shall out on the world. I have not written a letter for a cruel time; I have been, and am, so busy, drafting a long story (for me, I mean), about a hundred *Cornhill* pages, or say about as long as the Donkey book: *Prince Otto* it is called, and is,

[1] Fair copy of some of the *Child's Garden* verses.

1883.
AET. 33.

at the present hour, a sore burthen but a hopeful. If I had him all drafted, I should whistle and sing. But no: then I'll have to rewrite him; and then there will be the publishers, alas! But some time or other, I shall whistle and sing, I make no doubt.

I am going to make a fortune, it has not yet begun, for I am not yet clear of debt; but as soon as I can, I begin upon the fortune. I shall begin it with a halfpenny, and it shall end with horses and yachts and all the fun of the fair. This is the first real grey hair in my character: rapacity has begun to show, the greed of the protuberant guttler. Well, doubtless, when the hour strikes, we must all guttle and protube. But it comes hard on one who was always so willow-slender and as careless as the daisies.

Truly I am in excellent spirits. I have crushed through a financial crisis; Fanny is much better; I am in excellent health, and work from four to five hours a day—from one to two above my average, that is; and we all dwell together and make fortunes in the loveliest house you ever saw, with a garden like a fairy story, and a view like a classical landscape.

Little? Well, it is not large. And when you come to see us, you will probably have to bed at the hotel, which is hard by. But it is Eden, madam, Eden and Beulah and the Delectable Mountains and Eldorado and the Hesperidean Isles and Bimini.

We both look forward, my dear friend, with the greatest eagerness to have you here. It seems it is not to be this season; but I appoint you with an appointment for next season. You cannot see us else: remember that. Till my health has grown solid like an oak-tree, till my fortune begins really to spread its boughs like the same monarch of the woods (and the acorn, ay de mi! is not yet planted), I expect to be a prisoner among the palms.

Yes, it is like old times to be writing you from the Riviera, and after all that has come and gone, who can predict anything? How fortune tumbles men about! Yet I have not found that they change their friends, thank God.

1883.
AET. 33.

Both of our loves to your sister and yourself. As for me, if I am here and happy, I know to whom I owe it; I know who made my way for me in life, if that were all, and I remain, with love, your faithful friend,
ROBERT LOUIS STEVENSON.

TO EDMUND GOSSE

Chalet la Solitude, Hyères, [April 1883].

MY DEAR GOSSE,—I am very guilty; I should have written to you long ago; and now, though it must be done, I am so stupid that I can only boldly recapitulate. A phrase of three members is the outside of my syntax.

First, I liked the *Rover* better than any of your other verse. I believe you are right, and can make stories in verse. The last two stanzas and one or two in the beginning—but the two last above all—I thought excellent. I suggest a pursuit of the vein. If you want a good story to treat, get the *Memoirs of the Chevalier Johnstone*, and do his passage of the Tay; it would be excellent: the dinner in the field, the woman he has to follow, the dragoons, the timid boatmen, the brave lasses. It would go like a charm; look at it, and you will say you owe me one.

Second, Gilder asking me for fiction, I suddenly took a great resolve, and have packed off to him my new work, *The Silverado Squatters*. I do not for a moment suppose he will take it; but pray say all the good words you can for it. I should be awfully glad to get it taken. But if it does not mean dibbs at once, I shall be ruined for life. Pray write soon and beg Gilder your prettiest for a poor gentleman in pecuniary sloughs.

Fourth, next time I am supposed to be at death's door,

1883.
AET. 33.
write to me like a Christian, and let not your correspondence attend on business.—Yours ever, R. L. S.

P.S.—I see I have led you to conceive the *Squatters* are fiction. They are not, alas!

TO MR. AND MRS. THOMAS STEVENSON

Chalet Solitude, May 5, [1883].

MY DEAREST PEOPLE,—I have had a great piece of news. There has been offered for *Treasure Island*—how much do you suppose? I believe it would be an excellent jest to keep the answer till my next letter. For two cents I would do so. Shall I? Anyway, I'll turn the page first. No—well—A hundred pounds, all alive, O! A hundred jingling, tingling, golden, minted quid. Is not this wonderful? Add that I have now finished, in draft, the fifteenth chapter of my novel, and have only five before me, and you will see what cause of gratitude I have.

The weather, to look at the per contra sheet, continues vomitable; and Fanny is quite out of sorts. But, really, with such cause of gladness, I have not the heart to be dispirited by anything. My child's verse book is finished, dedication and all, and out of my hands—you may tell Cummy; *Silverado* is done, too, and cast upon the waters; and this novel so near completion, it does look as if I should support myself without trouble in the future. If I have only health, I can, I thank God. It is dreadful to be a great, big man, and not be able to buy bread.

O that this may last!

I have to-day paid my rent for the half year, till the middle of September, and got my lease: why they have been so long, I know not.

I wish you all sorts of good things.

When is our marriage day?—Your loving and ecstatic son, TREESURE EILAAN.

It has been for me a Treasure Island verily.

TO MR. AND MRS. THOMAS STEVENSON

La Solitude, Hyères, May 8, 1883.

MY DEAR PEOPLE,—I was disgusted to hear my father was not so well. I have a most troubled existence of work and business. But the work goes well, which is the great affair. I meant to have written a most delightful letter; too tired, however, and must stop. Perhaps I'll find time to add to it ere post.

I have returned refreshed from eating, but have little time, as Lloyd will go soon with the letters on his way to his tutor, Louis Robert (! ! ! !), with whom he learns Latin in French, and French, I suppose, in Latin, which seems to me a capital education. He, Lloyd, is a great bicycler already, and has been long distances; he is most new-fangled over his instrument, and does not willingly converse on other subjects.

Our lovely garden is a prey to snails; I have gathered about a bushel, which, not having the heart to slay, I steal forth withal and deposit near my neighbour's garden wall. As a case of casuistry, this presents many points of interest. I loathe the snails, but from loathing to actual butchery, trucidation of multitudes, there is still a step that I hesitate to take. What, then, to do with them? My neighbour's vineyard, pardy! It is a rich, villa, pleasure-garden of course; if it were a peasant's patch, the snails, I suppose, would have to perish.

The weather these last three days has been much better, though it is still windy and unkind. I keep splendidly well, and am cruelly busy, with mighty little time even for a walk. And to write at all, under such pressure, must be held to lean to virtue's side.

My financial prospects are shining. O if the health will hold, I should easily support myself.—Your ever affectionate son, R. L. S.

1883.
AET. 33.

TO EDMUND GOSSE

The following refers to an arrangement (see above, p. 265) made through Mr. Gosse for the publication of a part of the *Silverado Squatters* in the *New York Century Magazine*, of which Mr. Gilder was, and is, as is well known, the admirable editor:—

La Solitude, Hyères-les-Palmiers, Var,
[*May* 20, 1883].

MY DEAR GOSSE,—I enclose the receipt and the corrections. As for your letter and Gilder's, I must take an hour or so to think; the matter much importing—to me. The £40 was a heavenly thing.

I send the MS. by Henley, because he acts for me in all matters, and had the thing, like all my other books, in his detention. He is my unpaid agent—an admirable arrangement for me, and one that has rather more than doubled my income on the spot.

If I have been long silent, think how long you were so, and blush, sir, blush.

I was rendered unwell by the arrival of your cheque, and, like Pepys, 'my hand still shakes to write of it.' To this grateful emotion, and not to D.T., please attribute the raggedness of my hand.

This year I should be able to live and keep my family on my own earnings, and that in spite of eight months and more of perfect idleness at the end of last and beginning of this. It is a sweet thought.

This spot, our garden and our view, are sub-celestial. I sing daily with my Bunyan, that great bard,

'I dwell already the next door to Heaven!'

If you could see my roses, and my aloes, and my fig-marigolds, and my olives, and my view over a plain, and my view of certain mountains as graceful as Apollo, as severe as Zeus, you would not think the phrase exaggerated.

It is blowing to-day a *hot* mistral, which is the devil or a near connection of his.

This to catch the post.—Yours affectionately,

R. L. STEVENSON.

To Edmund Gosse

1883.
AET. 33.

La Solitude, Hyères-les-Palmiers, Var, France,
May 21, 1883.

MY DEAR GOSSE,—The night giveth advice, generally bad advice; but I have taken it. And I have written direct to Gilder to tell him to keep the book[1] back and go on with it in November at his leisure. I do not know if this will come in time; if it doesn't, of course things will go on in the way proposed. The £40, or, as I prefer to put it, the 1000 francs, has been such a piercing sun-ray as my whole grey life is gilt withal. On the back of it I can endure. If these good days of *Longman* and the *Century* only last, it will be a very green world, this that we dwell in and that philosophers miscall. I have no taste for that philosophy; give me large sums paid on the receipt of the MS. and copyright reserved, and what do I care about the non-bëent? Only I know it can't last. The devil always has an imp or two in every house, and my imps are getting lively. The good lady, the dear, kind lady, the sweet, excellent lady, Nemesis, whom alone I adore, has fixed her wooden eye upon me. I fall prone; spare me, Mother Nemesis! But catch her!

I must now go to bed; for I have had a whoreson influenza cold, and have to lie down all day, and get up only to meals and the delights, June delights, of business correspondence.

You said nothing about my subject for a poem. Don't you like it? My own fishy eye has been fixed on it for prose, but I believe it could be thrown out finely in verse, and hence I resign and pass the hand. Twig the compliment?—Yours affectionately R. L. S.

[1] *Silverado Squatters.*

1883.
AET. 33.

TO W. E. HENLEY

'Tushery' had been a name in use between Stevenson and Mr. Henley for romances of the *Ivanhoe* type. He now applies it to his own tale of the Wars of the Roses, *The Black Arrow*, written for Mr. Henderson's *Young Folks*, of which the office was in Red Lion Square.

[*Hyères, May* 1883.]

... THE influenza has busted me a good deal; I have no spring, and am headachy. So, as my good Red Lion Counter begged me for another Butcher's Boy—I turned me to—what thinkest 'ou?—to Tushery, by the mass! Ay, friend, a whole tale of tushery. And every tusher tushes me so free, that may I be tushed if the whole thing is worth a tush. *The Black Arrow: A Tale of Tunstall Forest* is his name: tush! a poor thing!

Will *Treasure Island* proofs be coming soon, think you?

I will now make a confession. It was the sight of your maimed strength and masterfulness that begot John Silver in *Treasure Island*. Of course, he is not in any other quality or feature the least like you; but the idea of the maimed man, ruling and dreaded by the sound, was entirely taken from you.

Otto is, as you say, not a thing to extend my public on. It is queer and a little, little bit free; and some of the parties are immoral; and the whole thing is not a romance, nor yet a comedy; nor yet a romantic comedy; but a kind of preparation of some of the elements of all three in a glass jar. I think it is not without merit, but I am not always on the level of my argument, and some parts are false, and much of the rest is thin; it is more a triumph for myself than anything else; for I see, beyond it, better stuff. I have nine chapters ready, or almost ready, for press. My feeling would be to get it placed anywhere for as much as could be got for it, and rather in the shadow, till one saw the look of it in print.—Ever yours, PRETTY SICK.

TO W. E. HENLEY

1883.
AET. 33.

La Solitude, Hyères-les-Palmiers, May 1883.

MY DEAR LAD,—The books came some time since, but I have not had the pluck to answer: a shower of small troubles having fallen in, or troubles that may be very large.

I have had to incur a huge vague debt for cleaning sewers; our house was (of course) riddled with hidden cesspools, but that was infallible. I have the fever, and feel the duty to work very heavy on me at times; yet go it must. I have had to leave *Fontainebleau*, when three hours would finish it, and go full-tilt at tushery for a while. But it will come soon.

I think I can give you a good article on Hokusai; but that is for afterwards; *Fontainebleau* is first in hand.

By the way, my view is to give the *Penny Whistles* to Crane or Greenaway. But Crane, I think, is likeliest; he is a fellow who, at least, always does his best.

Shall I ever have money enough to write a play?
O dire necessity!

A word in your ear: I don't like trying to support myself. I hate the strain and the anxiety; and when unexpected expenses are foisted on me, I feel the world is playing with false dice.—Now I must Tush, adieu,

AN ACHING, FEVERED, PENNY-JOURNALIST.

A lytle Jape of TUSHERIE.
By A. Tusher.

The pleasant river gushes
    Among the meadows green;
At home the author tushes;
    For him it flows unseen.

The Birds among the Bŭshes
    May wanton on the spray;
But vain for him who tushes
    The brightness of the day!

1883.
AET. 33.

The frog among the rushes
    Sits singing in the blue.
By 'r la'kin! but these tushes
    Are wearisome to do!

The task entirely crushes
    The spirit of the bard:
God pity him who tushes—
    His task is very hard.

The filthy gutter slushes,
    The clouds are full of rain,
But doomed is he who tushes
    To tush and tush again.

At morn with his hair-br*u*shes,
    Still 'tush' he says, and weeps;
At night again he tushes,
    And tushes till he sleeps.

And when at length he pŭshes
    Beyond the river dark—
'Las, to the man who tushes,
    'Tush' shall be God's remark!

TO W. E. HENLEY

The verses alluded to are some of those afterwards collected in *Underwoods*.

[*Chalet La Solitude, Hyères, May* 1883.]

DEAR HENLEY,—You may be surprised to hear that I am now a great writer of verses; that is, however, so. I have the mania now like my betters, and faith, if I live till I am forty, I shall have a book of rhymes like Pollock, Gosse, or whom you please. Really, I have begun to learn some of the rudiments of that trade, and have written three or four pretty enough pieces of octosyllabic nonsense, semi-serious, semi-smiling. A kind of prose Herrick, divested of the gift of verse, and you behold the Bard. But I like it.   R. L. S.

TO W. E. HENLEY

1883.
AET. 33.

The 'new dictionary' means, of course, the first instalments of the great Oxford Dictionary of the English Language, edited by Dr. J. A. H. Murray.

Hyères [June 1883].

DEAR LAD,—I was delighted to hear the good news about ——. Bravo, he goes uphill fast. Let him beware of vanity, and he will go higher; let him be still discontented, and let him (if it might be) see the merits and not the faults of his rivals, and he may swarm at last to the top-gallant. There is no other way. Admiration is the only road to excellence; and the critical spirit kills, but envy and injustice are putrefaction on its feet.

Thus far the moralist. The eager author now begs to know whether you may have got the other Whistles, and whether a fresh proof is to be taken; also whether in that case the dedication should not be printed therewith; *B*ulk *D*elights *P*ublishers (original aphorism; to be said sixteen times in succession as a test of sobriety).

Your wild and ravening commands were received; but cannot be obeyed. And anyway, I do assure you I am getting better every day; and if the weather would but turn, I should soon be observed to walk in hornpipes. Truly I am on the mend. I am still very careful. I have the new dictionary; a joy, a thing of beauty, and—bulk. I shall be raked i' the mools before it's finished; that is the only pity; but meanwhile I sing.

I beg to inform you that I, Robert Louis Stevenson, author of *Brashiana* and other works, am merely beginning to commence to prepare to make a first start at trying to understand my profession. O the height and depth of novelty and worth in any art! and O that I am privileged to swim and shoulder through such oceans! Could one get out of sight of land—all in the blue? Alas not, being anchored here in flesh, and the bonds of logic being still about us.

VOL. I.—S

1883.
AET. 33.

But what a great space and a great air there is in these small shallows where alone we venture! and how new each sight, squall, calm, or sunrise! An art is a fine fortune, a palace in a park, a band of music, health, and physical beauty; all but love—to any worthy practiser. I sleep upon my art for a pillow; I waken in my art; I am unready for death, because I hate to leave it. I love my wife, I do not know how much, nor can, nor shall, unless I lost her; but while I can conceive my being widowed, I refuse the offering of life without my art. I *am* not but in my art; it is me; I am the body of it merely.

And yet I produce nothing, am the author of *Brashiana* and other works: tiddy-iddity—as if the works one wrote were anything but 'prentice's experiments. Dear reader, I deceive you with husks, the real works and all the pleasure are still mine and incommunicable. After this break in my work, beginning to return to it, as from light sleep, I wax exclamatory, as you see.

   Sursum Corda:
   Heave ahead:
   Here's luck.
   Art and Blue Heaven,
   April and God's Larks.
   Green reeds and the sky-scattering river.
   A stately music.
   Enter God!   R. L. S.

Ay, but you know, until a man can write that 'Enter God,' he has made no art! None! Come, let us take counsel together and make some!

TO W. E. HENLEY

The first paragraph of the following refers to contributions of R. L. S. to the *Magazine of Art* under Mr. Henley's editorship:—

La Solitude, Hyères [*Summer* 1883].

DEAR LAD,—Glad you like *Fontainebleau*. I am going to be the means, under heaven, of aërating or literating your pages. The idea that because a thing is a picture-book all the writing should be on the wrong tack is *triste* but widespread. Thus Hokusai will be really a gossip on convention, or in great part. And the Skelt will be as like a Charles Lamb as I can get it. The writer should write, and not illustrate pictures: else it's bosh. . . .

1883.
AET. 33.

Your remarks about the ugly are my eye. Ugliness is only the prose of horror. It is when you are not able to write *Macbeth* that you write *Thérèse Raquin*. Fashions are external: the essence of art only varies in so far as fashion widens the field of its application; art is a mill whose thirlage, in different ages, widens and contracts; but, in any case and under any fashion, the great man produces beauty, terror, and mirth, and the little man produces cleverness (personalities, psychology) instead of beauty, ugliness instead of terror, and jokes instead of mirth. As it was in the beginning, is now, and shall be ever, world without end. Amen!

And even as you read, you say, 'Of course, *quelle rengaîne!*' R. L. S.

TO ALISON CUNNINGHAM

The persons mentioned below in the third paragraph are cousins of the writer and playmates of his childhood; two of them, named Lewis like himself, after their Balfour grandfather, had been nicknamed after their birthplaces 'Delhi' and 'Cramond' to avoid confusion :—

La Solitude, Hyères [Summer 1883].

MY DEAR CUMMY,—Yes, I own I am a real bad correspondent, and am as bad as can be in most directions.

I have been adding some more poems to your book. I wish they would look sharp about it; but, you see, they are trying to find a good artist to make the illustrations, without which no child would give a kick for it. It will be quite a fine work, I hope. The dedication is a poem too, and has been quite a long while written, but I do not mean you to see it till you get the book; keep the jelly

1883.
AET. 33.

for the last, you know, as you would often recommend in former days, so now you can take your own medicine.

I am very sorry to hear you have been so poorly; I have been very well; it used to be quite the other way, used it not? Do you remember making the whistle at Mount Chessie? I do not think it *was* my knife; I believe it was yours; but rhyme is a very great monarch, and goes before honesty, in these affairs at least. Do you remember, at Warriston, one autumn Sunday, when the beech nuts were on the ground, seeing heaven open? I would like to make a rhyme of that, but cannot.

Is it not strange to think of all the changes: Bob, Cramond, Delhi, Minnie, and Henrietta, all married, and fathers and mothers, and your humble servant just the one point better off? And such a little while ago all children together! The time goes swift and wonderfully even; and if we are no worse than we are, we should be grateful to the power that guides us. For more than a generation I have now been to the fore in this rough world, and been most tenderly helped, and done cruelly wrong, and yet escaped; and here I am still, the worse for wear, but with some fight in me still, and not unthankful—no, surely not unthankful, or I were then the worst of human beings!

My little dog is a very much better child in every way, both more loving and more amiable; but he is not fond of strangers, and is, like most of his kind, a great, specious humbug.

Fanny has been ill, but is much better again; she now goes donkey rides with an old woman, who compliments her on her French. That old woman—seventy odd—is in a parlous spiritual state.

Pretty soon, in the new sixpenny illustrated magazine, Wogg's picture is to appear: this is a great honour! And the poor soul, whose vanity would just explode if he could understand it, will never be a bit the wiser!— With much love, in which Fanny joins, believe me, your affectionate boy,   ROBERT LOUIS STEVENSON.

TO W. E. HENLEY

La Solitude, Hyères, Summer 1883.

DEAR LAD,—Snatches in return for yours; for this little once, I'm well to windward of you.

Seventeen chapters of *Otto* are now drafted, and finding I was working through my voice and getting screechy, I have turned back again to rewrite the earlier part. It has, I do believe, some merit: of what order, of course, I am the last to know; and, triumph of triumphs, my wife—my wife who hates and loathes and slates my women—admits a great part of my Countess to be on the spot.

Yes, I could borrow, but it is the joy of being before the public, for once. Really, £100 is a sight more than *Treasure Island* is worth.

The reason of my *dèche*? Well, if you begin one house, have to desert it, begin another, and are eight months without doing any work, you will be in a *dèche* too. I am not in a *dèche*, however; *distinguo*—I would fain distinguish; I am rather a swell, but *not solvent*. At a touch the edifice, *ædificium*, might collapse. If my creditors began to babble around me, I would sink with a slow strain of music into the crimson west. The difficulty in my elegant villa is to find oil, *oleum*, for the dam axles. But I've paid my rent until September; and beyond the chemist, the grocer, the baker, the doctor, the gardener, Lloyd's teacher, and the great chief creditor Death, I can snap my fingers at all men. Why will people spring bills on you? I try to make 'em charge me at the moment; they won't, the money goes, the debt remains.—The Required Play is in the *Merry Men*.

Q. E. F.

I thus render honour to your *flair*; it came on me of a clap; I do not see it yet beyond a kind of sunset glory. But it's there: passion, romance, the picturesque, involved: startling, simple, horrid: a sea-pink in sea-froth!

1883. *S'agit de la désenterrer.* 'Help!' cries a buried master-
AET. 33. piece.

Once I see my way to the year's end, clear, I turn to plays; till then I grind at letters; finish *Otto*; write, say, a couple of my *Traveller's Tales*; and then, if all my ships come home, I will attack the drama in earnest. I cannot mix the skeins. Thus, though I'm morally sure there is a play in *Otto*, I dare not look for it: I shoot straight at the story.

As a story, a comedy, I think *Otto* very well constructed; the echoes are very good, all the sentiments change round, and the points of view are continually, and, I think (if you please), happily contrasted. None of it is exactly funny, but some of it is smiling.   R. L. S.

TO EDMUND GOSSE

The reference is to Mr. Gosse's volume called *Seventeenth Century Studies.*

La Solitude, Hyères [*Summer* 1883].

MY DEAR GOSSE,—I have now leisurely read your volume; pretty soon, by the way, you will receive one of mine.

It is a pleasant, instructive, and scholarly volume. The three best being, quite out of sight—Crashaw, Otway, and Etherege. They are excellent; I hesitate between them; but perhaps Crashaw is the most brilliant.

Your Webster is not my Webster; nor your Herrick my Herrick. On these matters we must fire a gun to leeward, show our colours, and go by. Argument is impossible. They are two of my favourite authors: Herrick above all: I suppose they are two of yours. Well, Janus-like, they do behold us two with diverse countenances, few features are common to these different avatars; and we can but agree to differ, but still with gratitude to our entertainers, like two guests at the same dinner, one of whom takes clear and one white soup. By my way of thinking, neither of us need be wrong.

The other papers are all interesting, adequate, clear, and with a pleasant spice of the romantic. It is a book you may be well pleased to have so finished, and will do you much good. The Crashaw is capital: capital; I like the taste of it. Preface clean and dignified. The handling throughout workmanlike, with some four or five touches of preciosity, which I regret.

With my thanks for information, entertainment, and a pleasurable envy here and there.—Yours affectionately,

R. L. S.

TO W. E. HENLEY

During the height of the Provençal summer, Stevenson went with his wife to meet his parents at the Baths of Royat in Auvergne, where he stayed for six weeks, and where all passed pleasantly with no return of illness. Soon after he was settled again at Hyères, he had a great shock in the death of one of the oldest and most intimate of his friends of Edinburgh days, Mr. James Walter Ferrier (see the essay 'Old Mortality' in *Memories and Portraits*). It is in accordance with the expressed wish of this gentleman's surviving sister that publicity is given to the following letter:—

*La Solitude, Hyères-les-Palmiers,
Var, September* 19, 1883.

DEAR BOY,—Our letters vigorously cross: you will ere this have received a note to Coggie: God knows what was in it.

It is strange, a little before the first word you sent me —so late—kindly late, I know and feel—I was thinking in my bed, when I knew you I had six friends—Bob I had by nature; then came the good James Walter—with all his failings—the *gentleman* of the lot, alas to sink so low, alas to do so little, but now, thank God, in his quiet rest; next I found Baxter—well do I remember telling Walter I had unearthed 'a W.S. that I thought would do '—it was in the Academy Lane, and he questioned me as to the Signet's qualifications; fourth came Simpson; somewhere about the same time, I began to get intimate with Jenkin; last came Colvin. Then, one black winter afternoon, long Leslie Stephen, in his velvet jacket, met me in the *Spec.* by appointment, took me over to the infirmary, and in the crackling, blighting gaslight showed me that old head whose excellent representation I see before me in the photograph. Now when a man has six friends, to introduce a seventh is usually hopeless. Yet when you were presented, you took to them and they to you upon the nail. You must have been a fine fellow; but what a singular fortune I must have had in my six friends that you should take to all. I don't know if it is good Latin, most probably not: but this is enscrolled before my eyes for Walter: *Tandem e nubibus in apricum properat.* Rest, I suppose, I know, was all that remained; but O to look back, to remember all the mirth, all the kindness, all the humorous limitations and loved defects of that character; to think that he was young with me, sharing that weather-beaten, Fergussonian youth, looking forward through the clouds to the sunburst; and now clean gone from my path, silent—well, well. This has been a strange awakening. Last night, when I was alone in the house, with the window open on the lovely still night, I could have sworn he was in the room with me; I could show you the spot; and, what was very curious, I heard his rich laughter, a thing I had not called to mind for I know not how long.

I see his coral waistcoat studs that he wore the first time he dined in my house; I see his attitude, leaning back a little, already with something of a portly air, and laughing internally. How I admired him! And now in the West Kirk.

I am trying to write out this haunting bodily sense of absence; besides, what else should I write of?

Yes, looking back, I think of him as one who was good, though sometimes clouded. He was the only gentle one of all my friends, save perhaps the other Walter. And he was certainly the only modest man among the lot. He never gave himself away; he kept back his secret; there was always a gentle problem behind all. Dear, dear, what a wreck; and yet how pleasant is the retrospect! God doeth all things well, though by what strange, solemn, and murderous contrivances!

It is strange: he was the only man I ever loved who did not habitually interrupt. The fact draws my own portrait. And it is one of the many reasons why I count myself honoured by his friendship. A man like you *had* to like me; you could not help yourself; but Ferrier was above me, we were not equals; his true self humoured and smiled paternally upon my failings, even as I humoured and sorrowed over his.

Well, first his mother, then himself, they are gone: 'in their resting graves.'

When I come to think of it, I do not know what I said to his sister, and I fear to try again. Could you send her this? There is too much both about yourself and me in it; but that, if you do not mind, is but a mark of sincerity. It would let her know how entirely, in the mind of (I suppose) his oldest friend, the good, true Ferrier obliterates the memory of the other, who was only his 'lunatic brother.'

Judge of this for me, and do as you please; anyway, I will try to write to her again; my last was some kind of scrawl that I could not see for crying. This came upon me, remember, with terrible suddenness; I was surprised by this death; and it is fifteen or sixteen years since first I saw the handsome face in the *Spec.* I made sure, besides, to have died first. Love to you, your wife, and her sisters. —Ever yours, dear boy, R. L. S.

I never knew any man so superior to himself as poor James Walter. The best of him only came as a vision, like Corsica from the Corniche. He never gave his

1883.
AET. 33.

measure either morally or intellectually. The curse was on him. Even his friends did not know him but by fits. I have passed hours with him when he was so wise, good, and sweet, that I never knew the like of it in any other. And for a beautiful good humour he had no match. I remember breaking in upon him once with a whole red-hot story (in my worst manner), pouring words upon him by the hour about some truck not worth an egg that had befallen me; and suddenly, some half hour after, finding that the sweet fellow had some concern of his own of infinitely greater import, that he was patiently and smilingly waiting to consult me on. It sounds nothing; but the courtesy and the unselfishness were perfect. It makes me rage to think how few knew him, and how many had the chance to sneer at their better.

Well, he was not wasted, that we know; though if anything looked liker irony than this fitting of a man out with these rich qualities and faculties to be wrecked and aborted from the very stocks, I do not know the name of it. Yet we see that he has left an influence; the memory of his patient courtesy has often checked me in rudeness; has it not you?

You can form no idea of how handsome Walter was. At twenty he was splendid to see; then, too, he had the sense of power in him, and great hopes; he looked forward, ever jesting of course, but he looked to see himself where he had the right to expect. He believed in himself profoundly; but *he never disbelieved in others*. To the roughest Highland student he always had his fine, kind, open dignity of manner; and a good word behind his back.

The last time that I saw him before leaving for America —it was a sad blow to both of us. When he heard I was leaving, and that might be the last time we might meet— it almost was so—he was terribly upset, and came round at once. We sat late, in Baxter's empty house, where I was sleeping. My dear friend Walter Ferrier: O if I had only written to him more! if only one of us in these last days had been well! But I ever cherished the honour of his friendship, and now when he is gone, I know what I have lost still better. We live on, meaning to meet; but when the hope is gone, the pang comes.

1883.
AET. 33.

R. L. S.

TO EDMUND GOSSE

La Solitude, Hyères-les-Palmiers,
26th September 1883.

MY DEAR GOSSE,—It appears a bolt from Transatlantica is necessary to produce four lines from you. It is not flattering; but as I was always a bad correspondent, 'tis a vice to which I am lenient. I give you to know, however, that I have already twice (this makes three times) sent you what I please to call a letter, and received from you in return a subterfuge—or nothing. . . .

My present purpose, however, which must not be postponed, is to ask you to telegraph to the Americans.

After a summer of good health of a very radiant order, toothache and the death of a very old friend, which came upon me like a thunderclap, have rather shelved my powers. I stare upon the paper, not write. I wish I could write like your Sculptors; yet I am well aware that I should not try in that direction. A certain warmth (tepid enough) and a certain dash of the picturesque are my poor essential qualities; and if I went fooling after the too classical, I might lose even these. But I envied you that page.

I am, of course, deep in schemes; I was so ever. Execution alone somewhat halts. How much do you make per annum, I wonder? This year, for the first time, I shall pass £300; I may even get halfway to the next milestone. This seems but a faint remuneration; and the devil of it is, that I manage, with sickness, and moves, and education, and the like, to keep steadily in front of my income. However, I console myself with this, that if I were anything else under God's Heaven, and had the same crank health, I should make an even zero. If I had, with my present knowledge, twelve months of my old health, I would, could, and should do something neat. As it is, I have to tinker at my things in little sittings; and the rent, or the butcher, or something, is always calling me off to rattle up a pot-boiler. And then comes a back-set of my health, and I have to twiddle my fingers and play patience.

Well, I do not complain, but I do envy strong health where it is squandered. Treasure your strength, and may you never learn by experience the profound *ennui* and irritation of the shelved artist. For then, what is life? All that one has done to make one's life effective then doubles the itch of inefficiency.

I trust also you may be long without finding out the devil that there is in a bereavement. After love it is the one great surprise that life preserves for us. Now I don't think I can be astonished any more.—Yours affectionately,

R. L. S.

TO SIDNEY COLVIN

The following is in answer to a letter containing remarks on the proofs of the *Child's Garden*, then going round among some of his friends, and on the instalments of *Silverado Squatters* and the *Black Arrow*, which were appearing in the *Century Magazine* and *Young Folks* respectively. The proposal for an excursion among the Greek islands, to be made the subject of a book, had come, if I remember right, from a firm of American publishers, and was declined on the ground of health risks. The remarks on Professor Seeley's literary manner are *àpropos* of the *Expansion of England*, which I had lately sent him:—

La Solitude, Hyères-les-Palmiers, Var [*October* 1883].

COLVIN, COLVIN, COLVIN,—Yours received; also interesting copy of *P. Whistles.* 'In the multitude of councillors the Bible declares there is wisdom,' said my great-uncle, 'but I have always found in them distraction.' It is extraordinary how tastes vary: these proofs have been handed about, it appears, and I have had several letters; and—distraction. 'Æsop: the Miller and the Ass.'

Notes on details:—

1. I love the occasional trochaic line; and so did many excellent writers before me.

2. If you don't like 'A Good Boy,' I do.

3. In 'Escape at Bedtime,' I found two suggestions. 'Shove' for 'above' is a correction of the press; it was so written. 'Twinkled' is just the error; to the child the stars appear to be there; any word that suggests illusion is a horror.

4. I don't care; I take a different view of the vocative.

5. Bewildering and childering are good enough for me. These are rhymes, jingles; I don't go for eternity and the three unities.

I will delete some of those condemned, but not all. I don't care for the name Penny Whistles; I sent a sheaf to Henley when I sent 'em. But I've forgot the others. I would just as soon call 'em 'Rimes for Children' as anything else. I am not proud nor particular.

Your remarks on the *Black Arrow* are to the point. I am pleased you liked Crookback; he is a fellow whose hellish energy has always fired my attention. I wish Shakespeare had written the play after he had learned some of the rudiments of literature and art rather than before. Some day, I will re-tickle the Sable Missile, and shoot it, *moyennant finances*, once more into the air; I can lighten it of much, and devote some more attention to Dick o' Gloucester. It's great sport to write tushery.

By this I reckon you will have heard of my proposed excursiolorum to the Isles of Greece, the Isles of Greece, and kindred sites. If the excursiolorum goes on, that is, if *moyennant finances* comes off, I shall write to beg you to collect introductiolorums for me.

Distinguo: 1. *Silverado* was not written in America, but in Switzerland's icy mountains. 2. What you read is the bleeding and disembowelled remains of what I wrote. 3. The good stuff is all to come—so I think. 'The Sea Fogs,' 'The Hunter's Family,' Toils and Pleasures'—*belles pages.*—Yours ever, RAMNUGGER.

O!—Seeley is too clever to live, and the book a gem. But why has he read too much Arnold? Why will he avoid—obviously avoid—fine writing up to which he has led? This is a winking, curled-and-oiled, ultra-cultured, Oxford-don sort of an affectation that infuriates my honest soul. 'You see'—they say—'how unbombastic *we* are; we come right up to eloquence, and, when it's hanging on the pen, dammy, we scorn it!' It is literary Deronda-ism. If you don't want the woman, the image, or the phrase, mortify your vanity and avoid the appearance of wanting them.

TO W. H. LOW

Manhattan mentioned below is the name of a short-lived New York magazine, the editor of which had asked through Mr. Low for a contribution from R. L. S.

La Solitude, Hyères, October [1883].

MY DEAR LOW,— . . . Some day or other, in Cassell's *Magazine of Art*, you will see a paper which will interest you, and where your name appears. It is called 'Fontainebleau: Village Communities of Artists,' and the signature of R. L. Stevenson will be found annexed.

Please tell the editor of *Manhattan* the following secrets for me: 1*st*, That I am a beast; 2*nd*, that I owe him a letter; 3*rd*, that I have lost his, and cannot recall either his name or address; 4*th*, that I am very deep in engagements, which my absurd health makes it hard for me to overtake; but 5*th*, that I will bear him in mind; 6*th* and last, that I am a brute.

My address is still the same, and I live in a most sweet corner of the universe, sea and fine hills before me, and a rich variegated plain; and at my back a craggy hill, loaded with vast feudal ruins. I am very quiet; a person passing by my door half startles me; but I enjoy the most aromatic airs, and at night the most wonderful view into a moonlit garden. By day this garden fades into nothing, overpowered by its surroundings and the luminous distance; but at night and when the moon is out, that garden, the arbour, the flight of stairs that mount the artificial hillock, the plumed blue gum-trees that hang trembling, become the very skirts of Paradise. Angels I know frequent it; and it thrills all night with the flutes of silence. Damn that garden;—and by day it is gone.

Continue to testify boldly against realism. Down with Dagon, the fish god! All art swings down towards imitation, in these days, fatally. But the man who loves art with wisdom sees the joke; it is the lustful that tremble and respect her ladyship; but the honest and romantic lovers of the Muse can see a joke and sit down to laugh with Apollo.

The prospect of your return to Europe is very agreeable; and I was pleased by what you said about your parents. One of my oldest friends died recently, and this has given me new thoughts of death. Up to now I had rather thought of him as a mere personal enemy of my own; but now that I see him hunting after my friends, he looks altogether darker. My own father is not well; and Henley, of whom you must have heard me speak, is in a questionable state of health. These things are very solemn, and take some of the colour out of life. It is a great thing, after all, to be a man of reasonable honour and kindness. Do you remember once consulting me in Paris whether you had not better sacrifice honesty

1883.
AET. 33.

1883.
AET. 33.

to art; and how, after much confabulation, we agreed that your art would suffer if you did? We decided better than we knew. In this strange welter where we live, all hangs together by a million filaments; and to do reasonably well by others, is the first pre-requisite of art. Art is a virtue; and if I were the man I should be, my art would rise in the proportion of my life.

If you were privileged to give some happiness to your parents, I know your art will gain by it. *By God, it will!* *Sic subscribitur*,   R. L. S.

TO R. A. M. STEVENSON

La Solitude, Hyères-les-Palmiers [*October* 1883].

MY DEAR BOB,—Yes, I got both your letters at Lyons, but have been since then decading in several steps. Toothache; fever; Ferrier's death; lung. Now it is decided I am to leave to-morrow, penniless, for Nice to see Dr. Williams.

I was much struck by your last. I have written a breathless note on Realism for Henley; a fifth part of the subject hurriedly touched, which will show you how my thoughts are driving. You are now at last beginning to think upon the problems of executive, plastic art, for you are now for the first time attacking them. Hitherto you have spoken and thought of two things—technique and the *ars artium*, or common background of all arts. Studio work is the real touch. That is the genial error of the present French teaching. Realism I regard as a mere question of method. The 'brown foreground,' 'old mastery,' and the like, ranking with villanelles, as technical sports and pastimes. Real art, whether ideal or realistic, addresses precisely the same feeling, and seeks the same qualities—significance or charm. And the same—very same—inspiration is only methodically differentiated according as the artist is an arrant realist or an arrant idealist. Each, by his own method, seeks to save and perpetuate the same significance or charm; the one by suppressing, the other by forcing, detail. All other idealism is the brown foreground over again, and hence only art in the sense of a game, like cup and ball. All other realism is not art at all—but not at all. It is, then, an insincere and showy handicraft.

Were you to re-read some Balzac, as I have been doing, it would greatly help to clear your eyes. He was a man who never found his method. An inarticulate Shakespeare, smothered under forcible-feeble detail. It is astounding to the riper mind how bad he is, how feeble, how untrue, how tedious; and, of course, when he surrendered to his temperament, how good and powerful. And yet never plain nor clear. He could not consent to be dull, and thus became so. He would leave nothing undeveloped, and thus drowned out of sight of land amid the multitude of crying and incongruous details. There is but one art—to omit! O if I knew how to omit, I would ask no other knowledge. A man who knew how to omit would make an *Iliad* of a daily paper.

Your definition of seeing is quite right. It is the first part of omission to be partly blind. Artistic sight is judicious blindness. Sam Bough[1] must have been a jolly blind old boy. He would turn a corner, look for one-half or quarter minute, and then say, 'This'll do, lad.' Down he sat, there and then, with whole artistic plan, scheme of colour, and the like, and begin by laying a foundation of powerful and seemingly incongruous colour on the block. He saw, not the scene, but the water-colour sketch. Every artist by sixty should so behold nature. Where does he learn that? In the studio, I swear. He goes to nature for facts, relations, values—material; as a man, before writing a historical novel, reads up memoirs. But it is not by reading memoirs that he has learned the

[1] The well-known Scottish landscape painter, who had been a friend of Stevenson's in youth.

selective criterion. He has learned that in the practice of his art; and he will never learn it well, but when disengaged from the ardent struggle of immediate representation, of realistic and *ex facto* art. He learns it in the crystallisation of day-dreams; in changing, not in copying, fact; in the pursuit of the ideal, not in the study of nature. These temples of art are, as you say, inaccessible to the realistic climber. It is not by looking at the sea that you get

'The multitudinous seas incarnadine,'

nor by looking at Mont Blanc that you find

'And visited all night by troops of stars.'

A kind of ardour of the blood is the mother of all this; and according as this ardour is swayed by knowledge and seconded by craft, the art expression flows clear, and significance and charm, like a moon rising, are born above the barren juggle of mere symbols.

The painter must study more from nature than the man of words. But why? Because literature deals with men's business and passions which, in the game of life, we are irresistibly obliged to study; but painting with relations of light, and colour, and significances, and form, which, from the immemorial habit of the race, we pass over with an unregardful eye. Hence this crouching upon camp-stools, and these crusts.[1] But neither one nor other is a part of art, only preliminary studies.

I want you to help me to get people to understand that realism is a method, and only methodic in its consequences; when the realist is an artist, that is, and supposing the idealist with whom you compare him to be anything but a *farceur* and a *dilettante*. The two schools of working do, and should, lead to the choice of different subjects. But that is a consequence, not a

[1] *Croûtes*: crude studies or daubs from nature.

cause. See my chaotic note, which will appear, I fancy, in November in Henley's sheet.

Poor Ferrier, it bust me horrid. He was, after you, the oldest of my friends.

I am now very tired, and will go to bed having prelected freely. Fanny will finish. R. L. S.

TO THOMAS STEVENSON

Nothing exists to show that the purpose, here indicated, of resuming the abandoned *Lay Morals* of 1879 was ever carried into effect.

La Solitude, Hyères-les-Palmiers, Var, 12th October 1883.

MY DEAR FATHER,—I have just lunched; the day is exquisite, the air comes through the open window rich with odour, and I am by no means spiritually minded. Your letter, however, was very much valued, and has been read oftener than once. What you say about yourself I was glad to hear; a little decent resignation is not only becoming a Christian, but is likely to be excellent for the health of a Stevenson. To fret and fume is undignified, suicidally foolish, and theologically unpardonable; we are here not to make, but to tread predestined, pathways; we are the foam of a wave, and to preserve a proper equanimity is not merely the first part of submission to God, but the chief of possible kindnesses to those about us. I am lecturing myself, but you also. To do our best is one part, but to wash our hands smilingly of the consequence is the next part, of any sensible virtue.

I have come, for the moment, to a pause in my moral works; for I have many irons in the fire, and I wish to finish something to bring coin before I can afford to go on with what I think doubtfully to be a duty. It is a most difficult work; a touch of the parson will drive off those I hope to influence; a touch of overstrained laxity, besides disgusting, like a grimace, may do harm. Nothing that I have ever seen yet speaks directly and efficaciously to

1883.
AET. 33.

young men; and I do hope I may find the art and wisdom to fill up a gap. The great point, as I see it, is to ask as little as possible, and meet, if it may be, every view or absence of view; and it should be, must be, easy. Honesty is the one desideratum; but think how hard a one to meet. I think all the time of Ferrier and myself; these are the pair that I address. Poor Ferrier, so much a better man than I, and such a temporal wreck. But the thing of which we must divest our minds is to look partially upon others; all is to be viewed; and the creature judged, as he must be by his Creator, not dissected through a prism of morals, but in the unrefracted ray. So seen, and in relation to the almost omnipotent surroundings, who is to distinguish between F. and such a man as Dr. Candlish, or between such a man as David Hume and such an one as Robert Burns? To compare my poor and good Walter with myself is to make me startle; he, upon all grounds above the merely expedient, was the nobler being. Yet wrecked utterly ere the full age of manhood; and the last skirmishes so well fought, so humanly useless, so pathetically brave, only the leaps of an expiring lamp. All this is a very pointed instance. It shuts the mouth. I have learned more, in some ways, from him than from any other soul I ever met; and he, strange to think, was the best gentleman, in all kinder senses, that I ever knew. —Ever your affectionate son,

· ROBERT LOUIS STEVENSON.

TO W. H. LOW

The paper referred to at the beginning of the second paragraph is one on R. L. S. in the *Century Magazine*, the first seriously critical notice, says Mr. Low, which appeared of him in the States.

[*Chalet la Solitude, Hyères, Oct.* 23, 1883.]

MY DEAR LOW,—*C'est d'un bon camarade;* and I am much obliged to you for your two letters and the inclosure. Times are a lityle changed with all of us since the ever memorable days of Lavenue: hallowed be his name! hallowed his old Fleury!—of which you did not see—I think—as I did—the glorious apotheosis: advanced on a Tuesday to three francs, on the Thursday to six, and on Friday swept off, holus bolus, for the proprietor's private consumption. Well, we had the start of that proprietor. Many a good bottle came our way, and was, I think, worthily made welcome.

I am pleased that Mr. Gilder should like my literature; and I ask you particularly to thank Mr. Bunner (have I the name right?) for his notice, which was of that friendly, headlong sort that really pleases an author like what the French call a 'shake-hands.' It pleased me the more coming from the States, where I have met not much recognition, save from the buccaneers, and above all from pirates who misspell my name. I saw my book advertised in a number of the *Critic* as the work of one R. L. Stephenson; and, I own, I boiled. It is so easy to know the name of the man whose book you have stolen; for there it is, at full length, on the title-page of your booty. But no, damn him, not he! He calls me Stephenson. These woes I only refer to by the way, as they set a higher value on the *Century* notice.

I am now a person with an established ill-health—a wife—a dog possessed with an evil, a Gadarene spirit—a chalet on a hill, looking out over the Mediterranean—a certain reputation—and very obscure finances. Otherwise, very much the same, I guess; and were a bottle of Fleury a thing to be obtained, capable of developing theories along with a fit spirit even as of yore. Yet I now draw near to the Middle Ages; nearly three years ago, that fatal Thirty struck; and yet the great work is not yet done—not yet even conceived. But so, as one goes on, the wood seems to thicken, the footpath to narrow, and the House Beautiful on the hill's summit to draw further and further away. We learn, indeed, to use our means; but only to learn, along with it, the paralysing knowledge that these means are only applicable to two or three poor commonplace motives. Eight years ago, if I could have slung ink as I can now, I should have thought myself well on the road after Shakespeare; and now—I find I have only got a pair of walking-shoes and not yet begun to travel. And art is still away there on the mountain summit. But I need not continue; for, of course, this is your story just as much as it is mine; and, strange to think, it was Shakespeare's too, and Beethoven's, and Phidias's. It is a blessed thing that, in this forest of art, we can pursue our woodlice and sparrows, *and not catch them*, with almost the same fervour of exhilaration as that with which Sophocles hunted and brought down the Mastodon.

Tell me something of your work, and your wife.—My dear fellow, I am yours ever, R. L. STEVENSON.

My wife begs to be remembered to both of you; I cannot say as much for my dog, who has never seen you, but he would like, on general principles, to bite you.

TO W. E. HENLEY

By this time *Treasure Island* was out in book form, and the following is in reply to some reflections on its seamanship which had been conveyed to him through Mr. Henley:—

[*Hyères, November* 1883.]

MY DEAR LAD,—... Of course, my seamanship is jimmy: did I not beseech you I know not how often to find me an ancient mariner—and you, whose own wife's own brother is one of the ancientest, did nothing for me? As for my seamen, did Runciman ever know eighteenth century Buccaneers? No? Well, no more did I. But I have known and sailed with seamen too, and lived and eaten with them; and I made my put-up shot in no great ignorance, but as a put-up thing has to be made, *i.e.* to be coherent and picturesque, and damn the expense. Are they fairly lively on the wires? Then, favour me with your tongues. Are they wooden, and dim, and no sport? Then it is I that am silent, otherwise not. The work, strange as it may sound in the ear, is not a work of realism. The next thing I shall hear is that the etiquette is wrong in Otto's Court! With a warrant, and I mean it to be so, and the whole matter never cost me half a thought. I make these paper people to please myself, and Skelt, and God Almighty, and with no ulterior purpose. Yet am I mortal myself; for, as I remind you, I begged for a supervising mariner. However, my heart is in the right place. I have been to sea, but I never crossed the threshold of a court; and the courts shall be the way I want 'em.

I'm glad to think I owe you the review that pleased me best of all the reviews I ever had; the one I liked best before that was ——'s on the *Arabians*. These two are the flowers of the collection, according to me. To live reading such reviews and die eating ortolans—sich is my aspiration.

Whenever you come you will be equally welcome. I am trying to finish *Otto* ere you shall arrive, so as to take and be able to enjoy a well-earned—O yes, a well-earned —holiday. Longman fetched by Otto: is it a spoon or a spoilt horn? Momentous, if the latter; if the former, a spoon to dip much praise and pudding, and to give, I do think, much pleasure. The last part, now in hand, much smiles upon me.—Ever yours, R. L. S.

1883.
AET. 33.

TO MRS. THOMAS STEVENSON

La Solitude, Hyères, [November 1883].

MY DEAR MOTHER,—You must not blame me too much for my silence; I am over head and ears in work, and do not know what to do first. I have been hard at *Otto*, hard at *Silverado* proofs, which I have worked over again to a tremendous extent; cutting, adding, rewriting, until some of the worst chapters of the original are now, to my mind, as good as any. I was the more bound to make it good, as I had such liberal terms; it's not for want of trying if I have failed.

I got your letter on my birthday; indeed, that was how I found it out about three in the afternoon, when postie comes. Thank you for all you said. As for my wife, that was the best investment ever made by man; but 'in our branch of the family' we seem to marry well. I, considering my piles of work, am wonderfully well; I have not been so busy for I know not how long. I hope you will send me the money I asked however, as I am not only penniless, but shall remain so in all human probability for some considerable time. I have got in the mass of my expectations; and the £100 which is to float us on the new year can not come due till *Silverado* is all ready; I am delaying it myself for the moment; then will follow the binders and the travellers and an infinity of other nuisances; and only at the last, the jingling-tingling.

Do you know that *Treasure Island* has appeared? In the November number of Henley's Magazine, a capital number anyway, there is a funny publisher's puff of it for your book; also a bad article by me. Lang dotes on *Treasure Island*: 'Except *Tom Sawyer* and the *Odyssey*,' he writes, 'I never liked any romance so much.' I will inclose the letter though. The Bogue is angelic, although very dirty. It has rained—at last! It was jolly cold when the rain came.

I was overjoyed to hear such good news of my father. Let him go on at that! Ever your affectionate,

R. L. S.

TO SIDNEY COLVIN

La Solitude, Hyères-les-Palmiers, Var, [November 1883].

MY DEAR COLVIN,—I have been bad, but as you were worse, I feel no shame. I raise a blooming countenance, not the evidence of a self-righteous spirit.

I continue my uphill fight with the twin spirits of bankruptcy and indigestion. Duns rage about my portal, at least to fancy's ear.

I suppose you heard of Ferrier's death : my oldest friend, except Bob. It has much upset me. I did not fancy how much. I am strangely concerned about it.

My house is the loveliest spot in the universe; the moonlight nights we have are incredible ; love, poetry and music, and the Arabian Nights, inhabit just my corner of the world—nest there like mavises.

> Here lies
> The carcase
> of
> Robert Louis Stevenson,
> An active, austere, and not inelegant
> writer,
> who,
> at the termination of a long career,
> wealthy, wise, benevolent, and honoured by
> the attention of two hemispheres,
> yet owned it to have been his crowning favour
> TO INHABIT
> LA SOLITUDE.

(With the consent of the intelligent edility of Hyères, he has been interred, below this frugal stone, in the garden which he honoured for so long with his poetic presence.)

I must write more solemn letters. Adieu. Write.

R. L. S.

TO MRS. MILNE

The next is to a cousin who had been one of his favourite playmates in childhood, and had recognised some allusions in the proof slips of the *Child's Garden* (the piece called ' A Private Story ').

La Solitude, Hyères, [*November* 1883].

MY DEAR HENRIETTA,—Certainly ; who else would they be? More by token, on that particular occasion, you were sailing under the title of Princess Royal; I, after a furious contest, under that of Prince Alfred; and Willie, still a little sulky, as the Prince of Wales. We were all in a buck basket about half-way between the swing and the gate; and I can still see the Pirate Squadron heave in sight upon the weather bow.

I wrote a piece besides on Giant Bunker; but I was not happily inspired, and it is condemned. Perhaps I'll try again; he was a horrid fellow, Giant Bunker! and some of my happiest hours were passed in pursuit of him. You were a capital fellow to play: how few there were who could! None better than yourself. I shall never forget some of the days at Bridge of Allan; they were one golden dream. See 'A Good Boy' in the *Penny Whistles*, much of the sentiment of which is taken direct from one evening at B. of A. when we had had a great play with the little Glasgow girl. Hallowed be that fat book of fairy tales! Do you remember acting the Fair One with Golden Locks? What a romantic drama! Generally speaking, whenever I think of play, it is pretty certain that you will come into my head. I wrote a paper called 'Child's Play' once, where, I believe, you or Willie would recognise things. . . .

Surely Willie is just the man to marry; and if his wife wasn't a happy woman, I think I could tell her who was to blame. Is there no word of it? Well, these things are beyond arrangement; and the wind bloweth where it listeth—which, I observe, is generally towards the west in Scotland. Here it prefers a south-easterly course, and is called the Mistral—usually with an adjective in front. But if you will remember my yesterday's toothache and this morning's crick, you will be in a position to choose an adjective for yourself. Not that the wind is unhealthy; only when it comes strong, it is both very high and very cold, which makes it the d-v-l. But as I am writing to a lady, I had better avoid this topic; winds requiring a great scope of language.

Please remember me to all at home; give Ramsay a pennyworth of acidulated drops for his good taste.—And believe me, your affectionate cousin,

     ROBERT LOUIS STEVENSON.

1883.
AET. 33.

TO MISS FERRIER

La Solitude, Hyères, Var, November 22, 1883.

DEAR MISS FERRIER,—Many thanks for the photograph. It is—well, it is like most photographs. The sun is an artist of too much renown; and, at any rate, we who knew Walter 'in the brave days of old' will be difficult to please.

I was inexpressibly touched to get a letter from some lawyers as to some money. I have never had any account with my friends; some have gained and some lost; and I should feel there was something dishonest in a partial liquidation even if I could recollect the facts, *which I cannot*. But the fact of his having put aside this memorandum touched me greatly.

The mystery of his life is great. Our chemist in this place, who had been at Malvern, recognised the picture. You may remember Walter had a romantic affection for all pharmacies? and the bottles in the window were for him a poem? He said once that he knew no pleasure like driving through a lamplit city, waiting for the chemists to go by.

All these things return now.

He had a pretty full translation of Schiller's *Æsthetic Letters*, which we read together, as well as the second part of *Faust*, in Gladstone Terrace, he helping me with the German. There is no keepsake I should more value than the MS. of that translation. They were the best days I ever had with him, little dreaming all would so soon be over. It needs a blow like this to convict a man of mortality and its burthen. I always thought I should go by myself; not to survive. But now I feel as if the earth

1883.
AET. 33.

were undermined, and all my friends have lost one thickness of reality since that one passed. Those are happy who can take it otherwise; with that I found things all beginning to dislimn. Here we have no abiding city, and one felt as though he had—and O too much acted.

But if you tell me, he did not feel my silence. However, he must have done so; and my guilt is irreparable now. I thank God at least heartily that he did not resent it.

Please remember me to Sir Alexander and Lady Grant, to whose care I will address this. When next I am in Edinburgh I will take flowers, alas! to the West Kirk. Many a long hour we passed in graveyards, the man who has gone and I—or rather not that man—but the beautiful, genial, witty youth who so betrayed him.—Dear Miss Ferrier, I am yours most sincerely,

ROBERT LOUIS STEVENSON.

TO W. H. LOW

La Solitude, Hyères, Var, 13th December 1883.

MY DEAR LOW,—. . . I was much pleased with what you send about my work. Ill-health is a great handicapper in the race. I have never at command that press of spirits that are necessary to strike out a thing red-hot. *Silverado* is an example of stuff worried and pawed about, God knows how often, in poor health, and you can see for yourself the result: good pages, an imperfect fusion, a certain languor of the whole. Not, in short, art. I have told Roberts to send you a copy of the book when it appears, where there are some fair passages that will be new to you. My brief romance, *Prince Otto*—far my most difficult adventure up to now—is near an end. I have still one chapter to write *de fond en comble*, and three or four to strengthen or recast. The rest is done. I do not know if I have made a spoon, or only spoiled a horn;

but I am tempted to hope the first. If the present bargain hold, it will not see the light of day for some thirteen months. Then I shall be glad to know how it strikes you. There is a good deal of stuff in it, both dramatic and, I think, poetic; and the story is not like these purposeless fables of to-day, but is, at least, intended to stand firm upon a base of philosophy—or morals—as you please. It has been long gestated, and is wrought with care. *Enfin, nous verrons.* My labours have this year for the first time been rewarded with upwards of £350; that of itself, so base we are! encourages me; and the better tenor of my health yet more.—Remember me to Mrs. Low, and believe me, yours most sincerely,

ROBERT LOUIS STEVENSON.

TO THOMAS STEVENSON

La Solitude, December 20, 1883.

MY DEAR FATHER,—I do not know which of us is to blame; I suspect it is you this time. The last accounts of you were pretty good, I was pleased to see; I am, on the whole, very well—suffering a little still from my fever and liver complications, but better.

I have just finished re-reading a book, which I counsel you above all things *not* to read, as it has made me very ill, and would make you worse—Lockhart's *Scott.* It is worth reading, as all things are from time to time that keep us nose to nose with fact; though I think such reading may be abused, and that a great deal of life is better spent in reading of a light and yet chivalrous strain. Thus, no Waverley novel approaches in power, blackness, bitterness, and moral elevation to the diary and Lockhart's narrative of the end; and yet the Waverley novels are better reading for every day than the life. You may take a tonic daily, but not phlebotomy.

The great double danger of taking life too easily, and taking it too hard, how difficult it is to balance that! But we are all too little inclined to faith; we are all, in our serious moments, too much inclined to forget that all are sinners, and fall justly by their faults, and therefore that we have no more to do with that than with the thundercloud; only to trust, and do our best, and wear as smiling a face as may be for others and ourselves. But there is no royal road among this complicated business. Hegel the German got the best word of all philosophy with his antinomies: the contrary of everything is its postulate. That is, of course, grossly expressed, but gives a hint of the idea, which contains a great deal of the mysteries of religion, and a vast amount of the practical wisdom of life. For your part, there is no doubt as to your duty—to take things easy and be as happy as you can, for your sake, and my mother's, and that of many besides. Excuse this sermon.—Ever your loving son, R. L. S.

TO MR. AND MRS. THOMAS STEVENSON

La Solitude, December 25, 1883.

MY DEAR FATHER AND MOTHER,—This it is supposed will reach you about Christmas, and I believe I should include Lloyd in the greeting. But I want to lecture my father; he is not grateful enough; he is like Fanny; his resignation is not the 'true blue.' A man who has gained a stone; whose son is better, and, after so many fears to the contrary, I dare to say, a credit to him; whose business is arranged; whose marriage is a picture—what I should call resignation in such a case as his would be to 'take down his fiddle and play as lood as ever he could.' That and nought else. And now, you dear old pious ingrate, on this Christmas morning, think what your mercies have been; and do not walk too far before your breakfast—as far as to the top of India Street, then to the top of Dundas Street, and then to your ain stair heid; and do not forget that even as *laborare,* so *joculari, est orare*; and to be happy the first step to being pious.

I have as good as finished my novel, and a hard job it has been—but now practically over, *laus deo!* My financial prospects better than ever before; my excellent wife a touch dolorous, like Mr. Tommy; my Bogue quite converted, and myself in good spirits. O, send Curry Powder per Baxter.   R. L. S.

TO MRS. THOMAS STEVENSON

[La Solitude, Hyères], last Sunday of '83.

MY DEAR MOTHER,—I give my father up. I give him a parable: that the Waverley novels are better reading for every day than the tragic Life. And he takes it backside foremost, and shakes his head, and is gloomier than ever. Tell him that I give him up. I don't want no such a parent. This is not the man for my money. I do not call that by the name of religion which fills a man with bile. I write him a whole letter, bidding him beware of extremes, and telling him that his gloom is gallows-worthy; and I get back an answer—Perish the thought of it.

Here am I on the threshold of another year, when, according to all human foresight, I should long ago have been resolved into my elements; here am I, who you were persuaded was born to disgrace you—and, I will do you the justice to add, on no such insufficient grounds—no very burning discredit when all is done; here am I married, and the marriage recognised to be a blessing of the first order, A1 at Lloyd's. There is he, at his not first youth, able to take more exercise than I at thirty-three, and gaining a stone's weight, a thing of which I am incapable. There are you; has the man no gratitude? There is Smeoroch[1]: is he blind? Tell him from me that all this is

NOT THE TRUE BLUE!

---

[1] A favourite Skye terrier. Mr. Stevenson was a great lover of dogs.

1884.
AET. 34.

I will think more of his prayers when I see in him a spirit of *praise*. Piety is a more childlike and happy attitude than he admits. Martha, Martha, do you hear the knocking at the door? But Mary was happy. Even the Shorter Catechism, not the merriest epitome of religion, and a work exactly as pious although not quite so true as the multiplication table—even that dry-as-dust epitome begins with a heroic note. What is man's chief end? Let him study that; and ask himself if to refuse to enjoy God's kindest gifts is in the spirit indicated. Up, Dullard! It is better service to enjoy a novel than to mump.

I have been most unjust to the Shorter Catechism, I perceive. I wish to say that I keenly admire its merits as a performance; and that all that was in my mind was its peculiarly unreligious and unmoral texture; from which defect it can never, of course, exercise the least influence on the minds of children. But they learn fine style and some austere thinking unconsciously.—Ever your loving son, R. L. S.

TO MR. AND MRS. THOMAS STEVENSON

La Solitude, Hyères-les-Palmiers, Var, January 1 (1884).

MY DEAR PEOPLE,—A Good New Year to you. The year closes, leaving me with £50 in the bank, owing no man nothing, £100 more due to me in a week or so, and £150 more in the course of the month; and I can look back on a total receipt of £465, 0s. 6d. for the last twelve months!

And yet I am not happy!
Yet I beg! Here is my beggary:—
1. Sellar's Trial.
2. George Borrow's Book about Wales.
3. My Grandfather's Trip to Holland.
4. And (but this is, I fear, impossible) the Bell Rock Book.

When I think of how last year began, after four months of sickness and idleness, all my plans gone to water, myself starting alone, a kind of spectre, for Nice—should I not be grateful? Come, let us sing unto the Lord!

1884.
AET. 34.

Nor should I forget the expected visit, but I will not believe in that till it befall; I am no cultivator of disappointments, 'tis a herb that does not grow in my garden; but I get some good crops both of remorse and gratitude. The last I can recommend to all gardeners; it grows best in shiny weather, but once well grown, is very hardy; it does not require much labour; only that the husbandman should smoke his pipe about the flower-plots and admire God's pleasant wonders. Winter green (otherwise known as Resignation, or the 'false gratitude plant') springs in much the same soil; is little hardier, if at all; and requires to be so dug about and dunged, that there is little margin left for profit. The variety known as the Black Winter green (H. V. Stevensoniana) is rather for ornament than profit.

'John, do you see that bed of resignation?'—'It's doin' bravely, sir.'—'John, I will not have it in my garden; it flatters not the eye and comforts not the stomach; root it out.'—'Sir, I ha'e seen o' them that rase as high as nettles; gran' plants!'—'What then? Were they as tall as alps, if still unsavoury and bleak, what matters it? Out with it, then; and in its place put Laughter and a Good Conceit (that capital home evergreen), and a bush of Flowering Piety—but see it be the flowering sort—the other species is no ornament to any gentleman's Back Garden.'

JNO. BUNYAN.

TO SIDNEY COLVIN

In the interval between the last letter and this, the writer had been at death's door from a sudden attack of internal congestion, which happened during a visit to Nice early in January.

1884.
AET. 34.
After a slow recovery he had returned to his house at Hyères, and for a time seemed to be picking up again.

La Solitude, Hyères-les-Palmiers, Var, 9th March 1884.

MY DEAR S. C.,—You will already have received a not very sane note from me; so your patience was rewarded—may I say, your patient silence? However, now comes a letter, which on receipt, I thus acknowledge.

I have already expressed myself as to the political aspect. About Grahame, I feel happier; it does seem to have been really a good, neat, honest piece of work. We do not seem to be so badly off for commanders: Wolseley and Roberts, and this pile of Woods, Stewarts, Alisons, Grahames, and the like. Had we but ONE statesman on any side of the house!

Two chapters of *Otto* do remain: one to rewrite, one to create; and I am not yet able to tackle them. For me, it is my chief o' works; hence probably not so for others, since it only means that I have here attacked the greatest difficulties. But some chapters towards the end: three in particular—I do think come off. I find them stirring, dramatic, and not unpoetical. We shall see, however; as like as not, the effort will be more obvious than the success. For, of course, I strung myself hard to carry it out. The next will come easier, and possibly be more popular. I believe in the covering of much paper, each time with a definite and not too difficult artistic purpose; and then, from time to time, drawing oneself up and trying, in a superior effort, to combine the facilities thus acquired or improved. Thus one progresses. But, mind, it is very likely that the big effort, instead of being the masterpiece, may be the blotted copy, the gymnastic exercise. This no man can tell; only the brutal and licentious public, snouting in Mudie's wash-trough, can return a dubious answer.

I am to-day, thanks to a pure heaven and a beneficent, loud-talking, antiseptic mistral, on the high places as to health and spirits. Money holds out wonderfully. Fanny has gone for a drive to certain meadows which are now one sheet of jonquils : sea-bound meadows, the thought of which may freshen you in Bloomsbury. 'Ye have been fresh and fair, Ye have been filled with flowers'—I fear I misquote. Why do people babble? Surely Herrick, in his true vein, is superior to Martial himself, though Martial is a very pretty poet.

1884.
AET. 34.

Did you ever read St. Augustine? The first chapters of the *Confessions* are marked by a commanding genius : Shakespearian in depth. I was struck dumb, but, alas ! when you begin to wander into controversy, the poet drops out. His description of infancy is most seizing. And how is this : 'Sed majorum nugae negotia vocantur ; puerorum autem talia cum sint puniuntur a majoribus.' Which is quite after the heart of R. L. S. See also his splendid passage about the 'luminosus limen amicitiae' and the 'nebulae de limosa concupiscentia carnis'; going on '*Utrumque* in confuso aestuabat et rapiebat imbecillam aetatem per abrupta cupiditatum.' That 'Utrumque' is a real contribution to life's science. Lust *alone* is but a pigmy ; but it never, or rarely, attacks us single-handed.

Do you ever read (to go miles off, indeed) the incredible Barbey d'Aurevilly? A psychological Poe—to be for a moment Henley. I own with pleasure I prefer him with all his folly, rot, sentiment, and mixed metaphors, to the whole modern school in France. It makes me laugh when it's nonsense ; and when he gets an effect (though it's still nonsense and mere Poëry, not poesy) it wakens me. *Ce qui ne meurt pas* nearly killed me with laughing, and left me—well, it left me very nearly admiring the old ass. At least, it's the kind of thing one feels one couldn't do. The dreadful moonlight, when they all three sit silent in the room—by George, sir, it's imagined —and the brief scene between the husband and wife is all there. *Quant au fond*, the whole thing, of course, is a fever dream, and worthy of eternal laughter. Had the young man broken stones, and the two women been hard-working honest prostitutes, there had been an end of the whole immoral and baseless business: you could at least have respected them in that case.

I also read *Petronius Arbiter*, which is a rum work, not so immoral as most modern works, but singularly silly. I tackled some Tacitus too. I got them with a dreadful French crib on the same page with the text, which helps me along and drives me mad. The French do not even try to translate. They try to be much more classical than the classics, with astounding results of barrenness and tedium. Tacitus, I fear, was too solid for me. I liked the war part; but the dreary intriguing at Rome was too much. — R. L. S.

TO MR. DICK

This correspondent was for many years head clerk and confidential assistant in the family firm at Edinburgh.

La Solitude, Hyères, Var, 12th March 1884.

MY DEAR MR. DICK,—I have been a great while owing you a letter; but I am not without excuses, as you have heard. I overworked to get a piece of work finished before I had my holiday, thinking to enjoy it more; and instead of that, the machinery near hand came sundry in my hands! like Murdie's uniform. However, I am now, I think, in a fair way of recovery; I think I was made, what there is of me, of whipcord and thorn-switches; surely I am tough! But I fancy I shall not overdrive again, or not so long. It is my theory that work is highly beneficial, but that it should, if possible, and certainly for such partially broken-down instruments as the thing I call my body, be taken in batches, with a clear break and breathing space between. I always do vary my work, laying one thing aside to take up another, not merely because I believe it rests the brain, but because I have found it most beneficial to the result. Reading, Bacon says, makes a full man, but what makes me full on any subject is to banish it for a time from all my thoughts. However, what I now propose is, out of every quarter, to work two months' and rest the third. I believe I shall get more done, as I generally manage, on my present scheme, to have four months' impotent illness and two of imperfect health—one before, one after, I break·down. This, at least, is not an economical division of the year.

I re-read the other day that heartbreaking book, the *Life of Scott*. One should read such works now and then, but O, not often. As I live, I feel more and more that literature should be cheerful and brave-spirited, even if it cannot be made beautiful and pious and heroic. We wish it to be a green place; the *Waverley Novels* are better to re-read than the over-true life, fine as dear Sir Walter was. The Bible, in most parts, is a cheerful book; it is our little piping theologies, tracts, and sermons that are dull and dowie; and even the Shorter Catechism, which is scarcely a work of consolation, opens with the best and shortest and completest sermon ever written—upon Man's chief end.—Believe me, my dear Mr. Dick, very sincerely yours,   ROBERT LOUIS STEVENSON.

P.S.—You see I have changed my hand. I was threatened apparently with scrivener's cramp, and at any rate had got to write so small, that the revisal of my MS. tried my eyes, hence my signature alone remains upon the old model; for it appears that if I changed that, I should be cut off from my 'vivers.'   R. L. S.

1884.
AET. 34.

TO COSMO MONKHOUSE

This correspondent was a friend of old Savile Club days; the drift of his letter can easily be guessed from this reply. The reference to Lamb is to the essay on the Restoration dramatists.

La Solitude, Hyères-les-Palmiers, Var, March 16, 1884.

MY DEAR MONKHOUSE,—You see with what promptitude I plunge into correspondence; but the truth is, I am condemned to a complete inaction, stagnate dismally, and love a letter. Yours, which would have been welcome at any time, was thus doubly precious.

Dover sounds somewhat shiveringly in my ears. You should see the weather *I* have—cloudless, clear as crystal, with just a punkah-draft of the most aromatic air, all pine and gum tree. You would be ashamed of Dover; you would scruple to refer, sir, to a spot so paltry. To be idle at Dover is a strange pretension; pray, how do you warm yourself? If I were there I should grind knives or write blank verse, or—— But at least you do not bathe? It is idle to deny it: I have—I may say I nourish—a growing jealousy of the robust, large-legged, healthy Britain-dwellers, patient of grog, scorners of the timid umbrella, innocuously breathing fog: all which I once was, and I am ashamed to say liked it. How ignorant is youth! grossly rolling among unselected pleasures; and how nobler, purer, sweeter, and lighter, to sip the choice tonic, to recline in the luxurious invalid chair, and to tread, well-shawled, the little round of the constitutional. Seriously, do you like to repose? Ye gods, I hate it. I never rest with any acceptation; I do not know what people mean who say they like sleep and that damned bedtime which, since long ere I was breeched, has rung a knell to all my day's doings and beings. And when a man, seemingly sane, tells me he has 'fallen in love with stagnation,' I can only say to him, 'You will never be a Pirate!' This may not cause any regret to Mrs. Monkhouse; but in your own soul it will clang hollow—think of it! Never! After all boyhood's aspirations and youth's immoral day-dreams, you are condemned to sit down, grossly draw in your chair to the fat board, and be a beastly Burgess till you die. Can it be? Is there not some escape, some furlough from the Moral Law, some holiday jaunt contrivable into a Better Land? Shall we never shed blood? This prospect is too grey.

> 'Here lies a man who never did
> Anything but what he was bid;
> Who lived his life in paltry ease,
> And died of commonplace disease.'

To confess plainly, I had intended to spend my life (or any leisure I might have from Piracy upon the high seas) as the leader of a great horde of irregular cavalry, devastating whole valleys. I can still, looking back, see myself in many favourite attitudes; signalling for a boat from my pirate ship with a pocket-handkerchief, I at the jetty end, and one or two of my bold blades keeping the crowd at bay; or else turning in the saddle to look back at my whole command (some five thousand strong) following me at the hand-gallop up the road out of the burning valley: this last by moonlight.

Et point du tout. I am a poor scribe, and have scarce broken a commandment to mention, and have recently dined upon cold veal! As for you (who probably had some ambitions), I hear of you living at Dover, in lodgings, like the beasts of the field. But in heaven, when we get there, we shall have a good time, and see some real carnage. For heaven is — must be — that great Kingdom of Antinomia, which Lamb saw dimly adumbrated in the *Country Wife*, where the worm which never dies (the conscience) peacefully expires, and the sinner lies down beside the Ten Commandments. Till then, here a sheer hulk lies poor Tom Bowling, with neither health nor vice for anything more spirited than procrastination, which I may well call the Consolation Stakes of Wickedness; and by whose diligent practice, without the least amusement to ourselves, we can rob the orphan and bring down grey hairs with sorrow to the dust.

This astonishing gush of nonsense I now hasten to close, envelope, and expedite to Shakespeare's Cliff. Remember me to Shakespeare, and believe me, yours very sincerely,
ROBERT LOUIS STEVENSON.

TO EDMUND GOSSE

Mr. Gosse had written describing the office which he then occupied, a picturesque old-fashioned chamber in the upper stories of the Board of Trade.

La Solitude, Hyères-les-Palmiers, Var, March 17, 1884.

MY DEAR GOSSE,—Your office—office is profanely said —your bower upon the leads is divine. Have you, like Pepys, 'the right to fiddle' there? I see you mount the companion, barbiton in hand, and, fluttered about by city sparrows, pour forth your spirit in a voluntary. Now when the spring begins, you must lay in your flowers: how do you say about a potted hawthorn? Would it bloom? Wallflower is a choice pot-herb; lily-of-the-valley, too, and carnation, and Indian cress trailed about the window, is not only beautiful by colour, but the leaves are good to eat. I recommend thyme and rosemary for the aroma, which should not be left upon one side; they are good quiet growths.

On one of your tables keep a great map spread out; a chart is still better—it takes one further—the havens with their little anchors, the rocks, banks, and soundings, are adorably marine; and such furniture will suit your ship-shape habitation. I wish I could see those cabins; they smile upon me with the most intimate charm. From your leads, do you behold St. Paul's? I always like to see the Foolscap; it is London *per se* and no spot from which it is visible is without romance. Then it is good company for the man of letters, whose veritable nursing Pater-Noster is so near at hand.

I am all at a standstill; as idle as a painted ship, but not so pretty. My romance, which has so nearly butchered me in the writing, not even finished; though so near, thank God, that a few days of tolerable strength will see the roof upon that structure. I have worked very hard at it, and so do not expect any great public favour. *In moments of effort, one learns to do the easy things that people like.* There is the golden maxim; thus one should strain and then play, strain again and play again. The strain is for us, it educates; the play is for the reader, and pleases. Do you not feel so? We are ever threatened by two contrary faults: both deadly. To sink into what my forefathers would have called 'rank conformity,' and to pour forth cheap replicas, upon the one hand; upon the other, and still more insidiously present, to forget that art is a diversion and a decoration, that no triumph or effort is of value, nor anything worth reaching except charm.—Yours affectionately, R. L. S.

TO MISS FERRIER

La Solitude, Hyères-les-Palmiers, Var, [*March* 22, 1884].

MY DEAR MISS FERRIER,—Are you really going to fail us? This seems a dreadful thing. My poor wife, who is not well off for friends on this bare coast, has been promising herself, and I have been promising her, a rare acquisition. And now Miss Burn has failed, and you utter a very doubtful note. You do not know how delightful this place is, nor how anxious we are for a visit. Look at the names: 'The Solitude'—is that romantic? The palm-trees?—how is that for the gorgeous East? 'Var'? the name of a river—'the quiet waters by'! 'Tis true, they are in another department, and consist of stones and a biennial spate; but what a music, what a plash of brooks, for the imagination! We have hills; we have skies; the roses are putting forth, as yet sparsely; the meadows by the sea are one sheet of jonquils; the birds sing as in an English May—for, considering we are in France and serve up our song-birds, I am ashamed to say, on a little field of toast and with a sprig of thyme (my own receipt) in their most innocent and now unvocal bellies—considering all this, we have a wonderfully fair wood-music round this Solitude of ours. What can I say more?—All this awaits you. *Kennst du das Land*, in short.—Your sincere friend,

ROBERT LOUIS STEVENSON.

TO W. H. LOW

The verses enclosed were the set entitled 'The Canoe Speaks,' afterwards printed in *Underwoods*. Stevenson was suffering at this time from a temporary weakness of the eyesight.

La Solitude, Hyères-les-Palmiers, Var, [*April* 1884].

MY DEAR LOW,—The blind man in these sprawled lines sends greeting. I have been ill, as perhaps the papers told you. The news—'great news — glorious news—sec-ond ed-ition!'—went the round in England.

Anyway, I now thank you for your pictures, which, particularly the Arcadian one, we all (Bob included, he was here sick-nursing me) much liked.

Herewith are a set of verses which I thought pretty enough to send to press. Then I thought of the *Manhattan*, towards whom I have guilty and compunctious feelings. Last, I had the best thought of all—to send them to you in case you might think them suitable for illustration. It seemed to me quite in your vein. If so, good; if not, hand them on to *Manhattan*, *Century*, or *Lippincott*, at your pleasure, as all three desire my work or pretend to. But I trust the lines will not go unattended. Some riverside will haunt you; and O! be tender to my bathing girls. The lines are copied in my wife's hand, as I cannot see to write otherwise than with the pen of Cormoran, Gargantua, or Nimrod. Love to your wife.—Yours ever, R. L. S.

Copied it myself.

TO THOMAS STEVENSON

La Solitude, April 19, 1884.

MY DEAR FATHER,—Yesterday I very powerfully stated the *Heresis Stevensoniana*, or the complete body of divinity of the family theologian, to Miss Ferrier. She was much impressed; so was I. You are a great heresiarch; and I know no better. Whaur the devil did ye get thon about the soap? Is it altogether your own? I never heard it elsewhere; and yet I suspect it must have been held at some time or other, and if you were to look up you would probably find yourself condemned by some Council.

I am glad to hear you are so well. The hear is excellent. The *Cornhills* came; I made Miss Ferrier read us 'Thrawn Janet,' and was quite bowled over by my own works. The 'Merry Men' I mean to make much longer, with a whole new dénouement, not yet quite clear to me. 'The Story of a Lie,' I must rewrite entirely also, as it is too weak and ragged, yet is worth saving for the Admiral. Did I ever tell you that the Admiral was recognised in America?

When they are all on their legs this will make an excellent collection.

Has Davie never read *Guy Mannering*, *Rob Roy*, or *The Antiquary*? All of which are worth three *Waverleys*. I think *Kenilworth* better than *Waverley*; *Nigel*, too; and *Quentin Durward* about as good. But it shows a true piece of insight to prefer *Waverley*, for it *is* different; and though not quite coherent, better worked in parts than almost any other: surely more carefully. It is undeniable that the love of the slap-dash and the shoddy grew upon Scott with success. Perhaps it does on many of us, which may be the granite on which D.'s opinion stands. However, I hold it, in Patrick Walker's phrase, for an 'old, condemned, damnable error.' Dr. Simson was condemned by P. W. as being 'a bagful of' such. One of Patrick's amenities!

Another ground there may be to D.'s opinion; those who avoid (or seek to avoid) Scott's facility are apt to be continually straining and torturing their style to get in more of life. And to many the extra significance does not redeem the strain. DOCTOR STEVENSON.

TO COSMO MONKHOUSE

La Solitude, Hyères, [*April* 24, 1884].

DEAR MONKHOUSE,—If you are in love with repose, here is your occasion: change with me. I am too blind to read, hence no reading; I am too weak to walk, hence no walking; I am not allowed to speak, hence no talking; but the great simplification has yet to be named; for, if this goes on, I shall soon have nothing to eat—and hence, O Hallelujah! hence no eating. The offer is a fair one: I have not sold myself to the devil, for I could never find him. I am married, but so are you. I sometimes write verses, but so do you. Come! *Hic quies!* As for the commandments, I have broken them so small that they are the dust of my chambers; you walk upon them, triturate and toothless; and with the Golosh of Philosophy, they shall not bite your heel. True, the tenement is falling. Ay, friend, but yours also. Take a larger view; what is a year or two? dust in the balance! 'Tis done, behold you Cosmo Stevenson, and me R. L. Monkhouse; you at Hyères, I in London; you rejoicing in the clammiest repose, me proceeding to tear your tabernacle into rags, as I have already so admirably torn my own.

1884.
AET. 34.

My place to which I now introduce you—it is yours—is like a London house, high and very narrow; upon the lungs I will not linger; the heart is large enough for a ballroom; the belly greedy and inefficient; the brain stocked with the most damnable explosives, like a dynamiter's den. The whole place is well furnished, though not in a very pure taste; Corinthian much of it; showy and not strong.

About your place I shall try to find my way alone, an interesting exploration. Imagine me, as I go to bed, falling over a blood-stained remorse; opening that cupboard in the cerebellum and being welcomed by the spirit of your murdered uncle. I should probably not like your remorses; I wonder if you will like mine; I have a spirited assortment; they whistle in my ear o' nights like a north-easter. I trust yours don't dine with the family; mine are better mannered; you will hear nought of them till 2 A.M., except one, to be sure, that I have made a pet of, but he is small; I keep him in buttons, so as to avoid commentaries; you will like him much—if you like what is genuine.

Must we likewise change religions? Mine is a good article, with a trick of stopping; cathedral bell note; ornamental dial; supported by Venus and the Graces; quite a summer-parlour piety. Of yours, since your last, I fear there is little to be said.

There is one article I wish to take away with me: my spirits. They suit me. I don't want yours; I like my own; I have had them a long while in bottle. It is my only reservation.—Yours (as you decide),

R. L. MONKHOUSE.

1884.
AET. 34.

TO W. E. HENLEY

Hyères, May 1884.

DEAR BOY,—*Old Mortality*[1] is out, and I am glad to say Coggie likes it. We like her immensely.

I keep better, but no great shakes yet; cannot work—cannot: that is flat, not even verses: as for prose, that more active place is shut on me long since.

My view of life is essentially the comic; and the romantically comic. *As you Like It* is to me the most bird-haunted spot in letters; *Tempest* and *Twelfth Night* follow. These are what I mean by poetry and nature. I make an effort of my mind to be quite one with Molière, except upon the stage, where his inimitable *jeux de scène* beggar belief; but you will observe they are stage-plays —things *ad hoc*; not great Olympian debauches of the heart and fancy; hence more perfect, and not so great. Then I come, after great wanderings, to Carmosine and to Fantasio; to one part of La Dernière Aldini (which, by the by, we might dramatise in a week), to the notes that Meredith has found, Evan and the postillion, Evan and Rose, Harry in Germany. And to me these things are the good; beauty, touched with sex and laughter; beauty with God's earth for the background. Tragedy does not seem to me to come off; and when it does, it does so by the heroic illusion; the anti-masque has been omitted; laughter, which attends on all our steps in life, and sits by the deathbed, and certainly redacts the epitaph, laughter has been lost from these great-hearted lies. But the comedy which keeps the beauty and touches the terrors of our life (laughter and tragedy-in-a-good-humour having kissed), that is the last word of moved representation; embracing the greatest number of elements of fate and character; and telling its story, not with the one eye of pity, but with the two of pity and mirth.

R. L. S.

[1] The essay so called. See *Memories and Portraits*.

TO EDMUND GOSSE

1884.
AET. 34.

Early in May Stevenson had been again very dangerously ill from hemorrhage of the lungs, and lay for several weeks between life and death, until about the beginning of July he was brought sufficiently round to venture by slow stages on the journey to England, staying for two or three weeks at Royat on the way. His correspondent had lately been appointed Clark Reader in English Literature at Trinity College, Cambridge.

From my Bed, May 29, 1884.

DEAR GOSSE,—The news of the Professorate found me in the article of—well, of heads or tails; I am still in bed, and a very poor person. You must thus excuse my damned delay; but, I assure you, I was delighted. You will believe me the more, if I confess to you that my first sentiment was envy; yes, sir, on my blood-boltered couch I envied the professor. However, it was not of long duration; the double thought that you deserved and that you would thoroughly enjoy your success fell like balsam on my wounds. How came it that you never communicated my rejection of Gilder's offer for the Rhone? But it matters not. Such earthly vanities are over for the present. This has been a fine well-conducted illness. A month in bed; a month of silence; a fortnight of not stirring my right hand; a month of not moving without being lifted. Come! *Ça y est*: devilish like being dead.—Yours, dear Professor, academically,   R. L. S.

I am soon to be moved to Royat; an invalid valet goes with me! I got him cheap—second-hand.

In turning over my late friend Ferrier's commonplace book, I find three poems from *Viol and Flute* copied out in his hand: 'When Flower-time,' 'Love in Winter,' and 'Mistrust.' They are capital too. But I thought the fact would interest you. He was no poetist either; so it means the more. 'Love in W.!' I like the best.

1884.
AET. 34.

TO MR. AND MRS. THOMAS STEVENSON

Hotel Chabassière, Royat, [*July* 1884].

MY DEAR PEOPLE,—The weather has been demoniac; I have had a skiff of cold, and was finally obliged to take to bed entirely; to-day, however, it has cleared, the sun shines, and I begin to

(*Several days after.*)

I have been out once, but now am back in bed. I am better, and keep better, but the weather is a mere injustice. The imitation of Edinburgh is, at times, deceptive; there is a note among the chimney pots that suggests Howe Street; though I think the shrillest spot in Christendom was not upon the Howe Street side, but in front, just under the Miss Graemes' big chimney stack. It had a fine alto character—a sort of bleat that used to divide the marrow in my joints—say in the wee, slack hours. That music is now lost to us by rebuilding; another air that I remember, not regret, was the solo of the gas-burner in the little front room; a knickering, flighty, fleering, and yet spectral cackle. I mind it above all on winter afternoons, late, when the window was blue and spotted with rare rain-drops, and, looking out, the cold evening was seen blue all over, with the lamps of Queen's and Frederick's Street dotting it with yellow, and flaring eastward in the squalls. Heavens, how unhappy I have been in such circumstances—I, who have now positively forgotten the colour of unhappiness; who am full like a fed ox, and dull like a fresh turf, and have no more spiritual life, for good or evil, than a French bagman.

We are at Chabassière's, for of course it was nonsense to go up the hill when we could not walk.

The child's poems in a far extended form are likely soon to be heard of—which Cummy I dare say will be glad to know. They will make a book of about one hundred pages.—Ever your affectionate, R. L. S.

TO SIDNEY COLVIN

1884.
AET. 34.

I had reported to Stevenson a remark made by one of his greatest admirers, Sir E. Burne Jones, on some particular analogy, I forget what, between a passage of Defoe and one in *Treasure Island*.

[*Royat, July* 1884.]

... HERE is a quaint thing, I have read *Robinson, Colonel Jack, Moll Flanders, Memoirs of a Cavalier, History of the Plague, History of the Great Storm, Scotch Church and Union*. And there my knowledge of Defoe ends—except a book, the name of which I forget, about Peterborough in Spain, which Defoe obviously did not write, and could not have written if he wanted. To which of these does B. J. refer? I guess it must be the history of the Scottish Church. I jest; for, of course, I *know* it must be a book I have never read, and which this makes me keen to read—I mean *Captain Singleton*. Can it be got and sent to me? If *Treasure Island* is at all like it, it will be delightful. I was just the other day wondering at my folly in not remembering it, when I was writing *T. I.*, as a mine for pirate tips. *T. I.* came out of Kingsley's *At Last*, where I got the Dead Man's Chest—and that was the seed—and out of the great Captain Johnson's *History of Notorious Pirates*. The scenery is Californian in part, and in part *chic*.

I was downstairs to-day! So now I am a made man—till the next time.   R. L. STEVENSON.

If it was *Captain Singleton*, send it to me, won't you?

Later.—My life dwindles into a kind of valley of the shadow picnic. I cannot read; so much of the time (as to-day) I must not speak above my breath, that to play patience, or to see my wife play it, is become the be-all and the end-all of my dim career. To add to my gaiety, I may write letters, but there are few to answer.

Patience and Poesy are thus my rod and staff; with these I not unpleasantly support my days.

I am very dim, dumb, dowie, and damnable. I hate to be silenced; and if to talk by signs is my forte (as I contend), to understand them cannot be my wife's. Do not think me unhappy; I have not been so for years; but I am blurred, inhabit the debatable frontier of sleep, and have but dim designs upon activity. All is at a standstill; books closed, paper put aside, the voice, the eternal voice of R. L. S., well silenced. Hence this plaint reaches you with no very great meaning, no very great purpose, and written part in slumber by a heavy, dull, somnolent, superannuated son of a bedpost.

VII

LIFE AT BOURNEMOUTH

SEPTEMBER 1884—DECEMBER 1885

ARRIVING in England at the end of July 1884, Stevenson took up his quarters first for a few weeks at Richmond. He was compelled to abandon the hope of making his permanent home at Hyères, partly by the renewed failure there of his own health, partly by a bad outbreak of cholera which occurred in the old Provençal town about the time he left it. After consultation with several doctors, all of whom held out hopes of ultimate recovery despite the gravity of his present symptoms, he moved to Bournemouth. Here he found in the heaths and pine-woods some distant semblance of the landscape of his native Scotland, and in the sandy curves of the Channel coast a passable substitute for the bays and promontories of his beloved Mediterranean. At all events, he liked the place well enough to be willing to try it for a home; and such it became for all but three years, from September 1884 to August 1887. These, although in the matter of health the worst and most trying years of his life, were in the matter of work some of the most active and success-ful. For the first two or three months the Stevensons occupied a lodging on the West Cliff called Wensleydale; for the next four or five, from mid-November 1884 to March 1885, they were tenants of a house named Bonallie Towers, pleasantly situated amid the pinewoods of Branksome Park, and by its name recalling familiar Midlothian associations. Lastly, about Easter 1885, they entered into occupation of a house of their own, given by the elder Mr. Stevenson as a special gift to his daughter-in-law, and renamed by its new occupants Skerryvore, in reminiscence of one of the great lighthouse works carried out by the family firm off the Scottish coast.

During all the time of Stevenson's residence at Bournemouth he was compelled to lead the life, irksome to him above all men, but borne with invincible sweetness and patience, of a chronic invalid and almost constant prisoner to the house. A great part of his time had perforce to be spent in bed, and there almost all his literary work was produced. Often for days, and sometimes for whole weeks together, he was forbidden to speak aloud, and compelled to carry on conversation with his family and friends in whispers or with the help of pencil and paper. The few excursions to a distance which he attempted—most commonly to my house at the British Museum, once to Cambridge, once to Matlock, once to Exeter, and once in 1886 as far as Paris—these excursions generally ended in a breakdown and a hurried retreat to home and bed. Nevertheless, he was able in intervals of comparative ease to receive and enjoy the visits of friends from a distance both old and new—among the most welcome of the latter being Mr. Henry James, Mr. William Archer, and Mr. John S. Sargent; while among Bournemouth residents who attached themselves to him on terms of special intimacy and affection were the late Sir Percy and Lady Shelley and the family of Sir Henry Taylor the poet. At the same time, seizing and making the most of every week, nay, every day and hour of respite, he contrived to produce work surprising alike, under the circumstances, by quantity and quality. During the first two months of his life at Bournemouth the two plays *Admiral Guinea* and *Beau Austin* were written in collaboration with Mr. Henley, and many other dramatic schemes were broached which health and leisure failed him to carry out. In the course of the next few months he finished *Prince Otto*, *The Child's Garden of Verses*, and *More New Arabian Nights*, all three of which had been begun, and the two first nearly completed, before he left Hyères. He at the same time attacked two new tasks— a highway novel called *The Great North Road*, and a *Life of Wellington* for a series edited by Mr. Andrew Lang, both of which he had in the sequel to abandon; and a third, the boys' story of *Kidnapped*, which turned out one of the most brilliant of his successes. About midsummer of the year 1885 he was distressed by the sudden death of his old and kind friend Professor Fleeming Jenkin, and after a while undertook the task of writing a memoir of him to be prefixed to his collected papers. Towards the close of the same year he was busy with what proved to be the most popular of all his writings, *The Strange Case of Dr. Jekyll and Mr. Hyde*, and with the Christmas story of *Olalla*.

1884.
AET. 34.

TO MR. AND MRS. THOMAS STEVENSON

Wensleydale, Bournemouth, Sunday, 28th September 1884.

MY DEAR PEOPLE,—I keep better, and am to-day downstairs for the first time. I find the lockers entirely empty; not a cent to the front. Will you pray send us some? It blows an equinoctial gale, and has blown for nearly a week. Nimbus Britannicus; piping wind, lashing rain; the sea is a fine colour, and wind-bound ships lie at anchor under the Old Harry rocks, to make one glad to be ashore.

The Henleys are gone, and two plays practically done. I hope they may produce some of the ready.—I am, ever affectionate son, R. L. S.

TO W. E. HENLEY

There is no certain clue to the date of the following; neither has it been possible to make sure what was the enclosure mentioned. The special illness referred to seems to be that of the preceding May at Hyères.

[*Wensleydale, Bournemouth, October* 1884?]

DEAR BOY,—I trust this finds you well; it leaves me so-so. The weather is so cold that I must stick to bed, which is rotten and tedious, but can't be helped.

I find in the blotting book the enclosed, which I wrote to you the eve of my blood. Is it not strange? That night, when I naturally thought I was coopered, the thought of it was much in my mind; I thought it had gone; and I thought what a strange prophecy I had made in jest, and how it was indeed like to be the end of many letters. But I have written a good few since, and the spell is broken. I am just as pleased, for I earnestly desire to live. This pleasant middle age into whose port we are steering is quite to my fancy. I would cast anchor here, and go ashore for twenty years, and see the manners of the place. Youth was a great time, but somewhat fussy. Now in middle age (bar lucre) all seems mighty placid. It likes me; I spy a little bright café in one corner of the port, in front of which I now propose we should sit down. There is just enough of the bustle of the harbour and no more; and the ships are close in, regarding us with stern-windows—the ships that bring deals from Norway and parrots from the Indies. Let us sit down here for twenty years, with a packet of tobacco and a drink, and talk of art and women. By-and-by, the whole city will sink, and the ships too, and the table, and we also; but we shall have sat for twenty years and had a fine talk; and by that time, who knows? exhausted the subject.

I send you a book which (or I am mistook) will please you; it pleased me. But I do desire a book of adventure —a romance—and no man will get or write me one. Dumas I have read and re-read too often; Scott, too, and I am short. I want to hear swords clash. I want a book to begin in a good way; a book, I guess, like *Treasure Island,* alas! which I have never read, and cannot though I live to ninety. I would God that some one else had written it! By all that I can learn, it is the very book for my complaint. I like the way I hear it opens; and they tell me John Silver is good fun. And to me it is, and must ever be, a dream unrealised, a book unwritten. O my sighings after romance, or even Skeltery, and O! the weary age which will produce me neither!

CHAPTER I

The night was damp and cloudy, the ways foul. The single horseman, cloaked and booted, who pursued his way across Willesden Common, had not met a traveller, when the sound of wheels——

CHAPTER I

'Yes, sir,' said the old pilot, 'she must have dropped into the bay a little afore dawn. A queer craft she looks.'

1884.
AET. 34.

'She shows no colours,' returned the young gentleman musingly.

'They're a-lowering of a quarter-boat, Mr. Mark,' resumed the old salt. 'We shall soon know more of her.'

'Ay,' replied the young gentleman called Mark, 'and here, Mr. Seadrift, comes your sweet daughter Nancy tripping down the cliff.'

'God bless her kind heart, sir,' ejaculated old Seadrift.

CHAPTER I

The notary, Jean Rossignol, had been summoned to the top of a great house in the Isle St. Louis to make a will; and now, his duties finished, wrapped in a warm roquelaure and with a lantern swinging from one hand, he issued from the mansion on his homeward way. Little did he think what strange adventures were to befall him!——

That is how stories should begin. And I am offered HUSKS instead.

What should be:	What is:
The Filibuster's Cache.	Aunt Anne's Tea Cosy.
Jerry Abershaw.	Mrs. Brierly's Niece.
Blood Money: A Tale.	Society: A Novel.

R. L. S.

To the Rev. Professor Lewis Campbell

[*Wensleydale, Bournemouth, November* 1884.]

MY DEAR CAMPBELL,—The books came duly to hand. My wife has occupied the translation[1] ever since, nor have I yet been able to dislodge her. As for the primer, I have read it with a very strange result: that I find no fault. If you knew how, dogmatic and pugnacious, I stand warden on the literary art, you would the more appreciate your success and my—well, I will own it—disappointment. For I love to put people right (or

[1] Of Sophocles.

wrong) about the arts. But what you say of Tragedy and of Sophocles very amply satisfies me; it is well felt and well said; a little less technically than it is my weakness to desire to see it put, but clear and adequate. You are very right to express your admiration for the resource displayed in Œdipus King; it is a miracle. Would it not have been well to mention Voltaire's interesting onslaught, a thing which gives the best lesson of the difference of neighbour arts?—since all his criticisms, which had been fatal to a narrative, do not amount among them to exhibit one flaw in this masterpiece of drama. For the drama, it is perfect; though such a fable in a romance might make the reader crack his sides, so imperfect, so ethereally slight is the verisimilitude required of these conventional, rigid, and egg-dancing arts.

I was sorry to see no more of you; but shall conclude by hoping for better luck next time. My wife begs to be remembered to both of you.—Yours sincerely,
ROBERT LOUIS STEVENSON.

TO ANDREW CHATTO
Wensleydale, Bournemouth, October 3, 1884.

DEAR MR. CHATTO,—I have an offer of £25 for *Otto* from America. I do not know if you mean to have the American rights; from the nature of the contract, I think not; but if you understood that you were to sell the sheets, I will either hand over the bargain to you, or finish it myself and hand you over the money if you are pleased with the amount. You see, I leave this quite in your hands. To parody an old Scotch story of servant and master: if you don't know that you have a good author, I know that I have a good publisher. Your fair, open, and handsome dealings are a good point in my life, and do more for my crazy health than has yet been done by any doctor.—Very truly yours,
ROBERT LOUIS STEVENSON.

1884.
AET. 34.

TO W. H. LOW

It was some twenty months since the plan of publishing the *Child's Garden* in the first instance as a picture-book had been mooted (see above, p. 258). But it had never taken effect, and in the following March the volume appeared without illustrations in England, and also, I believe, in America.

Bonallie Towers, Branksome Park, Bournemouth, Hants, England, First week in November, I guess, 1884.

MY DEAR LOW,—Now, look here, the above is my address for three months, I hope; continue, on your part, if you please, to write to Edinburgh, which is safe; but if Mrs. Low thinks of coming to England, she might take a run down from London (four hours from Waterloo, main line) and stay a day or two with us among the pines. If not, I hope it will be only a pleasure deferred till you can join her.

My Children's Verses will be published here in a volume called *A Child's Garden*. The sheets are in hand; I will see if I cannot send you the lot, so that you might have a bit of a start. In that case I would do nothing to publish in the States, and you might try an illustrated edition there; which, if the book went fairly over here, might, when ready, be imported. But of this more fully ere long. You will see some verses of mine in the last *Magazine of Art*, with pictures by a young lady; rather pretty, I think. If we find a market for *Phasellulus loquitur*, we can try another. I hope it isn't necessary to put the verse into that rustic printing. I am Philistine enough to prefer clean printer's type; indeed, I can form no idea of the verses thus transcribed by the incult and tottering hand of the draughtsman, nor gather any impression beyond one of weariness to the eyes. Yet the other day, in the *Century*, I saw it imputed as a crime to Vedder that he had not thus travestied Omar Khayyàm. We live in a rum age of music without airs, stories without incident, pictures without beauty, American wood engravings that should have been etchings, and dry-point etchings that ought to have been mezzo-tints. I think of giving 'em literature without words; and I believe if you were to try invisible illustration, it would enjoy a considerable vogue. So long as an artist is on his head, is painting with a flute, or writes with an etcher's needle, or conducts the orchestra with a meat-axe, all is well; and plaudits shower along with roses. But any plain man who tries to follow the obtrusive canons of his art, is but a commonplace figure. To hell with him is the motto, or at least not that; for he will have his reward, but he will never be thought a person of parts.

January 3, 1885.

And here has this been lying near two months. I have failed to get together a preliminary copy of the Child's Verses for you, in spite of doughty efforts; but yesterday I sent you the first sheet of the definitive edition, and shall continue to send the others as they come. If you can, and care to, work them—why so, well. If not, I send you fodder. But the time presses; for though I will delay a little over the proofs, and though it is even possible they may delay the English issue until Easter, it will certainly not be later. Therefore perpend, and do not get caught out. Of course, if you can do pictures, it will be a great pleasure to me to see our names joined; and more than that, a great advantage, as I daresay you may be able to make a bargain for some share a little less spectral than the common for the poor author. But this is all as you shall choose; I give you *carte blanche* to do or not to do.—Yours most sincerely,

ROBERT LOUIS STEVENSON.

O, Sargent has been and painted my portrait; a very nice fellow he is, and is supposed to have done well; it is a poetical but very chicken-boned figure-head, as thus represented. R. L. S. Go on.

1884.
AET. 34.

P.P.S.—Your picture came; and let me thank you for it very much. I am so hunted I had near forgotten. I find it very graceful; and I mean to have it framed.

TO THOMAS STEVENSON

About this time Mr. Stevenson was in some hesitation as to letting himself be proposed for the office of President of the Royal Society of Edinburgh.

Bonallie Towers, Bournemouth, November 1884.

MY DEAR FATHER,—I have no hesitation in recommending you to let your name go up; please yourself about an address; though I think, if we could meet, we could arrange something suitable. What you propose would be well enough in a way, but so modest as to suggest a whine. From that point of view it would be better to change a little; but this, whether we meet or not, we must discuss. Tait, Chrystal, the Royal Society, and I, all think you amply deserve this honour and far more; it is not the True Blue to call this serious compliment a 'trial'; you should be glad of this recognition. As for resigning, that is easy enough if found necessary; but to refuse would be husky and unsatisfactory. *Sic subs.* R. L. S.

My cold is still very heavy; but I carry it well. Fanny is very very much out of sorts, principally through perpetual misery with me. I fear I have been a little in the dumps, which, *as you know, sir*, is a very great sin. I must try to be more cheerful; but my cough is so severe that I have sometimes most exhausting nights and very peevish wakenings. However, this shall be remedied, and last night I was distinctly better than the night before. There is, my dear Mr. Stevenson (so I moralise blandly as we sit together on the devil's garden-wall), no more abominable sin than this gloom, this plaguey peevishness; why (say I) what matters it if we be a little uncomfortable—that is no reason for mangling our unhappy wives. And then I turn and *girn* on the unfortunate Cassandra.—Your fellow culprit, R. L. S.

1884.
AET. 34.

TO W. E. HENLEY

The 'Arabs' mentioned below are the stories comprising the volume *More New Arabian Nights: The Dynamiter.*

Wensleydale, Bournemouth, November 1884.

DEAR HENLEY,—We are all to pieces in health, and heavily handicapped with Arabs. I have a dreadful cough, whose attacks leave me *ætat.* 90. I never let up on the Arabs, all the same, and rarely get less than eight pages out of hand, though hardly able to come downstairs for twittering knees.

I shall put in ——'s letter. He says so little of his circumstances that I am in an impossibility to give him advice more specific than a copybook. Give him my love, however, and tell him it is the mark of the parochial gentleman who has never travelled to find all wrong in a foreign land. Let him hold on, and he will find one country as good as another; and in the meanwhile let him resist the fatal British tendency to communicate his dissatisfaction with a country to its inhabitants. 'Tis a good idea, but it somehow fails to please. In a fortnight, if I can keep my spirit in the box at all, I should be nearly through this Arabian desert; so can tackle something fresh.—Yours ever, R. L. S.

TO THOMAS STEVENSON

Mr. Stevenson, the elder, had read the play of *Admiral Guinea*, written in September by his son and Mr. Henley in

1884.
AET. 34.

collaboration, and had protested, with his usual vehemence of feeling and expression, against the stage confrontation of profane blackguardry in the person of Pew with evangelical piety in that of the reformed slaving captain who gives his name to the piece.

Bonallie Towers, Branksome Park, Bournemouth (The three B's) [November 5, 1884].

MY DEAR FATHER,—Allow me to say, in a strictly Pickwickian sense, that you are a silly fellow. I am pained indeed, but how should I be offended? I think you exaggerate; I cannot forget that you had the same impression of the *Deacon*; and yet, when you saw it played, were less revolted than you looked for; and I will still hope that the *Admiral* also is not so bad as you suppose. There is one point, however, where I differ from you very frankly. Religion is in the world; I do not think you are the man to deny the importance of its rôle; and I have long decided not to leave it on one side in art. The opposition of the Admiral and Mr. Pew is not, to my eyes, either horrible or irreverent; but it may be, and it probably is, very ill done: what then? This is a failure; better luck next time; more power to the elbow, more discretion, more wisdom in the design, and the old defeat becomes the scene of the new victory. Concern yourself about no failure; they do not cost lives, as in engineering; they are the *pierres perdues* of successes. Fame is (truly) a vapour; do not think of it; if the writer means well and tries hard, no failure will injure him, whether with God or man.

I wish I could hear a brighter account of yourself; but I am inclined to acquit the *Admiral* of having a share in the responsibility. My very heavy cold is, I hope, drawing off; and the change to this charming house in the forest will, I hope, complete my re-establishment.—With love to all, believe me, your ever affectionate,

ROBERT LOUIS STEVENSON.

To Charles Baxter

1884.
AET. 34.

*Bonallie Towers, Branksome Park, Bournemouth,
November 11, [1884].*

MY DEAR CHARLES,—I am in my new house, thus proudly styled, as you perceive; but the deevil a tower ava' can be perceived (except out of window); this is not as it should be; one might have hoped, at least, a turret. We are all vilely unwell. I put in the dark watches imitating a donkey with some success, but little pleasure; and in the afternoon I indulge in a smart fever, accompanied by aches and shivers. There is thus little monotony to be deplored. I at least am a *regular* invalid; I would scorn to bray in the afternoon; I would indignantly refuse the proposal to fever in the night. What is bred in the bone will come out, sir, in the flesh; and the same spirit that prompted me to date my letter regulates the hour and character of my attacks.—I am, sir, yours,
THOMSON.

To Charles Baxter

The next, on the same subject, is written in the style and character of the Edinburgh ex-elder, Johnson.

Postmark, Bournemouth, 13th November 1884.

MY DEAR THOMSON,—It's a maist remarkable fac', but nae shüner had I written yon braggin', blawin' letter aboot ma business habits, when bang! that very day, ma hoast[1] begude in the aifternune. It is really remaurkable; it's providenshle, I believe. The ink wasnae fair dry, the words werenae weel ooten ma mouth, when bang, I got the lee. The mair ye think o't, Thomson, the less ye'll like the looks o't. Proavidence (I'm no' sayin') is all verra weel *in its place*; but if Proavidence has nae mainners, wha's to learn't? Proavidence is a fine thing, but hoo would you like Proavidence to keep your till for ye? The richt

---
[1] Cough.

1884.
AET. 34.

place for Proavidence is in the kirk; it has naething to do wi' private correspondence between twa gentlemen, nor freendly cracks, nor a wee bit word of sculduddery[1] ahint the door, nor, in shoart, wi' ony *hole-and-corner wark*, what I would call. I'm pairfec'ly willin' to meet in wi' Proavidence, I'll be prood to meet in wi' him, when my time's come and I cannae dae nae better; but if he's to come skinking aboot my stair-fit, damned, I micht as weel be deid for a' the comfort I'll can get in life. Cannae he no be made to understand that it's beneath him? Gosh, if I was in his business, I wouldnae steir my heid for a plain, auld ex-elder that, tak him the way he taks himsel,' 's just aboot as honest as he can weel afford, an' but for a wheen auld scandals, near forgotten noo, is a pairfec'ly respectable and thoroughly decent man. Or if I fashed wi' him ava', it wad be kind o' handsome like; a pun'-note under his stair door, or a bottle o' auld, blended malt to his bit marnin', as a teshtymonial like yon ye ken sae weel aboot, but mair successfu'.

Dear Thomson, have I ony money? If I have, *send it*, for the loard's sake.   JOHNSON.

TO MISS FERRIER

Bonallie Towers, Bournemouth, November 12, 1884.

MY DEAR COGGIE,—Many thanks for the two photos which now decorate my room. I was particularly glad to have the Bell Rock. I wonder if you saw me plunge, lance in rest, into a controversy thereanent? It was a very one-sided affair. I slept upon the field of battle, paraded, sang Te Deum, and came home after a review rather than a campaign.

Please tell Campbell I got his letter. The Wild Woman of the West has been much amiss and complaining sorely. I hope nothing more serious is wrong with

[1] Loose talk.

her than just my ill-health, and consequent anxiety and labour; but the deuce of it is, that the cause continues. I am about knocked out of time now: a miserable, snuffling, shivering, fever-stricken, nightmare-ridden, knee-jottering, hoast-hoast-hoasting shadow and remains of man. But we'll no gie ower jist yet a bittie. We've seen waur; and dod, mem, it's my belief that we'll see better. I dinna ken 'at I've muckle mair to say to ye, or, indeed, onything; but jist here's guid-fallowship, guid health, and the wale o' guid fortune to your bonny sel'; and my respecs to the Perfessor and his wife, and the Prinshiple, an' the Bell Rock, an' ony ither public chara'ters that I'm acquaunt wi'. R. L. S.

1884.
AET. 34.

TO EDMUND GOSSE

Just before the crippling fit of illness above recorded, Stevenson had accepted a commission from the *Pall Mall Gazette* for a 'crawler' or Christmas story of the blood-curdling kind. He had been unable to finish for this purpose the tale he had first intended; had tried the publishers with 'Markheim' (afterwards printed in the collection called *Merry Men*), which proved too short; had then furbished up as well as he could a tale drafted in the Pitlochry days, 'The Body-Snatcher'; which was advertised in the streets of London by sandwich men carrying posters so horrific that they were suppressed, if I remember right, by the police. Stevenson rightly thought the tale not up to his best mark, and would not take the full payment which had been bargained for. His correspondent was just about to start on a tour to the United States.

Bonallie Towers, Branksome Park, Bournemouth, Nov. 15, 1884.

MY DEAR GOSSE,—This Mr. Morley[1] of yours is a most desperate fellow. He has sent me (for my opinion) the most truculent advertisement I ever saw, in which the white hairs of Gladstone are dragged round Troy behind my chariot wheels. What can I say? I say nothing to

[1] Mr. Charles Morley, at this time manager or assistant-manager of the *Pall Mall Gazette*.

1884.
AET. 34.
him; and to you, I content myself with remarking that he seems a desperate fellow.

All luck to you on your American adventure; may you find health, wealth, and entertainment! If you see, as you likely will, Frank R. Stockton, pray greet him from me in words to this effect:—

> My Stockton if I failed to like,
> It were a sheer depravity,
> For I went down with the *Thomas Hyke*
> And up with the *Negative Gravity!*

I adore these tales.

I hear flourishing accounts of your success at Cambridge, so you leave with a good omen. Remember me to *green corn* if it is in season; if not, you had better hang yourself on a sour apple tree, for your voyage has been lost.—Yours affectionately, ROBERT LOUIS STEVENSON.

TO MISS FERRIER

The death here referred to is that of the correspondent's brother-in-law, Sir Alexander Grant, the well-known Aristotelian scholar and Principal of the University of Edinburgh.

[Bournemouth,] December 1884.

MY DEAR COGGIE,—We are very much distressed to hear of this which has befallen your family. As for Sir Alexander, I can but speak from my own feelings: he survived to finish his book, and to conduct, with such a great success, the ter-centenary. Ah, how many die just upon the threshold! Had he died a year ago, how great a disappointment! But all this is nothing to the survivors. Do please, as soon as you are able, let us know how it goes, and how it is likely to go with the family; and believe that both my wife and I are most anxious to have good news, or the best possible. I know very well how you must feel; you are passing a bad time.

Our news must seem very impertinent. We have both been ill; but I, at least, am better. The Bogue, who is let out every night for half an hour's yapping, is anchored in the moonlight, just before the door, and, under the belief that he is watchdog at a live farm beleaguered by moss-troopers, is simply raising Cain.

I can add nothing more, but just that we wish to hear as soon as you have nothing else to do—not to hurry, of course—if it takes three months, no matter, but bear us in mind.—With best love from both of us, ever your most affectionate friend, R. L. STEVENSON.

TO HENRY JAMES

The following to Mr. Henry James refers to the essay of R. L. S. called a 'Humble Remonstrance,' which had just appeared in *Longman's Magazine*. Mr. James had written holding out the prospect of a continuance of the friendly controversy which had thus been opened up between them on the aims and qualities of fiction.

Bonallie Towers, Branksome Park, Bournemouth,
December 8, 1884.

MY DEAR HENRY JAMES,—This is a very brave hearing from more points than one. The first point is that there is a hope of a sequel. For this I laboured. Seriously, from the dearth of information and thoughtful interest in the art of literature, those who try to practise it with any deliberate purpose run the risk of finding no fit audience. People suppose it is 'the stuff' that interests them; they think, for instance, that the prodigious fine thoughts and sentiments in Shakespeare impress by their own weight, not understanding that the unpolished diamond is but a stone. They think that striking situations, or good dialogue, are got by studying life; they will not rise to understand that they are prepared by deliberate artifice and set off by painful suppressions. Now, I want the whole thing well ventilated, for my own education and the public's; and I beg you to look as quick as you can, to follow me up with every circumstance of defeat where we differ, and (to prevent the flouting of the laity) to emphasise the points where we agree. I trust your paper will show me the way to a rejoinder; and that rejoinder I shall hope to make with so much art as to woo or drive you from your threatened silence. I would not ask better than to pass my life in beating out this quarter of corn with such a seconder as yourself.

Point the second—I am rejoiced indeed to hear you speak so kindly of my work; rejoiced and surprised. I seem to myself a very rude, left-handed countryman; not fit to be read, far less complimented, by a man so accomplished, so adroit, so craftsmanlike as you. You will happily never have cause to understand the despair with which a writer like myself considers (say) the park scene in Lady Barberina. Every touch surprises me by its intangible precision; and the effect when done, as light as syllabub, as distinct as a picture, fills me with envy. Each man among us prefers his own aim, and I prefer mine; but when we come to speak of performance, I recognise myself, compared with you, to be a lout and slouch of the first water.

Where we differ, both as to the design of stories and the delineation of character, I begin to lament. Of course, I am not so dull as to ask you to desert your walk; but could you not, in one novel, to oblige a sincere admirer, and to enrich his shelves with a beloved volume, could you not, and might you not, cast your characters in a mould a little more abstract and academic (dear Mrs. Pennyman had already, among your other work, a taste of what I mean), and pitch the incidents, I do not say in any stronger, but in a slightly more emphatic key —as it were an episode from one of the old (so-called) novels of adventure? I fear you will not; and I suppose I must sighingly admit you to be right. And yet, when I see, as it were, a book of Tom Jones handled with your exquisite precision and shot through with those side-lights of reflection in which you excel, I relinquish the dear vision with regret. Think upon it.

As you know, I belong to that besotted class of man, the invalid: this puts me to a stand in the way of visits. But it is possible that some day you may feel that a day near the sea and among pinewoods would be a pleasant change from town. If so, please let us know; and my wife and I will be delighted to put you up, and give you what we can to eat and drink (I have a fair bottle of claret). —On the back of which, believe me, yours sincerely,

1884.
AET. 34.

ROBERT LOUIS STEVENSON.

P.S.—I reopen this to say that I have re-read my paper, and cannot think I have at all succeeded in being either veracious or polite. I knew, of course, that I took your paper merely as a pin to hang my own remarks upon; but, alas! what a thing is any paper! What fine remarks can you not hang on mine! How I have sinned against proportion, and with every effort to the contrary, against the merest rudiments of courtesy to you! You are indeed a very acute reader to have divined the real attitude of my mind; and I can only conclude, not without closed eyes and shrinking shoulders, in the well-worn words

Lay on, Macduff!

TO MR. AND MRS. THOMAS STEVENSON

Bonallie Towers, Bournemouth, December 9, 1884.

MY DEAR PEOPLE,—The dreadful tragedy of the *Pall Mall* has come to a happy but ludicrous ending: I am to keep the money, the tale writ for them is to be buried certain fathoms deep, and they are to flash out before the world with our old friend of Kinnaird, 'The Body Snatcher.' When you come, please to bring—

(1) My *Montaigne*, or, at least, the two last volumes.
(2) My *Milton* in the three vols. in green.
(3) The *Shakespeare* that Babington sent me for a wedding-gift.
(4) Hazlitt's *Table Talk and Plain Speaker.*

If you care to get a box of books from Douglas and Foulis, let them be *solid*. *Croker Papers, Correspondence of Napoleon, History of Henry IV.*, Lang's *Folk Lore*, would be my desires.

I had a charming letter from Henry James about my *Longman* paper. I did not understand queries about the verses; the pictures to the Seagull I thought charming; those to the second have left me with a pain in my poor belly and a swimming in the head.

About money, I am afloat and no more, and I warn you, unless I have great luck, I shall have to fall upon you at the New Year like a hundredweight of bricks. Doctor, rent, chemist, are all threatening; sickness has bitterly delayed my work; and unless, as I say, I have the mischief's luck, I shall completely break down. *Verbum sapientibus.* I do not live cheaply, and I question if I ever shall; but if only I had a halfpenny worth of health, I could now easily suffice. The last breakdown of my head is what makes this bankruptcy probable.

Fanny is still out of sorts; Bogue better; self fair, but a stranger to the blessings of sleep.—Ever affectionate son, R. L. S.

TO W. E. HENLEY

Bonallie Towers, Bournemouth, [*December* 1884].

DEAR LAD,—I have made up my mind about the P. M. G., and send you a copy, which please keep or return. As for not giving a reduction, what are we? Are we artists or city men? Why do we sneer at stockbrokers? O nary; I will not take the £40. I took that as a fair price for my best work; I was not able to produce my best; and I will be damned if I steal with my eyes open. *Sufficit.* This is my lookout. As for the paper being rich, certainly it is; but I am honourable. It is no more above me in money than the poor slaveys and cads from whom I look for honesty are below me. Am I Pepys, that because I can find the countenance of 'some of our ablest merchants,' that because—and—pour forth languid twaddle and get paid for it, I, too, should 'cheerfully continue to steal'? I am not Pepys. I do not live much to God and honour; but I will not wilfully turn my back on both. I am, like all the rest of us, falling ever lower from the bright ideas I began with, falling into greed, into idleness, into middle-aged and slippered fireside cowardice; but is it you, my bold blade, that I hear crying this sordid and rank twaddle in my ear? Preaching the dankest Grundyism and upholding the rank customs of our trade—you, who are so cruel hard upon the customs of the publishers? O man, look at the Beam in our own Eyes; and whatever else you do, do not plead Satan's cause, or plead it for all; either embrace the bad, or respect the good when you see a poor devil trying for it. If this is the honesty of authors—to take what you can get and console yourself because publishers are rich—take my name from the rolls of that association. 'Tis a caucus of weaker thieves, jealous of the stronger.—Ever yours, THE ROARING R. L. S.

You will see from the enclosed that I have stuck to what I think my dues pretty tightly in spite of this flourish: these are my words for a poor ten-pound note!

TO W. E. HENLEY

Bonallie Towers, Bournemouth, [*Winter*, 1884].

MY DEAR LAD,—Here was I in bed; not writing, not hearing, and finding myself gently and agreeably ill used; and behold I learn you are bad yourself. Get your wife to send us a word how you are. I am better decidedly. Bogue got his Christmas card, and behaved well for three days after. It may interest the cynical to learn that I started my last hæmorrhage by too sedulous attentions to my dear Bogue. The stick was broken; and that night

Bogue, who was attracted by the extraordinary aching of his bones, and is always inclined to a serious view of his own ailments, announced with his customary pomp that he was dying. In this case, however, it was not the dog that died. (He had tried to bite his mother's ankles.) I have written a long and peculiarly solemn paper on the technical elements of style. It is path-breaking and epoch-making; but I do not think the public will be readily convoked to its perusal. Did I tell you that S. C. had risen to the paper on James? At last! O but I was pleased; he's (like Johnnie) been lang, lang o' comin', but here he is. He will not object to my future manœuvres in the same field, as he has to my former. All the family are here; my father better than I have seen him these two years; my mother the same as ever. I do trust you are better, and I am yours ever, R. L. S.

TO H. A. JONES

Bonallie Towers, Branksome Park,
Bournemouth, Dec. 30, 1884.

DEAR SIR,—I am so accustomed to hear nonsense spoken about all the arts, and the drama in particular, that I cannot refrain from saying 'Thank you' for your paper. In my answer to Mr. James, in the December *Longman*, you may see that I have merely touched, I think in a parenthesis, on the drama; but I believe enough was said to indicate our agreement in essentials.

Wishing you power and health to further enunciate and to act upon these principles, believe me, dear sir, yours truly, ROBERT LOUIS STEVENSON.

TO SIDNEY COLVIN

Bonallie Towers, Branksome Park,
Bournemouth, Jan. 4, 1885.

DEAR S. C.,—I am on my feet again, and getting on my boots to do the *Iron Duke*. Conceive my glee: I have refused the £100, and am to get some sort of royalty, not yet decided, instead. 'Tis for Longman's *English Worthies*, edited by A. Lang. Aw haw, haw!

1885.
AET. 35.

Now, look here, could you get me a loan of the Despatches, or is that a dream? I should have to mark passages I fear, and certainly note pages on the fly. If you think it a dream, will Bain get me a second-hand copy, or who would? The sooner, and cheaper, I can get it the better. If there is anything in your weird library that bears on either the man or the period, put it in a mortar and fire it here instanter; I shall catch. I shall want, of course, an infinity of books: among which, any lives there may be; a life of the Marquis Marmont (the Maréchal), *Marmont's Memoirs*, *Greville's Memoirs*, *Peel's Memoirs*, *Napier*, that blind man's history of England you once lent me, Hamley's *Waterloo*; can you get me any of these? Thiers, idle Thiers also. Can you help a man getting into his boots for such a huge campaign? How are you? A Good New Year to you. I mean to have a good one, but on whose funds I cannot fancy: not mine leastways, as I am a mere derelict and drift beam-on to bankruptcy.

For God's sake, remember the man who set out for to conquer Arthur Wellesley, with a broken bellows and an empty pocket.—Yours ever, R. L. STEVENSON.

TO THOMAS STEVENSON

Stevenson had been asked by his father to look over the proofs of a paper which the latter was about to read, as President of the Royal Society of Edinburgh, 'On the Principal Causes of Silting in Estuaries,' in connection with the Manchester Ship Canal Scheme.

[*Bonallie Towers, Bournemouth,*] 14*th January* 1885.

MY DEAR FATHER,—I am glad you like the changes. I own I was pleased with my hand's darg; you may observe, I have corrected several errors which (you may tell Mr. Dick) he had allowed to pass his eagle eye; I wish there may be none in mine; at least, the order is better. The second title, 'Some new Engineering Questions involved in the M. S. C. Scheme of last Session of P.', likes me the best. I think it a very good paper; and I am vain enough to think I have materially helped to polish the diamond. I ended by feeling quite proud of the paper, as if it had been mine; the next time you have as good a one, I will overhaul it for the wages of feeling as clever as I did when I had managed to understand and helped to set it clear. I wonder if I anywhere misapprehended you? I rather think not at the last; at the first shot I know I missed a point or two. Some of what may appear to you to be wanton changes, a little study will show to be necessary.

Yes, Carlyle was ashamed of himself as few men have been; and let all carpers look at what he did. He prepared all these papers for publication with his own hand; all his wife's complaints, all the evidence of his own misconduct: who else would have done so much? Is repentance, which God accepts, to have no avail with men? nor even with the dead? I have heard too much against the thrawn, discomfortable dog: dead he is, and we may be glad of it; but he was a better man than most of us, no less patently than he was a worse. To fill the world with whining is against all my views: I do not like impiety. But—but—there are two sides to all things, and the old scalded baby had his noble side.—Ever affectionate son,
R. L. S.

TO SIDNEY COLVIN

Bonallie Towers, Bournemouth, January 1885.

DEAR S. C.,—I have addressed a letter to the G. O. M. *à propos* of Wellington; and I became aware, you will be interested to hear, of an overwhelming respect for the old gentleman. I can *blaguer* his failures; but when you actually address him, and bring the two statures and records to confrontation, dismay is the result. By mere continuance of years, he must impose; the man who helped to rule England before I was conceived, strikes me with a new sense of greatness and antiquity, when I must actually beard him with the cold forms of correspondence. I shied at the necessity of calling him plain 'Sir'! Had he been 'My lord,' I had been happier; no, I am no equalitarian. Honour to whom honour is due; and if to none, why, then, honour to the old!

These, O Slade Professor, are my unvarnished sentiments: I was a little surprised to find them so extreme, and therefore I communicate the fact.

Belabour thy brains, as to whom it would be well to question. I have a small space; I wish to make a popular book, nowhere obscure, nowhere, if it can be helped, unhuman. It seems to me the most hopeful plan to tell the tale, so far as may be, by anecdote. He did not die till so recently, there must be hundreds who remember him, and thousands who have still ungarnered stories. Dear man, to the breach! Up, soldier of the iron dook, up, Slades, and at 'em! (which, conclusively, he did not say: the at 'em-ic theory is to be dismissed). You know piles of fellows who must reek with matter; help! help!—Yours ever, R. L. S.

TO SIDNEY COLVIN

In the two following letters are expressed some of the distress and bitterness with which, in common with most Englishmen, Stevenson felt the circumstances of Gordon's abandonment in the Soudan and the failure of the belated attempt to rescue him. The advice to go on with 'my book' refers, if I remember right, to some scheme for the republication in book form of stray magazine papers of mine of a more or less personal or biographical nature.

Bonallie Towers, Bournemouth, February 1885.

MY DEAR COLVIN,—You are indeed a backward correspondent, and much may be said against you. But in this

1885.
AET. 35.

weather, and O dear! in this political scene of degradation, much must be forgiven. I fear England is dead of Burgessry, and only walks about galvanised. I do not love to think of my countrymen these days; nor to remember myself. Why was I silent? I feel I have no right to blame any one; but I won't write to the G. O. M. I do really not see my way to any form of signature, unless 'your fellow criminal in the eyes of God,' which might disquiet the proprieties.

About your book, I have always said: go on. The drawing of character is a different thing from publishing the details of a private career. No one objects to the first, or should object, if his name be not put upon it; at the other, I draw the line. In a preface, if you chose, you might distinguish; it is, besides, a thing for which you are eminently well equipped, and which you would do with taste and incision. I long to see the book. People like themselves (to explain a little more); no one likes his life, which is a misbegotten issue, and a tale of failure. To see these failures either touched upon, or *coasted*, to get the idea of a spying eye and blabbing tongue about the house, is to lose all privacy in life. To see that thing, which we do love, our character, set forth, is ever gratifying. See how my *Talk and Talkers* went; every one liked his own portrait, and shrieked about other people's; so it will be with yours. If you are the least true to the essential, the sitter will be pleased; very likely not his friends, and that from *various motives*.   R. L. S.

When will your holiday be? I sent your letter to my wife, and forget. Keep us in mind, and I hope we shall be able to receive you.

TO J. A. SYMONDS

Bournemouth, February 1885.

MY DEAR SYMONDS,—Yes, we have both been very neglectful. I had horrid luck, catching two thundering influenzas in August and November. I recovered from the last with difficulty, but have come through this blustering winter with some general success; in the house, up and down. My wife, however, has been painfully upset by my health. Last year, of course, was cruelly trying to her nerves; Nice and Hyères are bad experiences; and though she is not ill, the doctor tells me that prolonged anxiety may do her a real mischief.

1885.
AET. 35.

I feel a little old and fagged, and chary of speech, and not very sure of spirit in my work; but considering what a year I have passed, and how I have twice sat on Charon's pierhead, I am surprising.

My father has presented us with a very pretty home in this place, into which we hope to move by May. My *Child's Verses* come out next week. *Otto* begins to appear in April; *More New Arabian Nights* as soon as possible. Moreover, I am neck deep in Wellington; also a story on the stocks, *The Great North Road*. O, I am busy! Lloyd is at college in Edinburgh. That is, I think, all that can be said by way of news.

Have you read *Huckleberry Finn*? It contains many excellent things; above all, the whole story of a healthy boy's dealings with his conscience, incredibly well done.

My own conscience is badly seared; a want of piety; yet I pray for it, tacitly, every day; believing it, after courage, the only gift worth having; and its want, in a man of any claims to honour, quite unpardonable. The tone of your letter seemed to me very sound. In these dark days of public dishonour, I do not know that one can do better than carry our private trials piously. What a picture is this of a nation! No man that I can see, on any side or party, seems to have the least sense of our ineffable shame: the desertion of the garrisons. I tell my little parable that Germany took England, and then there was an Indian Mutiny, and Bismarck said: 'Quite right: let Delhi and Calcutta and Bombay fall; and let the women and children be treated Sepoy fashion,' and people say, 'O, but that is very different!' And then I wish I were dead. Millais (I hear) was painting Gladstone when the news came of Gordon's death; Millais was much affected, and Gladstone said, 'Why? *It is the man's own temerity!*' Voilà le Bourgeois! le voilà nu! But why should I blame Gladstone, when I too am a Bourgeois? when I have held my peace? Why did I hold my peace? Because I am a sceptic: *i.e.* a Bourgeois. We believe in nothing, Symonds; you don't, and I don't; and these are two reasons, out of a handful of millions, why England stands before the world dripping with blood and daubed with dishonour. I will first try to take the beam out of my own eye, trusting that even private effort somehow betters and braces the general atmosphere. See, for example, if England has shown (I put it hypothetically) one spark of manly sensibility, they have been shamed into it by the spectacle of Gordon. Police-Officer Cole is the only man that I see to admire. I dedicate my *New Arabs* to him and Cox, in default of other great public characters.—Yours ever most affectionately,

ROBERT LOUIS STEVENSON.

TO EDMUND GOSSE

The following refers to an edition of Gray, with notes and a short prefatory Life by Mr. Gosse; and to the publication of the *Child's Garden of Verses*.

Bonallie Towers, Bournemouth, March 12, 1885.

MY DEAR GOSSE,—I was indeed much exercised how I could be worked into Gray; and lo! when I saw it, the passage seemed to have been written with a single eye to elucidate the—worst?—well, not a very good poem of Gray's. Your little life is excellent, clean, neat, efficient. I have read many of your notes, too, with pleasure. Your connection with Gray was a happy circumstance; it was a suitable conjunction.

I did not answer your letter from the States, for what 1885. was I to say? I liked getting it and reading it; I was AET. 35. rather flattered that you wrote it to me; and then I'll tell you what I did—I put it in the fire. Why? Well, just because it was very natural and expansive; and thinks I to myself, if I die one of these fine nights, this is just the letter that Gosse would not wish to go into the hands of third parties. Was I well inspired? And I did not answer it because you were in your high places, sailing with supreme dominion, and seeing life in a particular glory; and I was peddling in a corner, confined to the house, overwhelmed with necessary work, which I was not always doing well, and, in the very mild form in which the disease approaches me, touched with a sort of bustling cynicism. Why throw cold water? How ape your agreeable frame of mind? In short, I held my tongue.

I have now published on 101 small pages *The Complete Proof of Mr. R. L. Stevenson's Incapacity to Write Verse*, in a series of graduated examples with table of contents. I think I shall issue a companion volume of exercises: 'Analyse this poem. Collect and comminate the ugly words. Distinguish and condemn the *chevilles*. State Mr. Stevenson's faults of taste in regard to the measure. What reasons can you gather from this example for your belief that Mr. S. is unable to write any other measure?'

They look ghastly in the cold light of print; but there is something nice in the little ragged regiment for all; the blackguards seem to me to smile, to have a kind of childish treble note that sounds in my ears freshly; not song, if you will, but a child's voice.

I was glad you enjoyed your visit to the States. Most Englishmen go there with a confirmed design of patronage, as they go to France for that matter; and patronage will not pay. Besides, in this year of—grace, said I?— of disgrace, who should creep so low as an Englishman? 'It is not to be thought of that the flood'—ah,

1885.
AET. 35.

Wordsworth, you would change your note were you alive to-day!

I am now a beastly householder, but have not yet entered on my domain. When I do, the social revolution will probably cast me back upon my dung heap. There is a person called Hyndman whose eye is on me; his step is beHynd me as I go. I shall call my house Skerryvore when I get it: SKERRYVORE: *c'est bon pour la poéshie.* I will conclude with my favourite sentiment: 'The world is too much with me.'

ROBERT LOUIS STEVENSON,
The Hermit of Skerryvore.

Author of 'John Vane Tempest: a Romance,' 'Herbert and Henrietta: or the Nemesis of Sentiment,' 'The Life and Adventures of Colonel Bludyer Fortescue,' 'Happy Homes and Hairy Faces,' 'A Pound of Feathers and a Pound of Lead,' part author of 'Minn's Complete Capricious Correspondent: a Manual of Natty, Natural, and Knowing Letters,' and editor of the 'Poetical Remains of Samuel Burt Crabbe, known as the melodious Bottle-Holder.'

Uniform with the above:

'The Life and Remains of the Reverend Jacob Degray Squah,' author of 'Heave-yo for the New Jerusalem.' 'A Box of Candles; or the Patent Spiritual Safety Match,' and 'A Day with the Heavenly Harriers.'

TO W. H. LOW

The 'dedication' referred to is that of a forthcoming illustrated edition of Keats's *Lamia.*

Bonallie Towers, Bournemouth, March 13, 1885.

MY DEAR LOW,—Your success has been immense. I wish your letter had come two days ago: *Otto*, alas! has been disposed of a good while ago; but it was only day before yesterday that I settled the new volume of Arabs. However, for the future, you and the sons of the deified Scribner are the men for me. Really they have behaved most handsomely. I cannot lay my hand on the papers, or I would tell you exactly how it compares with my English bargain; but it compares well. Ah, if we had that copyright, I do believe it would go far to make me solvent, ill-health and all.

I wrote you a letter to the Rembrandt, in which I stated my views about the dedication in a very brief form. It will give me sincere pleasure, and will make the second dedication I have received, the other being from John Addington Symonds. It is a compliment I value much; I don't know any that I should prefer.

I am glad to hear you have windows to do; that is a fine business, I think; but, alas! the glass is so bad nowadays; realism invading even that, as well as the huge inferiority of our technical resource corrupting every tint. Still, anything that keeps a man to decoration is, in this age, good for the artist's spirit.

By the way, have you seen James and me on the novel? James, I think in the August or September—R. L. S. in the December *Longman*. I own I think the *école bête*, of which I am the champion, has the whip hand of the argument; but as James is to make a rejoinder, I must not boast. Anyway the controversy is amusing to see. I was terribly tied down to space, which has made the end congested and dull. I shall see if I can afford to send you the April *Contemporary*—but I dare say you see it anyway—as it will contain a paper of mine on style, a sort of continuation of old arguments on art in which you have wagged a most effective tongue. It is a sort of start upon my Treatise on the Art of Literature: a small, arid book that shall some day appear.

With every good wish from me and mine (should I not say 'she and hers'?) to you and yours, believe me yours ever, ROBERT LOUIS STEVENSON.

1885.
AET. 35.

TO P. G. HAMERTON

The work of his correspondent's which R. L. S. notices in the following is, of course, the sumptuous volume *Landscape*: Seeley & Co., 1885. The passages specially referred to will be found pp. 46-62 of that work.

Bournemouth, March 16, 1885.

MY DEAR HAMERTON,—Various things have been reminding me of my misconduct: First, Swan's application for your address; second, a sight of the sheets of your *Landscape* book; and last, your note to Swan, which he was so kind as to forward. I trust you will never suppose me to be guilty of anything more serious than an idleness, partially excusable. My ill-health makes my rate of life heavier than I can well meet, and yet stops me from earning more. My conscience, sometimes perhaps too easily stifled, but still (for my time of life and the public manners of the age) fairly well alive, forces me to perpetual and almost endless transcriptions. On the back of all this, my correspondence hangs like a thundercloud; and just when I think I am getting through my troubles, crack, down goes my health, I have a long, costly sickness, and begin the world again. It is fortunate for me I have a father, or I should long ago have died; but the opportunity of the aid makes the necessity none the more welcome. My father has presented me with a beautiful house here—or so I believe, for I have not yet seen it, being a cage bird but for nocturnal sorties in the garden. I hope we shall soon move into it, and I tell myself that some day perhaps we may have the pleasure of seeing you as our guest. I trust at least that you will take me as I am, a thoroughly bad correspondent, and a man, a hater, indeed, of rudeness in others, but too often rude in all unconsciousness himself; and that you will never cease to believe the sincere sympathy and admiration that I feel for you and for your work.

About the *Landscape*, which I had a glimpse of while

a friend of mine was preparing a review, I was greatly interested, and could write and wrangle for a year on every page; one passage particularly delighted me, the part about Ulysses—jolly. Then, you know, that is just what I fear I have come to think landscape ought to be in literature; so there we should be at odds. Or perhaps not so much as I suppose, as Montaigne says it is a pot with two handles, and I own I am wedded to the technical handle, which (I likewise own and freely) you do well to keep for a mistress. I should much like to talk with you about some other points; it is only in talk that one gets to understand. Your delightful Wordsworth trap I have tried on two hardened Wordsworthians, not that I am not one myself. By covering up the context, and asking them to guess what the passage was, both (and both are very clever people, one a writer, one a painter) pronounced it a guide-book. 'Do you think it an unusually good guide-book?' I asked, and both said, 'No, not at all!' Their grimace was a picture when I showed the original.

I trust your health and that of Mrs. Hamerton keep better; your last account was a poor one. I was unable to make out the visit I had hoped, as (I do not know if you heard of it) I had a very violent and dangerous hæmorrhage last spring. I am almost glad to have seen death so close with all my wits about me, and not in the customary lassitude and disenchantment of disease. Even thus clearly beheld I find him not so terrible as we suppose. But, indeed, with the passing of years, the decay of strength, the loss of all my old active and pleasant habits, there grows more and more upon me that belief in the kindness of this scheme of things, and the goodness of our veiled God, which is an excellent and pacifying compensation. I trust, if your health continues to trouble you, you may find some of the same belief. But perhaps my fine discovery is a piece of art, and belongs to a character cowardly, intolerant of certain feelings, and apt to self-deception. I don't think so, however; and when I feel what a weak and fallible vessel I was thrust into this hurly-burly, and with what marvellous kindness the wind has been tempered to my frailties, I think I should be a strange kind of ass to feel anything but gratitude.

I do not know why I should inflict this talk upon you; but when I summon the rebellious pen, he must go his own way; I am no Michael Scott, to rule the fiend of correspondence. Most days he will none of me; and when he comes, it is to rape me where he will.—Yours very sincerely, ROBERT LOUIS STEVENSON.

TO WILLIAM ARCHER

An anonymous review of the *Child's Garden*, appearing in March, gave R. L. S. so much pleasure that he wrote (in the four words, 'Now who are you?') to inquire the name of its writer, and learned that it was Mr. Archer; with whom he had hitherto had no acquaintance. He thereupon entered into friendly correspondence with his critic.

Bournemouth, March 29, 1885.

DEAR MR. ARCHER,—Yes, I have heard of you and read some of your work; but I am bound in particular to thank you for the notice of my verses. 'There,' I said, throwing it over to the friend who was staying with me, 'it's worth writing a book to draw an article like that.' Had you been as hard upon me as you were amiable, I try to tell myself I should have been no blinder to the merits of your notice. For I saw there, to admire and to be very grateful for, a most sober, agile pen; an enviable touch; the marks of a reader, such as one imagines for one's self in dreams, thoughtful, critical, and kind; and to put the top on this memorial column, a greater readiness to describe the author criticised than to display the talents of his censor.

I am a man *blasé* to injudicious praise (though I hope some of it may be judicious too), but I have to thank you for THE BEST CRITICISM I EVER HAD; and am therefore, dear Mr. Archer, the most grateful critickee now extant. ROBERT LOUIS STEVENSON.

P.S.—I congratulate you on living in the corner of all London that I like best. *À propos*, you are very right about my voluntary aversion from the painful sides of life. My childhood was in reality a very mixed experience, full of fever, nightmare, insomnia, painful days and interminable nights; and I can speak with less authority of gardens than of that other 'land of counterpane.' But to what end should we renew these sorrows? The sufferings of life may be handled by the very greatest in their hours of insight; it is of its pleasures that our common poems should be formed; these are the experiences that we should seek to recall or to provoke; and I say with Thoreau, 'What right have I to complain, who have not ceased to wonder?' and, to add a rider of my own, who have no remedy to offer. R. L. S.

TO MRS. FLEEMING JENKIN

The next two or three months yielded few or no letters of interest; the following refer to the death of Professor Fleeming Jenkin, who in Stevenson's early student days at Edinburgh had been both the warmest and the wisest of his elder friends (died June 12, 1885).

[*Skerryvore, Bournemouth, June* 1885.]

MY DEAR MRS. JENKIN,—You know how much and for how long I have loved, respected, and admired him; I am only able to feel a little with you. But I know how he would have wished us to feel. I never knew a better man, nor one to me more lovable; we shall all feel the loss more greatly as time goes on. It scarce seems life to me; what must it be to you? Yet one of the last things that he said to me was, that from all these sad bereavements of yours he had learned only more than ever to feel the goodness and what we, in our feebleness, call the support of God; he had been ripening so much—to other eyes

1885.
AET. 35.

than ours, we must suppose he was ripe, and try to feel it. I feel it is better not to say much more. It will be to me a great pride to write a notice of him : the last I can now do. What more in any way I can do for you, please to think and let me know. For his sake and for your own, I would not be a useless friend : I know, you know me a most warm one; please command me or my wife, in any way. Do not trouble to write to me ; Austin, I have no doubt, will do so, if you are, as I fear you will be, unfit.

My heart is sore for you. At least you know what you have been to him ; how he cherished and admired you ; how he was never so pleased as when he spoke of you ; with what a boy's love, up to the last, he loved you, This surely is a consolation. Yours is the cruel part—to survive; you must try and not grudge to him his better fortune, to go first. It is the sad part of such relations that one must remain and suffer; I cannot see my poor Jenkin without you. Nor you indeed without him ; but you may try to rejoice that he is spared that extremity. Perhaps I (as I was so much his confidant) know even better than you can do what your loss would have been to him ; he never spoke of you but his face changed ; it was—you were—his religion.

I write by this post to Austin and to the *Academy.*—Yours most sincerely, ROBERT LOUIS STEVENSON.

TO MRS. FLEEMING JENKIN

[*Skerryvore, Bournemouth, June* 1885.]

MY DEAR MRS. JENKIN,—I should have written sooner, but we are in a bustle, and I have been very tired, though still well. Your very kind note was most welcome to me. I shall be very much pleased to have you call me Louis, as he has now done for so many years. Sixteen, you say? is it so long? It seems too short now ; but of that we cannot judge, and must not complain.

I wish that either I or my wife could do anything for you; when we can, you will, I am sure, command us.

I trust that my notice gave you as little pain as was possible. I found I had so much to say, that I preferred to keep it for another place and make but a note in the *Academy*. To try to draw my friend at greater length, and say what he was to me and his intimates, what a good influence in life and what an example, is a desire that grows upon me. It was strange, as I wrote the note, how his old tests and criticisms haunted me; and it reminded me afresh with every few words how much I owe to him.

I had a note from Henley, very brief and very sad. We none of us yet feel the loss; but we know what he would have said and wished.

Do you know that Dew Smith has two photographs of him, neither very bad? and one giving a lively, though not flattering air of him in conversation? If you have not got them, would you like me to write to Dew and ask him to give you proofs?

I was so pleased that he and my wife made friends; that is a great pleasure. We found and have preserved one fragment (the head) of the drawing he made and tore up when he was last here. He had promised to come and stay with us this summer. May we not hope, at least, some time soon to have one from you?—Believe me, my dear Mrs. Jenkin, with the most real sympathy, your sincere friend,   ROBERT LOUIS STEVENSON.

Dear me, what happiness I owe to both of you!

TO W. H. LOW

In August of this year Stevenson made with his wife an excursion to the west (stopping at Dorchester on the way, for the pleasure of seeing Mr. Thomas Hardy at home), and was detained for several weeks at Exeter by a bad fit of hæmorrhage. His correspondence is not resumed until the autumn.

1885.
AET. 35.

Skerryvore, Bournemouth, October 22, 1885.

MY DEAR LOW,—I trust you are not annoyed with me beyond forgiveness; for indeed my silence has been devilish prolonged. I can only tell you that I have been nearly six months (more than six) in a strange condition of collapse, when it was impossible to do any work, and difficult (more difficult than you would suppose) to write the merest note. I am now better, but not yet my own man in the way of brains, and in health only so-so. I suppose I shall learn (I begin to think I am learning) to fight this vast, vague feather-bed of an obsession that now overlies and smothers me; but in the beginnings of these conflicts, the inexperienced wrestler is always worsted, and I own I have been quite extinct. I wish you to know, though it can be no excuse, that you are not the only one of my friends by many whom I have thus neglected; and even now, having come so very late into the possession of myself, with a substantial capital of debts, and my work still moving with a desperate slowness—as a child might fill a sandbag with its little handfuls—and my future deeply pledged, there is almost a touch of virtue in my borrowing these hours to write to you. Why I said 'hours' I know not; it would look blue for both of us if I made good the word.

I was writing your address the other day, ordering a copy of my next, *Prince Otto*, to go your way. I hope you have not seen it in parts; it was not meant to be so read; and only my poverty (dishonourably) consented to the serial evolution.

I will send you with this a copy of the English edition of the *Child's Garden*. I have heard there is some vile rule of the post-office in the States against inscriptions; so I send herewith a piece of doggerel which Mr. Bunner may, if he thinks fit, copy off the fly leaf.

Sargent was down again and painted a portrait of me walking about in my own dining-room, in my own velveteen jacket, and twisting as I go my own moustache;

at one corner a glimpse of my wife, in an Indian dress, and seated in a chair that was once my grandfather's; but since some months goes by the name of Henry James's, for it was there the novelist loved to sit—adds a touch of poesy and comicality. It is, I think, excellent, but is too eccentric to be exhibited. I am at one extreme corner; my wife, in this wild dress, and looking like a ghost, is at the extreme other end; between us an open door exhibits my palatial entrance hall and a part of my respected staircase. All this is touched in lovely, with that witty touch of Sargent's; but, of course, it looks dam queer as a whole.

Pray let me hear from you, and give me good news of yourself and your wife, to whom please remember me.—Yours most sincerely, my dear Low,

ROBERT LOUIS STEVENSON.

TO W. E. HENLEY

Prince Otto had been published in October of this year; and the following refers to two reviews of it—one of them by Mr. Henley, which to the writer's displeasure had been pruned by the editor before printing; the other by a writer in the *Saturday Review*, who declared that Otto was 'a fool and a wittol,' and could see nothing but false style in the story of Seraphina's flight through the forest.

[*Skerryvore, Bournemouth, Autumn* 1885.]

DEAR LAD,—If there was any more praise in what you wrote, I think [the editor] has done us both a service; some of it stops my throat. What, it would not have been the same if Dumas or Musset had done it, would it not? Well, no, I do not think it would, do you know, now; I am really of opinion it would not; and a dam good job too. Why, think what Musset would have made of Otto! Think how gallantly Dumas would have carried his crowd through! And whatever you do, don't quarrel with ——. It gives me much pleasure to see your work there; I think you do yourself great justice in that field; and I would let no annoyance, petty or justifiable, debar me from such a market. I think you do good there. Whether (considering our intimate relations) you would not do better to refrain from reviewing me, I will leave to yourself: were it all on my side, you could foresee my answer; but there is your side also, where you must be the judge.

As for the *Saturday*. Otto is no 'fool,' the reader is left in no doubt as to whether or not Seraphina was a Messalina (though much it would matter, if you come to that); and therefore on both these points the reviewer has been unjust. Secondly, the romance lies precisely in the freeing of two spirits from these court intrigues; and here I think the reviewer showed himself dull. Lastly, if Otto's speech is offensive to him, he is one of the large class of unmanly and ungenerous dogs who arrogate and defile the name of manly. As for the passages quoted, I do confess that some of them reek gorgonically; they are excessive, but they are not inelegant after all. However, had he attacked me only there, he would have scored.

Your criticism on Gondremark is, I fancy, right. I thought all your criticisms were indeed; only your praise —chokes me.—Yours ever, R. L. S.

TO WILLIAM ARCHER

The paper referred to in this and the following letters is one which Mr. Archer wrote over his own signature in the November number of *Time*, a magazine now extinct.

Skerryvore, Bournemouth, October 28, 1885.

DEAR MR. ARCHER,—I have read your paper with my customary admiration; it is very witty, very adroit; it contains a great deal that is excellently true (particularly the parts about my stories and the description of me as an artist in life); but you will not be surprised if I do not think it altogether just. It seems to me, in particular, that you have wilfully read all my works in terms of my earliest; my aim, even in style, has quite changed in the last six or seven years; and this I should have thought you would have noticed. Again, your first remark upon the affectation of the italic names; a practice only followed in my two affected little books of travel, where a typographical *minauderie* of the sort appeared to me in character; and what you say of it, then, is quite just. But why should you forget yourself and use these same italics as an index to my theology some pages further on? This is lightness of touch indeed; may I say, it is almost sharpness of practice?

Excuse these remarks. I have been on the whole much interested, and sometimes amused. Are you aware that the praiser of this 'brave gymnasium' has not seen a canoe nor taken a long walk since '79? that he is rarely out of the house nowadays, and carries his arm in a sling? Can you imagine that he is a backslidden communist, and is sure he will go to hell (if there be such an excellent institution) for the luxury in which he lives? And can you believe that, though it is gaily expressed, the thought is hag and skeleton in every moment of vacuity or depression? Can you conceive how profoundly I am irritated by the opposite affectation to my own, when I see strong men and rich men bleating about their sorrows and the burthen of life, in a world full of 'cancerous paupers,' and poor sick children, and the fatally bereaved, ay, and down even to such happy creatures as myself, who has yet been obliged to strip himself, one after another, of all the pleasures that he had chosen except smoking (and the days of that I know in my heart ought to be over), I forgot eating, which I still enjoy, and who sees the circle of impotence closing very slowly but quite steadily around him? In my view, one dank, dispirited word is harmful, a crime of *lèse- humanité*, a piece of acquired evil; every gay, every bright word or picture, like every pleasant air of music, is a piece of pleasure set

1885.
AET. 35.

afloat; the reader catches it, and, if he be healthy, goes on his way rejoicing; and it is the business of art so to send him, as often as possible.

For what you say, so kindly, so prettily, so precisely, of my style, I must in particular thank you; though even here, I am vexed you should not have remarked on my attempted change of manner: seemingly this attempt is still quite unsuccessful! Well, we shall fight it out on this line if it takes all summer.

And now for my last word: Mrs. Stevenson is very anxious that you should see me, and that she should see you, in the flesh. If you at all share in these views, I am a fixture, Write or telegraph (giving us time, however, to telegraph in reply, lest the day be impossible), and come down here to a bed and a dinner. What do you say, my dear critic? I shall be truly pleased to see you; and to explain at greater length what I meant by saying narrative was the most characteristic mood of literature, on which point I have great hopes I shall persuade you.—Yours truly,

ROBERT LOUIS STEVENSON.

P.S.—My opinion about Thoreau, and the passage in *The Week*, is perhaps a fad, but it is sincere and stable. I am still of the same mind five years later; did you observe that I had said 'modern' authors? and will you observe again that this passage touches the very joint of our division? It is one that appeals to me, deals with that part of life that I think the most important, and you, if I gather rightly, so much less so? You believe in the extreme moment of the facts that humanity has acquired and is acquiring; I think them of moment, but still of much less than those inherent or inherited brute principles and laws that sit upon us (in the character of conscience) as heavy as a shirt of mail, and that (in the character of the affections and the airy spirit of pleasure) make all the light of our lives. The house is, indeed, a great thing, and should be rearranged on sanitary principles; but my heart and all my interest are with the dweller, that ancient of days and day-old infant man.   R. L. S.

An excellent touch is p. 584. 'By instinct or design he eschews what demands constructive patience.' I believe it is both; my theory is that literature must always be most at home in treating movement and change ; hence I look for them.

TO THOMAS STEVENSON

[Skerryvore, Bournemouth,] October 28, 1885.

MY DEAREST FATHER,—Get the November number of *Time*, and you will see a review of me by a very clever fellow, who is quite furious at bottom because I am too orthodox, just as Purcell was savage because I am not orthodox enough. I fall between two stools. It is odd, too, to see how this man thinks me a full-blooded fox-hunter, and tells me my philosophy would fail if I lost my health or had to give up exercise!

An illustrated *Treasure Island* will be out next month. I have had an early copy, and the French pictures are admirable. The artist has got his types up in Hogarth; he is full of fire and spirit, can draw and can compose, and has understood the book as I meant it, all but one or two little accidents, such as making the *Hispaniola* a brig. I would send you my copy, *but I cannot*; it is my new toy, and I cannot divorce myself from this enjoyment.

I am keeping really better, and have been out about every second day, though the weather is cold and very wild.

I was delighted to hear you were keeping better; you and Archer would agree, more shame to you! (Archer is my pessimist critic.) Good-bye to all of you, with my best love. We had a dreadful overhauling of my conduct as a son the other night; and my wife stripped me of my illusions and made me admit I had been a detestable bad one. Of one thing in particular she convicted me in my own eyes: I mean, a most unkind reticence, which hung on me then, and I confess still hangs on me now, when I try to assure you that I do love you.—Ever your bad son,   ROBERT LOUIS STEVENSON.

TO HENRY JAMES

Skerryvore, Bournemouth, October 28, 1885.

MY DEAR HENRY JAMES,—At last, my wife being at a concert, and a story being done, I am at some liberty to write and give you of my views. And first, many thanks for the works that came to my sickbed. And second, and more important, as to the *Princess*.[1] Well, I think you are going to do it this time; I cannot, of course, foresee, but these two first numbers seem to me picturesque and sound and full of lineament, and very much a new departure. As for your young lady, she is all there; yes, sir, you can do low life, I believe. The prison was excellent; it was of that nature of touch that I sometimes achingly miss from your former work; with some of the grime, that is, and some of the emphasis of skeleton there is in nature. I pray you to take grime in a good sense; it need not be ignoble: dirt may have dignity; in nature it usually has; and your prison was imposing.

And now to the main point: why do we not see you? Do not fail us. Make an alarming sacrifice, and let us see 'Henry James's chair' properly occupied. I never sit in it myself (though it was my grandfather's); it has been consecrated to guests by your approval, and now stands at my elbow gaping. We have a new room, too, to introduce to you—our last baby, the drawing-room; it

[1] *Princess Casamassima.*

never cries, and has cut its teeth. Likewise, there is a cat now. It promises to be a monster of laziness and self-sufficiency.

Pray see, in the November *Time* (a dread name for a magazine of light reading), a very clever fellow, W. Archer, stating his views of me; the rosy-gilled 'athletico-æsthete'; and warning me, in a fatherly manner, that a rheumatic fever would try my philosophy (as indeed it would), and that my gospel would not do for 'those who are shut out from the exercise of any manly virtue save renunciation.' To those who know that rickety and cloistered spectre, the real R. L. S., the paper, besides being clever in itself, presents rare elements of sport. The critical parts are in particular very bright and neat, and often excellently true. Get it by all manner of means.

I hear on all sides I am to be attacked as an immoral writer; this is painful. Have I at last got, like you, to the pitch of being attacked? 'Tis the consecration I lack —and could do without. Not that Archer's paper is an attack, or what either he or I, I believe, would call one; 'tis the attacks on my morality (which I had thought a gem of the first water) I referred to.

Now, my dear James, come—come—come. The spirit (that is me) says, Come; and the bride (and that is my wife) says, Come; and the best thing you can do for us and yourself and your work is to get up and do so right away.—Yours affectionately,

ROBERT LOUIS STEVENSON.

TO WILLIAM ARCHER

[*Skerryvore, Bournemouth,*] *October* 30, 1885.

DEAR MR. ARCHER.—It is possible my father may be soon down with me; he is an old man and in bad health and spirits; and I could neither leave him alone, nor could we talk freely before him. If he should be here when you offer your visit, you will understand if I have to say no, and put you off.

I quite understand your not caring to refer to things of private knowledge. What still puzzles me is how you ('in the witness box'—ha! I like the phrase) should have made your argument actually hinge on a contention which the facts answered.

I am pleased to hear of the correctness of my guess. It is then as I supposed; you are of the school of the generous and not the sullen pessimists; and I can feel with you. I used myself to rage when I saw sick folk going by in their Bath-chairs; since I have been sick myself (and always when I was sick myself), I found life, even in its rough places, to have a property of easiness. That which we suffer ourselves has no longer the same air of monstrous injustice and wanton cruelty that suffering wears when we see it in the case of others. So we begin gradually to see that things are not black, but have their strange compensations; and when they draw towards their worst, the idea of death is like a bed to lie on. I should bear false witness if I did not declare life happy. And your wonderful statement that happiness tends to die out and misery to continue, which was what put me on the track of your frame of mind, is diagnostic of the happy man raging over the misery of others; it could never be written by the man who had tried what unhappiness was like. And at any rate, it was a slip of the pen: the ugliest word that science has to declare is a reserved indifference to happiness and misery in the individual; it declares no leaning toward the black, no iniquity on the large scale in fate's doings, rather a marble equality, dread not cruel, giving and taking away and reconciling.

Why have I not written my *Timon*? Well, here is my worst quarrel with you. You take my young books as my last word. The tendency to try to say more has passed unperceived (my fault, that). And you make no allowance for the slowness with which a man finds and tries to learn his tools. I began with a neat brisk little style, and a sharp little knack of partial observation; I have tried to expand my means, but still I can only utter a part of what I wish to say, and am bound to feel; and much of it will die unspoken. But if I had the pen of Shakespeare, I have no *Timon* to give forth. I feel kindly to the powers that be; I marvel they should use me so well; and when I think of the case of others, I wonder too, but in another vein, whether they may not, whether they must not, be like me, still with some compensation, some delight. To have suffered, nay, to suffer, sets a keen edge on what remains of the agreeable. This is a great truth, and has to be learned in the fire.—Yours very truly,

1885.
AET. 35.

                ROBERT LOUIS STEVENSON.

We expect you, remember that.

TO WILLIAM ARCHER

Skerryvore, Bournemouth, November 1, 1885.

DEAR MR. ARCHER,—You will see that I had already had a sight of your article and what were my thoughts.

One thing in your letter puzzles me. Are you, too, not in the witness-box? And if you are, why take a wilfully false hypothesis? If you knew I was a chronic invalid, why say that my philosophy was unsuitable to such a case? My call for facts is not so general as yours, but an essential fact should not be put the other way about.

The fact is, consciously or not, you doubt my honesty; you think I am making faces, and at heart disbelieve my utterances. And this I am disposed to think must spring from your not having had enough of pain, sorrow, and trouble in your existence. It is easy to have too much; easy also or possible to have too little; enough is required

1885.
AET. 35.

that a man may appreciate what elements of consolation and joy there are in everything but absolutely overpowering physical pain or disgrace, and how in almost all circumstances the human soul can play a fair part. You fear life, I fancy, on the principle of the hand of little employment. But perhaps my hypothesis is as unlike the truth as the one you chose. Well, if it be so, if you have had trials, sickness, the approach of death, the alienation of friends, poverty at the heels, and have not felt your soul turn round upon these things and spurn them under—you must be very differently made from me, and I earnestly believe from the majority of men. But at least you are in the right to wonder and complain.

To 'say all'? Stay here. All at once? That would require a word from the pen of Gargantua. We say each particular thing as it comes up, and 'with that sort of emphasis that for the time there seems to be no other.' Words will not otherwise serve us; no, nor even Shakespeare, who could not have put *As You Like It* and *Timon* into one without ruinous loss both of emphasis and substance. Is it quite fair then to keep your face so steadily on my most light-hearted works, and then say I recognise no evil? Yet in the paper on Burns, for instance, I show myself alive to some sorts of evil. But then, perhaps, they are not your sorts.

And again: 'to say all'? All: yes. Everything: no. The task were endless, the effect nil. But my all, in such a vast field as this of life, is what interests me, what stands out, what takes on itself a presence for my imagination or makes a figure in that little tricky abbreviation which is the best that my reason can conceive. That I must treat, or I shall be fooling with my readers: That, and not the all of some one else.

And here we come to the division: not only do I believe that literature should give joy, but I see a universe, I suppose, eternally different from yours; a solemn, a terrible, but a very joyous and noble universe, where suffering is not at least wantonly inflicted, though it falls with dispassionate partiality, but where it may be and generally is nobly borne; where, above all (this I believe; probably you don't: I think he may, with cancer), *any brave man may make* out a life which shall be happy for himself, and, by so being, beneficent to those about him. And if he fails, why should I hear him weeping? I mean if I fail, why should I weep? Why should *you* hear *me*? Then to me morals, the conscience, the affections, and the passions are, I will own frankly and sweepingly, so infinitely more important than the other parts of life, that I conceive men rather triflers who become immersed in the latter; and I will always think the man who keeps his lip stiff, and makes 'a happy fireside clime,' and carries a pleasant face about to friends and neighbours, infinitely greater (in the abstract) than an atrabilious Shakespeare or a backbiting Kant or Darwin. No offence to any of these gentlemen, two of whom probably (one for certain) came up to my standard.

And now enough said; it were hard if a poor man could not criticise another without having so much ink shed against him. But I shall still regret you should have written on an hypothesis you knew to be untenable, and that you should thus have made your paper, for those who do not know me, essentially unfair. The rich, fox-hunting squire speaks with one voice; the sick man of letters with another.—Yours very truly,

ROBERT LOUIS STEVENSON
(*Prometheus-Heine in minimis*).

P.S.—Here I go again. To me, the medicine bottles on my chimney and the blood on my handkerchief are accidents; they do not colour my view of life, as you would know, I think, if you had experience of sickness; they do not exist in my prospect; I would as soon drag them under the eyes of my readers as I would mention a pimple I might chance to have (saving your presence) on my posteriors. What does it prove? what does it change? it has not hurt, it has not changed me in any essential part; and I should think myself a trifler and in bad taste if I introduced the world to these unimportant privacies.

But, again, there is this mountain-range between us— *that you do not believe me.* It is not flattering, but the fault is probably in my literary art.

TO W. H. LOW

The 'other thing coming out' mentioned below in the last paragraph but one was *The Strange Case of Dr. Jekyll and Mr. Hyde.*

Skerryvore, Bournemouth, December 26, 1885.

MY DEAR LOW,—*Lamia* has not yet turned up, but your letter came to me this evening with a scent of the Boulevard Montparnasse that was irresistible. The sand of Lavenue's crumbled under my heel; and the bouquet of the old Fleury came back to me, and I remembered the day when I found a twenty franc piece under my fetish. Have you that fetish still? and has it brought you luck? I remembered, too, my first sight of you in a frock coat and a smoking-cap, when we passed the evening at the Café de Medicis; and my last when we sat and talked in the Parc Monceau; and all these things made me feel a little young again, which, to one who has been mostly in bed for a month, was a vivifying change.

Yes, you are lucky to have a bag that holds you comfortably. Mine is a strange contrivance; I don't die, damme, and I can't get along on both feet to save my soul; I am a chronic sickist; and my work cripples along between bed and the parlour, between the medicine bottle and the cupping glass. Well, I like my life all the same; and should like it none the worse if I could have another talk with you, though even my talks now are measured out to me by the minute hand like poisons in a minim glass.

A photograph will be taken of my ugly mug and sent to you for ulterior purposes: I have another thing coming out, which I did not put in the way of the Scribners, I can scarce tell how; but I was sick and penniless and rather back on the world, and mismanaged it. I trust they will forgive me.

I am sorry to hear of Mrs. Low's illness, and glad to hear of her recovery. I will announce the coming *Lamia* to Bob: he steams away at literature like smoke. I have a beautiful Bob on my walls, and a good Sargent, and a delightful Lemon; and your etching now hangs framed in the dining-room. So the arts surround me.—Yours,

R. L. S.

www.ingramcontent.com/pod-product-compliance
Lightning Source LLC
Chambersburg PA
CBHW030557300426
44111CB00009B/1015